EMIL AND KATHLEEN SICK SERIES IN
WESTERN HISTORY AND BIOGRAPHY

With support from the Center for the Study of the Pacific Northwest at the University of Washington, the Sick Series in Western History and Biography features scholarly books on the peoples and issues that have defined and shaped the American West. Through intellectually challenging and engaging books of general interest, the series seeks to deepen and expand our understanding of the American West as a region and its role in the making of the United States and the modern world.

*The Great Columbia Plain: A Historical Geography, 1805–1910*, by Donald W. Meinig

*Mills and Markets: A History of the Pacific coast Lumber Industry to 1900*,
by Thomas R. Cox

*Radical Heritage: Labor, Socialism, and Reform in Washington and British Columbia, 1885–1917*,
by Carlos A. Schwantes

*The Battle for Butte: Mining and Politics on the Northern Frontier, 1864–1906*,
by Michael P. Malone

*The Forging of a Black Community: Seattle's Central District from 1870 through
the Civil Rights Era*, by Quintard Taylor

*Warren G. Magnuson and the Shaping of Twentieth-Century America*, by Shelby Scates

*The Atomic West*, edited by Bruce Hevly and John M. Findlay

*Power and Place in the North American West*, edited by Richard White and John M. Findlay

*Henry M. Jackson: A Life in Politics*, by Robert G. Kaufman

*Parallel Destinies: Canadian-American Relations West of the Rockies*,
edited by John M. Findlay and Ken S. Coates

*Nikkei in the Pacific Northwest: Japanese Americans and Japanese Canadians in the Twentieth
Century*, edited by Louis Fiset and Gail M. Nomura

*Bringing Indians to the Book*, by Albert Furtwangler

*Death of Celilo Falls*, by Katrine Barber

*The Power of Promises: Perspectives on Indian Treaties of the Pacific Northwest*,
edited by Alexandra Harmon

*Warship under Sail: The USS* Decatur *in the Pacific West*,
by Lorraine McConaghy

*Shadow Tribe: The Making of Columbia River Indian Identity*,
by Andrew H. Fisher

*A Home for Every Child: Relinquishment, Adoption, and the Washington Children's Home Society,
1896–1915*, by Patricia Susan Hart

*Atomic Frontier Days: Hanford and the American West*,
by John M. Findlay and Bruce Hevly

*The Nature of Borders: Salmon, Boundaries, and Bandits on the Salish Sea*,
by Lissa K. Wadewitz

*Encounters in Avalanche Country: A History of Survival in the Mountain West, 1820–1920*
by Diana L. Di Stefano

*The Rising Tide of Color: Race, State Violence, and Radical Movements across the Pacific*,
edited by Moon-Ho Jung

# THE RISING TIDE OF COLOR

RACE, STATE VIOLENCE,
AND RADICAL MOVEMENTS
ACROSS THE PACIFIC

Edited by

MOON-HO JUNG

CENTER FOR THE STUDY OF THE PACIFIC NORTHWEST

*in association with*

UNIVERSITY OF WASHINGTON PRESS
SEATTLE AND LONDON

© 2014 by the University of Washington Press
Printed and bound in the USA
Design by Dustin Kilgore
Composed in Chaparral, a typeface designed by Carol Twombly
18  17  16  15  14     5  4  3  2  1

Center for the Study of the Pacific Northwest       University of Washington Press
PO Box 353587                                       www.washington.edu/uwpress
Seattle, WA 98195, USA

Library of Congress Cataloging-in-Publication Data
The rising tide of color : race, state violence, and radical movements across the Pacific / edited by Moon-Ho Jung.
    pages   cm. — (Emil and Kathleen Sick series in Western history and biography)
Includes bibliographical references and index.
ISBN 978-0-295-99360-7 (hardcover : alkaline paper) 1. Pacific Coast (U.S.)—Race relations. 2. Pacific Area—Race relations. 3. Pacific Coast (U.S.)—Politics and government. 4. Pacific Area—Politics and government. 5. Political violence—Pacific Coast (U.S.)—History. 6. Political violence—Pacific Area—History. 7. Social movements—Pacific Coast (U.S.)—History. 8. Social movements—Pacific Area—History. 9. Radicalism—Pacific Coast (U.S.)—History. 10. Radicalism—Pacific Area—History. I. Jung, Moon-Ho, 1969- II. Center for the Study of the Pacific Northwest.
F855.R47 2014
305.800979—dc23

                        2014007275

The paper used in this publication is acid-free and meets the minimum requirements of American National Standard for Information Sciences—Permanence of Paper for Printed Library Materials, ANSI Z39.48–1984.∞

To my 할머니 (grandmother)

# Contents

# Acknowledgments

THE ESSAYS COLLECTED HERE WERE FIRST PRESENTED IN MAY 2011 AT a conference called Race, Radicalism, and Repression on the Pacific coast and Beyond, organized and hosted by the Center for the Study of the Pacific Northwest (CSPN) and the Harry Bridges Center for Labor Studies at the University of Washington. Support from the UW Law School (especially Ron Collins), UW Libraries (especially Theresa Mudrock), UW Departments of English and History, and the Wing Luke Museum of the Asian Pacific American Experience helped to make the conference a resounding success. I thank Jim Gregory, Linda Nash, and Chandan Reddy for serving on the program committee with me. Andrew Hedden of the Harry Bridges Center contributed his artistic and organizing skills. Holly George, Wendi Lindquist, and especially Kim McKaig of CSPN took care of all of the details related to the conference. Kim also proofread the entire collection.

Putting together the collection has been a collective project. For their sharp insights and collegial support, I thank Luther Adams, Eiichiro Azuma, Mike Cheng, May Fu, Ruth Wilson Gilmore, Jennifer Guglielmo, Dan Martinez HoSang, Moon-Kie Jung, Dan Kanstroom, Richard S. Kim, Daryl Maeda, Kevin Mumford, Michael Omi, George Quibuyen (Geologic/Prometheus Brown), Vince Rafael, Chandan Reddy, Jeanette Roan, Dylan Rodríguez, Dave Roediger, Nayan Shah, Naoko Shibusawa, Mike Tagawa, Ben Wang, and Mark Wild. At the University of Washington Press, Marianne Keddington-Lang provided enthusiastic support in the beginning stages. With great care and incredible speed, Ranjit Arab and Mary C. Ribesky shepherded the project through review and production. I also thank the anonymous reader for a careful and helpful review of the entire collection, particularly my introduction. Kerrie Maynes was our sharp-eyed copyeditor. Kathy Woodward of the Simpson Center for the Humanities provided critical support for the conference and the collection, including funds for the index.

We are living through very depressing and violent times that can make us feel helpless and hopeless. Our collection tries to lay bare some of the intricate and insidious roots of white supremacy and state violence that have shaped the world we live in. But there is hope. There is always hope. The chapters that follow also seek to reveal the creative and ingenious ways that human beings have pursued a radically different world. From the day of my birth, my grandmother, my parents, and my brother have guided me to see injustice and to seek justice. Tefi Lamson and our daughters Mina and Seri brighten my world every day. They are the sources of my hope.

# THE RISING TIDE OF COLOR

# PART ONE

# Framing Race, State Violence, and Radical Movements

# Introduction

## Opening Salvo

MOON-HO JUNG

*Now this here's for those who choose fights*
*Whose fruits might never not ripen until after their life.*
*It's not right how they martyr our leaders*
*And target our children,*
*Disrespect our sisters*
*And wonder why we're militant.*
*Peace to my third world equivalent,*
*Even if I can't fight beside you*
*I write what I can*
*To get our fam in other lands to understand your pain,*
*'Cause your beef is mine and we're one and the same.*
*And I know about this privilege,*
*But if you're from where I'm from*
*Then you know a bigger burden comes with it.*
*And that's what I carry when you see me on a hustle,*
*I'm talking as a walking document of our struggle.*
. . . . . . . . . . . . . . . . . . . . . . . . . . . . . . . . . . .
*Right now I want to thank God for being me,*
*My soul won't rest until the colony is free.*
*1896 revolution incomplete,*
*Silence is defeat, my solution is to speak.*
*Resurrect the legacy of martyrs I beseech,*
*Time to choose a side, it's the mighty vs. the meek.*
*My big brother Free brought the word from the East,*
*We're the bullet in the middle of the belly of the beast.*

—BLUE SCHOLARS, "Opening Salvo," *Bayani* (2007)

ON THE EVENING OF MAY 14, 2011, AN OVERFLOWING CROWD GATHERED at the Wing Luke Museum of the Asian Pacific American Experience in Seattle to attend a screening of *Aoki*, a film about Richard Aoki, an Asian American Black Panther. Ben Wang and Mike Cheng, the filmmakers, were there. Mike Tagawa, a fellow Asian American Black Panther, was there. The screening, in fact, served as an informal reunion of former Panthers and fellow travelers, many of them clad proudly in their signature black leather jackets and berets. There were a lot of hugs, lots of genuine affection and camaraderie. When the lights went out and Aoki's image first appeared on the screen, the audience hollered and applauded, bestowing on the prominent (and, until recently, relatively unknown) Black Panther much love and respect. It was a beautiful scene.

Richard Aoki (1938–2009) grew up in a world shaped by race, state violence, and radical movements. When he was three years old, he and his family were driven out of the segregated neighborhoods of West Oakland and Berkeley, California, and incarcerated at the Tanforan Race Track and then in a concentration camp in Topaz, Utah. In the barren landscape of Utah, Aoki learned early on the contradictions of race and nation. His excitement over being picked to play George Washington in a school pageant dissipated when his father responded not with paternal pride but with violent rage. "I'll never forget that lesson: I should not think in terms of George Washington, this was not my country," he recalled. "In fact, 'my country' put me in this camp." In his household, he added, Franklin Delano Roosevelt was "the devil incarnate," the president responsible for the mass incarceration of Japanese Americans.[1] A moment of repression was simultaneously a radicalizing moment of new possibilities of seeing and engaging the world.

Aoki's personal journey, however, proved not so straightforward to the left. When he passed away in March 2009, caused most immediately by a self-inflicted gunshot wound in the context of a longer series of medical afflictions and complications, Aoki meticulously kept two uniforms hanging in his closet: a Black Panther leather jacket (with a "Free Huey" button) and a US Army uniform (with an American flag). At the end of a public memorial service two months later, filled with remembrances by radical activists, US Army color guards honored Aoki with the displaying and folding of an American flag, as "Taps" played in the background. How could a Third World revolutionary embrace the Stars and Stripes, which represents for many, especially Third World peoples, the most potent

emblem of empire and militarism in the twenty-first century?[2] Such iro-
nies and contradictions are not easy to comprehend, but they were no less
lived and remembered.

Aoki's personal story took a dramatic turn in August 2012, when journalist Seth Rosenfeld publicly alleged that Aoki had worked as an informant for the Federal Bureau of Investigation (FBI). Rosenfeld's charges,
made on the eve of a publicity drive for his new book, *Subversives: The FBI's
War on Student Radicals, and Reagan's Rise to Power*, appeared to be self-
serving, particularly with insinuations that his documentary evidence
could not sustain. Rosenfeld's article, for example, strongly implied that
Aoki had worked with the FBI to arm the Panthers and that his actions
had "contributed to fatal confrontations between the Panthers and the
police." Refutations and recriminations followed quickly and widely, generating media and activist attention for Rosenfeld and his book, though
not in ways that he might have anticipated or appreciated. In another
startling twist, weeks later Rosenfeld followed with a newly released FBI
file, Aoki's informant file, which seemed to demonstrate more conclusively
that Aoki had indeed worked as an informant.[3] In the aftermath of these
revelations, Aoki's image most likely would no longer be received with
unreserved warmth and reverence.

The essays collected here do not address Aoki directly, but his complicated life and afterlife point to this collection's overriding premise and
theme: that race, state violence, and radical movements have formed a
critical dynamic and dialectic in the shaping of US history. These essays
were first presented at a conference, Race, Radicalism, and Repression
on the Pacific coast and Beyond, organized and hosted by the Center for
the Study of the Pacific Northwest at the University of Washington. (The
screening of *Aoki* marked the conference's closing session.) The conference
sought in part to center in the study of race and politics the Pacific coast,
a region of the United States that generally receives little to no notice
in scholarly and nonscholarly conversations on race. Yet we know that
radical movements embracing and demanding racial justice—from the
Industrial Workers of the World and the International Longshore and
Warehouse Union to the Black Panthers and the Third World Liberation
Front strikes—have figured prominently in the history of the "left coast"
of the United States. These movements, integral elements of what reac-
tionary Lothrop Stoddard branded long ago as "the rising tide of color,"
have also generated violent responses, particularly state repression, that

reverberated across the United States and around the world.[4] Our collection is a preliminary attempt to make sense of that wider history of race, state violence, and radical movements across the Pacific.

BEYOND THE NATIONAL REDEMPTION OF RACE

In his widely celebrated speech on race in March 2008, then presidential candidate Barack Obama seemed to portend a new kind of politician, a figure capable of speaking about race honestly and critically. Less than a minute into the speech, however, it became clear that there would be nothing revolutionary uttered that day. After an introductory paean to America's Founding Fathers, Obama turned to "this nation's original sin of slavery." "Of course," he added quickly, "the answer to the slavery question was already embedded within our Constitution—a Constitution that had at i[t]s very core the ideal of equal citizenship under the law; a Constitution that promised its people liberty, and justice, and a union that could be and should be perfected over time." The person delivering the speech might have looked and sounded different, but his underlying message was the same. In racial matters, the United States was fundamentally about racial exclusion (the past) and national inclusion (the future), a promise supposedly inscribed in the Declaration of Independence and the Constitution.[5]

Obama was echoing a familiar refrain in American history and politics. The United States, and the US state in particular, has been depicted and perceived preponderantly as a neutral or benevolent force in matters of race. Beginning with Reconstruction—and perhaps even earlier with the Declaration of Independence and the Constitution, as Obama invoked—and culminating in the Civil Rights Act (1964) and the Voting Rights Act (1965), the US state has seemingly stepped forward to advance and sanctify the nation's supposed commitment to racial equality and racial justice. The federal government finally mustered a national resolve to defeat racism once and for all, to force desegregation on a recalcitrant South, so the story goes. That historical depiction, in turn, has been essential to making the US state appear nonracial and even antiracist from the nation's founding. It is like the pervasive image of Martin Luther King, Jr., in American culture today, frozen in time, speaking before the Lincoln Memorial in 1963 of a dream "deeply rooted in the American dream that one day this nation will rise up and live out the true meaning of its creed."[6]

It is a highly seductive image of the United States and of King, but it is fatally flawed and horribly distorted. King's critique ran much deeper, firmly rooted in a black radical tradition. On April 4, 1967, for example, he broke his public silence on the Vietnam War and received an avalanche of personal attacks in response. Linking domestic and foreign policies, and noting the irony that black and white soldiers were dying together in Southeast Asia while being disallowed from living and learning together in the United States, King said that he had to tell the truth. "I knew that I could never again raise my voice against the violence of the oppressed in the ghettos without having first spoken clearly to the greatest purveyor of violence in the world today—my own government," he said. Speaking as a "citizen of the world," King recalled a larger sense of history, "beyond the prophesying of smooth patriotism." "I speak for those whose land is being laid [to] waste, whose homes are being destroyed, whose culture is being subverted," he stated. "I speak for the poor of America who are paying the double price of smashed hopes at home and death and corruption in Vietnam."[7] For King, to struggle for racial justice meant embracing a sense of belonging beyond the nation-state and confronting the repressive machinations of that state.

How might predominant understandings of race, resistance, and the US state look different if approached from King's insights and from a decidedly Pacific framework? The essays collected herein wrestle with that central question through a variety of histories, geographies, and methods. Addressing disparate political, social, and cultural movements spanning the North American continent and across the Pacific Ocean, they begin to shed light on the breadth and complexity of radical politics in the twentieth century, a politics that often critiqued *and* appealed to conventional notions of race, gender, sexuality, class, and citizenship. Before I introduce the essays in greater detail, I first offer a brief genealogy of race, freedom, and state violence in the nineteenth century that might serve as a historical preface to the collection.

RACE AND FREEDOM ACROSS THE PACIFIC
(AND THE ATLANTIC)[8]

Securing and dominating commercial exchanges with the "Orient" had defined "America" and "Americans" since the late eighteenth century. Beginning in 1784, within months of the end of the Revolutionary War,

American merchants competed and formed alliances with their erstwhile enemies, the British, and other European powers to "open up" China. "The trade with the East has always been the richest jewel in the diadem of commerce," Thomas Hart Benton reminded his colleagues in the US Senate in 1846. The ultimate prize of continental expansion, he explained, was transpacific trade. "The van of the Caucasian race now top the Rocky Mountains, and spread down to the shores of the Pacific," Benton exhorted. "In a few years a great population will grow up there, luminous with the accumulated lights of European and American civilization.... The sun of civilization must shine across the sea: socially and commercially, the van of the Caucasians, and the rear of the Mongolians, must intermix." If his romantic vision did little to relieve the mounting frustration of American traders, diplomats, and missionaries in China, British military victories there accrued legal and commercial privileges for US delegates and citizens in 1844.[9]

While British guns led the attack on Chinese imperial authority, the United States scored a historic concession from Japan in 1854. Fresh from the US war with Mexico and the subsequent annexation of lands bordering the Pacific Ocean, secretary of state Daniel Webster dispatched commodore Matthew C. Perry to Edo (Tokyo) to realize a long-standing national hope—dating back at least to Andrew Jackson's presidency—of gaining access to Japanese ports and markets. Commanding four naval vessels, including two powered by steam, Perry entered Edo Bay in July 1853 and demanded a hearing with Japan's highest authorities. Reinforced by three additional warships, Perry returned seven months later and signed a treaty allowing US vessels to land in two Japanese ports and establishing a US consul in Japan. Although the Treaty of Kanagawa (Yokohama) failed to include a provision on foreign trade—Japanese authorities were very much aware of China's growing subjection to Western demands and products—it nonetheless marked a sea change in Japan's policies and politics. "The long doubtful attempt has been entirely successful," the *New York Times* rejoiced, "and to the United States belongs ... the honor of making the first international Treaty with Japan!" Bearing gifts and displaying military might, the United States had become a formidable champion of "free trade" across the Pacific.[10]

Imperial encounters and relations in Asia, in turn, profoundly affected the course of race, politics, and labor on the other side of the Pacific, for the "opening" of Asia encompassed the exchange of human bodies in addition to treaty rights and material goods. In the wake of the widening abolition of the slave trade and slavery, European and American shippers converged in southern China in the 1840s and 1850s to generate and to supply the demand for plantation workers in the Caribbean, especially Cuba. "There seems to be a rage at this time for speculating in Chinese ... the trade, which gives enormous profits, is engaging the attention of the first commercial houses and largest capitalists of this city," the US consul in Havana reported in 1855. "Chinese are coming in fast; and ... these laborers are, on some plantations, treated no better and even worse than negro slaves." And, to the consul's consternation, his countrymen dominated the trade from China. "For my part," he wrote to his superiors, "I assure you that I regret very much to see vessels under our flag engaged in such a traffic." The apotheosis of "free trade" in imperial discourse, as anthropologist Sidney W. Mintz has observed, emerged side by side with the gradual emancipation of enslaved labor and the simultaneous migration of indentured Asian labor.[11]

Asian workers, I have argued elsewhere, embodied the hopes, fears, and contradictions of emancipation in the middle decades of the nineteenth century. Originally introduced and justified as "free" improvements to enslaved labor, they also epitomized the backwardness of slavery, uniting proslavery and antislavery Americans in antebellum campaigns to denounce and prohibit what came to be known as the "coolie" trade. "What is the plain English of the whole system?" J. D. B. De Bow asked his southern brethren in 1859. "Is it not just this?—that the civilized and powerful races of the earth have discovered that the degraded, barbarous, and weak races, may be induced *voluntarily* to reduce themselves to a slavery more cruel than any that has yet disgraced the earth, and that humanity may compound with its conscience, by pleading that the act is one of *free will*?" Not to be outdone, US diplomats in China characterized the "coolie" trade as "irredeemable slavery under the form of freedom" that demanded US state intervention, both for humanity's sake and for the Chinese government's recognition of free trade's virtues. The racialization of Asian workers as "coolies" before the Civil War had the dual, imperial effect of rationalizing US slavery and its expansion southward and US diplomatic missions in China, Cuba, and beyond.[12]

The enjoined logics of free trade and free labor that posed Asia and Asian workers as antithetical *and* pivotal to both deepened during the Civil War and, in concert with military and political battles over slavery in the United States, increased the power of the federal government to define and advance freedom. Driven by years of horrifying accounts by US consuls in Chinese port cities, antislavery Republicans passed a major legislation against the "coolie" trade in February 1862. Although interpreting and enforcing the law would confound federal officials after the war, its sponsors emphasized the unequivocal need to suppress what they presented as a new slave trade. "Let us here, by legislation, declare it illegal—not a piracy; this bill does not so designate it," argued Thomas D. Eliot, a representative from Massachusetts, "and yet no statute pirate who has brought slaves from the coast of Africa more truly, in my judgment, deserves execration than those men who knowingly ... have engaged in the work of bringing coolies from their native homes to the island of Cuba." The law empowered US officials not only to prohibit the transport of Chinese subjects "known as 'coolies'" abroad but also to identify and facilitate the "free and voluntary emigration" of Chinese subjects. They presumably possessed the integrity and authority to distinguish the free from the unfree.[13]

In the meantime, US diplomats, backed by the military, made great strides in convincing Japan to allow commercial exchanges with foreigners. With British and French troops preparing for war against China yet again, Japanese leaders felt compelled to sign treaties with Western powers to shore up their authority within and without. Japan concluded a treaty with the United States in the summer of 1858 that opened five ports to foreign trade, established resident ministers in Edo and Washington, DC, and shielded US citizens from Japanese laws through extraterritorial rights. Such concessions, however, only produced greater tensions and concessions. In the summer of 1863, during the height of the US Civil War, Western ships, including a US warship, were fired upon in the Straits of Shimonoseki, located in Choshu, an outlying area of Japan leading the attack against the center of state power in Edo. Five Americans were killed. Undeterred by the unavailability of US naval vessels, most of which were in service against the Confederate South, secretary of state William H. Seward committed the US military to restore American honor. In September 1864, an alliance of British, French, Dutch, and American forces bombarded Choshu for four days and reopened the straits. The ensuing Convention of 1866 exacted more advantages for Western traders and legalized the right of Japanese subjects to travel abroad for the first time in more than two centuries.[14]

The conclusion of the Civil War emboldened the United States to exhibit, with greater force, its military prowess across the Pacific. By 1866, the US Navy shifted its focus back to reorganizing "efficient squadrons abroad ... for the protection of American interests and the assertion of American rights" on the high seas and in commercial ports around the world. The *Hartford*, the flagship of the Asiatic Squadron, apprehensively and conspicuously sailed through the Straits of Shimonoseki that summer to ensure the continued passage of commercial traffic. Four years later, secretary of state Hamilton Fish conceived a more ambitious naval expedition to Korea, ostensibly to negotiate a treaty with the "Hermit Kingdom" to protect shipwrecked American sailors. An awesome fleet of five heavily armed ships, with 1,230 men and eighty-five cannons aboard, set out to fulfill, in the ironic words of secretary of the navy George M. Robeson, a "peaceful" and "friendly" mission in the spring of 1871. The secretary not only promoted the expedition but also demanded improvements and investments in the US Navy to carry out others. "Barbarism will still respect nothing but power," he professed, "and barbaric civilization repels alike interference, association, and instruction." Americans, on the other hand, "carry with them affirmative, and sometimes aggressive, ideas of freedom and progress, antagonistic alike to the traditions, customs, and habits of the people, and the ideas and practices of the local governments." Their work on behalf of progress, he argued, required the US Navy's support.[15]

Fueled by racial dreams of proselytizing "freedom" and crushing "barbarism," the US expedition provoked a bloody war in Korea that exposed and underscored its imperial roots and routes. Using Chinese and Japanese ports as launching points and emulating Perry's confrontational tactics in Japan, rear admiral John Rodgers, the Asiatic Squadron's commander, directed his fleet in May 1871 to a militarily sensitive area of the Korean coast, only fifty miles from Seoul, Korea's capital. Rodgers and Frederick F. Low, the US minister to China heading the expedition, promptly demanded a hearing before the king's court and informed Korean emissaries that "the smaller vessels of the fleet will make explorations further on, in order that the large ships may move nearer the capital, in case the minister deems it necessary." When a visibly armed surveying party proceeded upriver toward Seoul on June 1, Korean forces made a "sudden and treacherous assault" on the Americans, according to Rodgers. A US contingent of nearly 1,000 men, many of them veterans of the Civil War, retaliated ten days later, killing at least 250 Koreans, seizing five forts, and ransacking and burning nearby villages. The intense, brutal war shocked even the battle-worn US forces and generated familiar racial and imperial justifications. "Human life is considered of little value," Low wrote of Koreans, "and soldiers, educated as they have been, meet death with the same indifference as the Indians of North America."[16]

Shortly after the Korean peninsula fell within the US sphere of influence—Low and Rodgers left Korea with threats of further action—the United States formalized its dominant and essentially colonial relations with Hawai'i. By 1850, seven decades after British captain James Cook had "discovered" Hawai'i in his search for a new passage to Asia, *haole* (white foreigners) had engineered a dramatic transformation of the islands. Acting as chief advisors to Hawaii's king, they had successfully pressed for the privatization of land and the passage of a labor law largely modeled on British West Indian indentureship. The devastating effects of war and emancipation on Louisiana's sugar industry in the 1860s, then, provided a major impetus to sugarcane production in Hawai'i. The Reciprocity Treaty (1876) between the United States and Hawai'i, which allowed Hawaiian sugar to enter the US market duty-free, signified and solidified the kingdom's growing dependence on the United States. Sugar production increased sharply, from 12,540 tons in 1875 to 289,544 tons in 1900. The Hawaiian islands had become, according to secretary of state James G. Blaine in 1881, "practically members of the American zollverein, an outlying district of the State of California." A subsequent treaty, ratified in 1887, granted the United States exclusive rights to develop a naval station at Pearl Harbor.[17]

If US military, diplomatic, and commercial endeavors across the Pacific sanctified free trade as an unquestioned hallmark of US foreign policy, the transport of Asian workers on those same imperial routes triggered intense political debates on the need to protect free labor in the United States. Hawaii's sugar industry, for example, relied almost exclusively on Chinese and Japanese migrant workers in the second half of the nineteenth century, made available in no small measure by decades of gunboat diplomacy in Asia. But the racialization of Asian workers as enslaved and slavish "coolies" appeared to pit the interests of free trade and free labor against one another. The Louisiana Sugar Planters Association vigorously protested the Reciprocity Treaty, which it claimed was supporting "the slave or coolie grown sugars of the tropics" at Louisiana's expense. Representative Randall Lee Gibson of Louisiana took up the lost cause in Washington, DC. "Will you not afford equal protection to the freedmen of Louisiana and freemen of that State against the unpaid labor, the slave labor of Cuba and the gang or cooly labor ... of the tropics, that is still more exacting?" he asked. He demanded the federal protection of "American" sugar, in the cause of "freedom and justice against slavery and injustice, American freedom against Cuban slavery and Hawaiian coolyism."[18]

Federal legislation excluding Asian workers from the United States proper resolved the discursive contradictions of free trade and free labor. Building on the anti-"coolie" rhetoric of the 1862 law that had cast the United States as a liberating empire across the seas, the US Congress began passing laws greatly extending federal authority on matters related to immigration. Prohibiting "coolies," previously a "foreign" concern, became a "domestic" priority, a security measure to protect a "free" United States. Representative Horace F. Page, a Republican from California, led the charge. In December 1874, he introduced a resolution, which was referred to the Committee on Foreign Affairs, to inquire "whether any legislation or other action on the part of the Government of the United States is necessary to prevent the immigration or importation of coolies under contract for servile labor, and Chinese women brought to the United States for the purpose of prostitution." Even after the passage of the law bearing his name, the Page Law (1875), barred US vessels and citizens from transporting contract laborers from Asia and women for the purpose of prostitution, Page was not satisfied. He and his colleagues continued to rail against "cooly slaves and serfs" in their campaign to prohibit Chinese migrations that resulted in the Chinese Exclusion Act in 1882, the same year the United States formalized a commercial treaty with Korea.[19] Free trade and free labor made the US empire and aggregated its claims to state power to wage wars and to stimulate and regulate the flows of goods and peoples.

THE RISING TIDE OF COLOR AT THE
DAWN OF THE TWENTIETH CENTURY

In 1903, W. E. B. Du Bois famously proclaimed in *The Souls of Black Folk*, "The problem of the twentieth century is the problem of the color-line,— the relation of the darker to the lighter races of men in Asia and Africa, in America and the islands of the sea." His prophetic observation tied US history to world history, opening a vista onto a wider world defined by white supremacy and colonialism. Seventeen years later in "The Souls of White Folk," a searing essay in his collection *Darkwater*, Du Bois declaimed the lunacy of war and state violence. "The cause of war is preparation for war," he argued, "and of all that Europe has done in a century there is nothing that has equaled in energy, thought, and time her preparation for wholesale murder." And Du Bois placed America firmly alongside Europe in its appetite for wholesale murder and the subjugation of the "darker nations." "She stands today shoulder to shoulder with Europe in Europe's worst sin against civilization," he stated. At the same time, Du Bois found hope in the world, a radicalism brewing within and beyond America. "A belief in humanity is a belief in colored men," he wrote in "The Souls of White Folk." And he warned unabashedly in that essay, "The Dark World is going to submit to its present treatment just as long as it must and not one moment longer."[20]

The global dynamics of race, state violence, and radical movements that Du Bois identified very much defined the closing of the nineteenth century and the opening of the twentieth. Heeding calls for a modern navy to rival the great European powers, in the 1880s and 1890s, Congress appropriated funds to overhaul the US Navy's fleet with new cruisers and battleships. The decades of military investment appeared to pay off in the waters of Manila Bay on May 1, 1898, in a brief battle that opened the Spanish-American War. The news of a resounding victory by commodore George Dewey and his Asiatic Squadron over the Spanish in the Philippines elated Americans back home and elicited national declarations of epochal triumph from coast to coast. "Dewey has silenced the batteries completely," assistant secretary of the navy Theodore Roosevelt, who had engineered Dewey's course to the Philippines, told a jubilant crowd in Washington, DC. "He simply smothered the Spanish fire from the beginning." The *Los Angeles Times* likewise boasted that Dewey's feats "served to show to Spain, and to the world, how utterly futile it is for the Spaniards to oppose the American arms."[21]

Defeating the vestiges of the Spanish Empire in the spring and summer of 1898, however, produced tensions and contradictions that neither Roosevelt nor Dewey had planned for. The US empire faced revolutions on the ground. Spain had been trying for three years to suppress anticolonial insurgencies in the Philippines and Cuba, campaigns that had left its forces depleted and besieged even before the Americans arrived. As

Dewey awaited reinforcements to wage war on land, Emilio Aguinaldo, the Filipino revolutionary leader exiled in Hong Kong, returned aboard a US cruiser and promptly declared the Philippines independent on June 12, 1898. The United States never recognized Aguinaldo's declaration and, with the arrival of US Army troops, saw Filipino revolutionaries no longer as necessary allies but as troublesome obstacles to the US mission. When US commanders prepared their final offensive on Manila, they had already agreed with their Spanish counterparts to keep Aguinaldo's troops out of the city, a plan that resulted in tense encounters and skirmishes between putative allies. The raising of the US flag over Manila in August 1898 hardly restored peace to what a US Army officer called "this revolutionary and insurrectionary city of ... 250,000 inhabitants of the most diverse nationality."[22] With the Spanish surrender materialized a greater enemy, a racial, revolutionary enemy.

The ensuing US-Philippine War was a race war, as historian Paul A. Kramer argues, in that US imperial forces engaged in a mutually reinforcing process of casting the indigenous enemy and themselves as racially different (and innately unequal) and justifying the tactics of colonial violence in racial terms. While Aguinaldo attempted to gain US recognition of his government in the months leading up to the signing of the Treaty of Paris between Spain and the United States in December 1898, US president William McKinley revealed his intent to claim sovereignty over the entire archipelago. The United States agreed to pay Spain twenty million dollars for the Philippines. McKinley, in turn, vowed that his nation came "not as invaders or conquerors, but as friends," and would strive to "win the confidence, respect, and affection of the inhabitants of the Philippines by assuring them in every possible way that full measure of individual rights and liberties which is the heritage of free peoples, and by proving to them that the mission of the United States is one of benevolent assimilation, substituting the mild sway of justice and right for arbitrary rule." His racializing language of uplift—and attendant demand of submission—found a receptive audience on the domestic front but not on the front lines, where a standoff between US and Filipino troops erupted in gunfire on February 4, 1899. A protracted war of US imperial conquest had begun.[23]

United States military personnel and politicians predictably turned to deeply entrenched racial idioms to make sense of an armed enemy in a distant land. "I feel sorry for these people and all that have come under the control of the United States," an African American sergeant wrote. "The first thing in the morning is the 'Nigger' and the last thing at night is the 'Nigger.'" White troops, another black soldier related, "talked with impunity of 'niggers' to our soldiers, never once thinking that they were talking to home 'niggers' and should they be brought to remember that at home this is the same vile epithet they hurl at us, they beg pardon and make some effiminate [sic] excuse about what the Filipino is called." Theodore Roosevelt, for his part, liked to draw a different racial analogy. "We have no more right to leave the Filipinos to butcher one another and sink slowly back into savagery," he preached before domestic audiences, "than we would have the right, in an excess of sentimentality, to declare the Sioux and Apaches free to expel all white settlers from the lands they once held." The US forces were fighting for "the greatness of the Nation— the greatness of the race."[24]

The new context (across the Pacific from the continental United States) and the new enemy (of "Asiatic" and mixed origins) also generated a new race vernacular conducive to perpetrating violence on Filipinos more specifically. The Philippines was not an extension of the Deep South or the American West, crowded as the islands were with, in Roosevelt's worldview, "half-caste and native Christians, warlike Moslems, with wild pagans." Indeed, the indefinability of "Filipinos" came to define the Philippines, a critical means to delegitimize the "insurrection" and "insurrectos." "The Filipinos are not a nation, but a variegated assemblage of different tribes and peoples, and their loyalty is still of the tribal type," concluded the Philippine Commission, a body delegated to investigate conditions on the islands in 1899. Self-government, thus, was out of the question for "the multiplicity of tribes … and the multifarious phases of civilization—ranging all the way from the highest to the lowest—exhibited by the natives of the several provinces and islands." United States troops on the ground had little use for ethnological distinctions, preferring to call all Filipinos "niggers" or, increasingly, "gu-gus" or "goo-goos." Derived from a Tagalog word for a slippery shampoo made of coconut oil or US soldiers' masculinist taunts of Filipinas making "goo-goo eyes," the word gained wide usage and eventually evolved to "gook," soon to become a staple of US military occupation in Asia, Latin America, and the Caribbean.[25]

"Gu-gus" turned more slippery in November 1899, when US generals first declared their mission accomplished and Aguinaldo adopted a new strategy of guerrilla warfare. Blending into the rural populace, which provided crucial networks of financial and material support, Filipino forces wreaked havoc on US designs to, as the Philippine Commission put it, prosecute "the war until the insurgents are reduced to submission." "The enemy existed unseen in the dripping jungle, in the moldering towns and in the smoky clearings on the hillsides, and since a natural prudence bade him not risk any open encounter, the enemy was not to be found," a US veteran recalled. "But they existed nonetheless." Filipinos had "that particular faculty of all Orientals to say one thing and meaning another," another stated, "professed to be 'mucho amigo' (good friends) to our faces, while secretly aiding the insurrection with all the means at their command." Organizing into guerrilla units further racialized Filipinos as "uncivilized" and, in turn, seemed to justify US soldiers' own embrace of "savage" warfare. "This struggle on the islands has been naught but a gigantic scheme of robbery and oppression," a black private observed in 1901. "Graves have been entered and searches have been made for riches; churches and cathedrals have been entered and robbed of their precious ornaments; homes have been pillaged and moneys and jewelry stolen."[26]

As the war dragged on, officially until 1902 and unofficially for at least another decade, the US military emulated European imperial powers that dealt with colonial subjects, whether armed or not, as potential insurgents. In December 1900, general Arthur MacArthur, the commanding US general and military governor, announced a "new and more stringent policy" toward breaking up the "organized system" sustaining Filipino guerrilla units, stating ominously that "whenever action is necessary the more drastic the application the better." Following MacArthur's orders, US commanders in many hostile areas adopted a tactic made notorious worldwide by Spanish general Valeriano "The Butcher" Weyler in Cuba in 1896 and revived more recently by British troops against the Boers in South Africa. With the largest military force dispatched across the Atlantic, Weyler had systematically forced the Cuban population into concentration camps to isolate the anticolonial insurgents, a campaign that President McKinley had denounced as tantamount to "extermination." American orders to Filipino peasants to relocate to "protected zones" differed little in form. Outside these "reconcentration camps," US troops torched residences and set crops ablaze wholesale, to cut off the guerrillas' food supply and to punish their supporters, and fired on anyone they came across.[27]

While US military officers ordered their men to make the Philippines into "a howling wilderness," as one described their objective, they and their supporters claimed over and over that the withdrawal of US forces would lead to anarchy in the Philippines. They came as an army of liberation, not of enslavement. "Should our power by any fatality be withdrawn ... the government of the Philippines would speedily lapse into anarchy, which would excuse, if it did not necessitate, the intervention of other powers, and the eventual division of the islands among them," the Philippine Commission stated. "Only through American occupation, therefore, is the idea of a free, self-governing, and unified Philippine commonwealth at all conceivable." Race necessitated imperial rule. "If England were to abandon all claim to influence the internal affairs of the Transvaal and give up the title to suzerainty ... the State would remain an organized community ... likely to work out its problems after the general fashion of modern society," the *New York Times* waxed benevolent. "If the United States should abandon the Philippines.... There is no reason ... to infer that anarchy, and the worst form of it, would not ensue." Unlike the Dutch descendants of South Africa, Filipinos seemed incapable of cultivating a "modern society" on their own.[28]

Although these utterances counterposed "modernity" and "anarchy" (equated with "disorder" and "backwardness"), anarchism as a radical critique and movement emerged in the "modern" world of Europe in the 1870s and 1880s. Following the dissolution of the First International in 1876 and emphasizing personal autonomy and "propaganda by the deed," revolutionary anarchism inspired and attracted working-class audiences across Europe, especially in Spain, Italy, and France. A wave of spectacular assassinations by self-identified anarchists in the 1890s placed anarchism firmly on the world map, a political force that state leaders ignored at their own peril. But, as Benedict Anderson argues, anarchism was not simply a metropolitan phenomenon. Colonial subjects and budding anticolonial nationalists, including prominent figures such as José Rizal of the Philippines, traveled on imperial routes to Europe, developing worldly visions and connections that exceeded and challenged the bounds of empire. The politics of metropoles and colonies, or "domestic" and "foreign" politics, were indivisible, something that Theodore Roosevelt, soon to ascend to the White House, recognized readily. "Those who would encourage anarchy at home most naturally strike hands with the enemies of our country abroad," he pronounced. "Fundamentally the causes which they champion are the same. The step encouraging the assassination of the guardians of the law at home, to the aiding and abetting of the shooting down of our soldiers abroad is but a short one."[29]

Framing any effort to resist imperial conquest as an act of sedition, the US state laid the groundwork for a repressive regime determined to gather intelligence and maintain a surveillance of the general population. The Sedition Act, passed by governor-general William Taft's civilian commission in November 1901, made it clear that McKinley's initial promise of extending a "full measure of individual rights and liberties" would ring hollow in the Philippines. The law prohibited "any person to advocate orally or by writing or printing or by like methods the independence of the Philippine Islands or their separation from the United States, either by peaceful or forcible means." Civil liberties had no place in the war-torn Philippines, islands full of active and potential revolutionaries. That particular context, historian Alfred W. McCoy argues, freed US military and civilian personnel to build "a modern surveillance state" unfathomable back home in North America. In February 1901, the War Department dispatched an officer from the Military Information Division (MID) to Manila, who, within a few months, hired undercover agents to report on the civilian population and systematized intelligence reports on opposition to US rule. On the eve of the US declaration of victory, the War Department further centralized its intelligence network, making Manila home to its first MID field office, which was ordered to report directly to MID headquarters in Washington, DC.[30]

The long war in the Philippines, a culmination of decades of US military and trade missions across the Pacific, generated an extensive infrastructure of intelligence and surveillance. In the beginning of the Spanish-American War, the MID had so little information on the Philippines that its officers hastily copied "confidential" excerpts from the *Encyclopaedia Britannica*. Within five years, the US Army Signal Corps laid 5,355 miles of cable on land and another 1,615 miles undersea across the archipelago, connecting nearly 300 telegraph and telephone stations. In 1903 alone, this network carried 3.1 million messages. A war against anarchy and anarchism was a war for information. And US soldiers admittedly committed torture in the Philippines, most infamously through the "water cure," in the name of gathering information. When governor-general Taft appeared before a US Senate committee investigating war atrocities in 1902, he conceded that the "so called water cure" had been employed "on some occasions to extract information." But, he explained, "there are some amusing instances of Filipinos who came in and said they would not say anything unless tortured; that they must have an excuse for saying what they proposed to say." In the end, Taft insisted, "there never was a war conducted, whether against inferior races or not, in which there were more compassion and more restraint and more generosity."[31] Institutionalizing a tradition of unilateral military intervention in Asia, the US-Philippine War produced a state with immense authority to repress radical movements, a development that would resonate and reverberate immediately and profoundly on the other side of the Pacific.

President William McKinley's assassination in 1901 by a self-professed anarchist, whose leftward drift had coincided with his brother's return from military service in the Philippines, sparked a new war, a global war against anarchism linking military action and immigration restrictions. "Anarchy is a crime against the whole human race, and all mankind should band against the Anarchist," the new president Theodore Roosevelt declared in December 1901. "His crime should be made an offense against the law of nations, like piracy and that form of man-stealing known as the slave trade; for it is of far blacker infamy than either." The Philippines demanded a strong military, which Roosevelt requested from Congress, since wars "with barbarous or semi-barbarous peoples ... [were] merely a most regrettable but necessary international police duty which must be performed for the sake of the welfare of mankind." To deal with anarchists closer to home, Roosevelt asked for a new immigration law, implying that the problem lay fundamentally beyond the United States. Anarchists, Roosevelt believed, "should be kept out of this country, and if found here they should be promptly deported to the country whence they came, and far-reaching provision should be made for the punishment of those who stay."[32]

Congress responded to Roosevelt's recommendations with a major immigration law in 1903, encompassing and expanding the list of "excluded classes" compiled over the previous quarter century. It now included

> All idiots, insane persons, epileptics, ... paupers; persons likely to
> become a public charge; professional beggars; persons afflicted with
> a loathsome or with a dangerous contagious disease; persons who
> have been convicted of a felony or other crime or misdemeanor
> involving moral turpitude; polygamists, anarchists, or persons

who believe in or advocate the overthrow by force or violence of the Government of the United States or of all government or of all forms of law, or the assassination of public officials; prostitutes, and persons who procure or attempt to bring in prostitutes or women for the purpose of prostitution; those who have been, within one year from the date of the application for admission to the United States, deported as being under offers, solicitations, promises or agreements to perform labor or service of some kind therein.

Reinforcing late-nineteenth-century representations of prostitutes and contract laborers as embodiments of enslavement after slavery, the 1903 law continued to dwell on these traditionally proscribed "classes." The Chinese, whose exclusion had inaugurated and enlarged the federal surveillance of bodies and borders beginning in 1882, were not included in the latest list, since "this Act shall not be construed to repeal, alter, or amend existing laws relating to the immigration, or exclusion of, Chinese persons or persons of Chinese descent."[33]

The law's most significant addition was anarchists, whom Roosevelt had denounced as "essentially seditious and treasonable." More than a century after fears of revolutionary ideas and peoples from France and Saint Domingue (Haiti) had led to the passage of the Alien and Sedition Acts in 1798, the US government again set explicit parameters on legitimate political ideology and political expression, beyond which noncitizens in particular became subject to federal scrutiny, exclusion, and deportation. The provisions specifically targeting anarchists prohibited the immigration and naturalization of anyone

who disbelieves in or who is opposed to all organized government, or who is a member of or affiliated with any organization entertaining and teaching such disbelief in or opposition to all organized government, or who advocates or teaches the duty, necessity, or propriety of the unlawful assaulting or killing of any officer or officers, either of specific individuals or of officers generally, of the Government of the United States or of any other organized government, because of his or their official character.[34]

An unmistakable response to McKinley's assassination, the law's anti-radical clauses established a vast and loose definition of what constituted criminal political beliefs and affiliations, a reflection and an extension of the sedition act in the Philippines, now cast onto the "domestic" population of the United States.

The 1903 immigration statute allocated immense administrative and discretionary powers to the federal government that would prove central in its mission to define and defend national security ever since. In particular, the bureaucrats who oversaw the admission and exclusion of all aliens—the commissioner-general of immigration and the immigration commissioners, officers, clerks, and other employees at individual ports of entry—held the ultimate authority to exclude or expel aliens, subject to no judicial oversight whatsoever. All aliens not "clearly and beyond a doubt entitled to land" were to receive hearings before a "board of special inquiry" of three immigration officers appointed by the immigration commissioners. These hearings were to be "separate and apart from the public," with the board's majority vote to be "final." Discontent aliens (or dissenting board members), however, could appeal the board's ruling through the immigration commissioners and the commissioner-general of immigration to the secretary of the treasury (changed later to the secretary of commerce and labor), "whose decision shall then be final." Such procedures and decisions concerned cases not only of exclusion but also of deportation. Any alien found to have entered the United States unlawfully within three years of landing was "to be taken into custody and returned to the country whence he came."[35]

Although the US Constitution enumerated no such authority, laws and legal cases on Chinese exclusion over the previous two decades had endowed the federal government with unilateral and exclusive power in all matters related to immigration and deportation, which were deemed foundational to national security. "To preserve its independence, and give security against foreign aggression and encroachment, is the highest duty of every nation ... whether from the foreign nation acting in its national character or from vast hordes of its people crowding in upon us," the US Supreme Court ruled in *Chae Chan Ping v. United States* (also known as the *Chinese Exclusion Case*, 1889). "The government, possessing the powers which are to be exercised for protection and security, is clothed with authority to determine the occasion on which the powers shall be called forth; and its determination, so far as the subjects affected are concerned, are [sic] necessarily conclusive upon all its departments and officers." If the US government categorized "foreigners of a different race" as "dangerous to its peace and security," the court reasoned, its designation and exclusion could not "be stayed because at the time there are no actual hostilities with the nation of which the foreigners are subjects." Sedition knew no bounds between war and peace. Four years later, the Supreme Court strongly affirmed the state's power "to expel or deport foreigners ... as absolute and unqualified as the right to prohibit and prevent their entrance into the country."[36]

In striking fashion, Chinese exclusion, long identified with white supremacy on the Pacific coast, had set the legal foundation for a massive state of repression targeting radical movements. Over the ensuing decades of the twentieth century, the US state would pass a barrage of laws on sedition and immigration, culminating in anticommunist crusades—and now the "war on terror"—that would haunt radical movements, particularly those seeking to overthrow white supremacy and colonialism. The turn of events must have pleased Lothrop Stoddard, who had prescribed in 1920 the need to contain "Pan-Colored" and "Colored-Bolshevist" alliances, the vanguard of "the rising tide of color." As "the arch-enemy of civilization and the race," Stoddard insisted, "Bolshevism must be crushed out with iron heels, no matter what the cost." The historical roots of J. Edgar Hoover's notorious characterization of the Black Panther Party as "the greatest threat to the internal security of the country" can be traced back to Stoddard, back to the Philippine Revolution and the US-Philippine War, and back to Chinese exclusion, if not earlier.[37] As the US state claimed authority to monitor, imprison, and deport radicals, it simultaneously racialized them, a cyclical process central and indeed essential to state repression in the twentieth century. It is those particular dynamics of race, state violence, and radical movements across the Pacific that the essays collected herein reveal and explore.


## RACE, STATE VIOLENCE,
## AND RADICAL MOVEMENTS ACROSS THE PACIFIC

Our iteration of *The Rising Tide of Color* does not pretend to offer a comprehensive picture of racial and radical politics in the twentieth century, but it begins to plot a historical process that Michael Omi and Howard Winant theorized years ago. In their seminal work, Omi and Winant proposed that we approach race as *"an unstable and 'de-centered' complex of social meanings constantly being transformed by political struggle."* Race was always in formation, they argued, both giving shape to and being shaped by social, economic, and political forces at particular historical moments. For most of US history, they observed, racially subordinated groups had no choice but to engage in a "racial *war of maneuver*," cultivating institutions, movements, and communities outside "the hegemonic racial state." Such maneuvers laid the groundwork for a racial "war of position," in the Gramscian sense, an open assault on the racial state for democratic transformation. Writing amid the "Reagan Revolution," Omi and Winant understood and underscored the dialectical relationship between the state, what they called the "racial state," and social movements in defining racial politics in the United States. The racial state did not embody and enact a linear, liberal progress toward equal rights and democracy. Rather, it has sought constantly to equilibrate (or stabilize) the racial order, according to Omi and Winant, through laws, policies, and "a repressive apparatus" in response to crises initiated by racially based social movements. State reform and state reaction proceeded apace, establishing "a new *unstable equilibrium*" in the racial order.[38]

The nine essays that follow open our eyes to a series of racial crises in the twentieth century, precipitated in no small measure by radical movements for racial justice. In the World War I era, anticolonial nationalists and labor organizers built powerful local movements in Hawai'i, on the Pacific coast, and elsewhere, motivated by and within a transpacific world of wars, migrations, and revolutions. Strengthening the repressive apparatus arising from earlier immigration laws and the US-Philippine War, the US state mobilized and expanded its antiradical laws and agents in the 1910s and 1920s to counter movements against white supremacy and colonialism. The racialized targets of antiradical repression, in turn, organized imaginatively around anarchism and communism in the 1930s, exploiting the political and cultural spaces opened up (and foreclosed) by a crisis in global capitalism and a US liberal state trying to address that crisis. Although local and global cries for social justice and democracy compelled the US state to disavow racism, colonialism, and violence in the middle decades of the twentieth century, its capacity to carry out and justify violence, particularly against peoples of color, increased to a scale unprecedented in the history of our planet. Out of those contradictions emerged interracial and global visions and solidarities in the decades following World War II—in working-class neighborhoods, in prisons, in Southeast Asia—even as the US state proved all too effective in rendering such radical movements illegible and illegitimate. These are some of the historical ruptures, continuities, and dialectics that our collection maps.

George Lipsitz, whose scholarship has shaped and advanced the study of race, social movements, and popular culture over the past quarter century, begins the collection with a piercing essay on the intellectual and political stakes of studying race, state violence, and radical movements in our current moment. An elaboration of his opening keynote address at our conference in May 2011, "Standing at the Crossroads" demands that we, as engaged scholars, pursue our work with *konesans* (knowledge) and *balans* (balance), concepts at the heart of Afro-diasporic traditions. *Konesans* flows not from empirical data or theoretical mastery but from experience and wisdom; *balans* does not seek neutrality or objectivity but generates opportunities to embrace and explain contradictions. Speaking to the current neoliberal, color-blind moment, Lipsitz identifies a series of political and intellectual "traps" that activists and scholars on the left can fall into, where oppositional rhetoric, political ideology, and radical posturing can devolve all too easily into individualized escapism, anti-democratic dogmatism, and shoddy scholarship. We need to study the history of race, state violence, and radical movements critically and rigorously, Lipsitz argues, to reveal their intimate connections over time and space, to understand and interrogate the relevance of the past to today's struggles. Wallowing in the past or romanticizing radical movements cannot define our agenda, he suggests, for the problems we face today are too profound and immense. The remaining essays in the collection, organized chronologically and thematically, strive to respond individually and collectively to Lipsitz's call.

Essays in the second section, "Traversing the Pacific," focus on specific locales to illustrate broader connections to a wider world of political and cultural movements across the Pacific in the early decades of the twentieth century. The US-Canadian borderlands of the Pacific Northwest, Kornel Chang demonstrates, was a hotbed of radical organizing during the World War I era, attracting and generating political discourses and practices across racial divides. The Industrial Workers of the World (IWW), perhaps the most notable and visible of them all, for example, embraced the concept of interracial working-class internationalism and extolled the virile and manly virtues of South Asian anticolonial revolutionaries and militant Japanese workers. The recuperation of Asian manhood likewise preoccupied South Asian radicals in the North American

West, Chang argues, as they sought to incite an armed revolution against the British Empire. At least in certain radical circles, Asian men came to represent nearly the ideal man, embodying qualities—masculine, courageous, determined, and revolutionary—that challenged and undermined their historical feminization. The political possibilities engendered by a common fixation on revolutionary manhood proved inherently limiting, though, Chang concludes, for neither Wobblies nor South Asian radicals could escape the binding logic of manliness and whiteness at the heart of race, nation, and empire. Claiming and reclaiming Asian manhood ultimately challenged *and* reproduced racial and gender norms, a political lesson along the lines that Audre Lorde would capture pithily: "The master's tools will never dismantle the master's house."[39]

If Wobblies tapped into circuits of knowledge across the Pacific—for example, by valorizing striking Japanese workers in Hawai'i—workers in Hawai'i likewise lived and struggled in transpacific contexts. Beginning at the turn of the twentieth century, Denise Khor argues in her chapter, "Dangerous Amusements," plantation workers in Hawai'i forged a counterpublic in part through the consumption of popular films, imported initially from Japan and increasingly from Hollywood. Silent films, introduced to Hawai'i by Japanese migrant entrepreneurs and translated into the local context by a cast of live narrators and musicians, produced, according to Khor, a homosocial space where plantation workers could congregate and cultivate a common consciousness critical of the plantation hierarchy. Particularly in the aftermath of spectacular plantation strikes, which transformed Japanese-owned movie theaters into union halls and makeshift homes for evicted workers and their families, the planter elite came to see the need to regulate and to suppress the theaters' presence and influence in the islands. Hawaii's elite, however, could never dictate the terms of cultural consumption and translation on the ground, Khor concludes, for workers rejected the educational films favored by their employers and subverted the racial and imperial messages at the heart of the American Western. It was ironically through silent Western films, a cultural archetype of US imperial expansion, that Japanese and Filipino workers developed a radical working-class culture that planters found so threatening.

The third section, "Forging Multiracial Fronts," shifts the focus geographically to the continental United States and chronologically to the 1930s, when those on the left waged a vibrant movement to contest and redefine state power to challenge white supremacy. In his captivating account of three anarchists, Kenyon Zimmer reveals how they subverted US immigration laws to claim and proclaim their statelessness and to reject a primary wage of whiteness: inclusion in the US nation-state. Branding and racializing Shmuel Marcus (Marcus Graham), Domenico Sallitto, and Vincenzo Ferrero as anarchists, the US state attempted to deport them, but the anarchists refused to play along. In places such as San Francisco, Zimmer argues, anarchists forged a multiracial struggle against the US state, in part because US immigration laws had positioned Asians, Mexicans, and anarchists in the same racializing and racialized category—subject to exclusion and deportation. If the legal and political campaigns in defense of the anarchists generated widespread support—and ideological tensions—on the left, they also continually frustrated US officials. By hiding his place of origin, in the case of Marcus, or dissembling their radical politics, Zimmer concludes, the three anarchists exposed the falsity of universal claims to national sovereignty. The federal government claimed the authority to expel anarchists, but it failed to find the means to carry out that power in these three cases. Through their cat-and-mouse game with the US state in the 1930s, Zimmer writes, Marcus, Ferrero, and Sallitto "remained defiantly within, but not of, the nation."

Christina Heatherton identifies similar tensions and dynamics at work in southern California in the early years of the Great Depression, when diverse and overlapping radical traditions converged to make race central to working-class struggles. In the throes of an economic crisis, she argues, workers of color, particularly Mexican workers, who repeatedly crossed borders and categories in the capitalist landscape—urban and rural, citizen and alien, employed and unemployed—banded together with white allies to challenge prevailing social relations of production and reproduction. They were inspired and propelled to action not only by dire circumstances but also by the organizing efforts of the Communist Party and vital memories and histories of revolutionary struggles, especially the Mexican Revolution. Through Unemployed Councils in Los Angeles and widespread strikes in the surrounding agricultural fields, according to Heatherton, working peoples of southern California simultaneously made claims on the state for relief and generated radical critiques of state repression at the heart of employers' drive to make the region a wide "open shop." On one level, the revolutionary movement to redefine relief—as a collective demand for immediate sustenance and wider transformations—marked an extension of the Mexican Revolution, which, she argues, had mobilized the masses against the presence and influence of US capital. On another level, Heatherton adds, it revealed the depths to which the communist movement resonated with peoples of color in the 1930s, fostering radical visions of social justice across racial and national divides.

The fourth section, "Seeing Radical Connections," retains the focus on California, the epicenter of segregated housing, militarized policing, and radical organizing in the twentieth century, particularly after World War II.[40] Emily K. Hobson's essay "Policing Gay LA" explains cogently how race and sexuality came to be segregated spatially and politically in postwar Los Angeles, a reflection and a product of the policies and tactics of the Los Angeles Police Department (LAPD) and of gay activists' embrace of "minority" identity. For decades through the 1950s, Hobson observes, the state campaign against "vice" concentrated on illicit sex work and visible homosexual contact in working-class neighborhoods of color. While middle-class white men found refuge in the private spaces of white neighborhoods, queer spaces emerged in racially diverse, working-class neighborhoods that increasingly subjected gay men, lesbians, and peoples of color to police surveillance and mass arrests. Those historical contexts, Hobson argues, generated a brief moment of radical possibility, when interracial mobilizations against the LAPD jointly confronted the policing of sexuality and the policing of race. The insurgent politics of contesting the state, however, soon gave way to a politics of respectability, including among liberal homophile activists, who positioned gay identities and communities—conceptually and physically—as analogous to and then apart from communities of color. The end result, Hobson concludes, was a wholesale disaggregation of race and sexuality, a process of historical forgetting that has endured and deepened through the era of gay liberation and beyond.

In "Carceral Migrations," Dan Berger investigates the transregional roots of black prisoner radicalism in the 1970s, specifically in the ways black subjection and black resistance came to be framed and understood around slavery. In the wake of civil rights legislation and amid the rise of the prison industrial complex, he argues, black prisoner activists integrated their personal and familial backgrounds in the US South and their impending or immediate incarceration in California to generate a radical critique of state violence—a disciplinary regime of coerced mobility and confinement at the heart of plantations in the Old South and of prisons in the Golden State. The invocation of slavery by Angela Davis, George Jackson, Ruchell Magee, and many others to condemn contemporary imprisonment in the American West represented more than a historical or literary metaphor. It simultaneously recalled a collective black memory and identity rooted in slavery—and resistance against slavery—and a larger history of slavery's centrality to the development of the United States and the modern world. Through their speeches, writings, and courtroom defenses, Berger argues, black prisoner activists engendered a penetrating rebuke of liberal narratives of race that tended to reduce and isolate white supremacy and white supremacists to the South. They drew attention to the deep connections between southern racial violence and what Daniel Martinez HoSang calls "blue state racism," a political lesson, Berger illustrates, enabled and embodied by black prisoner activists' own journeys from the South to the Pacific coast.[41]

The fifth and final section, "Fighting a State of Violence," highlights a series of transpacific movements in the 1960s and 1970s that likewise spawned radical critiques of the US state—"the greatest purveyor of violence in the world today," in Martin Luther King, Jr.'s words. Judy Tzu-Chun Wu's "Hypervisbility and Invisibility" builds on Edward W. Said's concept of orientalism—that the production of intellectual and cultural knowledge of the East defined and justified Western colonial identity and authority—to interpret efforts by various women from Southeast Asia and North America to forge a global sisterhood against the US empire. Through tours and conferences in Vietnam and Canada and through reports and reflections on those meetings in radical publications, Wu argues, women of different racial and political backgrounds cultivated a gendered analysis of war and empire that cumulatively replicated, inverted, and subverted an orientalist logic—what she calls "radical orientalism." Their renderings of the East during the height of the Vietnam War fixated particularly on the prominent roles assumed by women in Southeast Asia—mothers, wives, victims, heroines, and, perhaps most fundamentally, revolutionaries. Whether projected by Southeast Asian women themselves or projected onto them by women of the West, those representations, according to Wu, produced new identities, alliances, and discourses that exposed and exceeded racial and national boundaries. For women of color in the United States, especially Asian American women, she argues, personal encounters with "sisters" from Asia awakened them to a wider world of radical possibilities.

In "Radicalizing Currents," Simeon Man explores transpacific movements that allied and radicalized activists of different backgrounds in multiple locales. Although intended to diffuse the antiwar movement on the homefront, he argues, president Richard M. Nixon's policy to "Vietnamize" the war in Vietnam drove antiwar activists across the Pacific to the bases of the US military empire, where they forged alliances with local activists in Japan, Okinawa, and the Philippines. Man traces the trajectory of the Pacific Counseling Service (PCS) in particular, an organization founded in 1969 to lend support to disaffected GIs in the Bay Area. PCS organizers moved farther and farther to the left of their pacifist origins in the early 1970s, he argues, as their work with GIs on the Pacific coast and then in Asia and with local political movements in Asia compelled them to see the Vietnam War as a phase of a larger history of the US empire. Their organizing efforts in Okinawa and the Philippines especially exposed them to an urgent politics shaped by vexed histories of colonialism—histories that were, Man suggests, then being elided and renewed through the US state's pacts with the Japanese and Philippine states. Those emergent international relations proved crucial to the violent repression of radical movements afoot in Asia, he concludes, but they also helped to deepen global revolutionary alliances and commitments to liberate Third World peoples from the yoke of racism and imperialism.

*    *    *

As I compiled and edited this collection of essays, I found myself listening a lot to the music of Blue Scholars. This dynamic duo from Seattle has been releasing some of the most radical albums in hip hop over the past decade, articulating a historical appreciation of political struggle and a global vision of social justice that would make Lothrop Stoddard turn over in his grave. In their own ways, the essays collected here deliver a similar message of hope, a hope rooted not in simple prescriptions but in complex contradictions. The nine chapters of the collection emerged in part by happenstance—who chose to present at the conference, who decided (and who declined) to submit a revised essay afterward—but they testify collectively to the need to reorient the study of race in US history. By focusing on historical moments on the Pacific coast and across the Pacific, they call for interpretive frameworks beyond particular regions, nations, and empires, not for a new brand of national or regional exceptionalism. And there is a long list of topics and subjects that the collection surely could and should have addressed, foremost among them the struggles of American Indians to grapple with the dialectics of race, state violence, and radical movements. There is a lot of work to be done. If anything, I hope our collection serves as a resounding call for new histories, geographies, and identities toward building new radical possibilities in the twenty-first century. That is my hope.

1   Diane C. Fujino, *Samurai among Panthers: Richard Aoki on Race, Resistance, and a Paradoxical Life* (Minneapolis: University of Minnesota Press, 2012), 13, 19. I thank George Quibuyen (Geologic) of Blue Scholars for allowing me to quote from "Opening Salvo."

2   Fujino, *Samurai among Panthers*, 275–79.

3   Seth Rosenfeld, "Activist Richard Aoki Named as Informant," *San Francisco Chronicle*, August 20, 2012; Trevor Griffey, "When a Celebrated Activist Turns Out to Be an FBI Informant," *Truthout*, November 5, 2012, available at truth-out.org (accessed January 9, 2013). Griffey's article covers the varied responses to Rosenfeld's charges.

4   Lothrop Stoddard, *The Rising Tide of Color against White World-Supremacy* (New York: Charles Scribner's Sons, 1920).

5   Barack Obama, "Race Speech," March 18, 2008, http://www.constitutioncenter.org/amoreperfectunion/docs/Race_Speech_Transcript.pdf (accessed April 2, 2012).

6   James Melvin Washington, ed., *A Testament of Hope: The Essential Writings of Martin Luther King, Jr.* (San Francisco: HarperSanFrancisco, 1991), 219.

7   Nikhil Pal Singh, *Black Is a Country: Race and the Unfinished Struggle for Democracy* (Cambridge: Harvard University Press, 2004), 1–6; Washington, *Testament of Hope*, 233, 231, 238.

8   The following two sections of the introduction are adapted from my article "Seditious Subjects: Race, State Violence, and the U.S. Empire," *Journal of Asian American Studies* 14, no. 2 (June 2011): 221–47.

9   John Kuo Wei Tchen, *New York before Chinatown: Orientalism and the Shaping of American Culture, 1776–1882* (Baltimore: Johns Hopkins University Press, 1999), 25–40; *Congressional Globe*, 29th Congress, 1st Session, 916, 918; Stuart Creighton Miller, *The Unwelcome Immigrant: The American Image of the Chinese, 1785–1882* (Berkeley: University of California Press, 1969), 16–80; Gary Y. Okihiro, *Margins and Mainstreams: Asians in American History and Culture* (Seattle: University of Washington Press, 1994), 3–30; Bradford Perkins, *The Cambridge History of American Foreign Relations*, vol. 1, *The Creation of a Republican Empire, 1776–1865* (Cambridge: Cambridge University Press, 1993), 203.

10  "Extension of American Commerce—Proposed Mission to Japan and Corea," 28th Congress, 2nd Session, House of Representatives Document 138, 1–2; Walter LaFeber, *The Clash: A History of U.S.-Japan Relations* (New York: W. W. Norton and Company, 1997), 9–17; *New York Times*, July 11, 1854.

11  Wm. H. Robertson to Secretary of State William L. Marcy, August 6, 1855, 34th Congress, 1st Session, Senate Executive Document 99, 3; Wm. H. Robertson to Secretary

of State William L. Marcy, July 27, 1855, 34th Congress, 1st Session, House Executive Document 105, 68; Sidney W. Mintz, *Sweetness and Power: The Place of Sugar in Modern History* (New York: Penguin Books, 1985), 61–72.

12    Moon-Ho Jung, *Coolies and Cane: Race, Labor, and Sugar in the Age of Emancipation* (Baltimore: Johns Hopkins University Press, 2006), 11–33 (quotes from 26 and 30).

13    Jung, *Coolies and Cane*, 33–38 (quote from 37).

14    LaFeber, *Clash*, 17–29.

15    "Report of the Secretary of the Navy," December 3, 1866, 39th Congress, 2nd Session, House Executive Document 1, 9, 15–16; Gordon H. Chang, "Whose 'Barbarism'? Whose 'Treachery'? Race and Civilization in the Unknown United States–Korea War of 1871," *Journal of American History* 89, no. 4 (March 2003): 1335, 1338; George M. Robeson, "Report of the Secretary of the Navy," November 25, 1871, 42nd Congress, 2nd Session, House Executive Document 1, Part 3, 4, 12.

16    Chang, "Whose 'Barbarism'? Whose 'Treachery'?" 1335–56 (quotes from 1345 and 1356); Jno. Rodgers to George M. Robeson, June 3, 1871, 42nd Congress, 2nd Session, House Executive Document 1, Part 3, 276.

17    Gary Y. Okihiro, *Cane Fires: The Anti-Japanese Movement in Hawaii, 1865–1945* (Philadelphia: Temple University Press, 1991), 3–11; Moon-Kie Jung, *Reworking Race: The Making of Hawaii's Interracial Labor Movement* (New York: Columbia University Press, 2006), 12; Eric T. L. Love, *Race over Empire: Racism and U.S. Imperialism, 1865–1900* (Chapel Hill: University of North Carolina Press, 2004), 75–93 (Blaine quote from 93).

18    Jung, *Coolies and Cane*, 218.

19    George Anthony Peffer, *If They Don't Bring Their Women Here: Chinese Female Immigration before Exclusion* (Urbana: University of Illinois Press, 1999), 34–35; Jung, *Coolies and Cane*, 10–13, 33–38; Chang, "Whose 'Barbarism'? Whose 'Treachery'?" 1362.

20    W. E. B. Du Bois, *Writings: The Suppression of the African Slave-Trade, The Souls of Black Folk, Dusk of Dawn, Essays and Articles* (New York: Library of America, 1986), 372; W. E. B. Du Bois, *Darkwater: Voices from within the Veil* (New York: Washington Square Press, 2004), 33, 35–36.

21    Nathan Miller, *The U.S. Navy: A History*, 3rd ed. (Annapolis, MD: Naval Institute Press, 1997), 143–59; *New York Times*, May 2, 3, 7, 8, 1898; *Los Angeles Times*, May 3, 1898.

22    Brian McAllister Linn, *The Philippine War, 1899–1902* (Lawrence: University Press of Kansas, 2000), 8–25; Paul A. Kramer, *The Blood of Government: Race, Empire, the United States, and the Philippines* (Chapel Hill: University of North Carolina Press, 2006), 94–97; Alfred W. McCoy, "Policing the Imperial Periphery: Philippine Pacification and the Rise of the U.S. National Security State," in *Colonial Crucible: Empire in the Making of the Modern American State*, ed. Alfred W. McCoy and Francisco A. Scarano (Madison: University of Wisconsin Press, 2009), 106.

23    Kramer, *Blood of Government*, 89–111 (McKinley quote, 110).

24    Willard B. Gatewood, Jr., *"Smoked Yankees" and the Struggle for Empire: Letters from Negro Soldiers, 1898–1902* (Fayetteville: University of Arkansas Press, 1987), 257, 280; *New York Times*, September 24, 1899.

25    *New York Times*, April 11, 1899; Kramer, *Blood of Government*, 122–29; David R. Roedi-
      ger, *Towards the Abolition of Whiteness: Essays on Race, Politics, and Working Class His-
      tory* (London: Verso, 1994), 117–20.

26    Kramer, *Blood of Government*, 130–37 (veterans' quotes, 134); *New York Times*, Novem-
      ber 3, 1899; Gatewood,"*Smoked Yankees*," 305.

27    Linn, *The Philippine War*, 213–15; Kramer, *Blood of Government*, 152–54; Benedict
      Anderson, *Under Three Flags: Anarchism and the Anti-Colonial Imagination* (London:
      Verso, 2005), 146.

28    Linn, *Philippine War*, 313; *New York Times*, November 3 and September 26, 1899.

29    Anderson, *Under Three Flags*, 71–81; *New York Times*, September 24, 1899.

30    Kramer, *Blood of Government*, 175; McCoy, "Policing the Imperial Periphery," 108;
      Joan M. Jensen, *Army Surveillance in America, 1775–1980* (New Haven, CT: Yale Uni-
      versity Press, 1991), 101–103.

31    Jensen, *Army Surveillance in America*, 92; McCoy, "Policing the Imperial Periphery,"
      108; Stuart Creighton Miller,"*The Benevolent Assimilation*": *The American Conquest of
      the Philippines, 1899–1903* (New Haven, CT: Yale University Press, 1982), 213 (Taft
      quotes); Paul Kramer, "The Water Cure," *New Yorker*, February 25, 2008, 38–43.

32    Eric Rauchway, *Murdering McKinley: The Making of Theodore Roosevelt's America* (New
      York: Hill and Wang, 2003), 170; *New York Times*, December 4, 1901.

33    *The Statutes at Large of the United States of America, from December, 1901, to March,
      1903*, vol. 32, part 1 (Washington, DC: Government Printing Office, 1903), 1214–15,
      1221; Amy Dru Stanley, *From Bondage to Contract: Wage Labor, Marriage, and the Mar-
      ket in the Age of Slave Emancipation* (Cambridge: Cambridge University Press, 1998);
      Lucy E. Salyer, *Laws Harsh as Tigers: Chinese Immigrants and the Shaping of Modern
      Immigration Law* (Chapel Hill: University of North Carolina Press, 1995); Nayan
      Shah, *Contagious Divides: Epidemics and Race in San Francisco's Chinatown* (Berkeley:
      University of California Press, 2001); Erika Lee, *At America's Gates: Chinese Immigra-
      tion during the Exclusion Era, 1882–1943* (Chapel Hill: University of North Carolina
      Press, 2003).

34    *New York Times*, December 4, 1901; Daniel Kanstroom, *Deportation Nation: Outsid-
      ers in American History* (Cambridge, MA: Harvard University Press, 2007), 46–63;
      *Statutes at Large*, 1221–22.

35    *Statutes at Large*, 1219–20.

36    Kanstroom, *Deportation Nation*, 91–130; Chae Chan Ping v. United States, 130 US
      581 (1889); Fong Yue Ting v. United States, Wong Quan v. United States, Lee Joe v.
      United States, 149 US 698 (1893).

37    Mae M. Ngai, *Impossible Subjects: Illegal Aliens and the Making of Modern America*
      (Princeton: Princeton University Press, 2004); William Preston, Jr., *Aliens and Dis-
      senters: Federal Suppression of Radicals, 1903–1933*, 2nd ed. (Urbana: University of
      Illinois Press, 1994); Joshua Bloom and Waldo E. Martin, Jr., *Black against Empire:
      The History and Politics of the Black Panther Party* (Berkeley: University of California
      Press, 2013), 3 (Hoover quote).

38    Michael Omi and Howard Winant, *Racial Formation in the United States: From the
      1960s to the 1980s* (New York: Routledge, 1986), 68, 74, 79, 82 (emphases in original).

39  Audre Lorde, *Sister Outsider* (Berkeley: Crossing Press, 1984), 110.

40  See, e.g., Mike Davis, *City of Quartz: Excavating the Future in Los Angeles* (New York: Verso, 2006); Mark Wild, *Street Meeting: Multiethnic Neighborhoods in Early Twentieth-Century Los Angeles* (Berkeley: University of California Press, 2005); Scott Kurashige, *The Shifting Grounds of Race: Black and Japanese Americans in the Making of Multiethnic Los Angeles* (Princeton: Princeton University Press, 2008); João H. Costa Vargas, *Catching Hell in the City of Angels: Life and Meanings of Blackness in South Central Los Angeles* (Minneapolis: University of Minnesota Press, 2006); Ruth Wilson Gilmore, *Golden Gulag: Prisons, Surplus, Crisis, and Opposition in Globalizing California* (Berkeley: University of California Press, 2007).

41  Daniel Martinez HoSang, *Racial Propositions: Ballot Initiatives and the Making of Postwar California* (Berkeley: University of California Press, 2010), 264.

# 1

# "Standing at the Crossroads"

## Why Race, State Violence, and Radical Movements Matter Now

GEORGE LIPSITZ

AT THIS DANGEROUS MOMENT OF SEEMINGLY ENDLESS WAR COUPLED with cataclysmic economic crisis and impending environmental catastrophe, concerned scholars are creating new histories of race, state violence, and radical movements on the Pacific coast and beyond.[1] These inquiries critique and contest current conditions by exploring the historical origins and evolution of our present-day problems. They reveal how previous generations mobilized against economic exploitation and inequality, imperial wars, state repression, and racialized moral panics. This research reflects the ingenuity and intelligence of the individual scholars who author it, but it is also evidence that we are living through a time when traditional histories seem no longer to suffice either to explain our imperiled present or to provide reliable guidelines for the foreboding future. We have come to a new crossroads in history, a place where impoverished and outworn ideas, interpretations, and imaginaries are being challenged by new archives, analyses, and arguments appropriate for identifying, addressing, and redressing the injustices of our time.

At any crossroads, decisions must be made. In many cultures the crossroads is a dangerous but sacred location. People can lose their way at the places where different paths come together. At a crossroads, confusion abounds and collisions can occur. The right path often looks like the wrong path and the wrong path looks like the right path. Yet precisely because crossroads are places where decisions have to be made, they are sites replete with potential and possibility. At the crossroads, it is possible to see in more than one direction, to venture off on a new path, to change course.

In the Afro-diasporic tradition, negotiating the crossroads successfully requires both knowledge and balance, what the practitioners of *vodou* in Haiti describe as *konesans* and *balans*.[2] For people trained in Western ways of knowing, the word "knowledge" often connotes a blend of empirical facts with abstract theories. In that tradition, "balance" signifies neutrality and moderation. In the Afro-diasporic tradition, however, knowledge (*konesans*) entails blending experience with wisdom. It is a capacity acquired with age, developed through respect for those who precede us in life, for the people whose suffering, sacrifice, and struggle have made it possible for us to exist today. Mastery of *konesans* means acquiring the ability to place the present in its full temporal context as both the product of the past and the progenitor of the future. The world we inhabit was here before we arrived and it will be here long after we are gone. We cannot disavow the past's claims upon the present or deny our responsibility to the future. Yet focusing too much on the past can also be a problem, because it can become an alternative reality, a place of escape that hinders our ability to understand the present and act upon it. For that reason, *konesans* needs to be coupled with *balans*. Through *balans* we learn that moral excellence requires synthesis, recombination, and intersectionality, that we need to learn how to reconcile things that seem like opposites rather than simply choosing between them. Unlike Western ways of thinking, where "different from" is almost always considered "better than" or "worse than" and people try to make the "right" choice to the exclusion of all other possibilities, Afro-diasporic philosophy sees conflicts and contradictions as opportunities for creative combinations premised on privileging the "both/and" over the "either/or."[3] Like the physicians of antiquity who comprehended that the same things that cause diseases can be used to cure them, thinkers deploying *konesans* and *balans* understand that things that can kill us can also cure us, if we use them in the right ways. When viewed through the lens of *balans*, right and wrong or truths and lies are not mutually incommensurable opposites but rather different poles of a dialogically and dialectically connected totality. Everyone possesses a part of the truth, yet all understandings contain flaws. The moral judgment required by *balans* cannot be reduced to a set of rules to follow, but rather emerges organically through appreciating differences and embracing contradictions. *Balans* impels us to know and honor our history but to transcend its limitations. Through *konesans* and *balans* wisdom amounts to more than an accumulation of facts. Morality requires us to do more than simply avoid evil. *Konesans and balans* require discernment, deliberation, and constant decision making.

Students of history know that many things are best understood in retrospect. Looking backward helps us look forward. For scholars of race, state violence, and radical movements, *konesans* and *balans* can be especially important. There are many decisions to be made at that crossroads. We need to understand race but not to reify it, to study radicalism but not to celebrate it simplistically or cynically dismiss it. We need to reveal the history of repression without exaggerating its effects. Studying race presents particularly vexing problems. The sphere of the "racial" is a biological and anthropological fiction that functions as a social fact. It is a made-up category that produces all-too-real consequences. Racial projects excuse inequality; they justify unjust power. Racism inhibits and divides radical movements. People in power appeal to white racism as a way of convincing workers to believe that racial privileges will compensate for their class grievances, that attacks on the status quo entail unacceptable transgressions of deeply rooted racial norms. By rooting class hierarchies in racial categories, people in power can attribute inequalities and injustices to nature rather than history. To the degree that racism makes injustice and inequality seem natural, necessary, and inevitable, it becomes a crucible in which other cruelties are learned and legitimated. Class and gender stratification persist, in part, because racism exists. Yet we have been systematically taught *not* to study race. A long history of mystification in both scholarly practice and legal doctrine promotes color-blind pronouncements as the privileged ethical response to color-bound problems. As Kimberle Crenshaw and other critical race theorists have long argued, color blindness as an idea relies on little more than its incessant use by powerful people. It lacks any firm basis in reality, theory, or for that matter the Constitution. Color blindness is not so much a social theory or moral imperative as a rhetorical prophylactic designed to suppress discussion of race-bound solutions to race-bound problems.[4]

Yet it is not possible actually to avoid race in a racialized society. Racism does not disappear simply because aggrieved or dominant groups do not mention it. Its power only grows stronger. But the history of race and radicalism demonstrates that when racism is confronted and contested, all aggrieved groups can benefit. Explicit antiracism not only seeks to remove the expressly racist obstacles in the way of aggrieved communities of color, it also almost always participates in the creation of new democratic institutions, ideas, and practices. Antiracism advances radicalism and retards repression. Yet, while necessary, antiracism by itself can never be fully sufficient for countering completely the complex, intersectional, and differentiated hierarchies of societies stratified not only by race but also by class, gender, sexuality, ability-disability, language, and religion. Racism is always intersectional. It is the life of the party; it never goes anywhere alone. It augments and exacerbates sexism, class rule, homophobia, ableism, and nativism. Race-based approaches isolated from broader struggles can sometimes devolve into narrow racialisms that reify the very differences they purport to deconstruct, imposing an artificial and unreal homogeneity on a heterogeneous social group. Racism needs to be challenged, but narrow racialism needs to be resisted. The right thing can become the wrong thing without *konesans* and *balans*.

In similar fashion, historical research itself can be a knife that cuts both ways. If we grab a knife by the handle, it can serve as a useful tool, but if we grab it by the blade, we will only injure ourselves. Studying history can be a way of expanding our understanding of the present by revealing previously occluded causal connections between the present and the past. Yet if handled in an imbalanced way, historical thinking can keep us chained to the past and its inadequate and outmoded ways of thinking. Respect for the past can degenerate into uncritical nostalgia for it. Past radical movements have much to teach us through the ways in which they spoke to the specific contradictions of the times they emerged. Yet the ideas, analyses, and forms of organization they developed cannot simply be transplanted to the present.

Identifying the historical origin and evolution of the different forms of class suppression, political repression, and racial oppression we face today can help us see how the patterns of the past impede progress in the present. Nothing from the past ever disappears completely. Every aspect of history is still here in some form. Yet excessive preoccupation with the past can divert our attention away from important new changes, transformations, and innovations. All historical moments are marked by both rupture and continuity. Emphasizing rupture over continuity or continuity over rupture can be tactically valuable tools of evaluation and interpretation in any given instance, but the wisdom that comes from experience requires us to remember that both continuity and rupture are present in any given moment. Malcolm X used to say that racism is like a Cadillac; they make a new model every year. Just as a 1955 owner's manual would not be a good guide for fixing a 1965 vehicle, a 1955 mentality would not suffice to repair the racism of 1965. Yet a 1965 Cadillac is still a Cadillac, and the racism of 1965 is still racism. Deciding whether to emphasize rupture or continuity is a tactical and situational question, a decision that must be made on the basis of experiment, experience, *konesans*, and *balans*.

In researching the history of race, state violence, and radical movements, the right thing can easily become the wrong thing. Savoring the successes of past social movements can remind us that every problem has a solution and draw our attention to forgotten tactics, strategies, slogans, and organizational forms relevant to the present. Yet seeking a past that makes the present bearable can also lead to uncritical, romantic, and escapist accounts of past struggles. The victories of the past are worth remembering, but we need to reckon with the legacy of defeats as well. The same fervor that fuels radical solidarity can also promote dogmatism. The righteousness of people speaking truth to power has often descended into self-righteousness. Being inspired by partial victories of the past should not make us underestimate how large a price we pay for history's defeats.

Power is not something that only dominant groups possess. Oppositional movements do not simply struggle *against* hegemony; they struggle *for* hegemony. Discipline, determination, solidarity, and struggle produce power. Understanding power requires *konesans* and *balans*. Struggling for power makes it possible for people to resist repression and to open up new spaces for deliberative talk and face-to-face decision making. It can create new social relations and new prestige hierarchies. Social movements exercise power by occupying public spaces, disrupting daily life, discrediting official hierarchies, and promoting resistance against them. Yet sometimes in the turmoil of struggle the use of power by radical groups can make them too much like their opponents. The right thing can easily become the wrong thing. Tightly organized, secretive, and hierarchical organizations can be well suited to resisting infiltration by informers and provocateurs, but in the process they may cause groups to lose the loyalty of the rank and file by depriving people of the dignity that comes from participation in collective debate and decision making.

Similarly, a willingness to engage in bold exemplary actions can inspire the masses and shake them from their lethargy. Yet leaders committed to immediate action can come to despise the rank and file they purport to represent, to view them as too passive, too timid, and too complacent. In contrast, comparatively spontaneous and seemingly unorganized democratic uprisings can sometimes succeed splendidly in expressing the will of the masses at specific times, but they rarely lead to the establishment of institutions and organizations capable of sustaining the struggle over long periods of time. Activists sometimes deliberately provoke authorities in the hope that reaction will spark new radical action. Indeed, state repression often backfires and produces reactive solidarity inside aggrieved communities. Yet activists who boldly court repression can become resented by their own constituency for the unwanted and undeserved punishments that communities suffer in retaliation for the vanguard actions of activists. In addition, periods of repression can compel radical groups to degenerate into little more than elaborate legal defense committees that spend so much time trying to keep their leaders out of jail that they have no resources left for promoting actions from which new visions of how society might be organized can emerge. Delineating the long and dishonorable history of state repression helps explain an important part of how and why past radical social movements have failed, but excessive attention to repression absolves the movements themselves of their failures to develop the degrees of mass support they needed to make repression unlikely to succeed. An honest reckoning with the past will show that repression indeed had ruinous effects on radical movements, but the same record reveals that the survival of movements confronting repression has depended more on their ability to recruit and retain mass support than on the simple imbalance of power between themselves and their enemies. In both activism and scholarship about activism, *konesans* and *balans* are necessary tools.

Looking to the past intelligently requires us also to be aware of the contradictions of the present. Present-day problems can be productive in provoking scholars to view the past in new ways, to ask new questions and to look at previously understudied evidence. Yet the epistemological value of the past comes precisely from the fact that it is not the present. Historical research produces a distance from the present that comes from defamiliarization, from engagement with eras characterized by tones and textures different from our own. Defamiliarization opens up occluded alternatives and possibilities. A temporary detour to the past can enable us to return to the present armed with the imagination and insight that comes from viewing things through different lenses.

Historical inquiry helps us realize that seemingly new forms of racial repression have a history, that present patterns of arrest, incarceration, surveillance, silencing, terror, and torture did not start only yesterday. Yet today's problems will never be exactly the same as the problems of the past. The same is true of solutions. Radical resistance exists today against racism and repression in part because it is fueled by long histories of survival, affirmation, resistance, and continuing struggle. Yet cultivating our appreciation of continuities should not make us resistant to recognizing ruptures. Times of crisis, ferment, and upheaval produce new perceptions, personalities, and politics. They bring to the fore new identities, ideas, and imaginations suitable for fashioning new forms of struggle. The history we read can be an important part of how we understand the problems of the present, but it cannot be a substitute for the history we need to make based on the unique promise and peril of our own time.

## WHY *KONESANS* AND *BALANS* MATTER NOW

Like all time periods, the present is shaped by elements of both continuity and rupture, but today ruptures take center stage. The "now" in which we live is no ordinary time. It is a time of dramatic transformation and change. The crises that permeate the economy, the environment, the educational system, the criminal justice system, and the administration of empire portend radical reconfigurations of social institutions and social relations in the years ahead. We dwell in a world that seems to be unraveling at the seams. Our studies of race, state violence, and radical movements take place in the context of pervasive and growing threats to civil rights and human rights. Calculated cruelty and unbridled exploitation seem to have the upper hand everywhere. All around the world, armies and less formally organized armed combatants, paramilitary forces, and hired mercenaries target civilian populations for destruction. Multinational corporations and international agencies profit from the promotion of hunger and thirst by privatizing the agricultural commons. Male privilege and power around the globe feminize poverty, repress reproductive freedoms, and compel vulnerable women and children to remain in abusive family situations. In the world's wealthiest and most powerful nations, legal scholars, government officials, military officers, and elected leaders have now agreed to abandon the centuries-old principles of habeas corpus and due process. Some suspects are not allowed to confront their accusers or even know the nature of the charges against them. Government officials now openly condone and embrace forms of torture that they previously at least had to outsource or conduct surreptitiously because they wanted to maintain the pretense of obeying international law. Perpetual war, mass incarceration, and the shredding of the social safety net are fueled by appetites whetted by relentless exposure to vulgar and violent images, scenarios, and sensations in our political and popular culture. Even in the face of the worst economic crisis in decades, the corporate media devote more attention to the antics and dysfunctions of celebrities than to the predatory and morally bankrupt behavior of stockbrokers and mortgage lenders. Economic and political restructuring policies promote the looting of public resources by private interests and the organized abandonment of aggrieved populations. Revenge and punishment come disguised as justice, while consumer choice masquerades as political agency.

Our planet and its people will live with consequences of the decisions made about these crises for many years to come. The elites who hold the preponderance of wealth and power will dismiss every form of resistance as wrong. As W. E. B. Du Bois explained about the dilemma facing black people under the regime of slavery, "Everything Negroes did was wrong. If they fought for freedom, they were beasts; if they did not fight, they were born slaves. If they cowered on the plantations, they loved slavery; if they ran away, they were lazy loafers. If they sang, they were silly; if they scowled, they were impudent."[5] Yet while every form of resistance becomes portrayed as wrong, every policy of the powerful will be presented as right, no matter how disastrous the results. For the people in power, nothing succeeds like failure. Each new disaster becomes further justification for the implementation of even more draconian measures. Our society no longer produces prosperity or security for the majority of the population, but instead generates a compensatory "sadism in search of a story" through cycles of moral panics stoked by pathological responses to fears about difference. The people with power who control corporations and governments cannot fix the things they have broken. They cannot repair the terrible damages that their policies have inflicted on people and on the planet. In fact, their policies consistently perpetuate the problems they purport to prevent while continuously producing new ones they cannot solve. They have stopped even trying to solve these problems. Instead we are confronted with a general strike by capital aimed at looting public resources for private gain and substituting technocratic plutocracy for democracy. Thirty years of deregulation, privatization, and economic restructuring have radically redistributed wealth away from the working class and toward the upper classes. Because of the stagnation of real wages and the subsidies to the wealthy written into the US tax code, for example, the wealthiest 1 percent of the population gains a collective $673 billion every year while the bottom 80 percent loses an aggregate $743 billion yearly.[6] To deflect attention away from these policies, the corporate media and the corporate political system stage a seemingly endless succession of moral panics about putatively nonnormative behavior by aggrieved racial groups, immigrants, welfare recipients, sexual and religious minorities, the homeless, and the poor. Today the demonized groups even include public employees, teachers, firefighters, and police officers with pensions. The end result of these processes, as New Orleans activist Kalamu ya Salaam argues, is that people who control nothing are blamed for everything.[7] At the same time, the people who control nearly everything are blamed for nothing.

Policies expressly designed to redistribute wealth from the working masses to the upper classes have produced enormous luxury and locked-in advantages for the rich while imposing nearly insurmountable barriers to upward mobility on nearly everyone else. Yet the privileged are not satisfied with their privileges. They feel they do not have enough, and they are angry. Popular talk radio and cable television programs, letters to newspaper editors, and miscellaneous tweets and blogs present a constant litany of complaints from what must surely be the most miserable, mean-spirited, miserly, misanthropic, spiteful, sadistic, embittered, and angry group of "haves" in the history of the world. As James Baldwin observed decades ago at the start of this transformation of a flawed democracy into a ruthless plutocracy,

> Not even the people who are the most spectacular recipients of
> the benefits of prosperity are able to endure these benefits:
> They can neither understand them nor do without them, nor
> can they go beyond them, in order to preserve their values,
> however stifling and joyless these values have caused their lives
> to be. The bulk of the people desperately seek out representatives
> who are prepared to make up in cruelty what both they and the
> people lack in conviction.[8]

This political culture paralyzes the government at every level, fueling a race to the bottom in which each governing body tries to shift responsibility to the subunit below it. As my late colleague Clyde Woods observed again and again, the dominant neoliberal project in this era requires a fragmented, delinked, privatized, and devolved state dedicated to protecting the propertied and the privileged but unwilling and perhaps even unable to meet the needs of the majority of the population.[9] Yet at the same time, while the state devolves as a source of social well-being, it evolves into a centralized center of command and control through its policies of policing, surveillance, mass incarceration, and subsidies to capital. As Avery Gordon argues acerbically, "When the State abandons you, it never lets you out of its sight."[10]

The history of race, state violence, and radical movements helps us see how and why regressive policies designed to undermine opportunity and upward mobility inevitably become presented to the public in the form of thinly disguised racial projects. Today's racism is not exactly the same racism that the freedom struggles of the twentieth century challenged and changed, but it is still racism. The Arizona legislature exploits the vulnerabilities of undocumented workers by passing a bill that criminalizes the entire Mexican American population. This law requires police officers to use racial profiling, to demand proof of citizenship from individuals they suspect to be undocumented. The same legislature then attempts to outlaw antiracist ideas by banning courses in ethnic studies from the public schools. Taken together, these laws maintain on the one hand that *individual rights are so important* that schoolchildren cannot receive lessons pertaining to the history of the racial groups to which they belong, and on the other hand that *individual rights are also so unimportant* that all people who look like they might be of Mexican origin must be deprived of their constitutional rights collectively because they belong to a group that includes some individuals without proper legal documentation. In the "now" in which we live the chairman of the House Committee on Homeland Security says that there are too many mosques in America. A Kansas legislator jokes at an official hearing that illegal immigrants should be shot like wild pigs. In Hazelton, Pennsylvania, and Escondido, California, local government officials craft housing and traffic ordinances to harass, intimidate, and suppress entire Latino communities. In St. Bernard Parish outside of New Orleans, local leaders ban the construction of multiunit apartment buildings and attempt to make it illegal to rent housing to anyone other than blood relatives in order to keep the parish population white and to deny housing to New Orleans black people displaced by the flooding that followed Hurricane Katrina. Racist hate crimes have taken the lives of Luis Ramirez in Shenandoah, Pennsylvania; Raul and Breseida Flores in Arivaca, Arizona; and many others. The Supreme Court of the United States has outlawed voluntary local school desegregation programs in Seattle and Louisville. The state textbook review committee in Texas has removed Thurgood Marshall and Cesar Chavez from history and replaced them with Phyllis Schlafly and Newt Gingrich. The University of Texas is in the process of defunding its ethnic studies programs while increasing the budget of its Center for European Studies. The University of San Francisco is terminating its Upward Bound Program. Cornell University is reorganizing its Africana Studies and Research Center in order to destroy its connections to the community. The governor of Louisiana proposes to end the autonomy and the unique mission of the historically black campus of Southern University in New Orleans by incorporating it into a historically white institution. What happens to any of us now seems certain to happen to all of us soon. As Clyde Woods has argued, what we see in Baghdad, New Orleans, and Port-au-Prince today is what we will see everywhere tomorrow.[11] It is not simply that an injustice anywhere is an injustice everywhere, but that within a fully linked and integrated system of global finance, production, and consumption, unchallenged wrongdoing and undemocratic power anywhere become staging grounds and base camps for promoting wrongdoing everywhere.

ACTIVISM, IDEAS, AND CRISIS

The same progressive forces fueling the efflorescence of scholarship on race, state violence, and radical movements are also at work in the society at large. From large-scale actions such as the important antiwar demonstrations of 2003 and the massive mobilizations on behalf of immigrant rights in 2006, to the powerful new energies flowing through myriad small-scale activist projects designed to deepen democratic deliberation and decision making at the local level, popular efforts and activism everywhere are producing new individual and group identities and personalities, bold new ideas and imaginaries, and profoundly new analyses, interpretations, tactics, and strategies aimed at fashioning new forms of struggle. As the social democratic liberalism of the Democratic

Party increasingly reveals itself to be little more than conservatism on the installment plan—at best simply a slightly less vicious mixture of austerity and repression in the service of the same forms of privatization and empire—radicalism becomes the only sensible alternative. The legacy of New Deal liberalism has been fatally undermined by what the implementation of neoliberal policies has done to the economy. The New Deal was based on a bargain. The government became a primary source of capitalist accumulation through defense spending, highway building, the export-import bank, and other projects. Because state-sponsored and subsidized capital accumulation required political legitimation, the state made concessions to the working class through programs designed to promote education, employment, housing, and health. These concessions produced a high-employment and high-wage economy in which the purchasing power of the public fueled economic growth and expansion. Yet these gains were a knife that cut two ways. Policies portrayed as providing security to all workers actually advanced the interests of white males over all other groups. Federal home loans excluded borrowers from aggrieved communities of color. The Social Security Act and the Wagner Act denied farm workers and domestic workers access to old-age pensions, disability and survivors benefits, and protections for collective bargaining rights. Social welfare benefits that men secured collectively and automatically were available to women only if they applied as individuals. The seeming social inclusion of the New Deal welfare state created new forms of differentiated exclusion, exacerbating racial and gender division among workers. These exclusions provoked new feminist and antiracist mobilizations that led to the expansion of democratic opportunities in the 1960s.

Starting in the 1970s, new profitability and liquidity crises for capital convinced key representatives of the ruling class that the costs of legitimation had become too high, that they should pursue higher profits and seek a larger share of the national wealth for themselves by curtailing what they viewed as the excess democracy created during the New Deal and Civil Rights eras. They started to deny to white males what they had previously denied to women and racial minorities. Successful attacks on the power of organized labor to bargain freely over wages and working conditions, on environmental protection, on progressive tax policies, on corporate regulation, and on spending for social needs have produced the present perfect storm of crises that now prevail in every dimension of our individual and collective lives. Moreover, the economic crisis facing individuals, governments, and businesses is not just one more temporary downturn in the business cycle awaiting the next big boom, but rather a reckoning with the reality that the neoliberal economy leaves wages too low for consumer spending to ever rebound in any meaningful way. Corporate profits and corporate assets are at an all-time high, yet capital is staging a general strike, refusing to invest in productive economic activity and creating budget crises for governments in order to force the transfer of public assets to private interests, to expand profits not by selling goods to consumers but by policies of "budget reform." These reforms deplete public treasuries; rob workers of wages, pensions, and working conditions secured through collective bargaining agreements; and subsidize privatization policies that give private firms public resources and opportunities to make new profits by selling back to the public sector a whole range of things that used to be the province of the state, from classroom testing materials to health care and insurance policies, from the provision of electric power and water resources to policing and firefighting.[12] These programs will not produce prosperity or security for the majority of the population. They threaten to undermine the viability and credibility of the entire economic and political system. They make the labor of working people less rewarding while augmenting the rewards of ownership and investment. They promote the demoralization that comes from severing the connections that link work and reward in the lives of working people. They will, however, produce radicals and radicalism among the ranks of dispossessed people who have nowhere else to turn. As Aimé Césaire noted in the 1940s in his *Discourse on Colonialism*, "A civilization that proves incapable of solving the problems it creates is a decadent civilization. A civilization that chooses to close its eyes to its most crucial problems is a stricken civilization. A civilization that uses its principles for trickery and deceit is a dying civilization."[13] Only radical responses will suffice, because the crises we face and the social conditions we endure are not temporary defects in an otherwise smoothly functioning society, but rather basic breakdowns in the central systems that structure our shared social life. The choice we face at this crossroads is no longer either liberalism or radicalism, but rather radicalism or barbarism.

In the context of this moment of upheaval, transformation, and change, perhaps the most powerful motivation for studying the history of race, state violence, and radical movements is to discover what has worked successfully in the past, to establish an archive of tactics, strategies, slogans, and organizational forms that enabled aggrieved groups to win victories, to deploy power so that decision makers found themselves forced to say yes when they really wanted to say no.[14] Our current moment makes us especially eager to discover how past social movements were able to get beyond short-term ameliorative reforms and instead challenge dominant frames and carve away spaces for fundamentally new ways of knowing and being. Radical change has often been contagious. In pursuing freedom for themselves, radical mobilizations have helped win it for others. Race-based radical movements have been especially important because they have not just opposed race-specific obstacles in the paths of people of color but instead struggled for the creation of new democratic institutions, practices, and programs that helped democratize life chances and opportunities in society at large. We need to know, for example, the history of how the freedom dreams of enslaved people challenged the hegemony of white male propertied power and secured a commitment to equal protection for all in the wake of the Civil War. The abolition movement and a broader collective and coordinated struggle in the 1860s created new democratic institutions through the Charleston Convention of 1865, the activism of Union and Loyal Leagues, coalitions between freed slaves and poor whites in local and state governments, and the passage of the 1866 Civil Rights Law and the adoption of the Thirteenth, Fourteenth, and Fifteenth amendments. Formerly enslaved blacks recognized that it was not enough to win nominal freedom for themselves in a society premised on their subordination and exploitation, and that instead they needed to create new democratic institutions and practices for all. Similarly, the Black Freedom movement of the mid-twentieth century ended Jim Crow segregation in public accommodations and in the voting booth, but it also won measures that created new democratic opportunities for others through expanded aid to education, provisions protecting women from discrimination in employment and education, extension of the franchise to eighteen-year-olds, and expansion of federally supported education and health care programs.

Class-based mobilizations have similarly done their best work when they went beyond ameliorative changes and instead sought radical changes in social relations. Radical agitation and organization created the New Deal culture of unity that transformed immigrants and their children from unwanted aliens into redemptive insiders. Their successful mobilizations in the Age of the CIO (Congress of Industrial Organizations) undermined the hegemony of white Anglo-Saxon Protestant culture and secured collective bargaining rights for labor, insurance and old age pensions, and federal expenditures expanding housing opportunities. During the West Coast waterfront strikes of 1934, longshore workers replaced the humiliating shape-up system that forced them to compete with each other for jobs with the "low man out" system in which work was shared on the basis of giving the first opportunities to those who had worked the fewest hours and job assignments came from the union hiring hall rather than from management. The low man out system reigned on the docks for twenty-five years until employers turned to automation to destroy it and to eliminate the power of dock workers to exert control over products produced far away from their final markets. As long as the low man out system was in force, workers preempted the prerogatives of management, eclipsed employer favoritism and prejudice with worker solidarity, and enacted in their day-to-day work relations the shared dignity and equality that they otherwise could only envision. The workers' struggles on the docks expanded the sphere of politics beyond the electoral system (where they had little power) to the point of production (where their ability to stop production gave them enormous power). Through job-based unionism at the point of production, they exercised and enjoyed democratic control over the nature, purpose, and pace of their work.

Similarly, the history of feminism reveals how major changes happen, how decentralized yet collective mass action can bring about major changes. For centuries, rape and battering were considered private matters beyond the reach of the law. Through activism ranging from small local consciousness-raising groups to large world conferences on the status of women, and through legal strategies deployed in individual cases and class-action suits, feminists transformed rape and battering into criminal offenses that could be adjudicated in court. This movement not only won material protection for the dignity and autonomy of women but also undermined the public-private division upon which central forms of patriarchal violence and exploitation depend. Yet here, too, *konesans* and *balans* matter. As Kimberle Crenshaw argued in 1991, and as relentless activism by women of color survivors of domestic violence has shown ever since, policies based on the experiences and perceptions of white women that are set up to reduce rape and battering can actually *increase* the vulnerabilities of immigrants and women of color because deportation, the collateral punishments of criminal offenses, and shortages of affordable housing leave these women confronting circumstances very different from those facing the law's implied and inscribed person—imagined to be white and middle class—to be protected from domestic violence.[15]

These histories contain memories that flash up to us now in our current moment of danger.[16] They resonate in our time because they display many of the characteristics of the social movements that have emerged in this era. The uprising by the Zapatista Army of National Liberation (EZLN) in Chiapas in 1994, the Battle in Seattle against the World Trade Organization in 1999, the outpouring of queer activism in response to medical and political indifference to the AIDS epidemic, the work of activists against environmental racism, the mass demonstrations on behalf of immigrants in 2006, and the Occupy Wall Street movement in 2011 and 2012 are some of the most visible manifestations of a new approach to radical organization and mobilization. As Immanuel Wallerstein notes astutely in *After Liberalism*, throughout history the white US left has generally seen the primary contradiction in society as an opposition between capital and labor. It envisioned change as the task of a vanguard party that leads the masses, seizes state power for itself, and then tries to use the apparatuses of government to make radical changes. This tradition views democracy with distrust as a bourgeois diversion from unified class-based mobilization, but looks trustfully to the authority of scientific rationality and its promises of inevitable progress as part of the revolutionary process.[17] Contemporary struggles, by contrast, generally favor decentralized and dispersed mobilizations aimed at building the new society in the shell of the old rather than seeking to seize power first. They view the labor-capital antagonism as only one of several important contradictions in society, not as the single axis of emancipatory change. They generally do not believe in a scientific path to social progress, and are suspicious that increased productivity might come at the expense of the environment and would only exacerbate the conflation of commodities with human happiness. Struggles for human dignity loom large in the aims and practices of these groups; they tend to see democracy not as a bourgeois trick

achievements of this tradition and understandably paved the way for similar studies recuperating the importance of a part of the past generally excised from dominant historical narratives.[20] There is no gainsaying the important accomplishments of these groups, the logic of the vanguard form given the repressive apparatuses of capital and the state, or the courage and imagination of many of their adherents. Yet in connecting radical hopes for the future to the vanguard politics of the past, these studies can fail to reckon with the price the left has paid for the vanguard model, with how destructive it has been to democratic hopes and aspirations, with how responsible it has been for the bureaucratization and militarization of radical social movements, and with their resulting alienation from the masses they needed to mobilize.[21] In remembering the things that vanguardism enabled, these studies too often ignore all that it inhibited. The same forms of exemplary action that vanguard groups use to gain the attention and the admiration of the people also often separate them from their constituency. As Huey P. Newton noted in looking back at the experiences of the Black Panther Party, picking up weapons and wearing uniforms enabled the party to convince the community that the organization was serious about defending the people from police abuse. Yet those same actions also set the group apart from the people. The spectacle enabled supporters to remain spectators and made revolution seem like a series of actions rather than a process of shared development. "We saw ourselves as the revolutionary 'vanguard,'" Newton explained, "and did not fully understand then that only the *people* can create revolution."[22]

An uncritical approach to vanguard parties distorts our understanding of the significance of repression as well. For example, the anticommunism enacted through the Smith Act, McCarthyism, and COINTELPRO (Counterintelligence Program) did terrible damage to radical movements, but it did not destroy them. As George Rawick observed, exclusive focus on repression occludes how the vanguard politics of Marxist groups led them to lag behind events and helped forge their own alienation from the masses. Workers staging wildcat strikes in the 1950s and 1960s got little help from the radical parties whose entry into the CIO labor bureaucracy in the 1940s led them to cast their lot with the idea of a labor party led by trade union leaders in the postwar period. At a time when rank-and-file militancy had an enormous popular constituency, Marxist groups, in Rawick's words, "called upon workers to put up with not only the labor bureaucracy in the union, but in the party, and 'hopefully' in the state as well."[23]

The principles of *konesans* and *balans* require us to neither fully embrace nor completely reject the legacies of Leninism inscribed in the idea of the vanguard party. As Malcolm X observed, when a people are fighting for freedom there is no such thing as a bad device.[24] No form of organization and no means of struggle can be ruled out in advance. Yet tactics and forms of organization that produce short-term victories can set the stage for long-term defeats.[25] Moreover, vanguardism is not just a tactic; it is a way of knowing and a way of being. An overly developed identification with the vanguard tradition will obscure the value of some of the unique ways of knowing and ways of being that have emerged out of recent and contemporary mass mobilizations. As John Brown Childs argues, an ethics of respect lies at the heart of these recent movements. They differ from the vanguard tradition in several important ways. They counter the top-down militarized and bureaucratized model of the Leninist party with a rhizomatic approach that entails multiple and diverse points of entry and attachment, an approach that maintains varied emplacements while still moving in the same general direction. These groups are not trying to convert others to a single correct line or perspective, a practice that Childs describes as speaking without listening. Instead, they invite others into a shared conversation that no one controls but that changes everyone. Rather than looking for the one true answer implied by Lenin's question "What is to be done?" the ethics of respect encourage activists to seek the many different and unpredictable answers that flow in response to the questions "What is being done? And how?"[26] Radical social movements do require discipline, organization, and ideological clarity, as the vanguard tradition has always argued, but discipline, organization, and ideological clarity need to be tools forged by the people for their own purposes, not disciplinary apparatuses constructed for the people by their leaders.

## 2. The Syndicalist Trap

The collapse of the Soviet Union in 1989 coupled with the emergence of new systems of global capitalist investment, production, distribution, and politics in the 1990s led to a resurgence of syndicalist and anarchist mobilizations. Emphasizing decentralized organization, deliberative talk, and democratic decision making, these mobilizations seek to create alternative organizations at the local level, such as projects that promote sustainable development and workers' cooperatives. They have promoted popular scrutiny of government budgets and revived the 1960s practice of presenting Freedom Budgets that pose alternative courses of state action. They consistently oppose corporate actions, and challenge the procorporate policies of nongovernment organizations. This activism has provoked scholars to revisit the histories of anarchist and syndicalist organizations. This tradition offers an important alternative to the politics of the Leninist vanguard tradition, but scholars have not yet reckoned fully with the historical failures of anarchism and syndicalism to institutionalize their temporary gains inside organizations capable of sustaining the struggle during times when mass demonstrations and upheavals are not possible. Moreover, despite democratic impulses and aims, the anarchist and syndicalist traditions have also always been vulnerable to their own forms of vanguardism, especially by adventurists and provocateurs whose proclivity for dramatic "exemplary" actions undemocratically saddles entire movements with the consequences of the actions of an unelected few. The lack of clearly defined structures and lines of authority that are supposed to promote democratic participation in these groups can also reduce accountability.

Michael Miller Topp's research reveals the need for *konesans* and *balans* in the history of anarchism. In *Those Without a Country*, Topp reveals how small groups of Italian syndicalists displaced to the United States at the turn of the twentieth century exerted enormous influence on immigrant and working-class life through their important contributions to the mass strikes in Lawrence, Lowell, and Paterson led by the Industrial Workers of the World in 1912 and 1913 and to the defense committees organized during the 1920s to defend Nicola Sacco and Bartolomeo Vanzetti from politically inspired executions.[27] Small decentralized groups operating without firm ideological or programmatic guidelines enabled workers to stage creative confrontations that advanced the interests of the working class as a whole. Yet the same features that enabled syndicalism to succeed also inhibited its development. Without organizational discipline or ideological clarity, organizers unwisely encouraged workers to view their class injuries as insults to their gender or ethnicity. They built militancy around masculine self-assertion and ethnic solidarity. These qualities helped win new recruits whose participation produced victories, but at a cost. Syndicalists trained to view the class struggle as an injury to manhood were poorly positioned to organize in factories where women made up a majority of the workforce. Militants seething with ethnic resentments and eager for the kinds of physical conflicts that they associated with manhood could be easily diverted to other causes. Some found fulfillment in supporting Italy's invasions of Ethiopia and Libya. Others returned to their country of origin and satisfied their senses of wounded national pride by joining Mussolini's fascist movement. Syndicalists who participated in progressive left struggles over a thirty-year period ended up as fascists, not because they became converted to a radically different view of the world but rather because the radicalism that made sense to them carried too many traces of dominant thinking even when mobilized for oppositional purposes. The inevitably conflicted and contradictory process of radicalization can lead to reaction without *konesans* and *balans*.

In today's social movements, powerful subcurrents of syndicalism and anarchism have been central to the successes of the Occupy Wall Street protests. Mass meetings focused on collective education, deliberative talk, and democratic decision making have attracted a mass following, evidencing a hunger for both knowledge and action in the face of the ever-growing inequalities and injustices of neoliberal society. The absence of a hierarchical organization and a defined ideology in these actions opens up spaces for new politics, polities, and publics. A refusal to make concrete demands on state authorities emphasizes the degree to which participants believe that the state has been captured completely by corporate interests. The mass congregation that fuels occupation encourages the promotion of new social relationships across previously accepted boundaries and barriers of age, occupation, race, gender, citizenship status, class, and sexuality. A slogan that proclaims that the movement represents the 99 percent of the population that is not rich underscores brilliantly the maldistribution of wealth and power in society. It makes it possible for Occupy Wall Street to make a large number of allies. Yet at the same time, the movement's binary opposition between the wealthy and everyone else obscures the many fissures among the 99 percent that keep the system functioning and thriving. A movement that is focused largely on the action of congregating together is unlikely to develop the kinds of transformational demands, strategies, actions, experiences, and structures needed to contest power rather than merely to critique it. The same lack of organization and ideology that promotes inclusion also makes the movement susceptible to infiltration by provocateurs and informants while keeping it powerless to discipline them or disavow their actions convincingly. The movement's weaknesses flow from the same sources as its strengths.

The history of radicalism is replete with examples of movements that become trapped by their own metaphors. The populist upheavals of the late nineteenth century gained traction with the masses by drawing on evangelical Protestantism and comparing monopoly capitalists to the money changers that Jesus drove from the temple. Yet, as Bruce Palmer shows in *Man Over Money*, the very metaphor that made capitalist exploitation evident and deplorable to populists also led them to believe that the sins they opposed could not be remedied on earth, that rather than seeking an end to the evils they opposed they could rest assured that God would take care of the malefactors on Judgment Day. The very metaphor that gave power to the populists eventually disempowered them as well.[28] Occupy Wall Street has had remarkable success in crafting a popular and credible metaphor that brilliantly encapsulates the reasons why we need a mass radical movement. But whether that metaphor can actually lead to the construction of such a movement is a question that needs to be resolved in the terrains of *konesans* and *balans*.

## 3. The Isolated Scholar Trap

The historical study of race, state violence, and radical movements is not only about *what* we know, but also about *how* we know. As the increasingly indecent social relations of our time provoke scholars to excavate lost histories of race, state violence, and radicalism, we confront both the promise and the peril of academic work in this society. Scholars can do important work in showing that what might seem to be merely recent or ephemeral developments have a long history. They can reveal how racial projects have both inhibited and enabled radical mobilizations. They can demonstrate how radicalism has frequently functioned effectively to reframe dominant beliefs and frameworks. Yet good intentions do not guarantee good results. The segregation of academic institutions and intellectuals from popular constituencies creates dangerous forms of isolation. Without daily contact with organized struggles by large groups of people, scholarly research can become a form of collaboration with the social forces it aims to critique and contest. Isolated intellectuals derive their projects largely from their own alienation rather than from the questions that emerge out of concrete contestation and struggle by social movements. The credentialing and reward structures of scholarship can produce personalities who find it hard to work with others, who are uncomfortable crossing class lines, who cultivate personal quirks and qualities that make them stand out as being different from others, who detach themselves from the experiences and struggles of large groups. Academic prestige comes most easily to projects that display the mastery and difficulty of complex concepts, rather than to those that intervene productively in society. Too many intellectuals have learned to think globally, but to do nothing locally. Scholars can become self-impressed to the point of narcissism, self-loathing to the point of paranoia. They can become preoccupied with the personal to the point of turning all intellectual disagreements into moral hierarchies built on contempt, ridicule, and gossip. The units in which we work often seem more like interactive telenovelas than academic departments. Under these conditions, the purpose of academic work can become distorted into the creation of designer identities by individuals seeking security and comfort inside academic gated communities. They produce people who want to live comfortably in this society as it exists by branding themselves as radical and oppositional without actually engaging in radical or oppositional work. Some are suspicious of the communities from which they come and that they are asked to represent in scholarship. Most are fearful of what Seth Moglen aptly describes as "the torment of hope." They do not want to be disappointed by the radical movements that actually exist so they wait for the creation of some ideal future movement that will be worthy of their time and attention. They view any glimmer of hope as naive romanticism that underestimates the villainy of hegemonic power. They gravitate toward writing the autopsies of past social movements rather than toward contributing ideas and energy to current ones.[29]

We should want more out of our work than to be curators of the blasted hopes of the past or simply to be the authors of ever more eloquent chronicles of other people's suffering. We should want to address and redress that suffering in everything we do. Yet even this critique can become part of the problem if we do not deploy *konesans* and *balans*. Critiquing and condemning other academics can become a substitute for serious social engagement, an escape from broader social responsibilities. The academy has its contradictions, just like any other social site. Focusing on it as somehow uniquely corrupt or powerless or frivolous can cultivate a paralyzing sense of self-hatred. Energy and anger that should be directed against unjust social hierarchies can easily become channeled into contempt for colleagues whose shortcomings remind us of our own failings.

It can be constructive to resist valuing the importance of the university in society too much, but that resistance can easily become destructive when it leads us to succumb to cynical resignation that condemns the university's practices and ideologies but does not contest them. One reason for engaging directly with social movements is that their practical concerns and limitations help develop capacities for *konesans* and *balans*.

## 4. The Engaged Scholar Trap

The opposite of the isolated scholar is the engaged scholar. Yet the two are not as different as they sometimes appear. The engaged scholar grasps one important part of the truth. No one will do for us what we fail to do for ourselves. No plutocracy ever reforms itself. As Reverend Fred Shuttlesworth observed during the Montgomery Bus Boycott, "Rattlesnakes don't commit suicide."[30] Opinions, attitudes, analyses, and interpretations are most meaningful when they lead to action informed by intelligence. This is work that needs to be done out in the world, out along the highways and the hedges where we can look for people who are looking for us. Yet the *konesans* that comes from such work need to be informed by *balans*, by recognition of the important work that falls uniquely to scholars. The first thing that engaged scholarship needs to engage with is scholarship itself. A commitment to activism should not be an excuse for doing bad research. In fact, our scholarship should be better than that of our enemies, not just because it is likely to be attacked, but because the problems we attempt to solve are so profound that only the truth will suffice. An emphasis on intervention does not lessen the demands on knowledge. On the contrary, asking and answering questions important to people with whose struggles we identify compels us to do our work even better.[31] Exposing our ideas to large groups of people with firsthand knowledge of the conditions we study will bring scholars in contact quickly and consistently with multiple standpoints and perspectives. It will compel us to address issues that are important to the everyday life experiences of large numbers of people. This kind of research promotes an honest reckoning with the narrow range of experiences generally represented in academic conversations. It subjects preliminary findings to knowing critiques from interlocutors with knowledge otherwise inaccessible to scholars.

The universities in which we work are important sites in society. The ideas learned and legitimated inside the institutions of higher education help determine how society functions; we cannot abandon this terrain to our enemies. Yet work inside the university will not be easy in the years ahead. Precisely because scholarship holds tremendous relevance to the problems our society faces, it is certain to come under attack. The university is one of the few sites left in society not completely dominated (at least not yet) by the imperatives of market space and market time. We can certainly expect our enemies to play us against one another, to pressure us to make gains at each other's expense, to see our own social group as more oppressed than others, or to view other aggrieved groups as privileged insiders getting resources that should rightfully flow to us. As the university consolidates itself as a fiscalized, virtualized, and voca-tionalized investment opportunity, scholars will be asked increasingly to serve the interests of global capital rather than meeting the needs of laborers at home or abroad. In the face of these pressures we have to ask ourselves the question that Lauryn Hill asks in her song "That Thing": "How you gonna win if you ain't right within?"

Some forms of engagement amount to little more than escape. Many scholars have been injured deeply by the very communities they find themselves expected to represent in the university. Hurt by their com-munity's anti-intellectualism, materialism, prejudice, homophobia, suffo-cating family obligations, domestic abuse, and secret pledges of allegiance, they become drawn to strategies that seem to promise to free them from the burdens of the identities they are often asked to inhabit and repre-sent in the university. They internalize a reflexive resistance to obligation and accountability. Their personal commitments to seeing themselves as being radical and oppositional lead them to demand that activist groups purge themselves of all problems and contradictions before the struggle begins, that the movement provide them with a space of absolute personal comfort. This is a form of collaboration masquerading as critique. Noth-ing serves the neoliberal project better than self-branding individual-ism. Radical social movements emerge precisely when people recognize that they cannot exempt themselves from the collective consequences of unequal power, that they have to work alongside allies who are not perfect. Social movements see that the struggles they take on can be won only by love—not by an uncritical love that excuses the faults of our communities but rather by a determination to find something left to love in them even when they seem unlovable. Understanding the problems and contradictions that communities contain yet being determined to build on them is not something that can be done from the outside. Our commitment to loving aggrieved communities should rise to the exact dimension and degree that they are hated by the dominant culture.[32] This does not mean being uncritical. It does not entail accepting unacceptable behavior. It does not mean that we should cultivate narrow and partisan attachments to our own social groups at the expense of broader world-traversing and world-transcending obligations. But it does require what the martyred Salvadoran archbishop Oscar Romero described as accompaniment—walking down the road with people who are poor and marginalized and brutalized, taking the same risks they take, and linking our lives to their lives.[33]

Periods of heightened struggle produce repeated defeats. Defeats lead to demoralization. Demoralization leads to mutual blaming and shaming, especially of allies and comrades who are easier to hurt than our actual enemies on the other side. How we carry these burdens will determine a great deal about what our future looks like. There is of course no one formula for our work, no one-size-fits-all solution to the problems we face. We have always profited greatly from the fact that we do not speak with one voice, that we are not the same. Yet we have important work to do. Our task today is similar to the one that George Rawick explained to his fellow radical sociologists some forty years ago: "We must overcome our own pessimism, our own social isolation, our own fear of competing with mainstream sociology, our own fear of error. We must be willing to give intellectual blows when needed and to take and overcome them when they are aimed at us. The matters we deal with are not trivial, they will release human passion and energy, and we must not retreat behind our own desire for peace in order to avoid these realities."[34] We will make mistakes. We will be part of the problem as well as part of the solution. That is why *konesans* and *balans* matter.

## 5. The Trap of Feeling Good about Feeling Bad

Historical narratives that recount injustices and struggles against them do not always provoke progressive political responses. A long tradition in philosophy and the arts has taught people to derive aesthetic pleasure and an elevated sense of self-worth from the feelings of empathy, sympathy, and pity that depictions of painful social realities evoke. Rather than serving as provocations for action, these can produce political passivity and quiescence. The subject created by centuries of bourgeois culture is a besieged individual with a phobic relationship to the social aggregate. To this subject, narratives that reveal that social relations are unjust, that elites are powerful and corrupt, and that ordinary people suffer terribly because of their powerlessness produce desires for personal and private escapes, for ways of living comfortably *with* rather than in opposition to the power hierarchies of this world. The wickedness of the world only confirms the need to escape into a private realm of moral sentiment and vicarious pity. The aesthetic realm becomes an arena in which people learn to feel rather than to act, and where social conditions serve as mere prompts for affect. Works of expressive culture that seem to indict injustice and dignify the oppressed produce affective pleasures that substitute for social exchange. Once people decide how they feel about injustice, they no longer see a need to do something about it. Instead, they use their feelings of estrangement as proof that they are good people, that their feelings of empathy, sympathy, and pity absolve them of any responsibility to act. Felice Blake and Paula Ioanide describe this dynamic as "feeling good about feeling bad."[35]

Historians frequently craft narratives that appeal to these feelings, imagining that they are winning allies by engaging them in stories about struggle, sacrifice, and suffering. Yet giving people something to feel is not the same as giving them something to do. Empathy can be a knife that cuts two ways. As Nancy Armstrong shows in her analysis of the emergence of the novel as the key cultural device through which modern subjectivities were learned and legitimated, the compassion for others promoted by discourses of sympathy does not lead to actions against inequalities but instead to a greater commitment to their preservation.[36] There should be no heartwarming reconciliation across class lines in culture if those lines continue to divide people in social life. Much of modern literature, theatre, photography, film, and folklore has helped construct a pedagogy through which people learn to feel good about feeling bad. Historical work on aggrieved groups is likely to be translated into that framework unless a conscious process of *konesans* and *balans* marks it as a different kind of learning.

One way to avoid the trap of feeling good about feeling bad is to renegotiate the terms of cultural reception. Radical movements do not just promise future social change, they offer activists an opportunity to live differently right now. They are crucibles of new ways of knowing and new ways of being. They not only challenge the social distribution of resources and rights but also create countercultures from which new kinds of subjects and subjectivities can emerge. From the utility of group singing as a way of enacting the collective power envisioned by workers on strike and civil rights demonstrators, to the utility of agitprop theatre and spoken-word art, radical movements deploy expressive culture as a way of creating the seeds of a new society inside the shell of the old.

The scholarly approaches to culture that prevail in the academy generally treat expressive culture in isolation from the social conditions from which it emerges. Culture is seen as reactive, as a form of protest or a way to fight fear in the midst of struggle, but it is rarely seen as a productive part of the work that social movements carry out. Yet past and present works of expressive culture serve as archives of collective struggle, as repositories of collective memory, as sites of moral and political instruction, and as vehicles for calling communities into being through performance. Even when they do not touch directly on chronological accounts of the past, they are suffused with collective memories and vernacular traditions that connect the past with the present. Some of the most generative historical thinking about race, state violence, and radical movements comes from people who do not have standing in society as historians, who draw on the vernacular expressive cultures of aggrieved groups as ways of carrying on the struggle in the present.

For example, New Orleans spoken-word artist Sunni Patterson speaks of her art as something that finds the pulse of the people.[37] Along with other activists, teachers, and spoken-word artists in New Orleans, Patterson has helped form "story circles" that give voice to the right of the black working class in that city to participate in making the decisions that affect their lives. Similarly, the international Improvisation, Community, and Social Practice initiative headquartered at the University of Guelph in Canada has been promoting dialogues between artistic improvisers and human rights activists to build a participatory and democratic culture around human rights issues. Chicano artists and activists are fashioning a political performance culture through the practices of the fandango that promote the concept of *convivencia*—deliberate and intentional acts of convening outside of commercial culture. These efforts to create forms of art that find the pulse of the people are infused with traces of long histories of art-based community making inside radical movements, and it is important for historians to discern how they continue today and to learn from them as ways of understanding both the past and the present.

Patterson's artistry in the wake of the terrible destruction suffered by the black working class in New Orleans in the aftermath of Hurricane Katrina offers an exemplary model of how this work happens. In her poem "We Know This Place," Patterson connects the organized abandonment of her community in 2005 to the long history of racialized exploitation and brutality that preceded it. Her poem proclaims, "We know this place. It's ever changing yet forever the same: money and power and greed the game."[38] Knowing "this place" for Patterson means that perceptions of progress have proved illusory, that the familiar suffering caused by racism and repression remains as painful as ever. The place that she claims her community knows is in one sense a physical place, the New Orleans that for centuries has been the core of the Mississippi Delta economy, the financial and administrative center for slave owners and plantation owners, and the scene of relentless segregation, lynching, urban renewal, and police brutality. Yet the place that Patterson's poem proclaims that "we know" is also a political and discursive location, a place of subordination, psychic rage, and social death. "So we know this place," her poem continues, "for we have glanced more times than we'd like to share / into eyes that stare with nothing there / behind them but an unfulfilled wish and an unconscious yearning for life though death rests comfortably beside us."[39] We know this place because everything that happens in it is haunted by things that happened before. We cannot attribute the suffering in New Orleans in 2005 to any single decision by elected officials, the Army Corps of Engineers, emergency relief administrators, or police officers because it was the cumulative vulnerability of the black working class caused by the consequences of class subordination, racial oppression, and political suppression over centuries that guaranteed that any and every decision made during the crisis would hurt black people. The abandonment and dispossession of the black working class in New Orleans did not take place because of an aberrant response to an unexpected natural disaster, but rather stemmed from a large and long pattern of suppression firmly in place long before the hurricane hit.[40]

Yet when Patterson says "We know this place," she also means that the history of domination has also been the history of resistance. "Money, power, and greed" have long been the game, but we also inherit from history instructive legacies of radical refusal, resistance, organization, and mobilization. The place that Sunni Patterson knows is a place where Homer Plessy and other creoles of Haitian ancestry challenged segregation by defying the Louisiana Separate Car Act in the 1890s; the place where Audley "Queen Mother" Moore successfully defended Marcus Garvey's right to speak in the 1920s by mobilizing a crowd of armed black people to protect him; the place that served as the base of operations for Tom Dent, Richard Haley and Oretha Castle Haley, Lolis Elie, and Jerome Smith as they organized opposition to Jim Crow segregation in the 1960s in the parts of Louisiana and Mississippi that Fannie Lou Hamer described as the "home of the grave and the land of the tree."[41] We know this place of contestation and struggle, Patterson reminds us, because we inherit a long history of agitation and education that prepares us for the struggles that today's injustices demand of us. Ancestors—both real and adopted—have walked this path before us. The racialized repression and brutality that we confront today has a long history from which we can learn important lessons.

The forces responsible for provoking activism and activist scholarship create a seemingly endless array of new identities and identifications. Yet armed with *konesans* and *balans*, we can see that we know this place, that the history of race, state violence, and radical movements on the Pacific coast and beyond prepares us perfectly for the difficult work that we need to do in the months and years ahead. What scholars are saying in the chapters in this book and in the larger force field of scholarship that surrounds it is exactly what Sunni Patterson and aggrieved artists, intellectuals, and activists all over the world are saying. Patterson's poem ends with a call to action. She writes,

> Hold on to the prize, never put it down
> Be firm in the stance, no break no bow,
> Go to forward, Mama, make your move now
> Forward, dear children, 'cuz freedom is now.[42]

The work we need to do will not be easy. We will face many difficult days ahead. Yet we are well prepared for the challenges we face. Armed with *konesans* and *balans*, we know this place.

1    A partial list includes Manning Marable, *Malcolm X : A Life of Reinvention* (New York: Viking, 2011); Diane C. Fujino, *Heartbeat of Struggle: The Revolutionary Life of Yuri Kochiyama* (Minneapolis: University of Minnesota Press, 2004); Diane C. Fujino, *A Samurai among Panthers: Richard Aoki on Race, Resistance, and a Paradoxical Life* (Min-

neapolis: University of Minnesota Press, 2012); Daryl J. Maeda, *Chains of Babylon: The Rise of Asian America* (Minneapolis: University of Minnesota Press, 2009); Lee Bebout, *Mythohistorical Interventions: The Chicano Movement and Its Legacies* (Minneapolis: University of Minnesota Press, 2011); Minkah Makalani, *In the Cause of Freedom: Radical Black Internationalism from Harlem to London, 1917–1939* (Chapel Hill: University of North Carolina Press, 2011); Erik McDuffie, *Sojourning for Freedom: Black Women, American Communism, and the Making of Black Left Feminism* (Durham, NC: Duke University Press, 2011); Donna Murch, *Living for the City: Migration, Education, and the Rise of the Black Panther Party in Oakland, California* (Chapel Hill: University of North Carolina Press, 2010); Daniel Widener, *Black Arts West: Culture and Struggle in Postwar Los Angeles* (Durham, NC: Duke University Press, 2010); Eric Porter, *The Problem of the Future World: W. E. B. Du Bois and the Race Concept at Mid-century* (Durham, NC: Duke University Press, 2010); Kelly Lytle Hernández, *Migra! A History of the U.S. Border Patrol* (Berkeley: University of California Press, 2010); Jeffrey Haas, *The Assassination of Fred Hampton: How the FBI and Chicago Police Murdered a Black Panther* (Chicago: Chicago Review Press, 2011); Alyosha Goldstein, *Poverty in Common: The Politics of Community Action during the American Century* (Durham, NC: Duke University Press, 2012); Nico Slate, *Colored Cosmopolitanism: The Shared Struggle for Freedom in the United States and India* (Cambridge, MA: Harvard University Press, 2012); and Shelley Streeby, *Radical Sensations: World Movements, Violence, and Visual Culture* (Durham, NC: Duke University Press, 2013).

2  Karen McCarthy Brown, "Afro-Caribbean Spirituality: A Haitian Case Study," in *Vodou in Haitian Life and Culture: Invisible Powers*, ed. Patrick Bellegarde-Smith and Claudine Michel (Hounds Mill, Basingstoke: Palgrave Macmillan, 2006), 1–26. I am grateful to Claudine Michel for all of the guidance and instruction she has given me on the moral, spiritual, and epistemological significance of *vodou*.

3  Robert Farris Thompson, *The Flash of the Spirit* (New York: Oxford, 1984). Of course this way of thinking is not confined to diasporic Africans.

4  Kimberle Crenshaw, "Race, Reform, and Retrenchment: Transformation and Legitimation in Anti-Discrimination Law," in *Critical Race Theory: The Key Writings That Formed the Movement,* ed. Kimberle Crenshaw, Neil Gotanda, Gary Peller, and Kendall Thomas (New York: The New Press, 1995), 103–22.

5  W. E. B. Du Bois, *Black Reconstruction in America, 1860–1880* (New York: Free Press, 1998), 125.

6  Kevin Drum, "Plutocracy Now," *Mother Jones* 36, no. 2 (Apr. 2011): 63.

7  Kalamu ya Salaam, "Poetic Visions," Annual Meeting of the American Studies Association, Washington, DC, November 5, 2009 (Center for Black Studies Research DVD).

8  James Baldwin, *No Name in the Street* (New York: Vintage, 1972), 87.

9  Clyde Woods, "Les Miserables of New Orleans: Trap Economics and the Asset Stripping Blues, Part 1," in *In the Wake of Hurricane Katrina: New Paradigms and Social Visions,* ed. Clyde Woods (Baltimore, MD: Johns Hopkins University Press, 2010), 343–70.

10  Avery F. Gordon, "A World Map," text for Ashley Hunt's *A World Map in Which We*

See *An Atlas of Radical Cartography*, ed. Lize Mogel and Alexis Bhagat (Los Angeles: Journal of Aesthetics and Protest Press, 2007), 4.

11   Clyde Woods, "Reimagining the Hemispheric South," keynote address, American Cultures in Global Contexts Conference, Santa Barbara, California, January 20, 2011. Author's notes.

12   This is not to argue that the expansion of the prison system stems simply from the profits to be made from private prisons, although there is evidence that the private prison industry lobbied for Arizona SB 1070, which could potentially produce customers for them. For the best analysis of the growth of the prison system, see Ruth Wilson Gilmore, *Golden Gulag: Prisons, Surplus, Crisis, and Opposition in Globalizing California* (Berkeley: University of California Press, 2007).

13   Aime Cesaire, *Discourse on Colonialism* (New York: Monthly Review Press, 2001), 1.

14   Martin Luther King, Jr., *"All Labor Has Dignity,"* ed. Michael K. Honey (Boston: Beacon Press, 2011), 177. King used this phrase about power being the ability to make people in power say yes when they want to say no, which he borrowed from Walter Reuther, to suggest to sanitation workers in Memphis that a general strike would be an appropriate mechanism in their struggle.

15   See Kimberle Crenshaw, "Mapping the Margins: Intersectionality, Identity Politics, and Violence Against Women of Color," *Stanford Law Review* 43, no. 6 (July 1991): 1241–299. See also *Color of Violence: The Incite! Anthology* (Boston: South End, 2006), especially 208–49.

16   Walter Benjamin, *Illuminations* (New York: Shocken Books, 1968), 255.

17   Immanuel Wallerstein, *After Liberalism* (New York: W. W. Norton, 1995), 49.

18   W. E. B. Du Bois, *Black Reconstruction*; C. L. R. James, *American Civilization* (Malden, MA: Blackwell, 1993); Cedric Robinson, *Black Marxism: The Making of the Black Radical Tradition* (Chapel Hill: University of North Carolina Press, 2000); Clyde Woods, *Development Arrested: Race, Power, and the Blues in the Mississippi Delta* (New York: Verso, 1998); Gilmore, *Golden Gulag*.

19   Toni Cade Bambara, quoted in Alice A. Deck, "Toni Cade Bambara (1939–)," in *Black Women in America: An Historical Encyclopedia*, ed. Darlene Clark Hine, Elsa Barkley Brown, and Rosalyn Terborg-Penn (Bloomington: Indiana University Press, 1993), 80.

20   Robin D. G. Kelley, *Hammer and Hoe: Alabama Communists during the Great Depression* (Chapel Hill: University of North Carolina Press, 1990).

21   See Stan Weir, *Singlejack Solidarity* (Minneapolis: University of Minnesota Press, 2004); and George Lipsitz, *A Rainbow at Midnight: Labor and Culture in the 1940s* (Urbana: University of Illinois Press, 1994).

22   David Hilliard, with Keith Zimmerman and Kent Zimmerman, *Huey: Spirit of the Panther* (New York: Thunder's Mouth Press, 2006), 127.

23   George Rawick, *Listening to Revolt: Selected Writings* (Chicago: Charles H. Kerr, 2010), 67.

24   Quoted in Peter Guralnick, *Dream Boogie* (Boston: Little & Brown and Company, 2005), 537.

25   During the review process that vetted this piece for publication, one reviewer challenged my seeming dismissal of vanguardism as misguided, arguing that Leninism is different from Stalinism and that progressive changes have been made and

continue to be made following the vanguard model. This view is held by many of the scholars of race, state violence, and radicalism whom I admire and respect tremendously. Yet I still insist that we need to confront the destructive results of leftist vanguards in the United States and around the world. Works that raise these issues include Weir, *Singlejack Solidarity*; Michael Schneider, "Vanguard, Vanguard, Who's Got the Vanguard," *Liberation* 17 (May and Aug. 1972); and Francois George, "Oublier Lenin," *Les Temps Modernes* 29 (Apr. 1973): 1735–72.

26 John Brown Childs, *Transcommunality: From the Politics of Conversion to the Ethics of Respect* (Philadelphia: Temple University Press, 2003), especially 9–27.

27 Michael Miller Topp, *Those Without a Country: The Political Culture of Italian American Syndicalists* (Minneapolis: University of Minnesota Press, 2001).

28 Bruce Palmer, *Man Over Money: The Southern Populist Critique of American Capitalism* (Chapel Hill: University of North Carolina Press, 1980).

29 Seth Moglen, *Mourning Modernity: Literary Modernism and the Injuries of American Capitalism* (Stanford: Stanford University Press, 2007).

30 Andrew Manis, *A Fire You Can't Put Out: The Civil Rights Life of Birmingham's Reverend Fred Shuttlesworth* (Tuscaloosa: University of Alabama Press, 2001), 79.

31 See Rawick, *Listening to Revolt*.

32 I draw the idea of "something left to love" from Tricia Rose's generative reading of Lorraine Hansberry's *A Raisin in the Sun* in a talk delivered at the Domesticity, Affect, Intimacy, and Justice Conference at the University of California, Santa Barbara, October 24, 2008.

33 See Staughton Lynd and Alice Lynd, *Stepping Stones: Memoir of a Life Together* (Lanham, MD: Lexington Books, 2009); Maria Lopez Vigil, *Oscar Romero: Memories in Mosaic* (London: Darton, Longman, and Todd, 2000).

34 Rawick, *Listening to Revolt*, 71.

35 I thank Paula Ioanide and Felice Blake for this wonderful phrase and for the important idea it encapsulates.

36 Nancy Armstrong, *How Novels Think: The Limits of Individualism* (New York: Columbia University Press, 2005), 25.

37 Sunni Patterson, presentation at the Annual Meeting of the American Studies Association, Washington, DC, November 5, 2009.

38 Sunni Patterson, "We Know This Place," in *In the Wake of Hurricane Katrina: New Paradigms and Social Visions*, ed. Clyde Woods (Baltimore, MD: Johns Hopkins University Press, 2010), 293–95.

39 Patterson, "We Know This Place."

40 See Woods, *In the Wake of Hurricane Katrina*.

41 Blair Kelley, *Right to Ride: Streetcar Boycotts and African American Citizenship in the Era of Plessy v. Ferguson* (Chapel Hill: University of North Carolina Press, 2010), 51–86; Tony Martin, *Race First: The Ideological and Organizational Struggles of Marcus Garvey* (Dover, MA: The Majority Press, 1986), 210; Kim Lacy Rogers, *Righteous Lives: Narratives of the New Orleans Civil Rights Movement* (New York: New York University Press, 1995); Lynne Olsen, *Freedom's Daughters* (New York: Simon and Schuster, 2001), 255; Chana Kai Lee, *For Freedom's Sake* (Urbana: University of Illinois Press, 2000); Tom

Dent, *Southern Journey: A Return to the Civil Rights Movement* (Athens: University of Georgia Press, 2001). In another case of the knife cutting two ways, Plessy challenged the Louisiana segregation law by arguing that his light skin and large number of white ancestors made him not black and therefore able to sit in the white car. This is a part of the complicated history of creoles of color in Louisiana who possessed a kind of whiteness before the Civil War but increasingly became treated as black and only black afterward.

42  Patterson, "We Know This Place," 295.

# PART TWO

# Traversing the Pacific

# 2

# Mobilizing Revolutionary Manhood

## Race, Gender, and Resistance in the Pacific Northwest Borderlands

KORNEL CHANG

IN 1908, THE *VANCOUVER WORLD* REPORTED THAT SOUTH ASIAN ANTI-colonial activists were "subscribing money for seditious purposes" in British Columbia and turning the province into a veritable "centre for revolutionary agitation." Elaborating on this new foreign menace, the paper claimed that "there is a certain school there, ostensibly for the instruction of Indians in English which is actually being managed by agitators for the purpose of imbuing Sikhs with revolutionary ideas."[1] The Colonial Office in London, similarly, maintained that a clandestine revolutionary network was operating out of the Pacific Northwest. "I have been informed that it is likely bombs are manufactured in Vancouver and also probably in Victoria," testified a colonial official. "Men have been taught there on the Coast how to make bombs, and are capable of readily assembling the parts when same have been successfully smuggled across the Pacific."[2] Such accounts recast the problem of transpacific Asian migrations, from one concerned with the invasion of inassimilable aliens to one about foreign insurgency and sedition.

The threat of foreign subversion, both real and imagined, was amplified when the US Immigration Bureau learned that South Asian revolutionaries were joining forces with other radical groups in the region. In 1914, US immigrant inspector Charles Riley reported that, "as evidence of their proficiency in the art of 'blowing people up,' I was assured that most of the members of the Hindu nationalist party were also 'IWW's.'"[3] He was, of course, referring to the Industrial Workers of the World, a radical labor organization that had recently made waves by mobilizing workers to take direct action against some of the most powerful corporations in the North American West.[4] American and Canadian authorities as well as British colonial officials in London and India deemed the possible merger between white labor militants and "Hindu seditionists" an existential threat to nation and empire.

The claims of interracial and interradical unity and the danger it posed were no doubt exaggerated to justify the wave of state repression that was to come.[5] But if these fears were inflated, they were not entirely unfounded either. In the first two decades of the twentieth century, the Industrial Workers of the World (IWW) and South Asian anticolonial revolutionaries in the Pacific Northwest rallied together at times to resist and challenge capitalist relations and Western imperialism. For white labor radicals, the South Asian independence struggle provided a way to imagine a world-wide revolution against global capitalism. The militant anticolonialism of the South Asian revolutionaries that called for the immediate overthrow of British rule in India resonated deeply with IWW leaders and activists, for it spoke to their own hopes for a revolutionary workers' internationalism. South Asian revolutionaries, in turn, adopted strands of the class-based internationalism of the IWW, among other ideas, to foster a transnational nationalist consciousness among colonial subjects in exile. This was, then, a case of a workers' internationalism finding expression in a global anticolonial movement, and vice versa.

The affinities that brought white and South Asian radicals together were also forged through the language of revolutionary manhood. In the Pacific Northwest, IWW activists made concerted efforts to redeem Asian manhood by insisting on Asian workers' capacity for direct action and working-class militancy. In doing so, they were seeking to make the case for Asian migrants as manly unionists who were deserving of class inclusion. To recuperate Asian manhood these activists drew on a familiar, albeit amorphous, language of working-class manhood with its emphasis on fearlessness, physical prowess, and individual initiative. But the IWW would also expand upon it by including anti-imperial agitation and resistance as outward signs of a "virile syndicalism."[6] As such, rebellion against empire and seizing one's political independence were now considered alongside sabotage and striking on the job as expressions of direct action. This was hardly a stretch, since the cultural construct of revolutionary manhood bore a close resemblance to a radical working-class manhood, and because some, though clearly not all, IWW leaders and activists equated resistance to imperialism with resistance to capitalism.

This discursive device, which was employed haphazardly rather than programmatically, enabled the IWW to incorporate, if only tenuously, Asian radicals as well as Asian workers into its movement.

The IWW's efforts to rehabilitate Asian manhood intersected and, on certain occasions, overlapped with the gender politics of South Asian revolutionary nationalism. Indeed, at the same time white labor radicals were trying to overcome anti-Asian racism with gender, South Asian revolutionaries were involved in the reclamation of their own manhood so as to stake their claim to self-determination. Beginning in the last quarter of the nineteenth century, British colonial authorities worked deliberately to deracinate the manhood of South Asian nationalists as part of an imperial strategy to undermine the nationalist movement on the subcontinent and beyond. As historian Mrinalini Sinha has brilliantly shown, by portraying their colonial subjects as effeminate and childlike, symbolized by the Orientalist trope of the "effeminate babu," British colonizers rendered South Asians unfit for self-rule.[7] South Asian revolutionary nationalists in the North American West responded to the emasculating politics of the British colonial state with a call to arms, seeing insurrectionary uprising as a chance to reclaim their manhood. This shared imagining of a gendered insurgency in which the promise of liberation would be realized through the manhood acts of virile subaltern men produced moments of interracial unity and interradical cooperation in the Pacific Northwest.

At the same time, white and South Asian radicals articulated different, even competing, conceptions of manhood that revealed important fissures between the two groups. These conflicting versions of manhood reflected the differing political commitments of white and South Asian radicals. The former were engaged in a class struggle, and the latter in an anticolonial cause, and as such white and South Asian radicals called on gender to perform ideological work that was at once complementary and contradictory. In making the case for the class inclusion of Japanese workers, for example, IWW activists referred to their manly self-restraint and their willingness to suffer persecution as outward signs of a virtuous, honorable manhood. On the other hand, most South Asian revolutionaries regarded long-suffering as an indication of weakness and unmanliness. To inspire their countrymen to topple British imperial rule on the subcontinent, their notion of revolutionary manhood emphasized the capacity to exercise force in the face of injustice that corresponded more closely with a virile masculinity.[8]

The vision of a gendered insurgency that brought white and Asian radicals together in solidarity in the Pacific Northwest paradoxically served to limit the possibilities of a lasting alliance, forestalled ultimately by its own racial and gendered underpinnings. Closely bound up with the ascendant ideas of manhood at the turn of the twentieth century, these gendered revolutionary discourses inescapably reproduced the historical coupling of whiteness and manliness.[9] In the case of the South Asian revolutionary nationalists, the strategy to resist British imperial domination through the language of virile manhood rehearsed the hegemonic logic of colonial masculinity, which was deployed precisely to delegitimize their claims to independence.

This essay explores the convergent and divergent radicalisms of the South Asian diasporic revolutionary movement and the IWW in the Pacific Northwest, demonstrating how they were animated by, and in turn animated, larger struggles being staged across the Pacific and across the globe. South Asian revolutionaries and other Asian nationalists and white labor radicals reconfigured the imperial pathways they traveled on to mount challenges to global capitalism and Euro-American imperial domination in the early twentieth century. But because their challenges adopted as much as they transcended the rationales of Western imperial modernity, they produced crosscutting social movements that were as fragmented as they were united in the face of tightening imperial control. This was the condition of a subaltern politics that was simultaneously born out of and against a Euro-American colonial modernity.

## REVOLUTIONARIES IN THE DIASPORA

In the late nineteenth century, colonial India experienced a massive groundswell of nationalist sentiment and activities. Nationalist organizations, revolutionary clubs, and political newspapers and journals sprouted across India. While most of these expressions of nationalism repudiated violence, a small segment called for violent retribution resulting in several high-profile assassination attempts on British crown officials on the subcontinent. The colonial state used the attacks as a pretext for a full-scale government crackdown on political dissent, as imperial authorities proceeded to round up and imprison "extremists," censor nationalist literature, and shut down nationalist organizations.[10] This state repression led to the mass exodus of nationalist activists and intellectuals, who fled to North America, Asia, Europe, and Africa to continue the struggle for independence away from the immediate gaze of the colonial state.

Inspired by rising discontent over British imperial rule, South Asian nationalists mobilized a worldwide movement in the first two decades of the twentieth century. This transnational nationalist community was far from homogenous, fracturing along political, religious, and ethnic lines.[11] Yet, despite these cleavages, diasporic nationalists of various political persuasions were connected across space and time through the aspiration of a free India. The revolutionary paper *Ghadar* spoke to this imagined transnational nationalist community when it declared, "In London, Paris, Geneva, New York, San Francisco, Vancouver, Fiji, and Natal, in all these places patriots are working with a singleness of purpose for their country."[12]

The borderlands of the North American West emerged as a critical node within this global network of nationalist mobilization, becoming a site for arguably the most radical brand of nationalist politics and resistance in the South Asian diaspora.[13] The director of Criminal Intelligence in India, C. J. Stevenson-Moore, called the area the "chief school for revolutionary Indians." Indeed, it became known as a staging ground for anticolonial insurgency on the Indian subcontinent. "Many revolutionary activities in India," he explained, "were believed to be plotted in Pacific coast cities." Citing specific intelligence, Stevenson-Moore noted that "when Lord Hardinge's party was made object to a bomb attack in New Delhi, it was suspected that the bomb had been produced in Seattle."[14]

By the eve of World War I, a loosely organized revolutionary structure had emerged, with the movement's leadership organized around cities on the Pacific Rim. South Asian revolutionaries circulated across the Pacific and beyond, forging anticolonial connections and relationships through which certain sites became nodes in a revolutionary geography. Vancouver, Victoria, Seattle, San Francisco, Manila, and Tokyo became links in a transnational chain that anticolonial supporters hoped would end in an insurrection against British rule in India.[15] The siting of anticolonial diasporic politics was determined in part by South Asian radicals' imaginings of the United States and Japan as emblematic anticolonial projects. South Asian revolutionaries drew eclectically from a number of different intellectual traditions and sources, but iconic American revolutionary figures—George Washington, Patrick Henry, and Thomas Paine—were especially prominent in their revolutionary writings and thoughts. In the

United States, revolutionaries found inspiration in a nation born of rebellion against an empire—in fact, the very same empire they were squaring off against. In the case of Japan, South Asian radicals saw the country's stunning military victory over Russia in 1905 as proof that Asian nations and peoples could match and perhaps in time eclipse the West, and as such made Japan a valuable model to study for South Asian revolutionaries.[16]

In the North American West, revolutionary nationalists traveled up and down the Pacific coast, delivering proindependence lectures in immigrant temples, societies, and reading rooms. The prominent Ghadar revolutionary Har Dayal, who led the radical movement from San Francisco, toured the Pacific Northwest in 1913 as part of an effort to raise revolutionary consciousness among South Asian immigrants in the western US-Canadian borderlands.[17] The US Immigration Bureau described Dayal as "a very violent Anglophone of frankly anarchist views" who was "delivering a course of lectures in Oregon and Washington, advocating anarchism."[18] In 1909, anticolonial activists Taraknath Das and Guru Kumar established the United India House in Seattle, "where lectures were given every Saturday by [Das] and other Bengali students to the Sikh laborers." The mass meetings where such lectures were delivered also furnished opportunities for revolutionaries to inform nonreading compatriots of recently published nationalist articles and books. In one of the rallies protesting Canadian immigration restriction, Sohan Lal read to the audience anti-British poems and essays from various revolutionary periodicals.[19] South Asian anticolonial nationalists also coordinated grassroots propaganda campaigns in the immigrant enclaves of Victoria and Vancouver, "preaching sedition from house to house," according to a British informant.[20]

The immigrant communities in these cities supplied the base from which to coordinate outreach to migrant workers. Anticolonial activists followed South Asian laborers into the hinterlands, bringing the gospel of Indian freedom to their work camps and bunkhouses. It should be said that the revolutionary literati were not consistently of one mind on this outreach. As evidenced by the frustrations expressed by certain members of the revolutionary vanguard, there were those who doubted the workers' capacity for political consciousness and minimized their potential for revolutionary action. This distinct class bias resulted in a somewhat disjointed campaign that was perhaps not as robust as it could have been. In 1913, for example, Guru Kumar lamented the "dearth of earnest workers" among the "Sikhs in the field." Nevertheless, there was a core group of revolutionary activists who, in identifying imperialism as a mode of capitalist exploitation, were committed to enlisting migrant workers into the liberation struggle. As Maia Ramnath writes, they linked the "racial discrimination toward a low-wage immigrant labor force to an explicitly anti-imperialist revolutionary program, rather than simply calling for inclusion in the existing society."[21]

Taraknath Das, for one, believed that the nationalist outreach to migrant workers was yielding its desired results, insisting that Sikh laborers, once "the backbone of the British Empire in India," were now coming "in contact with free people and institutions of free nations" and assimilating "the idea of liberty." This political awakening, he argued, was crucial to winning "over the native Indian army to the nationalist side." As Das explained, "We all know that the national uprising of 1857 would have been successful in throwing off the foreign yoke if our own people had not engaged in helping the tyrants ... now the problem before us is to see whether the native troops of the British government which number over 200,000 will again join hands with the tyrants or not. We believe not, if work could be carried on in giving the idea of the benefits of independence among the native troops."[22] British colonial officials were keenly aware of the effect that this organizing drive in the North American West could have on the Indian countryside. "Sikh laborers on the Pacific coast might come in time to assume a greater importance particularly in view of the indirect effects likely to be produced in the Punjab and elsewhere in India by a prolonged and carefully planned campaign of misrepresentation conducted by men like Taraknath Das and Guru Ditta Kumar among the Sikh immigrants in British Columba."[23]

In trying to rally various South Asian constituencies—Hindus, Muslims, and Sikhs—of different class backgrounds to the anticolonial cause, revolutionaries in the Pacific Northwest pursued a strategy that focused on the immigration question. The United States and Canada devised new policies and regulations to exclude South Asian immigrants in the early twentieth century. In Seattle, immigration officials carved out South Asian migrant illegality from existing statues within US immigration law. In 1908, for example, the Immigration Service excluded three hundred South Asian immigrants on the grounds that they were "liable to become a public charge at time of entry"—the LPC clause.[24] United States officials also interpreted clauses on physical and mental defect, disease, contract labor, and moral turpitude as broadly as possible to exclude South Asians. A departmental memorandum explained: "Since at least 1909 it has been the general policy of the Immigration Service to exclude Hindus. If such aliens were not found to belong to some of the definitely fixed and excluded classes such as paupers, criminals, or contagiously diseased, ground for exclusion was found either in the fact that they were person of poor physique (afflicted with physical defects affecting ability to earn a living) or that they were likely to become public charges."[25]

South Asian revolutionary activists exploited the issue of immigration restriction to build popular support for their cause. They organized mass meetings and demonstrations protesting the law's discriminatory features; they provided legal and social support for South Asian detainees who were ordered for deportation; and they established organizations for the express purpose of supporting the immigration rights of South Asians. In 1908, Taraknath Das organized a mass protest in Vancouver that brought together Canadian Sikhs, Hindus, and Muslims to challenge the Continuous Journey Order, which barred immigrants not coming directly from their country of origin. The technical language obscured the order's racist intent, for there was not a single steamship line providing direct service from India to Canada at this time. It was a method of achieving South Asian exclusion without explicitly discriminating against Crown subjects. Das and other revolutionaries challenged the order-in-council, contending that South Asians were entitled to free movement to and within territories under British jurisdiction by virtue of their status as British subjects. Part of the reason that revolutionaries struggled so mightily against immigration restriction—in addition to the fact that it made for good anti-imperial politics—was that they understood that the right of mobility was not simply about freedom of movement but that it was bound up with the freedom to organize and resist from abroad. By viewing immigration restriction as a concerted imperial strategy to contain the diasporic nationalist movement, they anticipated Hannah Arendt's dictum that "Freedom of movement ... is the indispensable precondition for action" by half a century.[26]

Revolutionaries were venerated for their willingness to confront Dominion authorities in Canada and US officials head on, making their anticolonial message more attractive in turn. Colonial intelligence pointed to this alarming trend in Vancouver, where revolutionaries "had worked up the Sikh labourers there to such an extent that those of them who had been soldiers in the Indian army and had war medals and army discharge certificates in their possession, burnt them on a bonfire at a public meeting; at the same time denouncing the British in violent terms."[27] The real danger behind this kind of political agitation, according to J. C. Kerr, assistant to the director of Criminal Intelligence, "lies in the fact that the Indians concerned are Sikhs, many of whom have formerly served in the Indian army, and that on their return to India they are likely to sow the seeds of disaffection amongst the classes from which the Sikh regiments are recruited."[28] Prior to their emigration, Punjabi Sikhs served in the imperial military and police force. As such, they seemed hardly the ideal group for fomenting a revolutionary movement.[29] However, by highlighting immigration restriction as an egregious abuse of colonial power, revolutionaries managed to persuade members of the Sikh immigrant community to join their anticolonial cause.

A GENDERED INSURGENCY

In contrast to more moderate nationalists and reformers, such as those associated with the Indian National Congress and Mohandas Gandhi's nonviolent resistance movement in South Africa, anticolonial activists in British Columbia, Washington, and California called for the immediate overthrow of British rule in India and considered revolutionary violence a legitimate response to colonial power. As revolutionary activist Hussain Rahim declared, "When these Canadians, Australians, and New Zealanders do not allow us to enter their country, why should we not drive them from India? We should take those steps and we could start a struggle and exclude those people from India."[30] This belligerent declaration was reminiscent of the defiant language that Rahim voiced at his own deportation hearing several years earlier when he had shouted, "You drive us Hindus out of Canada and we will drive out every white man out of India." As this quote suggests, revolutionaries encouraged a shared sense of predicament stemming from their common colonial subjugation, emphasizing that South Asians everywhere, whether "Hindustanis, Mohammedans, or Sikhs," were all equally victims of white colonial oppression.[31]

This highly militant and capacious sense of national belonging, forming a radical transnational nationalist consciousness, was largely imparted through the language of revolutionary manhood and as such South Asian anticolonial resistance was, at least in part, constituted through gender.

Revolutionary activists very consciously represented the South Asian as a martial type full of virility, militancy, and physical prowess. Gendered tropes and metaphors were therefore a staple of revolutionary publicity appearing frequently in the *Ghadar* and the *Free Hindusthan*. The masthead of the *Ghadar*, for example, read, "O People of India Arise and Take Your Sword." The elements of this gendered revolutionary discourse could also be readily identifiable in a poem the revolutionary paper published in 1913:

O people of India take this ship to shore
Drive away the storm of troubles from you.
All the world has risen up and we are left behind.
You also build up your home and independence with your life-blood.
Throw away your heavy feeling.
O heroes get up and take the lead.
All your gardens up and take the lead.
Start to water them again and build them up.
There is still life left among us to rise again.
But we must not leave it too late.
All over the world they call us useless.
Get up heroes and bring forward the name of your country.
Wake up the sleeping and the lover your countrymen far away.
Bring to light the land of India.
Bring her forward before the eyes of all the world.

This anticolonial vision of masculine South Asian brothers locked in arms, in which a self-sacrificing manhood would emancipate the nation, helped smooth over, however ephemerally, the myriad divisions fracturing the nationalist movement.

These gendered analogies and metaphors were a carefully scripted response to the colonial politics of masculinity that rendered South Asian nationalists slavish and submissive and therefore incapable of self-rule. This discursive strategy may have also been designed to reach their target constituency in the Pacific Northwest: the martial language of revolutionary manhood would have surely resonated with many South Asian Sikh immigrants, for it hewed closely to their virile self-image.[32] In the late nineteenth century, British colonizers tried to discredit the growing demands of an Indian elite by denigrating their masculinity, with their rhetorical assaults coalescing around an effeminate imagery.

Figure 2.1. This image
was the front cover of a
Ghadarite collection of
poems and songs published
by the Ghadar Party in
San Francisco in 1913.
Reprinted from *Ghadar
Di Gunj* (Jalander: Desh
Bhagat Yadgar Hall, 1993).

"It was the shift in British colonial attitudes towards Western-educated
Indians," Mrinalini Sinha argues, "from mediators between the colonial
administration and the rest of the Indian population to an unrepresen-
tative and artificial minority representing nothing but the anomalies of
their own situation, that was signaled by the late nineteenth-century
concept of the 'effeminate babu.'"[33] The effeminate babu stood, then, for
the degenerate Bengali male, and the Indian middle class, more broadly—
personifying a pretentious and superficially refined group who reputedly
lacked internalized controls for manly conduct. The Indian middle class
responded to this imperial iconography by introducing a reformist agenda
that included building gymnasiums and promoting strenuous activity, as
ways to address the perceived crisis in Indian masculinity.[34]

South Asian revolutionaries in the North American West (and elsewhere), on the other hand, called for the redemption of national manhood

through armed struggle, by literally taking up the sword. For revolutionaries, the anticolonial struggle was *the* test of South Asian manhood and, as such, revolutionary violence was simultaneously an act of masculine regeneration. "We have a right to create revolution in India," Das declared. "The only question is whether we have the desire and power to carry it out." Contending that their "national life is at stake," with the "British government in India [having] already adopted all possible repressive measures to crush our national aspirations," he implored his "dear brothers of Hindusthan" to "be united together and exert our best energies to get Swaraj—absolute self-government."[35] In his article "Hindu Fitness for Self-Rule," Das harkened back to revolutionary men of the past: "Luther, Mazzini, Patrick Henry, Thomas Paine, and other workers for the cause of humanity," who "were invariably in the minority at the beginning and came out victorious in the end."[36] In this imagining of anticolonial resistance, the comity of brotherhood, manly duty, and courage, and the prerogative of self-rule were inextricably intertwined.

But if South Asian revolutionaries projected the image of a masculine nationalist hero to contest a concerted imperial campaign to emasculate them, their discursive formation was also fraught with tensions and contradictions that limited its effectiveness. As postcolonial and feminist historians have persuasively argued, the nationalist strategy to assert a subaltern masculinity—and tie it to the prerogative of self-determination—through a discourse of virile manhood had the contradictory effect of reproducing the operative logic of colonial masculinity, of tightening the links between gender, nation, and empire, that is. In fact, many South Asian revolutionaries adopted a similar feminizing rhetoric to call the masculinity of their more moderate, reformist-minded countrymen into question, for what they perceived to be their tepid response to British imperial rule on the subcontinent.[37]

## REDEEMING ASIAN MANHOOD

The gender politics of the South Asian revolutionary nationalists overlapped, although never neatly or unproblematically, with the cultural campaign of the Industrial Workers of the World to redeem Asian manhood. Unlike other labor organizations in the region, the IWW looked to organize Asian workers and was committed to the ideal of interracial unionism. In 1911, an activist editorialized that "union[s] could pass reso-

Figure 2.2. Cartoon published in the Industrial Workers of the World newspaper *Solidarity*, June 30, 1917. Collective action and brotherly solidarity are represented as sources of (male) worker power.

lutions galore or try to kill the Orientals there, like some fools did about four years ago at Vancouver, but so long as labor is bought and sold upon the market, so long will the master class bring these people in to compete with us as sellers of labor power." The IWW therefore called on white workers to "do away with racial prejudice and imaginary boundary lines, recognize that all workers belong to the international nation of wealth producers, and clearly see that our only enemy is the capitalist class and the only boundary line is between exploiter and exploited."[38]

IWW activists took this vision of an interracial working-class internationalism directly into the logging, mining, and railway construction camps straddling the US-Canadian boundary, organizing white and Asian workers alike on both sides of the imaginary line. In doing so, they challenged at once the boundaries of race, class, and nation extant in the Pacific Northwest borderlands. These were, as a prominent activist insisted, nothing more than artifices of the ruling classes to keep workers divided and powerless. "The financier recognizes no boundary lines,

Figure 2.3. The portrayal of physical prowess and strength was a prominent motif in IWW iconography. Industrial Workers of the World pamphlet, 1933.

no colors or creeds or races when it comes to profitable investments," he explained. "But he makes use of all ancient superstitions and prejudice in the form of patriotism, religion and race hatreds to protect his investments."[39] Actualizing these aspirations and ideas, IWW leaders "Big" Bill Haywood, Elizabeth Gurley Flynn, and John Riordan frequently moved back and forth across the northern boundary to give speeches, organize workers, and participate in strikes and protests. As a result of such intentional cross-border outreach, the IWW, by 1909, was able to established nine locals across British Columbia, combining for a Canadian membership of close to 4,000.[40]

In their appeals for an interracial working-class internationalism, the IWW transformed Asian migrants into manly unionists deserving of class inclusion. IWW leaders and activists understood that their fight had to be waged on cultural as well as political grounds, that their success in building an interracial and international labor movement would depend on their ability to chip away at the dominant representation of the Asian worker as "coolie" labor—perhaps the most preeminent figure of degraded manhood during this time. His was a manhood tainted by a fusion of race and class failing. Unskilled and footloose, his "sojourning," among other things, was a mark of his degradation. As the Seattle *Union Record* noted scornfully, "Deprive a Jap of work in one place and he will hustle until he gets another."[41]

White labor leaders across the political spectrum denied Asian migrants entry to their unions precisely on these grounds, insisting that they lacked the accoutrements of manhood for working-class membership. The socialist paper *Western Clarion*, for example, made the case explicitly when it editorialized: "The desire of the capitalist for cheap and servile labor here is, no doubt, just as strong as elsewhere.... Industries have been prostituted by Asiatic corruption to such a low level that white workmen are debarred from honorable competition."[42] Merging the two most potent symbols of degradation in the late nineteenth century—the prostitute and the "coolie"—Chinese, Japanese, and South Asian laborers were represented as thoroughly unmanly and therefore beyond the redemption of working-class organization and acculturation.[43] The willingness to subject themselves to grinding poverty and a condition of dependence and insecurity, and their engagement in "women's work" all served as indisputable proof of their unmanliness, justifying their exclusion from the revolutionary vanguard of radical working-class organizations as well as the more conservative craft unionism of the American Federation of Labor (AFL).[44]

Seeking to facilitate their acceptance into the region's working class, IWW leaders and activists contested the "coolie" trope and produced an alternative discourse of Asian manhood, especially around militant Japanese workers. Elizabeth Gurley Flynn projected an image of the Asian laborer as a highly class-conscious workingman who challenged the prerogatives of the capitalist boss at every turn. "He will go to work in a fruit country and he will wait until the fruit is ripe and then if it isn't picked at once it will spoil, out walks the Jap and he doesn't savvy anything but more wages; and he usually gets more wages."[45] In the same vein, the *Industrial Worker* called the Japanese the "most merciless" of any seasonal laborer while discussing how an employer "bewails the mistake ... in getting Japanese who will exact everything possible, if they have but a half a chance." Taking on the charge that the Japanese were perennial strikebreakers, the leader of the IWW local in Spokane, J. H. Walsh, insisted,

"The average Japanese simply will not scab. He knows too much, and is too much of a man."[46] Flynn concurred, contending of the Japanese that "once a union man always a union man."[47]

IWW writers and activists also used these occasions to offer an incisive critique of the color-consciousness of conservative craft unionism. In an article titled "Silly Race Prejudice," Walsh denounced the AFL porters' union for their efforts to expel Japanese labor from industrial competition. He asked, "Will any man explain just why, as long as the Japanese are here, it would not be better to unite with them to fight the common enemy, the master, than to waste time, energy and strength in fighting another group of workers simply on account of their color—to the huge delight of the employer?" Walsh opined. "If the porters' union were but half as class conscious as the average Japanese worker, there would be better wages and better conditions for the porter than the wretched ones they are now forced to submit to."[48] Turning the tables on conservative white unionists and their exclusionary policies, the IWW called the manliness of the AFL into question, insisting that it was they who failed to measure up to the standard of manhood. "The American Federation of Labor," the *Industrial Worker* claimed, "is run in the interest of the employing class, and the bosses, big and little, are there to keep down the spirit and fighting blood of the workers." Thus, "any man who has the nerve and the backbone to stand up for what's right should leave this aggregation who have long since become merely a cat's paw for the bosses."[49]

Reversing traditional stereotypes, the IWW portrayed Asian workers as labor radicals who were willing to challenge the capitalist system while depicting white laborers as corporate lackeys devoid of manly courage. Using labor relations at the Port Blakely mills as an example, IWW activists argued that the Japanese possessed the quality of "stick" that was essential to becoming a manly unionist. "The Japanese decided to ask for a raise of 20 cents per day. One morning they all rolled up their blankets ready to leave camp if their demands were not granted. The 20 cent raise was granted." In contrast, they contended, at the very same mill, "white" men were treated and driven like "Mexican peons" and earning lower wages than the Japanese. They asked, "How long will it be before the body of 5,000 American laborers will have the energy and manhood to strike in a body? Many of those patriotic Americans in Washington and in the Northwest, for instance, who will follow the harvest, eat rotten food, and sleep in their masters' straw stacks, will be among the fools who cry out against the 'foreigner' and the Japanese!" And this was why a "yellow skin" was to be preferred a "thousand times" to a "yellow heart."[50]

The frequent references to Japanese labor radicalism came amid growing Japanese labor activism and agitation across the Pacific world. From industrial centers in Japan to the agricultural fields on the Pacific coast of North America, Japanese workers clashed with industrialists and landowners, engaging in high-profile strikes, work stoppages, and other forms of labor protests that highlighted their militancy and class consciousness.[51] Collectively, these episodes of Japanese labor uprisings would approximate the IWW's vision of workers' internationalism and frame the worldwide struggle against capitalism. They would also provide IWW activists with useable examples of Asian labor resistance from which to imagine and project an Asian manhood worthy of class inclusion and solidarity.

Among the most potent of these sources came from the sugar plantations of Hawai'i, where thousands of Japanese laborers had walked off their jobs for several months in 1909 after their demands for a wage increase went unmet. The Japanese couched their demands in the slogan "equal pay for equal work," insisting that they be paid the same as the Portuguese and Puerto Rican laborers who performed similar work on the plantation. Sugar planters responded with force, mobilizing state power against the "intransigent" Japanese workers. Labor leaders were arrested and imprisoned and the rank and file were beat back by police violence and surveillance. The repression eventually took its toll on the strikers, as the workers agreed to go back to work three months later. However, their efforts were not entirely in vain. Several months following the end of the strike, the planters agreed to bring up their wages and to abolish the system of wage differentiation based on nationality.[52]

The dramatic uprising of Japanese sugar workers on the Hawaiian Islands gained the attention and admiration of IWW activists in the Pacific Northwest. For them, it served as proof that Japanese workers were capable of direct action—the telltale sign of a virile working-class manhood. "The Japanese workers in the sugar plantations, and the agricultural laborers generally, in the islands, have formed a union called the 'Higher Wages Association.' They have been conducting a strike, many features of which show the discipline and fighting spirit of our Japanese fellow workers." In particular, the IWW emphasized the manly virtues of Yasutaro Soga and Fred Makino, the leaders of the movement, praising their willingness to suffer persecution for the cause of class liberation. According to the *Industrial Worker*, "Their foremost fighters may suffer imprisonment," but "such persecution will only be one more shake to rouse the sleeping giant of Labor." Moreover, by highlighting details of the Japanese strike of 1909, the IWW once again destabilized the racial logic that made manly unionism indistinguishable from whiteness. "An attempt is being made by the employers to break the strike by means of 'white' scabs!" On the other hand, the Japanese "who are supposed to be slavish for revolt," IWW propagandists argued, "are rapidly showing the world that they are the most merciless in their demands of the employer."[53] Furthering the case for workers' internationalism, white labor radicals pointed to the fact that the "Japanese government have vied with the American employers" in persecuting the strikers to show that "the struggle is on class lines between the workers and the employers without regard to nation or race."[54]

Throughout the duration of the strike, T. Takahashi, a Japanese labor activist from Chicago, wrote updates for the *Industrial Worker*, narrating the epic struggle between the island's sugar planters and Japanese workers for the paper's working-class readership. Describing the situation in Hawai'i as a "war between working-class and capitalist class," Takahashi reported that the "brutal police force" was unable to "crush the vigor of the awakening giant, the Japanese strikers." In his accounts, Takahashi used martial language and imagery to great effect, reinvigorating Japanese manhood by tying it to class warfare and militancy. "The capitalists of the island with the aid of governmental force succeeded at first battle, but our boys, whose spirit is expressed in their song, 'We rather die and scatter like cherry blossoms than to be a coward of shame,' existing like mere brick and stone, will never rest till they shall win."[55] The writings and images put forth by IWW activists and propagandists attested to the symbolic importance of the Pacific in their imagining of a virile Asian manhood in an age of exclusion.

## CONVERGING ON REVOLUTIONARY MANHOOD

The IWW's attempts to collapse the color line through a shared sense of working-class manhood also opened the possibilities to new political alliances and mixing of white and Asian radicals. Like with the striking Japanese laborers in  Hawai'i, IWW activists venerated South Asian revolutionaries for their militant radicalism that took an aggressive stand against their oppressors. Indeed, the IWW held up the South Asian revolutionary as a paragon of virile manhood. "There may not be as much sedition among the Hindus of British Columbia as among Canadian-born Socialists who rant of the flag as 'a bloody rag'; but our Socialistic seditionists have never yet been accused of collecting two million dollars to send home to India to buy rifles for the revolution."[56] The running admiration and support of South Asian anticolonialists did not correspond neatly to their efforts to broaden the labor movement, but in both instances, gender served as the binding agent; it was the shared traits of militancy, confrontation, and direct action that brought virile white and Asian radicals together in moments of interracial and interradical solidarity. As a spokesperson for the IWW boasted, "Our workers—revolutionists, you would call them—are at work among the Hindu in India."[57]

The rendering of the South Asian as a masculine heroic insurgent helped to distance him from and complicate his racial identification as an "Asiatic," and facilitated an interracial alliance that brought South Asian revolutionaries in contact with white labor radicals and their aspirations and ideas, and vice versa. Leading revolutionaries Hussain Rahim, Har Dayal, and Taraknath Das cultivated close ties with intellectuals, unionists, and activists associated with the IWW and the Sociality Party in Canada and the United States. Das began publishing his anticolonial newspaper the *Free Hindusthan* with financial assistance from the Socialist Party in Canada (SPC), and when he needed to relocate to avoid government censors in 1908, the *Western Clarion* offered the use of its offices in Seattle. The editors of the socialist paper also furnished Das with space in their newspaper to air his anticolonial views. In the case of Hussain Rahim, his radical ties so worried Dominion officials they tried to deport him on a number of different occasions. Confirming their worst fears, Rahim went on to engage in free speech fights, raise funds, translate organizing literature, and recruit members for the IWW and the SPC in British Columbia. His efforts earned him a seat on the SPC's executive committee, which made him the first nonwhite person to enter the party's leadership structure.[58] In this capacity, Rahim was believed to be the key figure in the spread of subversive ideas among the South Asian immigrant population. "The Hindus have up to the present never identified themselves with any particular political party and the introduction by Rahim of the socialist propaganda into this community is," a Dominion official stated, "I consider a very serious matter, as the majority of these people are uneducated and ignorant and easily led like sheep by a man like Rahim."[59]

Rahim and other revolutionary leaders served as a bridge between white labor radicals and South Asian migrant workers. In 1913, Agnes Laut, reporting for the *Saturday Night,* wrote that she saw "long lists of subscriptions from Hindu workmen to the IWW strike funds" during her investigations into the activities of the IWW in British Columbia.[60] The two groups met and interacted at meetings and demonstrations jointly held by the IWW, the SPC, and South Asian revolutionaries. At these venues, white and Asian radicals tried to rally their respective constituencies around a common purpose, insisting that the struggles against capitalism and imperialism were one and the same. This mixing raised concerns that the disparate radicals in the region were merging into a single movement—a nightmare scenario for Dominion and British colonial authorities. As an official reported alarmingly, "It is stated on good authority that the Hindus are preparing to take an active part in strikes and other anti-war demonstrations fomented by the IWW, Bolshevik and kindred groups in this country."[61]

White labor radicals of the IWW did little to temper these fears of interracial radicalism, touting their alliances with South Asian and other Asian insurgents. "The Chinese are awakening to freedom," an IWW activist declared. "They recently celebrated the first anniversary of the overthrow of the Manchu. Saturday night is the night arranged for them to meet in the IWW hall and take up the matter of uniting their forces with their fellow workers of this city." This newfound revolutionary consciousness was exemplified by Chinese nationalists such as Arthur Wann, who was recognized for his exceptional courage in the IWW free speech fights in Vancouver. As one observer recalled, "He fearlessly took the box in the vast sea of humanity on the Powell Street grounds and defiantly delivered a most revolutionary address in the teeth of the police." The socialist *B.C. Federationist* also echoed these sentiments, asserting, "China will not be long in awakening with revolutionaries like this. Comrade Wann is quite hopeful of being enrolled on the exchange with all Socialists and revolutionary papers in the States and Canada, and already has the encouragement of a few."[62]

As was the case with South Asian revolutionaries, radical Chinese nationalists helped to bridge the racial gap between white and Chinese workers, bringing their compatriots into the union. In testimonials given by veteran IWW members in Vancouver, they recalled that in some years the organization had as many Chinese members as white ones. They remembered in 1919 specifically that "the Chinese and whites went thru one very successful strike in the lumber mills together … at which time they got a very satisfactory increase in wages."[63] The IWW did its part by translating organizing literature into Chinese (as well as Punjabi). Some IWW locals also hired Chinese (as well as other Asian) organizers to recruit directly among their countrymen. Perhaps not on par with its discursive strategy to redeem Asian manhood, the IWW nonetheless made significant efforts to organize and ally with Chinese, Japanese, and South Asian workers in the Pacific Northwest.

## THE LIMITS OF REVOLUTIONARY MANHOOD

Despite these moments of interracial and interradical solidarity, uniting white and Asian radicals behind a single movement proved difficult. To start with, organizers faced the logistical challenges posed by cultural and linguistic divides, though they were certainly not insurmountable. Beyond that, there was the problem of convincing their respective constituencies of their common purpose. There were, to be sure, instances when the programmatic aims and political commitments of white and South Asian radicals came into alignment, such as when IWW activists identified the racial character of colonial exploitation in India, thereby recognizing that Western imperialism could not simply be reduced to a materialist dialectic. Another convergence emerged when South Asian anticolonial intellectuals attributed a capitalist logic to British imperialism, to its insatiable drive for resources and markets that subordinated other classes and groups of people around the world. But these synergies were cultivated neither consistently nor deep enough to bridge the gulf between anticapitalist and anti-imperialist forces in the region, resulting in a short-lived interracial coalition.

These tensions and fissures were aggravated by the contradictions within a gendered discourse of racial inclusion that was deployed to surmount intraclass divisions and unite revolutionary struggles in the Pacific Northwest. In the case of the IWW, however much the organization preached the gospel of racial equality and workers' internationalism, its leaders and members could not entirely transcend the dominant culture of white male supremacy. In a borderland society that was defined, to a very great degree, by an intense and at times fanatical anti-Asian racism, signaled in the oft-repeated calls for a "white man's country," this was no doubt a tall order. But the fact was, for all their eloquent pronouncements for interracial unionism and solidarity, IWW activists found themselves denigrating Asian labor much in the same manner as their white labor counterparts in the AFL.

The *Industrial Worker*, for example, reproduced some of the most common racial tropes of Chinese labor in an article "Chinese Displace American Sailors: Ships Are Manned by Orientals while American Seamen Starve on Shore," which told the story of how Chinese sailors were displacing American sailors on transpacific steamship liners by underselling their labor. "Chinese sailors receive about $20 a month," said the report. "That is sufficient to keep their fit for the day's toll." On the other hand, "American sailors, on the Pacific, have a scale calling for $72.50 a month," in addition to demands for "good, wholesome food." With the white workers, there was also the "danger of them organizing into unions that sometimes made it disagreeable for the bosses." Compared to white workers, "Chinese workers are more docile when dealing with the bosses," the article explained.[64]

The interlocking of race and gender in the IWW's revolutionary discourse undermined and limited the possibilities for interracial unity. For even as white labor radicals could imagine building alliances with virile Asian radicals, the gendered discourse they employed reproduced the historical links between whiteness and manliness. And, as such, the discursive strategy to promote class unity through a redeemed Asian manhood was forestalled by its own racial and gendered logic. Being closely aligned with the ascendant ideas of manhood at the turn of the twentieth century in which manhood and whiteness were coterminous, the radical manhood of the IWW was also, by extension, a racialized manhood. By appealing to a virile manhood in their efforts to overcome race, white labor radicals employed notions of race and gender that rehearsed the ruling logic of white male supremacy. Asian manhood represented at best a paler (or darker) version of white manhood.[65]

Take for example the case of Seattle labor activist K. Sasaki, who in many ways epitomized virile working-class manhood. He worked tirelessly to organize Japanese railway workers, challenged unfair employment practices, and reached out to white labor leaders in the hope of building a cross-racial labor movement in the Pacific Northwest. Yet his manhood continued to be questioned. Indeed, despite Sasaki's long list of accomplishments and working-class credentials, white laborers continued to demand proof of his manhood, insisting that "if the Jap [Sasaki] wants to become a unionist he has only to prove himself a man."[66] Against the standard of a racialized manhood, Asian laborers would always fail to measure up. Invigorating anticapitalist resistance and challenging the color line through gender had the paradoxical effect of reinscribing racial divisions within the labor movement, and ultimately dimmed the possibilities of a lasting political alliance.

Thus, even in cases in which Asian workers were shown to be acting out their manhood, they were invariably racialized as categorically distinct. In 1909, a Chinese crew working on the steamship *Lillie,* traveling between the Gulf of Mexico and the eastern seaboard of the United States, threatened to strike unless their demands for higher wages were met. The *Industrial Worker* reported that the "captain was forced to pay the increase asked," thereby making the Chinese sailors the "highest paid crew," more than all the other white crews on the gulf. Nevertheless, as the title suggests, "Whites Cheaper than Chinks," by expecting higher standards from white sailors, white labor radicals used the Chinese as a benchmark of degradation and unmanliness.[67] Indeed, the IWW continued to reify the Chinese as "coolies" in their writings and speeches. Referring to white contract laborers in Alaska, IWW activists were incredulous to learn that they accepted "the same identical contracts that were printed to enslaved Chinese coolies." They noted that while the "Wa Chong Co. of Seattle prefer to have yellow cannery workers," the terms were so appalling that even "the Orientals refuse to labor for them." To further shame and discipline this particular group of white workers, they made invidious racial comparisons, seeking to capture the full extent of their degradation. As the *Industrial Worker* reported, "White workers in cannery live on Chinese food and contract to obey orders of the Chinese boss."[68]

The racial and gendered persistence of revolutionary manhood undermined the IWW's internationalist vision for emancipation. Indeed, despite the organization's inclusive proclamations, the boundaries of race and gender continued to hamper white labor radicals from accepting Asians as social equals. This helps explain why at one of their regular meetings at the IWW meeting hall in Vancouver, "not a man in the hall and there must have been at least 150 men present" could recall ever having "gotten acquainted with an Oriental while on the job."[69] It was reminiscent of the dilemma that the socialist editor of the *B.C. Federationist,* Richard P.

Pettipiece, found himself in when investigative reporter Agnes Laut probed about his commitment to racial egalitarianism in 1913. She asked Pettipiece, "Have you no objection to these Asiatic people coming in and cutting your wages?" His response was a forceful and unambiguous case for interracial unionism. "Not a bit," he answered. "That day of narrow outlook has gone past in the labor world. We aim to unite the laborers of all nations in one solid army against capital." He stated emphatically, "Let them come in, we say! They will make so many more votes to overthrow capital! It isn't labor that opposes the Oriental. No—you bet! Let 'em come in! We'll take care of them! We'll take 'em right in our ranks!"

Pettipiece's response to the reporter's second question, however, betrayed his earlier antiracist sentiments. "Would you like your little daughter to sit in the same class at school as a Hindu or Jap?" the reporter queried. "No, I would not," he answered soberly. To make certain that his calls for interracial unionism would not be mistaken as an appeal for social equality, he clarified, "As a father, I don't want the Hindu in here any more than you do as a woman. Let the Asiatics have separate schools. As a citizen, I do not want the Asiatic." Attempting to reconcile this statement with his earlier antiracist pronouncements, he elaborated, "You can't assimilate him to our civilization; but this labor movement is no longer provincial. It is a world movement; and labor has found that we might better have the cheap Asiatics come in here and organized into our fighting ranks, than have the cheap products of Asiatic labor come in here and undersell our labor products." His ambivalence toward Asian migrants was perhaps best reflected in his final response to the question when he said, "Hindus are not dangerous as laborers, only as neighbors."[70] Pettipiece's attempts to distinguish between political/economic and social equality, by constructing the Asian as at once a good unionist and a dangerous neighbor, rested on the liberal distinction between public and private. But we know that these were rarely, if ever, hermetically sealed realms. Indeed, as recent scholarship has revealed, efforts to ban and demonize interracial intimacies were tantamount to strategies of political exclusion, of divesting nonwhite peoples of their civil rights and civil liberties.[71]

CONCLUSION

In the first two decades of the twentieth century, labor militants of the IWW and South Asian revolutionary nationalists organized against capitalist relations and Western imperialism in the North American West and beyond. Both campaigns—one a class struggle, and the other an anticolonial struggle—made assertions of a virile Asian manhood as part of an effort to overcome anti-Asian racism and the colonial politics of masculinity, which stood as barriers to class solidarity and national autonomy. These gendered strategies of class inclusion and revolutionary mobilization helped white and South Asian radicals to imagine themselves as part of a broader gendered insurgency in which virile subaltern men united against capitalist and imperialist oppression in the North American West and on the Indian subcontinent. But if representations of radical and revolutionary manhood were critical to mobilizing a militant subaltern politics, they also performed complex and contradictory work that reproduced dominant systems of meaning underpinning capitalist relations and imperial rule. Indeed, because these struggles took place under the terms of the ruling elite, strategies of recuperating Asian manhood inescapably reinforced normative race, class, and gender relations. This was a case, then, in which white and South Asian radicals contested the dominant meanings of race, class, and manhood without exceeding or transforming their fundamental logic, resulting in a transnational subaltern politics that disrupted but ultimately reinforced the hegemonic discourse of race and gender.

1    Earlier versions of this chapter were presented at the Race, Resistance, and Repression conference at the University of Washington and the Graduate Asian American Studies Program at the University of Pennsylvania. I am grateful to the audiences for their feedback. I want to thank Mrinalini Sinha, Beryl Satter, and Ruth Feldstein for helping me think through the gender piece. Finally, a special thanks to Moon-Ho Jung for reading and commenting on multiple drafts of the chapter. *Vancouver World*, January 12, 1908.

2    Letter from R. O. Montgomery to Richard McBride, July 27, 1915, National Archives of Canada (NAC), RG 6, Series E, Volume 524, File 251.

3    Letter from Charles H. Riley to Inspector in Charge, Portland, Oregon, January 14, 1914, National Archives and Records Administration, Washington, DC (hereafter NARA), RG 85, Entry 9, File 53572, Folder 92.

4    Melvin Dubofsky, *We Shall Be All: A History of the Industrial Workers of the World*, 2nd ed. (Urbana: University of Illinois Press, 1988); Robert L. Tyler, *Rebels of the Woods: The IWW in the Pacific Northwest* (Eugene: University of Oregon Press, 1967); Mark Leier, *Where the Fraser River Flows: A History of the Industrial Workers of the World in British Columbia* (Vancouver: New Star Books, 1990).

5    On state repression of South Asian radicalism in the North American West, see

Joan M. Jensen, *Passage from India: Asian Indian Immigrants in North America* (New Haven, CT: Yale University Press, 1988); Seema Sohi, "Race, Surveillance, and Indian Anticolonialism in the Transnational Western U.S.-Canadian Borderlands," *Journal of American History* 98, no. 2 (2011): 420–36; Kornel S. Chang, *Pacific Connections: The Making of the U.S.-Canadian Borderlands* (Berkeley: University of California Press, 2012), 165–73.

6    On the different cultures of working-class manhood in the North American West, see Susan Johnson, *Roaring Camp: The Social World of the California Gold Rush* (New York: W. W. Norton, 2000); Gunther Peck, *Reinventing Free Labor: Padrones and Immigrant Workers in the North American West, 1880–1930* (Cambridge: Cambridge University Press, 2000), 117–57; and essays in *Across the Great Divide: Cultures of Manhood in the American West*, ed. Matthew Basso, Laura McCall, and Dee Garceau (New York: Routledge, 2001). On the "virile syndicalism" of the IWW, see Francis Shor, "Masculine Power and Virile Syndicalism: A Gendered Analysis of the IWW in Australia," *Labour History* 63 (Nov. 1992): 83–99.

7    Mrinalini Sinha, *Colonial Masculinity: The "Manly Englishman" and the "Effeminate Bengali" in the Late Nineteenth Century* (Manchester: Manchester University Press, 1995). Sinha's insights build on the seminal work of Edward Said, *Orientalism* (New York: Vintage, 1979).

8    On the construction and contest over the meaning of manhood in colonial India, see Mrinalini Sinha, "Giving Masculinity a History: Some Contributions from the Historiography of Colonial India," *Gender and History* 11, no. 3 (Nov. 1999): 445–60.

9    On masculinity and how it became a cultural vehicle for gendered white supremacy at the turn of the twentieth century, see Gail Bederman, *Manliness and Civilization: A Cultural History of Gender and Race in the United States, 1880–1917* (Chicago: University of Chicago Press, 1995); Kristin Hoganson, *Fighting for American Manhood: How Gender Politics Provoked the Spanish-American and Philippine American Wars* (New Haven, CT: Yale University Press, 1998). On the racialized working-class manhood of the IWW, see Neil Foley, *White Scourge: Mexicans, Blacks, and Poor Whites in Texas Cotton Culture* (Berkeley: University of California Press, 1999), 92–117; David Roediger, "Gaining a Hearing for Black-White Unity: Covington Hall and the Complexities of Race, Gender, and Class," in *Towards the Abolition of Whiteness* (New York: Verso, 1994); Todd DePastino, *Citizen Hobo: How a Century of Homelessness Shaped America* (Chicago: University of Chicago Press, 2003), 95–126.

10   On the development of nationalist institutions and organizations in British India and the Crown's responses to them, see Ramesh Majumdar, *History of the Freedom Movement in India*, 3 vols. (Calcutta: Firma K. L. Mukhopadhyay, 1963); Richard Popplewell, *Intelligence and Imperial Defence: British Intelligence and the Defence of the Indian Empire, 1904–1924* (London: F. Cass, 1995); James Kerr, *Political Trouble in India, 1907–1917* (Delhi: Oriental Publishers, 1973).

11   On the competing nationalist discourses in India, see Partha Chatterjee, *Nation and Its Fragments: Colonial and Postcolonial Histories* (Princeton: Princeton University Press, 1993); Prasenjit Duara, *Rescuing History from the Nation: Questioning Narratives of Modern China* (Chicago: University of Chicago Press, 1995), 205–27; Dipesh

Chakrabarty, *Provincializing Europe: Postcolonial Thought and Historical Difference* (Princeton: Princeton University Press, 2000).

12   "Translated Copies of the Ghadar," City of Vancouver Archives (hereafter CVA), MSS. 69, 509-D-7, File 1.

13   On revolutionaries in the diaspora, see Harish K. Puri, *Ghadar Movement: Ideology, Organization and Strategy* (Amritsar: Garu Nanak Dev University Press, 1983); Arun C. Bose *Indian Revolutionaries Abroad, 1905–1922* (New Delhi: Northern Book Centre, 2002); Maia Ramnath, *Haj to Utopia: How the Ghadar Movement Charted Global Radicalism and Attempted to Overthrow the British Empire* (Berkeley: University of California Press, 2011).

14   "Note on the Anti-British Movement among Natives of India in America," as part of letter from Secretary to the Government of India to His Majesty's Under Secretary of State for India, February 27, 1913, London, UK, India Office and Library Records (hereafter IOLR), Judicial and Public Department Proceedings (hereafter JPDP), File 12/1.

15   Letter from Secretary of State to Viceroy, Home Department, April 1913, IOLR, JPDP, File 126/1913.

16   Tapan K. Mukherjee, *Taraknath Das: Life and Letters of a Revolutionary Exile* (Bengal: Jadavpur University, 1998), 7–8. On the rise of pan-Asianist thought among South Asian nationalists, see Cemil Aydin, *The Politics of Anti-Western in Asia: Visions of World Order in Pan-Islamic and Pan-Asian Thought* (New York: Columbia University Press, 2007), 93–126.

17   For histories of Har Dayal's political activities in the American West, see Puri, *Ghadar Movement*; and also Emily C. Brown, *Har Dayal: Hindu Revolutionary and Rationalist* (Tucson: University of Arizona Press, 1975).

18   US Immigration Bureau Memorandum, April 4, 1914, NARA, RG 85, Entry 9, File 53572, Folder 92.

19   Copies of the declarations [of Sikhs re tyranny], December 13, 1914, CVA, Mss. 69, 509-D-7, File 1.

20   Translated Letter of Ganga Ram, October 20, 1916, NAC, RG 13, Volume 1157, File 9133, Box 50.

21   Ramnath, *Haj to Utopia*, 62.

22   See "Circular No. 12 of 1912, Indian Agitation in America (Continuation of Circular No. 5 of 1908)," IOLR, JPDP, File 126/1913.

23   Letter to the Under Secretary of State of India, April 25, 1913, IOLR, JPDP, File 126/1913.

24   Letter from Ellis D. Bruler to the Commissioner-General of Immigration, January 11, 1911, NARA, RG 85, Entry 9, File 51388, Folder 5.

25   Memorandum, for the Secretary of State, April 7, 1913, NARA, RG 85, Entry 9, File 51388, Folder 5.

26   This was the specific lesson Taraknath Das drew from his earlier expulsion from Japan, where he had first settled after being exiled from India. He was part of a small but growing community of South Asian expatriates following the Russo-Japanese War. However, having recently renewed the Anglo-Japanese alliance, the Meiji gov-

ernment came under pressure to avoid providing a safe haven for people considered enemies of the Crown. As a result, Das and other South Asian revolutionaries were forced to continue the independence struggle elsewhere. See Mukherjee, *Taraknath Das*, 7–8.

27  "Notes on the Personal Views of J. A. W.," May 22, 1912, IOLR, JPDP, File 126/1913.

28  See "Circular No. 12 of 1912, Indian Agitation in America (Continuation of Circular No. 5 of 1908)," IOLR, JPDP, File 126/1913, 7.

29  In describing their political attitudes, historian Harish Puri has argued that "these people had little political consciousness and nationalist interest when they arrived in North America. They had come from closed village communities and their aspirations related mainly to earning money" (Puri, *Ghadar Movement*, 18).

30  "Report of Proceedings at Meeting of Hindus Held in O'Brien Hall, Vancouver, B.C.," September 29, 1913, NARA, RG 85, Entry 9, File 51388, Folder 5.

31  When Rahim first tried to enter British Columbia, Dominion officials held him for deportation because they had found in his possession letters from Taraknath Das and instructions on how to make explosives. He was, however, able to successfully appeal the deportation ruling, which allowed him to remain in British Columbia, where he was instrumental in building a revolutionary network. Circular No. 12 of 1912. "Indian Agitation in America," as part of a letter from the Government of India to His Majesty's Under Secretary of State for India, February 27, 1913, IOLR, JPDP, File 12/1.

32  In a collaboration between the colonizers and the colonized, in which both groups benefited (though highly unevenly) from its projection, the Punjabi Sikh was held up as the masculine ideal of the warrior-hero that imputed South Asian Sikh identity with martial valor, physical confidence, and a self-sacrificing manhood. See Tony Ballantyne, *Between Colonialism and Diaspora: Sikh Cultural Formations in an Imperial World* (Durham, NC: Duke University Press, 2006).

33  Sinha, *Colonial Masculinity*, 21.

34  On the efforts of Bengali middle-class reformers and intellectuals to recuperate Bengali masculinity, see John Rosseli, "The Self-Image of Effeteness: Physical Education and Nationalism in Nineteenth-Century Bengal," *Past and Present* 86 (Feb. 1988): 121–48.

35  "Copies of the Free Hindusthan," July 21, 1908, NAC, RG 2, Vol. 955, PC#1619.

36  *Western Clarion*, February 29, 1908.

37  Sinha, *Colonial Masculinity*; Frances Gouda, "Good Mothers, Medeas, or Jezebels: Feminine Imagery in Colonial and Anticolonial Rhetoric in the Dutch East Indies, 1900–1942," in *Domesticating the Empire: Race, Gender, and Family Life in French and Dutch Colonialism*, ed. Frances Gouda and Julia Clancy-Smith (Charlottesville: University Press of Virginia, 1998); Wilson Chacko Jacob, *Working Out Egypt: Effendi Masculinity and the Subject Formation in Colonial Modernity, 1870–1940* (Durham, NC: Duke University Press, 2010).

38  *Industrial Worker*, November 31, 1912.

39  *Industrial Worker*, February 3, 1917.

40  Paul Phillips, *No Power Greater: A Century of Labour in British Columbia* (Vancouver:

Boag Foundation, 1967), 46; and Andrew R. McCormack, *Reformers, Rebels, and Revo-lutionaries: The Western Canadian Radical Movement, 1899–1919* (Toronto: University of Toronto Press, 1977), 99. The transnational aspirations of the IWW were recognized in the opening moments of its founding convention when Canadian delegate John Riordan convincingly argued that the union be named the "Industrial Workers of the World" instead of the narrow, nation-based proposal of "Industrial Workers of America."

41 *Union Record*, May 4, 1900. The IWW, on the other hand, attributed workers' transience to the acute conditions of industrial capitalism, rejecting the notion that it was evidence of moral or personal failing, as some social reformers and labor leaders claimed.

42 *Western Clarion*, March 14, 1913. It should be noted that the Socialist Party's position regarding Asian immigrants was far from monolithic and was riddled with tensions and contradictions. There were a number of members who called for the end of racist union policies and who saw it, in the words of one Socialist organizer, "just as necessary to organize the colored races as the white." See *B. C. Federationist*, October 31, 1907.

43 On the figure of the "coolie" and how it facilitated America's transition from slave to "free" labor, see Moon-Ho Jung, *Coolies and Cane: Race, Labor, and Sugar in the Age of Emancipation* (Baltimore, MD: John Hopkins University Press, 2006). On how the prostitute emerged as the preeminent symbol of bonded labor in an age of emancipation, see Amy Stanley, *From Bondage to Contract: Wage Labor, Marriage, and the Market in the Age of Emancipation* (Cambridge: Cambridge University Press 1998), 218–63.

44 As a white labor activist noted, "Domestic service, house cleaning, sweeping, and a multitude of such duties that generally fall to the lot of widows, old women and girls are monopolized by Japs." Their unmanliness, moreover, was forcing white women into a life of immorality. See *Union Record*, March 9, 1907.

45 *Industrial Worker*, June 29, 1909.

46 *Industrial Worker*, August 26, 1909.

47 *Industrial Worker*, June 29, 1909.

48 *Industrial Worker*, April 22, 1909.

49 *Industrial Worker*, April 15, 1909.

50 *Industrial Worker*, May 20, 1909.

51 Chinese and South Asian laborers also engaged in acts of working-class resistance but the activities of Japanese workers, being the mainstay of the migrant workforce at the time in the North American West and Hawai'i, were greater in number (and visibility) and therefore garnered most of the attention of IWW leaders and activists. On Chinese labor resistance in the Americas, see Jung, *Coolies and Cane*, 184–214.

52 On Japanese labor militancy in Hawai'i, see Gary Okihiro, *Cane Fires: The Anti-Japanese Movement in Hawaii, 1865–1945* (Philadelphia: Temple University Press), 43–45; and Moon-Kie Jung, *Reworking Race: The Making of Hawaii's Interracial Labor Movement* (New York: Columbia University Press, 2006).

53 *Industrial Worker*, May 20, 1909.

54  *Industrial Worker*, August 26, 1909.

55  *Industrial Worker*, July 15, 1909.

56  Agnes Laut, *Am I My Brother's Keeper? A Study of British Columbia's Labor and Oriental Problems* (Toronto: Saturday Night, 1913), 36.

57  Ibid., 24.

58  See Peter Campbell, "East Meets Left: South Asian Militants and the Socialist Party of Canada in British Columbia, 1904–1914," *International Journal of Canadian Studies* 20 (Fall 1999): 35–66.

59  Letter from W. C. Hopkinson to W. W. Cory, April 1, 1912, NAC, RG 7, G-21, Vol. 202, File 332, Part 6.

60  Ibid.

61  Letter from Chief, Military Intelligence Branch to Labor Department, Attention Mr. Parker, NARA, RG 85, Entry 9, File 53854, Folder 133-A/B.

62  *B. C. Federationist*, December 12, 1912.

63  "Testimonial Meeting on the Oriental," March 4, 1924, Hoover Institution Archives, Stanford University, Race Relations Survey, Box 24, Folder 16.

64  *Industrial Worker*, January 14, 1922.

65  DePastino, *Citizen Hobo*, 120. To see how the personhood of Theodore Roosevelt both reflected and produced racial manhood at the turn of the twentieth century, see Bederman, *Manliness and Civilization*, 170–216.

66  *Seattle Union Record*, September 21, 1907.

67  *Industrial Worker*, April 1, 1909.

68  *Industrial Worker*, October 7, 1922.

69  "Testimonial Meeting on the Oriental," March 4, 1924, Hoover Institution Archives, Stanford University, Race Relations Survey, Box 24, Folder 16.

70  Laut, *Am I My Brother's Keeper?*, 24.

71  Hannah Rosen, *Terror in the Heart of Freedom: Citizenship, Sexual Violence, and the Meaning of Race in the Postemancipation South* (Chapel Hill: University of North Carolina Press, 2009); Nayan Shah, *Stranger Intimacy: Contesting Race, Sexuality, and the Law in the North American West* (Berkeley: University of California Press, 2011).

# 3

# Dangerous Amusements

## Hawaii's Theaters, Labor Strikes, and Counterpublic Culture, 1909–1934

DENISE KHOR

THE MOMENTUM FOR THE FIRST MAJOR ORGANIZED LABOR STRIKE IN Hawaiian history began in a theater. On November 1, 1908, local merchants and newspaper editors convened a small meeting, with not more than fourteen persons, at the Asahi Theatre in Honolulu. Built in 1899, the Asahi-za, or Asahi Theatre, was the first Japanese theater in Honolulu. Originally established with two thousand dollars collected from ten stockholders, it held a capacity of three hundred people and employed approximately forty contract actors. The Chinatown fire destroyed the structure in 1900, but the proprietors rebuilt the theater as a two-story building with a large wooden stage and balcony in 1908. In addition to local productions, the Asahi Theatre featured a vast repertoire of amusements from Japan. Professional theatrical troupes traveled from Tokyo to Honolulu to perform *shibai* (Japanese theatrical performance) as early as 1893. Moving pictures produced in Japan's developing film industry reached the islands in the early part of the twentieth century. The Asahi Theatre was a destination, a port of arrival, for these transpacific circulations. It was an institution created by the earliest generation of migrants from Japan that nurtured a public sphere emerging for the Japanese in Hawai'i.[1]

The November meeting in the Asahi Theatre was momentous as the first organized effort to unionize Japanese workers on Hawaii's sugar cane fields. Among the attendees at this initial meeting was Motoyuki Negoro, a recent graduate of the law school at the University of California, Berkeley. He drafted the primary treatise of the labor movement, titled "How About the Higher Wages," and published it in the Japanese language newspaper *Nippu Jiji* in 1908. Negoro emphasized the disproportionately low wages of the workers in relation to the high profits of the sugar industrialists and urged the Japanese state to act on behalf of its subjects, who were, as he wrote, "not born to be the slaves of capitalists in Hawaii." The Higher Wages Association, Zokyu Kisei Kai, was formed the following December, with Negoro elected as treasurer and Fred Kinsaburo Makino as chairman. The next meeting at the Asahi Theatre took place on December 12 and drew a crowd of an estimated 1,700 workers, organizers, and supporters. In the subsequent months, leaders of the Higher Wages Association would return time and again to the Asahi Theatre to hold mass rallies and deliver fiery speeches.

In addition to a physical space for the oration of political speeches, theaters in Hawai'i also staged theatrical performances that circulated the messages of the Higher Wages Association leadership. *A Play to Be Given in Formosa Fifty Years Hence* was featured at the Honolulu Theatre on January 15, 1909. The production was written by Negoro and described by the antilabor *Hawaii Shinpo* as a "so-called higher wage drama purposed to incite the less-informed class of our community."[2] According to Nora Conaty, this *shimpa*, a political drama that adapted the realism of kabuki to social themes, began with a scene depicting the wage disparity between Japanese and Portuguese workers of the cane fields. It narrated the gathering of workers, their realizations of injustice, and the potential of collective action. Scenes of the drama also condemned Sometaro Sheba, who had collaborated in real life with the Hawaiian Sugar Planters' Association (HSPA) to oppose the Higher Wages Association. In the end, Sheba meets a gruesome death and, amid waving banners and singing, the laborers win their higher wages.[3] The play contributed to a public dialogue that urgently connected the delivery of galvanizing speeches at mass rallies, the circulation of pamphlets and literature to the plantation towns, and the publication of political writings by the eleven Japanese language newspapers of Hawai'i.[4]

Honolulu authorities quickly recognized the dangers posed by the production of these materials dramatizing the labor movement. Negoro's play, along with writings from the Japanese-language *Nippu Jiji*, was identified as an article of criminal conspiracy and used as evidence in a trial in 1909 that resulted in a ten-month prison sentence for Negoro and key members of the Higher Wages Association.[5]

When the first 1,500 strikers voted to leave the fields of Aiea plantation on May 9, 1909, tensions quickly escalated and the theaters of Honolulu assumed a new role in the labor movement. The HSPA responded swiftly to the start of the four-month-long strike by evicting laborers from their houses and hiring strikebreakers at double the wage rate. Workers of Waipahu, Waialua, Kahuku, Waianae, and Ewa soon followed, and an estimated seven thousand laborers joined by the end of the month. Many of the evicted workers left the plantation towns and converged in the port cities of Oahu. Workers on the other islands, along with the Aiea Merchants Association and the Honolulu Retail Merchants Association, donated money to a strike fund totaling forty-two thousand dollars. To further support the strikers, Chinese merchants in Honolulu extended credit with generous lending terms. The trade unionists in Honolulu for the first time expressed solidarity with Japanese strikers even though they had long opposed Japanese workers leaving the plantations for the building trades. The theaters, including the Asahi Theatre, continued to perform an integral role during the strike. The buildings were converted into strike camps and makeshift shelters for the evicted laborers. Workers braced for the strike's culmination in the same theater where the movement had first started.[6]

A film culture in Hawai'i—drawn together by the Japanese-operated theaters, the exhibition of popular films, and the audiences who left the cane fields to occupy seats in the theaters—facilitated the formation of a counterpublic that mediated the most volatile years of labor unrest in prewar Hawai'i. The theaters of Hawai'i played a prominent role in the radical labor organizing of the island's workers. The significance of these theaters was palpable, especially in the plantation towns, where the majority of Hawaii's agricultural workers resided. While the term "counterpublic" names the ways that theaters in Hawai'i emerged as contested sites of class struggle, it also signals my approach to the study of film spectatorship and the working-class culture and labor history of Hawai'i.

Debates in film studies have generated significant analyses of the cinema's "public" dimensions and connections to cultural, social, and political history.[7] In her study of silent film spectatorship, film scholar Miriam Hansen draws on Oskar Negt's and Alexander Kluge's work on the public sphere to consider the multiple publics of silent cinema. She problematizes the notion of a singular public organized "from above" to explore the possibilities, and indeed the actualities, of an alternative or plurality of cinematic publics. Hansen suggests that the terms of this public formation of cinema can be apprehended not only in the apparatus of

Figure 3.1. Photograph of a labor rally held in rural Hawai'i during the 1909 strike. From Motoyuki Negoro, *Meiji yonjūichi, ni-nen Hawai Hōjin katsuyakushi* (Honolulu: N.p., 1915). From the University of Hawai'i Library.

Figure 3.2. Asahi Theatre, Honolulu, ca. 1915.
Photographer unknown. Courtesy of the Bishop Museum.

the cinema but also in the "social horizon of experience" and in relation to the "experiencing subjects themselves, on the basis of their context of living." Such an approach defines film spectatorship in social rather than textual terms, and also allows for counterpublic formations since "it entails the very moment in which reception can gain a momentum of its own, and give rise to formations not necessarily anticipated in the context of production."[8] Building on these insights, this chapter considers the overlapping and competing cinematic publics in Hawai'i.

Labor historians have long contended that the end of the contract labor system in Hawai'i at the start of the twentieth century introduced greater mobility and resources to workers of the cane fields, as many were no longer bound to contracts or debt. As a result, workers increasingly demonstrated their discontent with working conditions by absconding and organizing. As historian Edward Beechert notes, there were also greater numbers of labor "disturbances" of an "improvised quality" and that "served as training grounds for the more comprehensive demands of later and larger actions."[9] These transformations also took place as new transit lines and new forms of mass commercial culture gradually eroded the isolation of the plantations. The circulation of cheap amusements and the development of theaters in Hawai'i contributed to these new and significant changes. By widening the traditional scope of labor history in Hawai'i, this chapter also looks beyond the well-documented union leadership and the flashpoints of organized strikes to consider the participatory politics and public spaces of mass-oriented consumption.

Drawing on oral histories, immigrant newspapers, and the records of the Hawaiian Sugar Planters' Association, I suggest that theaters and film exhibition formed a significant aspect of workers' struggles in Hawai'i. Japanese proprietors built some of the earliest theaters in Honolulu, brought roving film projectors to the rural plantation towns, and promoted countless film shows for the island's workers. They drew on resources from the transpacific migration routes of their communities and established a formidable presence in the culture and commerce of early twentieth-century Hawai'i. In 1908, these quotidian developments collided with the interests of the sugar planter oligarchy in Hawai'i as plantation workers and labor activists began to use these theaters to rally and foster their organizing.

With an estimated two million dollar loss in the first major organized labor strike, the public gatherings in Hawaii's theaters, and the cinematic desires of workers, did not go unnoticed by the capitalists of the island's largest agricultural industry. Sugar planters expanded social welfare reform efforts to regulate workers' leisure, building film censor bureaus and regulating film exhibition across the plantation towns. These efforts competed against the popular shows that attracted the largest crowds. Moreover, the particular appeal of silent western films, their ideas and images of individualism and American manhood, turned many of the theaters into heterogeneous male publics. Audiences—whether resident or migrant, Japanese or Filipino, cane hauler or mill worker—could gather in the same plantation theaters and view the same popular films. The sugar planter oligarchy, in turn, came to perceive the collective facet of the cinematic experience as a threat to its interests. Workers imagined and planned their struggles long before arriving in the union hall. Significantly, these developments, as the sugar planters would learn, took root in the theaters and show houses of Hawai'i.

JAPANESE THEATERS IN HAWAI'I AND
THE TRANSNATIONAL ROUTES OF JAPANESE FILMS

During the decades of struggle between Hawaii's workers and the planter oligarchy, Japanese immigrants were at the forefront in building the stages that connected the worlds of labor and leisure. Japanese entrepreneurs joined the ranks of multiethnic early film exhibitors, operated venues to distribute and view projected film, and facilitated the earliest transnational networks to bring a polyglot of films to audiences across the Pacific and the continental United States. In Honolulu, Japanese proprietors established the earliest theaters in the burgeoning port city. The *Husted's Directory of Honolulu* in 1902 listed only four theaters in Honolulu at the time. Alongside the popular vaudeville Orpheum Theatre and the elite Hawaiian Opera House, described as an "artistic ornament of Honolulu" for the "circuit of all first-class companies going to the colonies," the directory listed "Chinese Theatre" and "Japanese Theatre," neither of which was noted in any greater detail.[10]

Japanese in the film trades of Hawai'i were particularly well positioned given a strong transpacific theatrical tradition. The local press noted a professional touring company from Japan, listed as "Japanese Theatre Company," arriving in Honolulu in 1893. With a large segment of the Japanese population working and residing outside of the port city, these

performance companies and theater troupes also traveled to the plantation towns, making use of informal, makeshift, and outdoor theaters. As
one observer in 1901 eloquently put it, the *shibai* was shown in the "front
yard [that had] turned into an auditorium surrounded by gay curtains,
and with no roof except the spreading branches of a giant algaroba tree."
When moving pictures from Japan first arrived in Hawai'i, the film shows
followed these theatrical antecedents and were staged as transitory and
ephemeral exhibitions. Mae Itamura collected tickets and traveled with
Japanese film exhibitors to the plantation camps in Maui. "If that camp
had a small theater, we played in the theater," she recalled. "Those days
we had lots of small places, you know. Keahau, Pulehu, Kailua 1, Kailua 2,
Camp 10, Camp 4, Camp 2." In camps without theaters, however, Itamura
remembered that a viewing space was built outdoors. They set up a manual
projector and screen, and used borrowed benches to demarcate the walls
of the makeshift theater space. Passing through these rural areas around
twice a month, the exhibitors drew large crowds. Itamura estimated that
over a hundred people were at these shows and included non-Japanese
audiences. "Everybody came," she recounted, "Filipinos and all."[11]

By the 1920s and 1930s, a significant number of Japanese proprietors
operated the film trades in Hawai'i. Japanese immigrants and their
descendants constituted 42.7 percent of Hawaii's entire population in
1920, and 37.9 percent in 1930. The Japanese business directories from the
1930s abounded with listings for theater operators, film exchanges and
distributors, and independent show promoters. A review of these sources
reveals that there were as many Japanese film proprietors working on the
island of Hawai'i as in the bustling port cities of Oahu. In Hilo, Japanese
language newspapers promoted the exhibition of "different moving magic
lantern shows" as early as 1909. The island of Hawai'i, also known as the
Big Island, had the largest concentration of the fifty-two sugar plantations
organized under the Hawaiian Sugar Planters' Association.[12]

While initially confined to labor in the cane fields, Japanese workers
increasingly left the plantations. Because of the dominance of the HSPA
in the agriculture of Hawai'i, independent farming was not a viable option
for economic mobility, as it had been for successful Issei in California. For
the Japanese in Hawai'i, the film trade was a reputable and viable pathway
to entrepreneurship and financial independence. It was a business that
Hatsuzo Tanimoto, who operated a dozen rural theaters in Hawai'i in the
1930s, passed on to his sons. Given his ineligibility for naturalized citizen-

ship, Tanimoto regarded the theaters as a route to setting down roots in Hawaiʻi. Before an audience at a theater opening in 1931, the Issei proprietor, who had lived in Hawaiʻi for forty years, declared that he had spent all his money in the territory, built a mansion in which he expected to live and die, and, perhaps most significantly, had "said goodbye to Japan."[13] These dynamics of film entrepreneurship for Tanimoto were particularly salient, as many Japanese by the first decade of the twentieth century had come to see a future in the islands, despite the migrant labor system established by Hawaiian capitalists. Moreover, many Japanese began to see Hawaiʻi as a more permanent home after passage to California became less tenable with the enactment of the 1908 immigration exclusion law.[14]

The plantation economy opened a substantial niche for the Japanese in the film trades as the HSPA grew increasingly interested in the new developments in leisure for their workers. Following the 1920 labor strike, a massive strike involving Japanese and Filipino workers, planters turned to the models of welfare capitalism that industrial employers across the mainland were developing as a way to promote loyalty to the company and preempt unionism. Each plantation in Hawaiʻi was instructed to develop the social welfare of workers, which was to include movies, since, according to HSPA representative Donald Bowman, "amusement is craved by all nationalities ... and motion picture theatres have proven most successful and should be installed by all the large settlements." Plantation managers worked with independent proprietors to supply their company towns with the mandated amusements for "social improvement," which was additionally advantageous given that plantation managers were subject to taxation unless they "had someone else operate or conduct the shows ... and pay the special tax as 'proprietors of theaters.'" Throughout the 1920s and 1930s, sugar planters turned to numerous proprietors of Japanese descent to furnish these services for popular amusement.[15]

Despite the financial advantages of such arrangements, the HSPA found theaters difficult to control and regulate. In the planter's records, reports abounded of men bringing amusements and motion pictures to laborers without permission from city officials or plantation managers. The County of Hawaiʻi had established licensing requirements in 1909 for all persons who operated "stereopticons, moving picture machines and other devices by which pictures or images are thrown upon wall or screen or are produced by light through transparent plate ... for which an admission fee is charged." However, sugar planters found these regulations in constant violation. For instance, a man described as "a Japanese called Takaoka from Pahoa" was reported to the county for lacking a proper license while showing a film in Laupahoehoe. Similar citations were given to K. Kawachi and Kim M. Shik, who was described as "a Korean who showed pictures in our house in Papaaloa and who had not procured a license." In another instance, a building inspector informed a manager on the island of Hawai'i that "moving picture shows were shown in your camps by men who have no license," prompting the plantation manager to vow to "stop these outside men."[16]

Planters also had particular trouble with several prominent figures in the Japanese community of Hawai'i. Born in Kailua-Kona in 1895, Sanji Abe was a Japanese pioneer in many respects—his civic involvement included work for the Hilo police department (first as an interpreter then as a deputy sheriff) and then service in the US Army during World War I. As president of the Society of American Citizens of Japanese Ancestry (known as the Nisei Club), he became in 1941 the first American of Japanese descent to enter the Hawai'i Territorial Senate as a Republican senator from Hilo. Before Abe's entry into the political theater of Hawai'i, he had worked extensively in Hawaii's internationalist world of the movies. In addition to establishing the Yamato Theatre, he became president of the International Theatrical Company in 1939 and owner of Honolulu's Kokusai Theatre in 1941. As a distributor of films from Japan, his travels to Tokyo were reported with great enthusiasm by the local press. The *Honolulu Advertiser* published headlines such as "Sanji Abe Is Touring Japan" and reported on Abe's travels on the luxury liner *Asama Maru* and his prominence in business circles in Japan.[17]

Abe was the owner of Yamato Theatre, or Yamato-za, established in Hilo in 1922 as the first theater exclusively devoted to the exhibition of Japanese films on the island of Hawai'i. Twice a month, Abe leased trucks to transport workers of the cane fields to his Japanese film exhibitions. These films were exhibited in Hawai'i exactly as they were exhibited in Japan, with a *benshi* who provided introductory remarks, narration, and explanation. Many film scholars regard the *benshi* to be a feature that distinguished Japanese cinema from other national cinemas.[18] Kamesuke Nakahama, born in Yamaguchi prefecture in 1895, worked as a *benshi* in Hawai'i starting in 1923. He described his performances as voicing the titles as they appeared on the screen, furthering the plot with previously written comments, and, perhaps most importantly, improvising in relation to the mood of the audience. This indeterminate aspect of Japanese film exhibition made spectatorship dynamic and unpredictable. With the gathering of Japanese and non-Japanese audiences in Hawai'i, the *benshi* could have narrated, adapted, or even completely transformed the original film to the varying contexts of Hawai'i and to audiences who required their own sets of translations. The *benshi*'s original function in Japan, in fact, was to explain to Japanese audiences the unfamiliar contexts and references in the foreign films exhibited at the turn of the century. Nevertheless, the *benshi* Nakahama asserted that "the movie taught certain Japanese moral values ... [and] through this process, the audience would reaffirm being Japanese."[19]

Hawaii's sugar planters recognized the unsettling politics emerging in the theaters that their proprietors facilitated. Films that promoted "being Japanese," as the *benshi* Nakahama suggested, could also potentially nurture the transnational ties that were crucial to a sense of ethnic solidarity galvanizing many Japanese workers. The mainstream press labeled the 1909 strike as "blood unionism," even attributing these connections to race and nationality to inflame anti-Japanese public sentiments. The performance of Japanese language and culture was highly contested in the Americanization campaigns of the 1920s. The planter oligarchy had initially supported Japanese-language schools and Buddhist temples, believing that these institutions bolstered worker morale. When Buddhist priests sided with striking workers in 1920, and the supporting role of other Japanese cultural institutions became clear, the planters abandoned their earlier support and decried "being Japanese" as anti-American.[20]

In the 1930s, Sanji Abe used his theater to celebrate the arrival of sailors from the Imperial Japanese Navy and presented a program of films that federal authorities labeled "nationalistic." These ceremonies commemorating the arrival of military ships from Japan were held as early as 1875, but became more frequent public rituals after World War I, when the ships began making regular trips to the ports of San Francisco and Los Angeles. Nationalism also resurged in the Japanese immigrant community with the Sino-Japanese War of 1937. In recognition of Abe and the potential dangers of these cheap amusements from Japan, plantation managers in 1939 notified the Japanese proprietor of their intention to relinquish ties and cancel his film contract. Upon receiving the bad news, the outspoken Abe requested the courtesy of being allowed to exhibit Japanese films at least once a month to workers. Recognizing his growing prominence in Hawai'i, planters granted Abe his "courtesy" in order to, as one official put it, *"ease out* this gentleman's connection with us."[21]

## SOCIAL REFORM AND REGULATING THE PLANTATION THEATER

Despite the need to use their services for "social welfare," sugar planters grew increasingly unsettled by the presence of the Japanese showmen and their world of cheap amusements. These latent tensions emerged in the daily accounts maintained by the HSPA. Beginning in 1923, a flurry of correspondence was exchanged over Nabasuke Tabata's proposal to build a moving picture theater at the Laupahoehoe plantation town. In the records kept by the HSPA, sugar planters laid bare their troubles. Amid the gentlemanly decorum of business transactions, officials came to regard Tabata as, in the words of one official, "a nuisance from the plantation environment that we should take every reasonable means to elimi-nate."[22] These expressed troubles are suggestive of the tangible stakes in the Japanese proprietor's endeavor. Miriam Hansen has argued that the notion of an alternative public sphere can be discerned in the slippage between the historical and the theoretical. More than a methodological problem in film studies, this relationship marks a heuristic advantage to conceptualizing the possibilities for transformation. "Even if there were no empirical traces of autonomous public formations," according to Han-sen, "they could be inferred from the force of negation, from the hege-monic efforts to suppress or assimilate any conditions that might allow for an alternative self-regulated, local, and socially specific organization of experience."[23] The forces of negation in the planters' record, I believe, sug-gest an alternative public sphere taking shape in and off the cane fields.

When Robert Hutchinson received the proposal for the moving picture theater, there were over nine hundred laborers who toiled in the cane fields and resided in the twelve camps of the company town that he man-aged for the Laupahoehoe Sugar Company. The plantation led the way in new irrigation and cane cultivation techniques, which contributed to an impressive yield in sugar of twelve thousand tons in 1918. Hutchinson's company town was regarded as a sterling example of welfare capitalism envisioned by the HSPA. The manager oversaw improvements in housing, health, and sanitation. Amenities such as garden spaces, playgrounds, and bathhouses were also built for "social improvement." Over 60 per-cent of laborers at Laupahoehoe Sugar were from the Philippines, and over 75 percent were foreign-born. While the majority of laborers were single young men from Asia, the sugar planters themselves were consistently white and often descended from missionary families. Similar to the majority of plantation managers working on the Big Island's Hamakua coast, Hutchinson was Scottish by descent. Born in 1872 in Edinburgh, he was educated at the notable Royal High School before arriving in Hawai'i in 1894. He became head overseer of the Laupahoehoe Sugar Company in 1910 and manager in 1915.[24]

Hutchinson was a part of the ruling elite on the island of Hawai'i. Compared to the salaries of the workers, those of the managers were not only extraordinary but also allowed the planters to achieve opulent colonial living standards. Plantation managers tended to reside in large houses that were located at a venerable distance from the camps and maintained by domestic servants, many of whom were men of Asian descent and also workers in the cane fields. The managers' living standards played a crucial role in the "imagined community" of whiteness in Hawai'i. As Evelyn Nakano Glenn explains, the term *haole*, which meant "stranger" or "foreigner" in the Hawaiian language and referred to any nonnative Hawaiian person, developed as a racial category through the plantation experience and the need for the small proprietorial and managerial class to distinguish itself from workers. The planters' living standards and employment of domestic servants were a material and symbolic marker of social distance. Even the Anglo-Europeans who first arrived in Hawai'i as laborers and nonelite classes emulated many of these standards, which ultimately helped to consolidate their newly acquired racial privilege. In addition, many of the plantation managers on the island of Hawai'i, according to Sally Engle Merry, shared close connections to the governing body. In fact, many members of the judiciary were themselves sugar planters. Together, this distinct class and generation "shared the values of capitalism and work, Christian moral reformism, and hierarchical ideas of race and gender of the elites in the local community."[25]

Nabasuke Tabata was neither a worker nor a servant on the Laupaphoehoe plantation. His request of Hutchinson was to build a moving-picture theater on a third of an acre of land he had purchased a few years earlier. As a property owner, Tabata represented a minority in the Japanese immigrant community. In Hawai'i, the five major sugar cane companies owned nearly all of the cane fields in the territory, as well as the region's banking, insurance, transportation, utilities, and merchandising institutions.

During the territorial period, fewer than eighty individuals held half of the land ownership in Hawai'i. Property consolidated and bound together the ruling oligarchy of the islands. With his plot of land, Tabata was a part of a growing yet small group whose social distance from managers such as Robert Hutchinson was closing. According to 1930 census figures, 18 percent of property holders in Hawai'i were persons of Japanese descent. Tabata hoped to erect a building that held a film projector and, adhering to the planter's own reform agenda, was of "public benefit." It would ideally be "fit for holding meetings, movie shows, and Japanese performances." These plans, Tabata assured Hutchinson, raised no concern for planters and held no "detriment to plantation interests."[26]

Officials, however, took little solace in Tabata's assurances. The sugar planters had increasingly developed tighter controls over the new developments in leisure, intervening in the rural settlements by creating a countervailing force to the popular and contestatory public cultures that abetted sugar plantation workers. The HSPA adopted models of welfare capitalism to allay labor unrest and promote ideals of Christian charity and Americanism. By adapting blue laws, which were first established in Hawai'i by American missionaries in response to the perceived rowdiness of American whalers and merchants from the transpacific maritime trade routes, planters created restrictions on Sunday shows. Sugar planters, in fact, had long turned to religious worship to promote stability, order, and work ethic, particularly since the majority of the laborers were single men. Christian missionaries were permitted on the plantations to proselytize and deliver sermons to Chinese and Native Hawaiian workers in the earliest years of the plantation economy. Churches and chapels were ubiquitous across the plantation towns by the twentieth century. Until the 1920 strike, sugar planters also granted rent-free lands or monetary subsidies to Buddhist temples and Shinto shrines, as some leaders served as emissaries to quell worker discontent on behalf of the planters.[27] Adapting Christian and moral values to film exhibition, planters created new ordinances that required film exhibitors to obtain a special application and screen only select films "of an educational or biblical character." In addition, the sugar planters also established a film censorship bureau intended to "supply all plantations with a class of films that will appeal to the laborer and at the same time be *clean*."[28]

Plantation managers often endorsed the exhibition of select films. The managers of camps at Kekaha and Waialua, for instance, commissioned a film exchange called World Enterprises that specialized in public health, hygiene, travelogue, education shorts, and other films deemed "wholesome entertainment features." Directed at filmgoers in the Kekaha plantation theater, however, the planter-initiated film campaign was an utter failure. The "wholesome features" and lessons in American work and living provided by the film exchange did not captivate or attract an audience. Quite quickly, the sugar planters had to cancel the movie orders. "Lack of interest," as the manager noted, "made us drop the whole thing."[29]

## SUBVERTING WESTERNS, SUBVERTING PLANTERS

The "clean" and educational Americanization films that were frequently referenced in planters' records were rarely mentioned in the recollections left by the laborers and families of the plantation era. Instead, residents of Hawaii's plantation towns most often recounted attending theaters to view popular Hollywood films. Offering a particularly vivid account, Francis Nagasawa, a resident of Kukuihaele plantation town, remembered the exhibition of silent western films and the enthusiastic crowds of Filipino laborers:

> The shed adjacent to the theater housed the generator which pumped the electricity with deafening roar to the movie projector. The frame of the movie was first captioned with English and the accompanying picture followed it. The motions of the actors were jerky perhaps because they hadn't perfected the timing mechanism for smooth sequence of motion. Movie was all cowboy [sic]. I can remember only one super-star called Tom Mix. The climax came at the end when the damsel in distress gives a big hug and kiss to her hero who had rescued her from the villains. The Filipino bachelors brought the house down with whistles and stumping of the feet on the wooden floor.

Despite the sugar planters' best efforts to "gradually build up in educating [laborers] to call for better grade pictures," as one report noted, audiences clearly staged their own desires in the plantation theater. These popular films held a significant place in the collective experience of Hawaii's plantation residents and served as a counterpoint to the "wholesome features" promoted by planter reform measures.[30]

The preference of laborers for these amusements was hardly surprising. While films promoted by planter reform measures were predominately nonnarrative, western films featured a narrative of, arguably, the most recognizable and enduring of American myths. Scholarship on the western film has looked at the genre as an ideological fantasy of the "myth of the frontier" that originated in the colonial period and came to represent a unique American character by the writings of, most notably, Frederick Jackson Turner. As a popular genre, westerns espoused the racial ideology of Anglo-Saxon supremacy and colonial expansion. These ideological features of the films were indeed prominent given the political economy of their initial creation. As Richard Abel points out, western film productions were first created to bolster a fledgling American film industry during a period when foreign films, especially French Pathé titles, rivaled Hollywood. American filmmakers sought to compete in the marketplace by creating a film product distinct from its foreign rivals. Based on these economic concerns, by 1909 western films were made to be "quintessentially American" in formal and ideological terms.[31]

For plantation theater audiences, the dominant features of the silent western film projected a stark contrast to working and living conditions in Hawaii's sugar plantations. With the mechanized production of sugar cultivation, planters had objectified workers as being bereft of personhood. "I can see no difference between the importation of foreign workers," as one official famously remarked, "and the importation of a jute bag from India." Western films presented these "foreign workers" with narratives that differentiated one person from another and invested heroic qualities in the individual. While the films' reverence of the western landscape furnished, as Ella Shohat and Robert Stam have suggested, the ideological premises of the genre as an empty stage for expansionist fantasies, the wide-open frontier on the screen appeared as an inversion of life in the carefully regulated plantation camps.[32]

The exhibition of films during the silent-film era was typically accompanied by a rich variety of sound that included lecturers, song and theater performers, musicians, pianists, and orchestras. As late as the mid-1930s, well after the development of synchronized sound in cinema, a single film was typically not a "main attraction" but a part of a program that included live stage performance, short films, serials, and newsreels. These features of film exhibition during the silent era could localize or even complicate or disrupt audience identification with the dominant messages of the film genre. American films, including silent westerns, thus resembled Japanese films in some measure. Both featured a mode of exhibition that diverted the attention of audiences from the screen to the stage.

In the early twentieth century, the plantation theater caused dramatic changes to the spatial and social isolation of the plantation towns. Lacking the streetcars and trolleys of Honolulu, those living in rural areas had been comparatively constrained. Tadao Kawamoto, who was born in Kauai and worked in the cane fields of McBryde Sugar Company, recalled that the popular films brought many of the laborers from the camps to the theater in a neighboring town. Workers devised new ways to ride the railways that transported the sugar cane. Kawamoto recalled, "When we get through the show, all of us boys used to lift the boxcar off the rails [to ride back to the camp].... When the next day the plantation field overseer should come over there and see that, well, nobody touch the car, because that car stay on the rail." Given the dispersed geography of the rural settlements and the unavailability of automobiles, Toden Higa, who was born in Okinawa and resided in Paaihau, remembered that "we walked all the way to Pauilo ... [when cinema] was no sound, only pictures." The theater pulled together the dispersed residents and workers of the plantation towns and provided a common arena for public interaction and congregation.[33]

As popular amusements, silent western films not only drew workers from the cane fields to the theater but also unsettled the racial divisions upheld by the planter oligarchy. Like Nagasawa's vivid memory of the silent western films and crowds of Filipino laborers, Louis Jacintho remembered that his father, a Portuguese immigrant who operated a steam plow for Koloa Sugar, went to the plantation theater every Saturday for a "double header cowboy movie [with] Tom Mix, or Hoot Gibson, Ken Maynard." Robert Kunimura, who grew up in the segregated Japanese camp in Koloa, similarly recalled the popularity of these particular films, which cost a mere ten cents.[34]

In their policies and practices, the officials of the sugar industry sought every imaginable means to remap these heterogeneous spaces. They sought to create a rigid racial hierarchy that subjected workers to what Moon-Kie Jung calls "differentiating racisms." White workers exclusively occupied the highest professional position of the industry's economic structure, while Portuguese, Japanese, and Filipinos occupied positions in descending order of status and power. Salaries, benefits, housing, resources, and the opportunity for advancement were unevenly allocated based on racial categories. But while work gangs, housing barracks, and even sports teams were segregated according to ethnicity, race, and nationality, the plantation theater brought the workers of the cane fields together.[35]

In the plantation theater, audiences gathered in the same space to view the same popular films. The cinema was a collective show. As silent-era productions, western films were not restricted by language or illiteracy. The films developed into a lingua franca of sorts on the plantations. They had the potential to facilitate a shared "talk," to unite rather than partition the workers of the cane fields. This talk perhaps resembled something of the Hawaiian Creole English that developed as a common language among the successive generations of sugar plantation workers from China, Japan, Portugal, Puerto Rico, and the Philippines.[36]

The particular appeal of the silent western film turned many of the plantation theaters into male publics that unnerved planters. As scholars such as Lee Clark Mitchell and Andrew Brodie Smith have argued, the western has been the most persistent genre to grapple with the ideas and images of American manhood and masculinity. In their focus on male companionship and displays of masculine virility against the myth of the frontier, silent-era westerns were intended to appeal to the screen desires of male audiences.[37] In the debates over Tabata's building proposal in the mid-1920s, officials imagined, and indeed feared, that the plantation theater would convene a separate sphere for male association and congregation. Manager Hutchinson cautioned of "a meeting place for plantation men" in the Japanese proprietor's theater. This male public could also be drawn together in the theater, given, he surmised, the "possibility of liquor and gambling entering it." The peril of this potential of cinema was evident to the beleaguered plantation management. Plantation camp police, as both Santiago Ramos and Robert Owan recalled, regularly patrolled and monitored the local theater in Kahuku. These public gathering sites for male workers were also subject to policing through antilabor legislation, including a 1925 trespassing law in Hawai'i that was, according to labor historian Edward Beechert, "the most effective labor control bill."[38]

Indeed, ideas of masculinity had a significant role in the union hall. Leaders of Hawaii's labor movement connected the workers' struggles to an ideology of growing into manhood, of embodying a particular type of masculinity. When Motoyuki Negoro delivered his labor treatises in 1909, he emphasized the desire of the Japanese laborer in Hawai'i to "become a full fledged man." With the changing gender ratio on the plantations, higher wage proponents argued that improved livelihoods were a particular necessity for the workingman who was also the head of a family. "A laborer's wages," asserted the Federation of Japanese Labor in 1920, "should be sufficient to support him and his family in decency and comfort." These appeals to manhood were prominent in the politics of American labor unions and the working-class radicalism of the early twentieth century. The "American standard of living," the popular creed of US labor unions, equated workers' struggles with an ideology of masculinity, whiteness, and domesticity. While Japanese and Filipino workers in Hawai'i were largely excluded from mainstream union membership, and even situated as the primary threat to a racialized wage standard, they mobilized these ideas to claim equal wages and improved working conditions.[39]

In the end, the connection between the plantation theater and workers' struggles was made abundantly clear in the debates over Nabasuke Tabata's proposal to build a theater next to the Laupahoehoe plantation. As one official explicitly concluded, "We do not think, for a moment, that the suggestion of leasing the place for 15 years should be considered as you might have a source of danger right in the middle of your Plantation in case of a strike." Indeed, sugar planters astutely recognized the role of the plantation theater in the labor movement. Following the first major organized labor strike in 1909, workers of the cane fields returned time and again to the stages of Hawaii's theaters. In 1920, workers convened the first cross-racial and dual union strike that involved over 77 percent of the labor force and lasted over five months. Japanese union organizers convened a "well attended meeting" at Valley Isle Theater in Maui. Workers from the Philippines, who formed the Filipino Federation of Labor, gathered to hear Pablo Manlapit in Hilo's Gaiety Theatre. At the Asahi Theatre in Honolulu, the crowd erupted as members of the Japanese Federation of Labor paraded onto the stage a disloyal Japanese worker who had crossed the strike line and returned to the cane fields. Labor leaders also continued to use the theaters as provisional strike camps. When a strike erupted in 1924 on Kauai, twenty-three evicted laborers were arrested on charges of vagrancy for sleeping in the lobby of a Japanese-owned theater.[40]

For sugar planters, some of the dangers posed by Hawaii's theaters and its working-class publics were put to rest with Tabata, whose request they ultimately refused. The planters provided no explanation, simply stating in a letter, "We regret that we feel that we are unable to meet [Tabata] in this matter." With the onset of the Great Depression and the untimely death of the elder Tabata, the Tabata family put their distressed holdings up for sale. In the most dire and desperate times of the 1930s, the wealthy planters offered six thousand dollars for the property that the Tabata family had reluctantly put up for sale for eleven thousand. In 1934, the planters finally seized all of the property owned by the Tabata family through debt capital.[41]

Nevertheless, the expression of apprehension about Tabata's theater and the caution of the planters concerning their laborers' seemingly benign cinematic desires are evidence of an emergent counterpublic in the cane fields. During the most volatile years of labor unrest in prewar Hawai'i, sugar planters intended for theaters and cheap amusements to stave off working-class group formation. They drew on the models of welfare capitalism sweeping across the mainland and promoted leisure and play in an effort to quell discontent and encourage company loyalty. Their intervening efforts to develop film censorship and regulation, however, were largely failed endeavors, for the plantation theater continued to thrive as a popular and contested site for workers' desires. Despite their reform measures, sugar planters were unable to prevent audiences from consuming popular amusements. They could neither oversee the new arenas of public congregation nor contain the potential in silent western films to nurture the shared bonds between workers. Ultimately, this facet of cinema as a collective experience would become critical to the labor movement in Hawai'i. Robert Hasegawa, whose family bore witness to the entire half century of labor struggle in Hawai'i as workers, translators, Japanese language teachers, and union administrators, remarked that the International Longshoremen's and Warehousemen's Union strike in 1946, which labor historians regard as the first successful interracial labor movement in Hawai'i, came into being only because of the cultural shifts that took place decades earlier when, as he put it, "we kids started to mix together."[42]

1    According to Jack Y. Tasaka, various plays with costumes imported from Japan were performed at the original Asahi Theatre, which earned a thousand dollars every week. The theater built after the 1900 fire was eventually taken over by Matsuo Seichi in 1912. See East-West Journal, August 13, 2003, 20–26. Details about the history of the Asahi Theatre appear in Lowell Angell, Theatres of Hawai'i (Charleston, WV: Arcadia Publishing, 2011); and Michael Okihiro, A'ala: The Story of a Japanese

Community in Hawaii (Honolulu: Japanese Cultural Center of Hawaiʻi, 2003).

2    The Hawaii Shinpo is quoted in Fourth Report of the Commissioner of Labor on Hawaii, 1910 (Washington, DC: Government Printing Office, 1911), 85.

3    Nora Conaty, "Old Shibai: Japanese Theater in Hawaiʻi," Hawaiian Journal of History 38 (2004): 121–41.

4    On the role of the Japanese language press in the 1909 strike, see Kelli Y. Nakamura, "'Violence and Press Incendiarism': Media and Labor Conflicts in the 1909 Strike," Hawaiian Journal of History 25 (2011): 69–99.

5    The arrest of Negoro and the seventeen labor leaders in 1909 received national press coverage. See "Japanese Conspire to Control Hawaii," New York Times, July 12, 1909, 1; "Japanese Imprison Sheriff," New York Times, July 13, 1909, 2; "Indictment Against Japs," Billings Daily Gazette, June 13, 1909, 1; "Twelve Japanese Held as Plotters," New York Times, June 14, 1909, 1; "Who Will Develop the Wealth of Hawaii? An Interesting Situation Due to Japanese Revolt," New York Times, June 27, 1909, 2; "Ten Months for Japanese," Washington Post, August 22, 1909, 13; "Japanese Sent to Prison," New York Times, August 22, 1909, 2.

6    On the formation of the Higher Wages Association and the "Great Strike of 1909," see Take and Allan Beekman, "Hawaii's Great Japanese Strike," in Kodomo No Tame Ni—For the Sake of the Children: The Japanese-American Experience in Hawaiʻi, ed. Dennis Ogawa (Honolulu: University of Hawaiʻi Press, 1978); Alan Moriyama, "The 1909 and 1920 Strikes of Japanese Sugar," in Counterpoint: Perspectives on Asian America, ed. Emma Gee (Los Angeles: Asian American Studies Center, 1976), 169–80; Edward Beechert, Working in Hawaii: A Labor History (Honolulu: University of Hawaiʻi Press, 1985), 161–76; and Gary Y. Okihiro, Cane Fires: The Anti-Japanese Movement in Hawaii, 1865–1945 (Philadelphia: Temple University Press, 1991), 65–81.

7    For a review of the debates on the "historical turn" in cinema studies, see the special issue of Cinema Journal 44 (Fall 2004), which included nuanced contributions by Sumiko Higashi, Charles Musser, Richard Abel, Jane Gaines, and Lee Grieveson.

8    Miriam Hansen, "Early Silent Cinema: Whose Public Sphere?" New German Critique 29 (1983): 147–84; Miriam Hansen, Babel and Babylon: Spectatorship in American Silent Film (Cambridge, MA: Harvard University Press, 1991).

9    Beechert, Working in Hawaii, 161.

10   Husted's Directory of Honolulu and Territory of Hawaii (Honolulu: Hawaiian Gazette Company, 1902), 143, 238.

11   Conaty, "Old Shibai," 123; "Japanese Show Their Paces in Native Vaudeville," Pacific Commercial Advertiser (Honolulu), May 2, 1901; Mae Itamura, oral history interview, 1980, "Stores and Storekeepers of Paia and Puunene, Maui," Ethnic Studies Oral History Project, University of Hawaiʻi, Manoa.

12   Robert C. Schmitt, Demographic Statistics of Hawaii, 1778–1965 (Honolulu: University of Hawaiʻi Press, 1968), 120; Kikujiro Clifferd Kondo, Dr. K. C. Kondo's Classified Japanese Business Directory of Territory of Hawaii: 1937–1938 (Honolulu, 1937); Kikujiro Clifferd Kondo, Dr. K. C. Kondo's Classified Japanese Business Directory of Territory of Hawaii: 1940–1941 (Honolulu, 1940); Empire Theatre advertisement, Hawaii Shokumin Shimbun, September 3, 1909. The Hawaiian Sugar Planters' Association was

established as a voluntary organization for the sugar plantation owners in 1895. The documents in the HSPA Plantation Archives, currently held at the University of Hawaiʻi at Manoa, were donated by the HSPA in 1995.

13   "Honomu Thrilled When Talkies Make Debut in Remodeled Theatre," *Honolulu Advertiser*, September 15, 1931.

14   Okihiro, *Cane Fires*, 65–194.

15   Donald Bowman, "General Welfare Work," *Hawaiian Planters Record* 23 (September 1920); circular from American Factors, August 20, 1919, PSC 12/6 AmFac, Plantation Department 1919, Hawaiian Sugar Planters' Association Plantation Archives (HSPAP), Hawaiian Collection, University of Hawaiʻi, Manoa.

16   Ordinance No. 31, March 4, 1909, LSC 7/7 Moving Picture House, 1923–1930, HSPAP; John K. Akau to R. A. Hutchinson, May 14, 1928, LSC 7/7 Moving Picture House 1923–1930, HSPAP; R. A. Hutchinson to County of Hawaiʻi, October 21, 1925, LSC 7/7 Moving Picture House 1923–1930, HSPAP; County Treasurer to Laupahoehoe Sugar Company, October 22, 1925, LSC 7/7 Moving Picture House 1923–1930, HSPAP; R. A. Hutchinson to County of Hawaiʻi, August 23, 1926, LSC 7/7 Moving Picture House 1923–1930, HSPAP; John K. Akau to R. A. Hutchinson, May 14, 1928, LSC 7/7 Moving Picture House 1923–1930, HSPAP.

17   "Sanji Abe First Big Islander Out for Senate," *Honolulu Advertiser*, May 2, 1940; "Sanji Abe Is Touring Japan," *Honolulu Advertiser*, July 9, 1940; "Abe Due Saturday," *Honolulu Advertiser*, August 20, 1940.

18   There is a contentious debate over the *benshi* as an original feature of Japanese cinema. See Hiroshi Komatsu, "Some Characteristics of Japanese Cinema Before World War I," in *Reframing Japanese Cinema: Authorship, Genre, History*, ed. Arthur Nolletti and David Desser (Bloomington: Indiana University Press, 1992); Joseph L. Anderson, "Spoken Silents in the Japanese Cinema; or, Talking to Pictures: Essaying the *Katsuben*, Contextualizing the Texts," in Nolletti and Desser, *Reframing Japanese Cinema*; and Tadao Sato, "Japanese Cinema and the Traditional Arts: Imagery, Technique, and Cultural Context," in *Cinematic Landscapes: Observations on the Visual Arts and Cinema of China and Japan*, ed. Linda C. Ehrlich and David Desser (Austin: University of Texas Press, 1994).

19   Naomi Sodetani, "Benshi and Me," in Okihiro, *Aʻala: The Story of a Japanese Community in Hawaii* (Honolulu: Japanese Cultural Center of Hawaiʻi), 41–44.

20   Eileen H. Tamura, "The English-Only Effort, the Anti-Japanese Campaign, and Language Acquisition in the Education of Japanese Americans in Hawaii, 1915–40," *History of Education Quarterly* 33 (1993): 37–58; Noriko Asato, "Mandating Americanization: Japanese Language Schools and the Federal Survey of Education in Hawaii, 1916–1920," *History of Education Quarterly* 43 (2003): 10–38; Okihiro, *Cane Fires*, 129–62.

21   Bob Dye, "The Case of Sanji Abe," *Honolulu*, November 2002; Brian Masaru Hayashi, *Democratizing the Enemy: The Japanese American Internment* (Princeton: Princeton University Press, 2004), 50; Yuji Ichioka, "Japanese Immigrant Nationalism: The Issei and the Sino-Japanese War, 1937–1941," *California History* 69 (1990): 260–75; L. W. Wishard to Consolidated Amusement Company, August 8, 1939, LSC 36/10 Kai, C, Gen Corr, Out 1939, HSPAP.

22    John E. Russell to R. A. Hutchinson, May 23, 1933, LSC 4/8 Tabata, HSPAP.

23    Hansen, *Babel and Babylon*, 91.

24    Christina R. N. Lothian, *Laupahoehoe* (N.p., 1977); George Nellist, *The Story of Hawaii and Its Builders: An Historical Outline of Hawaii with Biographical Sketches of Its Men of Note and Substantial Achievement, Past and Present, who have Contributed to the Progress of the Territory* (Honolulu: Honolulu Star Bulletin, 1925).

25    Evelyn Nakano Glenn, *Unequal Freedom: How Race and Gender Shaped American Citizenship and Labor* (Cambridge, MA: Harvard University Press, 2002), 207–15; Sally Engle Merry, *Colonizing Hawaii: The Cultural Power of Law* (Princeton: Princeton University Press, 2000), 118.

26    John Whitehead, "Western Progressives, Old South Planters, or Colonial Oppressors: The Enigma of Hawai'i's 'Big Five,' 1898–1940," *Western Historical Quarterly* 30 (1999): 295–326; US Census M. C. G., "Population and Land Ownership, 1930," in Milton C. George, *The Development of Hilo, Hawaii, T.H.: A Modern Tropical Sugar Port, Or, A Slice through Time at a Place Called Hilo* (Ann Arbor, MI: Edwards Letter Shop, 1948), 16; Lease of Papaaloa Theatre, April 29, 1926, LSC Moving Picture House, 1923–1930, HSPAP; R. A. Hutchinson to Directors of Laupahoehoe Sugar Company, May 12, 1926, LSC Moving Picture House, 1923–1930, HSPAP.

27    On Christianity and the Hawaiian plantations, see Tin-Yuke Char, "S. P. Aheong, Hawaii's First Chinese Christian Evangelist," *Hawaiian Journal of History* 11 (1977); Ronald Takaki, *Pau Hana: Plantation Life and Labor in Hawaii, 1835–1920* (Honolulu: University of Hawai'i Press, 1983).

28    Donald Bowman to Onomea Sugar Company, September 2, 1920, MKC 1/3 Ono, C, HSPA, Labor and Stats 1920–1928, HSPAP.

29    World Enterprises to Kekaha Sugar Co., April 1, 1940, KSC Film Service 1939–1940 26/12, HSPAP.

30    KSC 26/12 Film Service 1939–1940, HSPAP; Francis Nagasawa, oral history interview (1988), *Memoirs of the Hawaii Hiroshima Heritage Study Group*, Japanese Cultural Center of Hawai'i, Honolulu.

31    Richard Abel, "'Our Country'/Whose Country? The 'Americanisation' Project of Early Westerns," in *Back in the Saddle Again: New Essays on the Western*, ed. Edward Buscombe and Roberta E. Pearson (London: British Film Institute, 1998), 77–95.

32    Ella Shohat and Robert Stam, *Unthinking Eurocentrism: Multiculturalism and the Media* (New York: Routledge, 1994), 114–20.

33    Toden Higa, oral history interview by Michiko Kodama, in *Uchinanchu: A History of Okinawans in Hawaii* (Honolulu: Ethnic Studies Program, University of Hawai'i at Manoa, 1981), 517.

34    Louis Jacintho, oral history interview by Warren Nishimoto (1987), in "Koloa: an Oral History of a Kaua'i Community" (Mantra: Center for Oral History, Social Science Research Institution, University of Hawai'i, 1988), 119; Robert Kunimura, oral history interview with Warren Nishimoto (1987), in "Koloa," 953.

35    Moon-Kie Jung, *Reworking Race: The Making of Hawaii's Interracial Labor Movement* (New York: Columbia University Press, 2006).

36    Louis Jacintho, oral history interview by Warren Nishimoto (1987), in "Koloa," 119;

Robert Kunimura, oral history interview by Warren Nishimoto (1987), in "Koloa," 953; Jung, *Reworking Race*. The prominent union organizer John Reinecke wrote a master's thesis in 1930 about the makeshift language, or "creole dialect," that fused Japanese, Portuguese, and Tagalog loan words with Hawaiian English among the workers of the sugar cane plantations. He posited that with their limited occupational mobility and the unavailability of translators, workers found it more important to communicate with each other than to learn "standard" English to talk with managers and *haoles*. The thesis was later published as *Language and Dialect in Hawaii: A Sociolinguistic History to 1935* (Honolulu: University of Hawai'i Press, 1969). See also John Reinecke and Stanley Tsuzaki, "Hawaiian Loanwords in Hawaiian English of the 1930's," *Oceanic Linguistics* 6 (1967): 80–115.

37    Lee Clark Mitchell, *Westerns: Making the Man in Fiction and Film* (Chicago: University of Chicago Press, 1996); Andrew Brodie Smith, *Shooting Cowboys and Indians: Silent Western Films, American Culture, and the Birth of Hollywood* (Boulder: University of Colorado Press, 2003).

38    R. A. Hutchinson to Directors of Laupahoehoe Sugar Company, May 12, 1926, LSC 7/7 Moving Picture House, HSPAP; Santiago Ramos, oral history interview by Jeannette Fukuzawa (1978), Joseph F. Smith Library Archives and Special Collections, Brigham Young University Hawai'i, Lai'ie, 5; Robert Owan, oral history interview by Paul White and Kenneth W. Baldridge (1978), Joseph F. Smith Library Archives and Special Collections, Brigham Young University Hawai'i, Lai'ie, 17; Beechert, *Working in Hawaii*, 215.

39    Okihiro, *Cane Fires*, 46; Federation of Japanese Labor in Hawaii, *Controversy Between Japanese Labor and the Sugar Planters of Hawaii* (Honolulu: Nippu Jiji, 1920), 2. Significantly, labor leaders in 1920 also advocated for both male and female workers. They demanded wage increases to $1.25 per day for men and 95 cents per day for women. In addition, the union stipulated a demand for maternity leave and wage compensation for female laborers after delivery. These resolutions were articulated in the Federation of Japanese Labor in Hawai'i, *The Voice of Labor in Hawaii* (Honolulu: Nippu Jiji, 1920). See also Melinda Tria Kerkvliet, *Unbending Cane: Pablo Manlapit: A Filipino Labor Leader in Hawaii* (Honolulu: University of Hawai'i Press, 2002), 24; Lawrence Glickman, "Inventing the 'American Standard of Living': Gender, Race and Working-Class Identity, 1880–1925," *Labor History* 34 (1993): 221–35; Nayan Shah, *Contagious Divides: Epidemics and Race in San Francisco's Chinatown* (Berkeley: University of California Press, 2001), 158–78. Throughout the early twentieth century, Asian workers were excluded from the American Federation of Labor and the Knights of Labor. In contrast, the Industrial Workers of the World (IWW) and the Congress of Industrial Organizations (CIO) supported Asian workers' efforts to organize. See Daniel Rosenberg, "The IWW and Organization of Asian Workers in Early Twentieth-Century America," *Labor History* 36 (1995): 77–87.

40    E. H. Wodehouse to R. A. Hutchinson, May 6, 1926, LSC 7/7 Moving Picture House, 1923–1930, HSPAP; "Maui Japanese Plan to Join Labor Union," *Maui News*, November 21, 1919, 1; Masayo Umezawa Duus, *The Japanese Conspiracy: The Oahu Sugar Strike of 1920* (Berkeley: University of California Press, 1999), 50; "Situation Survey,"

March 6, 1920, Military Intelligence Correspondence, 1917–1941, Record Group 165, National Archives, College Park; John Reinecke, *The Filipino Piecemeal Sugar Strike of 1924–1925* (Honolulu: University of Hawai'i Press, 1996), 63.

41   R. A. Hutchinson to Kango Kawasaki, May 27, 1926, LSC 7/7 Moving Picture House, 1923–1930, HSPAP; R. A. Hutchinson to John E. Russell, May 15, 1934, LSC 4/8 Tabata, HSPAP.

42   Robert Hasegawa, oral history interview, "Unity in the Family," in *Talking Hawaii's Story: Oral Histories of an Island People,* ed. Mishi Kodama-Nishimoto, Warren S. Nishimoto, and Cynthia A. Oshiro (Honolulu: University of Hawai'i Press, 2009), 91.

# PART THREE

# Forging Multiracial Fronts

# 4

## Positively Stateless

### Marcus Graham, the Ferrero-Sallitto Case, and Anarchist Challenges to Race and Deportation

KENYON ZIMMER

ON JANUARY 14, 1938, A MAN KNOWN TO THE CALIFORNIA DISTRICT COURT as "Marcus Graham, alias Fred S. Graham, alias Robert Parson, alias Robert Parsons, alias Shoel Marcus"—none of these his birth name—rose from the defendant's chair to address the judge before his sentence for contempt was read. Despite his perilous status as an immigrant, a Jew, and a radical, Graham (as he was most commonly known) was anything but contrite. "My guilt here proves the inadequacy of this government," he declared. "I admit I am an anarchist." Never one to mince words, he then denounced the very foundations of the modern nation-state and its claims to legitimacy:

> This court substantiates as correct the position of the anarchists
> toward the government as an administrative organ not serving
> the interests of, but against the people, not of truth, not of justice
> but of rank injustice.... The very existence of government, its courts,
> its jails, its army, and the multitude's poverty and deprivation
> bespeaks its uselessness and harmfulness and furthermore
> condemns its moral right to exist at all. Naturally, then, as an
> Anarchist, I am no partner to the making of Laws of any country
> and therefore can at no time be flaunting laws or be asked to obey
> them—unless by force. And by force, not by reason, governments
> enforce all their laws.

Graham was sentenced to six months and removed, but not before a reporter for the *Oakland Tribune* noted "the helpless fury of the immigration officers" present, "who want to deport him, but can't make Graham tell where he came from."[1]

This odd courtroom drama was only the latest chapter in nearly two decades of American authorities' efforts to expel Graham from the United States, and in the government's much longer campaign to marginalize, exclude, and deport alien anarchists. The curious deportation cases of Marcus Graham and his Bay Area compatriots highlight the entanglement of race, nation, and political ideology. They also illustrate the limits of state power and show how statelessness could be leveraged to marginalized people's advantage. Anarchist ideology and praxis deliberately embodied the antithesis of the nation-state, and its adherents advocated statelessness not as it was conceived by Hannah Arendt and subsequent writers—as a nightmarish status imposed by those in power to control and terrorize the powerless—but rather as a condition that the powerless should strive to generalize. Foreign-born anarchists therefore reconstituted themselves as a unique category of immigrants: willful "anticitizens" who rejected political inclusion in both the American nation-state and their states of origin. These "stateless hybrids" or "others within," to borrow Coco Fusco's terminology, were living proof of "the failure of essentialist, nationalist, and other separatist paradigms that have structured our understanding of identity and difference for centuries."[2]

Many scholars have emphasized the historical link between race and American citizenship, especially the role of the state in conferring whiteness to European immigrants by granting them access to naturalization and the franchise. Far less attention has been paid to those, like many anarchists, who knowingly forfeited the most basic "wages of whiteness"—citizenship and suffrage—and thereby placed themselves outside of the politically and racially defined "American nation."[3] James C. Scott observes, "The huge literature on state-making, contemporary and historic, pays virtually no attention to its obverse: the history of deliberate and reactive statelessness ...[,] of those who got away, and state-making cannot be understood apart from it."[4] This is the story of some who "got away," and did so in a most peculiar manner: by refusing to leave.

STORY OF AN UNDESIRABLE

Marcus Graham, whose given name was in fact Shmuel Marcus, was born in the Romanian city of Dorohoi in 1893 to Orthodox Jewish parents. In

1907 his family migrated to Philadelphia, where he became a garment cutter and socialist before joining the sizable local Yiddish-speaking anarchist movement. An intractable revolutionary and opponent of the First World War, Graham left the country with several comrades to avoid registering for the draft and carried out antiwar agitation in Montreal and Toronto, where he adopted the pseudonym Robert Parsons. In 1919 he relocated to New York to join a small group producing an illegal newspaper, *The Anarchist Soviet Bulletin*. The paper condemned American military intervention in revolutionary Russia and called on American workers to arm themselves, organize "anarchist soviets," and launch a general strike to topple the US government. In response to the race riots of 1919 the group also urged the "Workers of America Colored or White" to recognize that racial antagonisms in northern industry resulted from divisions created by exclusionary labor union and employer practices, and to "realize that when we are killing one another it only benefits capitalism and help to keep them [*sic*] in richness, while we are suffering in want and misery."[5] Appearing in the midst of the postwar Red Scare, these calls for interracial insurrection led to Graham's first encounter with authorities.

On April 15, 1919, he was arrested in Paterson, New Jersey, after a suspicious policeman demanded to see the contents of his suitcase, which contained 2,500 copies of the *Bulletin*. During his interrogation Graham falsely claimed that his name was Robert Parsons and that he was a Canadian citizen born in Montreal. On May 1 he was transferred to Ellis Island to await deportation to Canada, but two weeks later he posted one thousand dollars bail and returned to the task of secretly editing the *Bulletin*. Several other members of his group were arrested over the following months for distributing the paper; two were deported to Russia in December, and another, Mollie Steimer, was a defendant in the landmark Supreme Court case *Abrams v. United States* and deported in November 1921.[6]

British authorities meanwhile reported that the Canadian address "Parsons" had given was false and there was no record that he held Canadian citizenship. Nevertheless, on November 18, 1919, the Bureau of Immigration issued a deportation warrant for the return of "Robert Parson (or Parsons)" to Canada.[7] Graham, however, jumped his bond and disappeared. When Britain's Trade Union Congress and Labour Party formed hundreds of Councils of Action in August 1920 to organize a threatened general strike in the event of Allied intervention in the Polish-Soviet

War, Graham mistook this movement for an impending revolution and surreptitiously traveled to London. Three months later, disillusioned, he returned to New York by way of Canada just as surreptitiously. In January 1921, now writing under the name Fred S. Graham, he relaunched the *Bulletin* under a new title, *Free Society*.[8] A month later, immigration inspectors caught up with Graham on the steps of the New York Public Library and returned him to Ellis Island, where he endured a twenty-four-hour interrogation during which he was stripped naked and beaten. Throughout, he refused to divulge where his group printed their paper and continued to insist that he was a Canadian named Parsons.[9] Knowing this to be false, the Bureau of Immigration concluded that their captive was "a Russian subject." But even if this had been correct, the United States had no diplomatic relations with the new Soviet government, and the Russians, who were conducting their own crackdown on political opposition, refused entry to most Russian anarchist deportees after March 1921. Ignorant of Graham's place of birth as well as his real name, the state found its own borders—the very thing that made deportation an effective weapon against most "undesirables"—working against it. So long as authorities could not locate a country obligated to accept Graham, they would be unable to deport him. After six months of consternation, the Bureau of Immigration again released "Parsons" on bond.[10]

The federal government agreed with anarchists like Graham insofar as it, too, insisted that they could not be loyal US citizens. Their statelessness was therefore reaffirmed and imposed from above as well as from below. In 1903, following the assassination of president William McKinley by the novice anarchist Leon Czolgosz, Congress passed the Anarchist Exclusion Act, barring foreign-born anarchists from entering the country or becoming naturalized (despite the fact that Czolgosz was born and raised in the United States). However, the statute proved difficult to enforce until wartime revisions in 1917 and 1918 expanded it to allow for the denaturalization and deportation of immigrants if at any time they came to "believe in, advise, advocate, or teach … the overthrow by force or violence of the Government of the United States or of all forms of law," or simply "disbelieved in" or were "opposed to all organized government." All foreign-born anarchists, who made up the majority of the American movement, were thereafter illegal aliens by definition.[11]

Recent scholarship describes how the juridical creation of statelessness and illegal aliens is part of an ongoing project to define national identity, and in the United States this process has been intimately linked to racialized notions of "the nation." Within this context, Rachel Ida Buff notes, even immigration exclusion based on political ideology was "a component of a racial regime governing entrance and exit."[12] For "new immigrant" anarchists such as Graham, this was true in a triple sense: First, the entire apparatus of exclusion and deportation was created in the 1880s and 1890s to enforce expanding race-based prohibitions on Asian immigration, which was then expanded to encompass anarchists and other "excludable classes." Second, "new immigrants" from eastern and southern Europe were, prior to World War II, categorized as belonging to distinct (but nevertheless "white") races innately inferior to the Nordic, Anglo-Saxon, or Caucasian race (depending on which popular typology was employed). Many American nativists attributed immigrant radicalism to the biological deficiencies of these "communistic and revolutionary races."[13]

Finally, anarchists were also often racialized *as anarchists*. Lauren Basson notes, "Some policymakers, local authorities, and journalists conceptualized anarchism not simply as a foreign, radical political doctrine to which people voluntarily adhered, but as an aberrant, racialized trait that placed its adherents outside the ascriptive boundaries of the nation." These views gained widespread scientific credibility and influence through the theories of Italian criminologist Cesare Lombroso, who diagnosed the anarchist as a specific "criminal type" characterized by mental and physiognomic abnormalities, all rooted in biological "atavism" and therefore heritable. If this did not construct anarchists as a "race" in conventional terms, it did make them targets of what Stefan Kühl calls "eugenic racism" by ascribing to them a phenotypically recognizable genetic defect that threatened to undermine white supremacy through racial degeneration. Anarchism was thus removed from the realm of political ideology and inscribed onto immigrant bodies, mandating the exclusion of anarchists from both the American nation and its gene pool.[14]

Attorney general A. Mitchell Palmer, who orchestrated the Red Scare of 1919–1920, invoked these biological notions of foreign radicalism while defending his actions before Congress: "Most of the individuals involved in this movement are aliens or foreign-born citizens.... Out of the sly and crafty eyes of many of them leap cupidity, cruelty, insanity, and crime; from their lopsided faces, sloping brows, and misshapen features may be recognized the unmistakable criminal type." Alien anarchists were the very first group targeted in Palmer's nationwide raids, and thousands of suspected radicals were, like Marcus Graham, rounded up and held for deportation. Hundreds were expelled among much fanfare, including high-profile anarchists such as Emma Goldman and Luigi Galleani. These expulsions highlighted immigrants' vulnerability to exclusionary statutes, but deportation proved to be less than the "absolute weapon against the foreign-born radical" that authorities had hoped for. Ultimately, fewer than 1,000 of those arrested (only about a third of them ideological anarchists) were deported, leaving the vast majority of alien anarchists at liberty within the United States.[15] Moreover, several anarchist deportees simply undid the government's work by reentering the United States clandestinely, illustrating a persistent shortcoming in the logic of deportation.[16]

Nativist, eugenicist, and antiradical influence next led to passage of the most sweeping immigration restrictions in American history. The Immigration Acts of 1921 and 1924 banned virtually all immigration from Asia and Africa, and set extremely low quotas on the number of southern and eastern European migrants that could enter the United States each year. In doing so, these laws simultaneously constructed all Europeans as members of a single white race with privileges not available to nonwhites, but also clearly marked European "new immigrants" as less desirable than migrants from western and northern Europe.[17] Anarchists and other excluded classes, however, remained distinct from and outside of this "American race." This exclusion only reinforced the antistatist and antiracist sentiments of anarchists such as Marcus Graham, who in 1924 joined the International Group of New York, a newly formed organization composed primarily of immigrant Italian, Jewish, and Spanish anarchists.

However, Graham was a confrontational and controversial figure; according to a contemporary, "nature endowed him with a measure of obstinacy, chutzpah and with a hot revolutionary temperament." Some in the movement strongly disliked him, and his extreme revolutionary views put him "on the fringe always alone," even among fellow anarchists.[18] Possessing a strong artistic streak, Graham felt more at home among the Rebel Poets, a loose collection of radical writers founded in 1928 by anarchist writers Ralph Cheyney and Lucia Trent. The following year the Rebel Poets helped Graham publish *An Anthology of Revolutionary Poetry*, an impressive compendium for which he had been collecting material ever since his first release from Ellis Island. Cheyney and Trent approvingly described the book as "an anthology of WORLD patriotism."[19]

In addition to its international scope, the volume stood out from contemporary collections of radical and "proletarian" poetry as being by far the most inclusive of African American voices. Graham was an enthusiastic supporter of the poets of the Harlem Renaissance, and the anthology featured poems by Countee Cullen (who was a member of the book's publication committee), Paul Laurence Dunbar, Fenton Johnson, Georgia Douglas Johnson, James Weldon Johnson, Claude McKay, and Rebel Poets member Langston Hughes. Graham gave a copy of the anthology to Hughes bearing the inscription, "With great admiration for a great poet," and Hughes penned three recently rediscovered poems on its flyleaves.[20]

In 1930, Graham was "hitch-hiking from city to city," promoting the anthology and placing copies in libraries. After he took a brief detour into Mexico, however, an immigration inspector in Yuma, Arizona, arrested Graham for possession of suspected anarchist literature—that is, copies of the anthology—and sought a warrant to deport him to Mexico. An ad hoc defense committee composed of radical writers and the American Civil Liberties Union (ACLU) quickly came to Graham's aid, and after two weeks a Bureau of Immigration board of review dismissed the application on the grounds that the outstanding deportation warrant from 1919 took precedence—regardless of the fact that it could not be executed.[21] Again, Graham proved capable of crisscrossing the United States' borders undetected and, once apprehended on American soil, impossible to remove. Defiant of the authorities, in late 1931 he launched a high-profile cross-country lecture tour that wrapped up in San Francisco in April 1932.

By this time Graham had also established a close relationship with the Italian American followers of Luigi Galleani, whose uncompromising strain of anarchism he found more to his liking than the gradualist and pragmatic approach of most of his fellow Jewish comrades. He contributed English-language articles (under his real name, "Sh. Marcus") to the Galleanisti's main newspaper, L'Adunanta dei Refrattari (Cry of the Refractaries), which also publicized his lectures. When Graham arrived in the Bay Area, therefore, he was presented with an exciting offer by local Italian anarchists: the editorship of a new publication to be produced by San Francisco's own International Group. He immediately accepted, and was soon at the center of the most diverse anarchist community in the United States.

Allison Varzally notes that within California's complex and shifting racial landscape during the interwar years, Jews such as Graham were "closest to a still developing color line" and the most likely of European migrants to form interracial social and political solidarities. Bay Area Italian anarchists also had a rich history of multiethnic organizing that included supporting and struggling alongside Asian and Mexican migrants, and Italian immigrants were themselves stigmatized as "the Chinese of Europe."[22] A common subjection to white supremacy, especially in the form of exclusion and state repression, facilitated these connections between Asians who were "aliens ineligible for citizenship," Mexican "illegals," and immigrant anarchists who under existing statutes were both ineligible for naturalization and illegal aliens. The movement that Graham now joined was therefore based in San Francisco's Latin Quarter of North Beach, but also extended into Chinatown, Berkeley, Oakland, and the Central Valley. Although the Red Scare had broken up many local anarchist groups and deported some of their leading figures, activity had quickly rebounded. In 1921 a Bureau of Investigation agent noted disapprovingly, "There is quite a large colony of [anarchists] in and around the Bay Cities," and in 1927 a visiting anarchist found active Italian, Russian, Jewish, and Chinese groups there.[23]

Italians constituted the largest group, numbering around three hundred in 1930. Most originated from northern Italy and adhered to Luigi Galleani's brand of anarchism. In 1927 they launched their own monthly newspaper, *L'Emancipazione* (Emancipation), and by 1931 the paper was distributing three thousand copies of each issue to over two thousand subscribers.[24] *L'Emancipazione*'s founder and editor was Vincenzo Ferrero, a cook born in 1885 in the northern Italian city of Asti who emigrated to New York in 1905. Although not radical prior to his arrival, Ferrero "immediately plunged into anarchist activity" and relocated to San Francisco before World War I. There he was briefly arrested in 1917 on spurious charges of "vagrancy" after delivering a street corner anticonscription speech, but otherwise emerged from the Red Scare unscathed.[25]

The Gruppo Emancipazione also attracted a new generation of antifascist exiles, including Domenico Sallitto, who belonged to a socialist circle in his native Sicily before leaving in 1920, at age eighteen, to escape Fascist violence. In New York, Sallitto became both a metal worker and an anarchist. He also joined that city's International Group, where he met his American-born wife, Lea, and probably encountered Graham as well. In 1930 Domenico and Lea moved to Oakland, where he found employment as an apricot picker and joined the Gruppo Emancipazione.[26] Ferrero, Sallitto, and the rest of the group were particularly alarmed by the spread of Fascism among Italian Americans, who helped to elect Angelo Rossi, a vocal admirer of Mussolini, as San Francisco's mayor in 1931. *L'Emancipazione* chronicled the crimes of Mussolini's regime, praised attempts against Il Duce's life, and denounced local manifestations of Fascist support. On December 2, 1929, Ferrero was himself arrested with a comrade while trying to disrupt a Fascist demonstration in Berkeley, and in 1932 San Francisco's Italian consul labeled him "without a doubt the worst and most dangerous element among [the] many anarchists residing in this district."[27]

Against Fascist nationalism, Italian anarchists sustained a commitment to "overcoming all race hatred for the solidarity of all peoples, [and] the destruction of all borders: to inaugurate the true and sincere pact of human solidarity." This stance was reflected in practice. Drawing on their own experiences, as well as the model of the International Group of New York, the Gruppo Emancipazione convened a picnic in October 1927 with the purpose of forming a coalition of all the region's anarchists. According to *L'Emancipazione*'s description of the event, "They ate, they sang, they debated. Laughter and voices mingled in the air. The Spanish, Russian, Yiddish, French, Chinese and Italian, instead of the Discord of Babel, seemed to harmonize together." At a more formal gathering in December representatives of Italian, Russian, Polish, Jewish, and Chinese organizations founded the International Group of San Francisco. Within a month a "Mexican group in Berkeley" and "some French-language comrades" had joined, and a handful of Spaniards and Germans followed.[28]

According to Ferrero, "Each national group had its own members but attended picnics and lectures together and worked together in common causes." The Russian anarchists' reading room at 2787 Folsom Street became the "Club Rooms" of the International Group, which were open to the public six evenings a week and hosted monthly "comraderies" with spaghetti, concerts, and dancing. The remarkable cosmopolitan atmosphere of the International Group can be glimpsed in the program for a fundraiser held in April 1933 that included a "three-act play in the Russian language," a "piano solo by Macario Jr.," a "Recitation by S. Menico

[Domenico Sallitto]," "Songs in German and English," and a "Popular Bala-laika Orchestra."[29] Interethnic and interracial bonds were personal as well as political; Chinese member Eddie Wong and Polish Jewish member Bella Friedman, for instance, married after meeting in the group (but only once they had moved to New York, as such marriages were banned under California's antimiscegenation statute until 1948).[30]

Like Graham, members of the International Group had suffered from authorities' renewed post–Red Scare interest in enforcing anarchist exclusion. Chinese-born anarchists, most of them students, had been active in San Francisco's Chinatown since at least 1919; in 1925 they formed Pingshe (The Equality Society) and, in 1927, began publishing the paper *Pingdeng* (Equality) as part of a transpacific Chinese anarchist network.[31] As one of the constituent parts of the International Group, Pingshe was also concerned with local and multiethnic endeavors. In March 1928 two of its members, Chen Shuyao and Cai Xian (who went by the name Liu Zhongshi, or "Jonesie" and "Red Jones" to his non-Chinese comrades), were arrested while handing out English-language leaflets condemning the American government's attempts to deport the Italian antifascist and anarchist Armando Borghi. The men's apartment, which doubled as the offices of *Pingdeng*, was raided, and deportation proceedings were initiated against the pair as alien anarchists. The International Group, however, secured bail for them after a week, and their deportations were canceled after false documents were procured—likely with assistance from comrades—showing that they had been born in the United States.[32] By reinventing themselves as "paper sons" of America, these Chinese anarchists shielded themselves from deportation and, ironically, were therefore able to continue their agitation more openly than ever before.[33]

English increasingly served as the common, if somewhat awkward, tongue of the International Group and its activities. After some hesitation, the Gruppo Emancipazione decided to replace *L'Emancipazione* with an English-language paper controlled by the International Group as whole, and asked Marcus Graham, who had experience with such publications, to become its editor. In January 1933 the first issue of *Man!* appeared, taking its name from the Greek humanist philosopher Protagoras's declaration "Man is the measurement of everything" ("man" being the standard translation of the original genderless term *anthrōpos*, rather than a self-conscious assertion of masculinity). Under Graham's direction *Man!* became one of the preeminent anarchist publications in the country.

Despite his abrasiveness, Graham could also be charismatic. He was "unusually well educated, remarkably well read, and an apparent deep thinker," in the words of one reporter. "With it all, he carries a conviction of sincerity." Most Bay Area anarchists admired his intransigence, though many did not share his more eccentric stances, such as veganism or opposition to industrial machinery. So closely did the politics of the Italian Galleanisti and the new editor align that some critics claimed *Man!* was "an Italian paper with English vocabulary," even though it was edited by a Romanian Jew. Nevertheless, as editor, Graham proved remarkably tolerant of differing opinions, and according to his private correspondence the paper reached "the largest reading circle that any libertarian publication may perhaps ever had."[34]

*Man!* consistently championed revolutionary self-activity, while condemning the rising tide of statism across the world, be it in the form of Fascism, Stalinism, or the welfare state. The New Deal, according to *Man!*, was "nothing but a new lease on life to safely continue an injust [sic] system of life," using "an enormous conscription of public wealth to repair the abysmal cracks made into the private fortunes of the basic capitalistic institutions of the nation."[35] The International Group was divided over the revived labor movement of the 1930s, however. Graham and the followers of Galleani believed that unions served as "a protective barrier against any spontaneous revolution action that may arise from among the exploited toilers," and Graham denounced anarchist union organizers—including Rose Pesotta of the International Ladies' Garment Workers' Union (ILGWU)—for participating in the "fascist scheme" of the National Recovery Act and holding paid union positions.[36] Most of the group's Polish, Russian, and Chinese members by contrast were anarcho-syndicalists and advocates of revolutionary unionism.

Yet they were all united in their rejection of racism; an Italian writer for *Man!* insisted, "The respect of man for man, no matter his descent, is the first requirement of civilization."[37] In addition to the International Group's embrace of Chinese, Mexicans, and other "nonwhites," it also defended the Scottsboro Boys and condemned "the mistreatment and shameful degradation that the Negro of the South is forced to undergo." Recalling his journeys through southern states a few years prior, Marcus Graham wrote of his own feelings of shame, humiliation, and anger that Jim Crow had aroused: "I shall never forget the degrading experiences that I underwent as a white man, at witnessing the mistreatment and shameful degradation that the Negro of the South is forced to undergo." Here Graham categorized himself as unambiguously "white," reflecting a larger shift in interwar Jewish American racial self-identification that reinforced the categories on which Jim Crow was built, but he took no comfort in being granted the "wages of whiteness."[38] Nor did he have a firm claim to these privileges, as the attempt in Arizona to deport him during that journey demonstrated.

Moreover, other immigrant contributors to *Man!* went further in their critiques, such as one who deconstructed "the Racial Myth" by explaining in strikingly modern terms how "race, or more correctly racism, [is] the mystification and exaggeration of the simple fact, that people differ somewhat in the pigment content of their skins or in other small ways."[39] Unlike many American socialists or Italian American syndicalists, most immigrant anarchists were inoculated against popular notions of racial difference due to both their personal experiences and to the influence of European anarchist writers such as Peter Kropotkin, Élisée Reclus, and Gigi Damiani, who celebrated the diversity and essential unity of humankind and strenuously objected to scientific racism.[40]

*Man!*'s antiracist salvos were also responses to Adolf Hitler's rise to power in Germany, which coincided with the paper's appearance. A Jewish contributor proclaimed, "The ideal of Anarchism should be to unite all isolated peoples in one solidified humanity.... Only in this manner can we expect to extirpate the silly egotism which every Nordic idiot carries in his manly chest. And only in this order of society can we ever think of eradicating the racial animosity which every national 'banner' brings upon our stricken world."[41] When fire was allegedly set to the Reichstag building by the Dutch communist Marinus van der Lubbe in February 1933, therefore, *Man!* praised the act. Although Hitler used the arson as a pretext to eliminate his political opposition, Graham interpreted it "as a signal for the German working class to rise against the bloody dictatorship of the Nazis," and believed that by condemning van der Lubbe, Germany's communists and socialists had abandoned a true revolutionist, dampened opposition to the Nazis, and created the conditions for their own repression and the spread of Fascism. In March 1934 the editor challenged the local branches of the Communist Party (CPUSA) and Socialist Party to debate the topic at the San Francisco Labor College.[42]

Graham's timing could not have been worse. In March 1934 the International Longshoremen's Association and San Francisco's shipping indus-

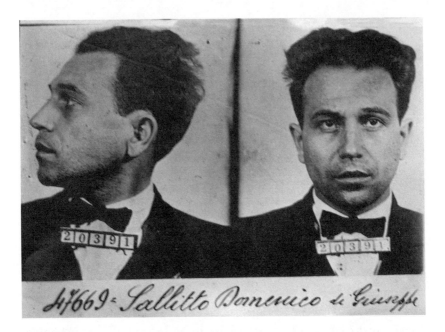

Figure 4.1. Domenico Sallitto, 1934. Archivio Centrale dello Stato, Rome. Courtesy of the Ministero per i Beni e le Attività Culturali.

Figure 4.2. Vincenzo Ferrero, 1934. Archivio Centrale dello Stato, Rome.

try were engaged in intense negotiations, and the threat of a coast-wide dockworkers' strike hung in the air, as did rumors that the impending conflict was a communist plot to foment revolution. It was an inauspicious moment for a public debate on the actions of a self-confessed communist and arsonist. Nevertheless, the event was held on the evening of March 25, with Graham speaking on behalf of the anarchist position. The debate was chaired by Domenico Sallitto, and in the audience was Patrick J. Farrelly, an undercover immigration inspector dispatched by anxious authorities. Two weeks later Farrelly, apparently hesitant to pursue a case against the elusive Graham, took out a warrant for the arrest of Sallitto as an alien anarchist.

The Italian had already fallen on hard times. In 1932 his wife had given birth to a daughter, but succumbed to tuberculosis and died less than two months later. Sallitto and his daughter, Nina, soon had to move in with Vincenzo Ferrero at 1000 Jefferson Avenue in Oakland, where the two men opened a small Italian restaurant. Ferrero cooked, and Sallitto worked as "the salad man" and waiter. The pair never turned a customer away; comrades and workers who were "down and out" were fed regardless of ability to pay, and Sallitto had to supplement his earnings by playing guitar or mandolin at nearby bars. The restaurant also rented out space on its mezzanine level to a distribution company and the offices of *Man!*.[43]

When immigration inspectors raided Sallitto's address on the night of April 11, 1934, therefore, they arrested both him and Ferrero after discovering issues of *L'Emancipazione* and *Man!* in the latter's room. Both men were held for deportation at Angel Island. Within days, foreign-born subscribers to *Man!* across the country were also visited and threatened by agents of the Bureau of Investigation, who "evidently ... obtained the mailing list from the local Post Office." Marcus Graham appealed to the ACLU, and the harassment ceased following a protest lodged with general commissioner of immigration Daniel McCormack. ACLU attorneys also obtained writs of habeas corpus for Ferrero and Sallitto, who were each released on a one-thousand-dollar bond.[44]

Over the next three months San Francisco was rocked by the threatened waterfront strike that in July became a general strike. *Man!* supported the rank-and-file strikers but condemned the unions' "deceitful mis-leaders"—who called off the general strike after four days and advised workers to submit to arbitration—for "selling out" their members. Despite the fact that the longshoremen succeeded in unionizing ports down the entire West Coast, some of San Francisco's anarchists viewed the strike as a wasted opportunity.[45]

The strike also increased local pressure on the Bureau of Immigration. Inspectors opened cases against a number of immigrant strikers, including Australian-born organizer Harry Bridges. Sallitto's attorney discovered, appended to his client's case file, correspondence between the district commissioner of immigration at San Francisco and General Commissioner McCormack in which the local official reported that conservative California newspapers and "civic organizations" had taken an interest in the cases of Ferrero and Sallitto, "and should they succeed in overcoming the order of deportation, we shall have to be prepared to 'take it on the chin' as the publicity will be very much against our department." These letters further noted that San Francisco's Italian consul was "very much interested in the deportation" of the two outspoken antifascists, and that Italy "would be only too glad" to issue passports for their repatriation.[46]

## DEFENDING FERRERO AND SALLITTO

For Ferrero and Sallitto deportation to Italy would have meant certain imprisonment, or worse. Italian legislation passed in 1926 and 1931 made it a crime for Italian citizens abroad to "carry on in foreign countries any activities whatsoever capable of prejudicing national interests," punishable by up to twenty-four years imprisonment and the loss of all civil rights—though the death penalty could be imposed for acts "tending" to incite insurrection.[47] For aid, Sallitto contacted Valerio Isca, a childhood friend from Sicily and anarchist in New York. Isca immediately communicated with New York attorney Isaac Shorr, himself a "ponderous philosophical anarchist" and subscriber to *Man!*, and Carol Weiss King, a crusading civil libertarian who, like Shorr, had a long history of defending immigrant radicals.[48] On the lawyers' advice Ferrero and Sallitto had their cases moved to New York and were transferred to Ellis Island, while comrades in the Bay Area looked after Sallitto's daughter until his case was resolved. Isca also organized the Ferrero-Sallitto Defense Conference and, with the aid of ILGWU organizer Rose Pesotta, arranged for the union to provide the men's bail money.[49]

The case quickly gained national attention. The *New York Post* charged, "It will be murder if the Department of Labor insists on deporting Vincent Ferrero and Domenic Sallitto to Italy," and rallies held in Union Square

and at Chicago's Hull House drew crowds of up to two thousand supporters. With the 1927 executions of the anarchists Sacco and Vanzetti still
fresh in their memories, liberals, unions, radicals, and immigrant rights
groups were eager to defend the two Italians in a clear-cut instance of
political persecution. Branches of the Ferrero-Sallitto Defense Conference
were formed in San Francisco, Chicago, Cleveland, and Philadelphia. Its
most active organizational affiliates were the ACLU and the Communist-
organized American Committee for Protection of Foreign Born (ACPFB),
which retained the services of Shorr and King for the case. The conference
claimed to be "supported by the largest number of trade union locals ever
assembled in a defense conference of this kind," and its union affiliates
included the Artists Union of America, the Women's Trade Union League,
and numerous individual locals belonging to the ILGWU, the Furriers
Union, the United Auto Workers, and the Progressive Miners of America.
The Communists' International Labor Defense joined alongside anti-Communist anarchist and Socialist groups, as well as the Greater New York
Federation of Churches. The conference calculated that its constituent
organizations represented a combined membership of 500,000.[50]

Prominent progressive intellectuals and writers also joined the campaign. One hundred signed their names to a letter of protest that was delivered to secretary of labor Frances Perkins, whose office had the final say
on deportation decisions prior to 1940. The signatories included Sherwood
Anderson, Alice Stone Blackwell, Kenneth Burke, John Dewey, W. E. B.
Du Bois, Max Eastman, Waldo Frank, Granville Hicks, Arthur Gar-
field Hays, Freda Kirchway, Sinclair Lewis, Dorothy Parker, Upton Sinclair, Ida B. Tarbell, Norman Thomas, Mary Heaton Vorse, and Marcus
Graham's personal acquaintances Countee Cullen and Langston Hughes.[51]

The defense campaign did its best to minimize Ferrero and Sallitto's
radicalism. The two anarchists were described only as "workers" or "anti-
fascists," and their supporters cast them as "two confused Italians" who
were hapless victims of antiradical hysteria.[52] Ferrero and Sallitto at times
contributed to these misconceptions; the New York Post quoted Ferrero—
"A slim, worried, bewildered little man"—saying, "As for us being Anarchists! That is silly. We are against Mussolini. We are anti-Fascists, that's
all." Defenders also appealed to the sanctity of family, as Sallitto's deportation and imprisonment would have left his young daughter orphaned.
(Immigration authorities had, in fact, threatened to have Nina placed in
an orphanage if he did not cooperate.)[53]

Additionally, the Ferrero-Sallitto Defense Conference framed its appeal within a strikingly unanarchistic discourse about political asylum and constitutional rights. Civil libertarians Charles Erskine Scott Wood and Sara Bard Fields wrote an open letter to General Commissioner McCormack declaring the entire affair "a disgraceful violation of the principle of political asylum, one of the fundamental principles of the republic." The *Nation* argued, "The law which would make these men liable to deportation should never have been passed and should now be repealed.... The evidence in both cases is so flimsy that they should be dropped on legal grounds; from a humane point of view their continuance is nothing less than brutal." The progressive *Emporia Gazette* agreed, stating that "so long as the right of free speech is guaranteed to disagreeable and objectionable people denouncing the President for his foibles and follies, the right of these rag-tagged and bob-tailed anarchists should be protected in the courts."[54]

This rhetoric of American values fit well within the evolving agendas of both the ACLU and the CPUSA. Although the ACLU had been founded during the Red Scare by radicals who used confrontation and direct action to pressure the courts and government, in the 1930s it altered course and came to view the New Deal government as an important ally.[55] This coincided with the Communist International's official embrace, in 1935, of the Popular Front, during which the CPUSA also supported the New Deal and wrapped itself in the language of patriotism and Americanism.[56] The case therefore appeared to be a quintessential 1930s Popular Front crusade. Beneath the surface, however, the Defense Conference was fraught with conflict.

Its entire approach was predicated on the defendants' legal claim to whiteness and the protections afforded to white immigrant "Americans in waiting." However much these cosmopolitan antifascists despised claims of racial superiority, they nevertheless benefitted from assumptions on the part of both their defenders and the American government that they had a legal right to be treated as members of a privileged white race. Furthermore, these same rights and protections were imparted by a nation-state that Ferrero and Sallitto opposed on principle. For them the state was itself the enemy, not a partner or protector. The International Group had proclaimed, "Only when man shall begin to understand the true functions of the state—[then] this most ferocious of all invented unnatural monsters that preys upon the credulity of deluded mankind will stand revealed as the greatest barrier in the struggle for social emancipation." Before the arrests both *L'Adunata dei Refrattari* and *Man!* had mocked "the great humanitarian" and "'ultra' liberal" Secretary of Labor Perkins for authorizing the repression of strikes and the deportation of immigrants, and afterward Ferrero and Sallitto were portrayed in anarchist accounts as "two victims of persecution instituted by the New Deal."[57] Even while fighting on the legal front, the anarchists utilized their own transnational networks to develop an extralegal contingency plan; in May 1935 "trusted sources" informed Italy's ministero dell'interno that anarchists in Geneva had made arrangements to smuggle Ferrero and Sallitto into France via Spain, should the need arise.[58]

Moreover, the Gruppo Emancipazione and International Group had consistently refused to cooperate with Bay Area Communists, even in the face of a common Fascist enemy. The arrests of Ferrero and Sallitto had, after all, been precipitated by a disagreement between anarchists and Communists, and irreconcilable differences remained, making collaboration difficult. When criticized by a fellow anarchist for working "arm-in-arm with the Stalinists of the League for Protection of the Foreign Born," Ferrero lamely objected, "I do not know if its members belong to political parties, and I never bothered to ask.... The fact remains that I am responsible for my actions and they are responsible of theirs: the compromise, here, is none." *Man!* had also attacked Rose Pesotta and mainstream labor unions, but the Defense Conference relied heavily on the support of both. Meanwhile, the Northern California branch of the ACLU was involved in its own turf war with the local CPUSA branch.[59] In retrospect, it is remarkable that this coalition held together at all.

But the Immigration and Naturalization Service (INS), as the Bureau of Immigration had been renamed in 1933, was also far from monolithic. Within the decentralized structure of the INS suspected violations of immigration law were reported to local immigration inspectors who apprehended and questioned suspects, compiled and considered the evidence against them, and issued rulings. These local inspectors functioned as "'street-level bureaucrats' who became 'de facto policy makers,'" acting largely at their own discretion. During the New Deal they often worked at cross-purposes with the liberal Secretary Perkins and Commissioner McCormack, who did their best to relax deportation enforcement and find loopholes in existing provisions.[60] President Franklin D. Roosevelt, for his part, neither ordered nor approved of deportations on the basis of political radicalism, which he felt were "against the Constitution." However, Perkins had earned the ire of conservatives for her lenient immigration enforcement, and the American Legion "and other patriotic organizations" accused her of "coddling of anarchists, communists and followers of other foreign-born 'isms,'" making specific reference to the Ferrero-Sallitto case. William Randolph Hearst's newspapers also demanded to know why the two anarchists remained in the country.[61] Perkins, under intense scrutiny, was forced to follow the letter, if not the spirit, of the law.

Sallitto's defense strategy also centered on the letter of the law. The entire case against him rested on the testimony of Inspector Farrelly, who claimed that as chairman of the van der Lubbe debate Sallitto had used the phrase "we anarchists." Sallitto's attorneys, however, produced four witnesses who swore that he had said no such thing. This forced Farrelly, who relied entirely on his own "mental notes," to admit that he could not recall the exact words spoken.[62] No additional evidence connecting Sallitto to the International Group or anarchist activity had been presented. Therefore, when a small group of anarchists crashed a dinner attended by Secretary Perkins in New York City, she surprised them by privately advising, "As far as Sallitto is concerned, we have no proof that he is an anarchist, so he will be released and his bail returned. As for Ferrero, we have ample proof that he is an anarchist—he was the editor of an anarchist paper, and so on. My advice is to have him disappear, and we will not look for him. You will lose a thousand dollars [in bail], but it can't be helped." As promised, in January 1938 the INS ruled there was insufficient evidence that Sallitto belonged to an excludable class and canceled his warrant. He had, in effect, "passed" for an acceptable immigrant, and returned to California with Aurora Alleva, an American-born daughter of Italian anarchists and secretary of the Ferrero-Sallitto Defense Conference, who became his lifelong companion. The annual convention of the state's Daughters of the American Revolution responded by passing a petition urging action be taken against Perkins for her unwillingness to deport illegal aliens, including "the cancellation of a warrant of deportation of Vincent [sic] Sallitto, self-admitted anarchist dedicated to the overthrow of our government."[63]

Ferrero's defense, meanwhile, took a novel turn. On December 6, 1937, Brooklyn's Democratic congressman Emanuel Celler, a longtime champion of immigrant rights, introduced House Resolution 8631, "A Bill for the Relief of Vincenzo Ferrero." The brainchild of attorney Carol King, the bill would have bypassed the Anarchist Exclusion Act by authorizing and directing the secretary of labor "to cancel the warrant of arrest and the order of deportation heretofore issued against Vincenzo Ferrero" and establish that "for the purposes of the immigration and naturalization laws, such alien shall be deemed to have been lawfully admitted to the United States for permanent residence as a political refugee." The resolution was referred to the House Committee on Immigration and Naturalization, which heard arguments in February and March of 1938.

On the opening day of hearings Democratic committee chair Samuel Dickstein noted that the committee had received "quite a lot of correspondence from all sections of the country, including Canada, in behalf of Vincenzo Ferrero." Congressman Celler similarly noted that there were "something over a hundred" organizations on record supporting the bill. This did not sway the rabid immigration restrictionist Charles Kramer of California, who argued in favor of Ferrero's deportation before launching into a nativist tirade against "all these aliens working in this country with so many citizens unemployed and on our relief rolls." Other committee members were vexed by Fererro's failure to apply for naturalization. When pressed on the issue, the anarchist replied, "I am under the impression that a man when he is living peacefully and successfully in the community where he is residing, when he respects every other one and is respected, and he tries to help others as much as possible, and he has no request to be helped, but if the help is coming he is grateful, I think that is indeed citizenship of the place where he is living." After further questions on this topic, Ferrero simply insisted, "I am a citizen without papers."[64]

Unimpressed, William R. Poage of Texas charged Ferrero with being "unwilling to assume the obligations of citizenship, although you were willing to take all the benefits for 33 years." Of course, Ferrero never enjoyed "all the benefits of citizenship," not the least being immunity from deportation. Nevertheless, the anarchist's failure to embrace American citizenship marked him in the congressman's eyes as unworthy of potential access to the protections of that citizenship, or even of refugee status—in effect, his failure to capitalize on his presumed legal whiteness put that whiteness and its privileges into question. Oddly, only the rabidly antiradical Republican Noah Mason of Illinois, who within a few months would become a founding member of the House Un-American Activities Committee, came to Ferrero's defense. While admitting the anarchist's "idea of citizenship is a rather peculiar one," he concluded that "if the gentleman himself does not want to assume the obligation of voting but is willing to assume all other obligations of citizenship, I do not know that that should be a reason for deportation."[65] The congressman was evidently oblivious to the radical implications of Ferrero's alternative vision of cosmopolitan citizenship "without papers."

However, committee members implicitly agreed that they could not support the bill if Ferrero actually belonged to an excludable class. The real question they considered, therefore, was whether Ferrero met the legal definition of an anarchist. Emmanuel Celler alleged, "There is no showing anywhere that Vincenzo Ferrero remains an anarchist; that at any time he advocated the use of force or violence either in the spoken word or in his paper." Carol King conceded that her client might be an anarchist, but challenged the well-established precedent that "philosophical anarchists" properly fell within exclusionary statutes, and insisted that Ferrero had never advocated violence. When her client was asked directly if he believed in overthrowing the government by force, Ferrero disingenuously replied, "I believe that force never solved any question and I do not think it ever will." But he refused to deny the broad outline of his anarchist ideals, explaining, "I believe that government should be placed, according to my estimation ... on the individual.... The individual should make his own rules and his own discipline, his own mode, in accordance with everybody else, and everybody else should have the same privilege." He asked, with feigned surprise, "What I describe today [is] anarchy? Well, I must be wrong then."[66]

As the committee deliberated, Ferrero was forced to justify his actions to fellow anarchists. He claimed, "Of the project of the bill, personally, I do not care as I have never cared. It will probably fail, and I hope that it does, so that agitation will be able to resume with moral results that will far exceed material ones, even though I myself may have to leave, which is most likely." As Ferrero predicted, the committee declined to make a recommendation, and the bill never reached the congressional floor. He was once more ordered to report for deportation. Having exhausted every legal and legislative avenue his attorneys could devise, Ferrero took Perkins's advice and disappeared; months later the Defense Conference announced that he had "fled from the United States, and is now a refugee in another country." Ferrero had in fact secretly crossed into Canada, but not too long after smuggled himself back across the border, one of an estimated "several thousand" Europeans to do so annually.[67] He eventually returned to the Bay Area, where his identity and illegal status were successfully kept secret by comrades for the next forty-six years. But the International Group's troubles did not end there.

## THE MAN WITHOUT A COUNTRY

In March 1936, in the midst of the Ferrero-Sallitto case, emboldened immigration inspectors ordered Marcus Graham to report for deportation under his 1919 warrant. Graham complied, but was released after several weeks once officials again found it impossible to proceed. During his incarceration *Man!* continued to appear, secretly edited out of New York by Alleva and Sallitto (at the very same time that the INS was struggling to produce evidence of Sallitto's anarchism!). After his release Graham relocated the paper to Los Angeles, where INS agents once more arrested him on October 6, 1937.[68] Graham was released on bail, and the defense committee that had secured his release in 1930 was reconstituted under the auspices of the Southern California branch of the ACLU as the Marcus Graham Freedom of the Press Committee.

Graham's case attracted a wide range of artists and writers, including many who had campaigned for Ferrero and Sallitto—and, before them, Sacco and Vanzetti. A number were involved with or included in Graham's *Anthology of Revolutionary Poetry*, including Alice Stone Blackwell, Countee Cullen, and Edna St. Vincent Millay (who in 1935 had purchased a subscription to *Man!* and copies of all its back issues). Other committee members included Sherwood Anderson, John Dewey, John Dos Passos, John Haynes Holmes, Dorothy Parker, and Norman Thomas. Radicals and writers in France and Spain also formed branches of the committee. The ACLU, which considered Graham's case one of "the chief issues of national importance pending in the courts," took the lead in his defense.[69]

Missing were the labor unions and Popular Front groups that lined up behind Ferrero and Sallitto; unlike his Italian comrades, Graham continued to openly proclaim his anarchism and his disdain for both union officials and Communists. Moreover, the ACLU framed his defense around First Amendment guarantees of freedom of speech rather than political asylum or immigrant rights. While Graham had little interest in constitutional protections and surely bristled at appeals on his behalf that described him as "a poor and inoffensive idealist,"[70] his disdain for the law made him a willing if cynical accomplice to the ACLU's mission to protect unpopular speech.

The INS meanwhile employed a new strategy, subpoenaing Graham to appear in district court on January 13, 1938, to "produce his birth certificate and his passports for entry into the United States," and to answer questions put to him by an immigration inspector "touching on his birthplace, his entry into the United States, his citizenship and his right to be and remain in the United States." Graham reported as ordered but refused to answer any questions, and was charged with contempt of court. The next day his contempt case was heard before the liberal district court judge Leon R. Yankwich. Graham's ACLU attorney argued that the Fifth Amendment protected Graham from giving testimony that might incriminate him, but Yankwich ruled that such protections did not apply to deportation proceedings, which were civil rather than criminal proceedings. Yankwich therefore found Graham guilty of contempt, but allowed him to make his defiant statement to the court quoted at the opening of this chapter. The judge then sentenced Graham to six months in the Orange County Jail, "where," a reporter noted, "mysteriously, the jailers apparently had the problem all solved by listing Graham's birthplace, correctly or incorrectly, as Canada."[71]

Graham was released on bond pending appeal, and in October the Ninth Circuit Court of Appeals partially reversed Yankwich's finding. Establishing an important precedent, it found that "the fact that deportation proceedings are civil in their nature does not prevent the privilege against self incrimination from being raised by a witness called upon to testify therein." However, it also ruled that only questions capable of soliciting incriminating answers fell under this protection. Graham's case was therefore referred back to the lower court, which was directed to determine which questions Graham might answer that would not "tend to incriminate him."[72] On June 26, 1939, Graham's rehearing came before Yankwich, but the ACLU requested that it be reassigned to another judge on the grounds that Yankwich was prejudiced against its client. The judge testily responded, "I'm tired of being harassed and threatened over this case!" He then stood and "flung the entire file of the case toward the lawyer and angrily ordered the case transferred forthwith." Another judge heard the case that afternoon, and ruled that Graham could answer questions regarding his place of birth, citizenship status, and "true and correct name," among others. Graham again refused to comply, was again ruled in contempt, and was again released on bond pending appeal. The *Oakland Tribune* ran the story under the headline "'Man Without a Country' Still Evades Deportation."[73]

When Graham's appeal was heard in June 1940, federal officials still wrongly believed that Graham was "a native of Russia," but they understandably lacked evidence to convince the courts of this, and the anarchist's "sphinx-like attitude" continued to frustrate their efforts. After the case was once more referred back to the lower court and the contempt charges were once more appealed, the Ninth Circuit Court ruled against Graham and he was forced to serve the six-month sentence. Nonetheless, his resistance had finally broken the will of immigration authorities; in 1941 the ACLU noted that the "deportation order of twenty years' standing, brought against an alleged anarchist, Marcus Graham, ... has apparently been suspended," and the case was never revived.[74]

Just as Graham was securing his freedom for the final time, he was dismayed to discover that, having gone through nine printers over the previous seven years, he could not find an establishment still willing to print *Man!* and had to suspend the publication. Ever the rebel, he confided to a friend, "I need hardly relate to you how I feel about this—but we are proud to go down with our colors flying [in] defiance to everything that is unjust and untrue."[75] The paper's closure was cold comfort for the immigration officials who had pursued Graham for more than two decades, however. They never overcame the confounding obstacle of a man who, by refusing to reveal his birthplace, became functionally stateless. Graham thus lived up to *Man!*'s claim that its editor was "a man without a country—and truly so, since the entire world is the only country he recognizes as his, and also that of every human being."[76]

Ironically, unbeknownst to both him and the US government, Graham—or rather, Shmuel Marcus—had been made quite literally stateless when in March 1938 the anti-Semitic government of his native Romania revoked the citizenship of some 270,000 Romanian Jews.[77] However, Graham had preemptively countered Romania's use of statelessness as an instrument of racial terror and genocide through his own positive assertion of a radical statelessness. By renouncing his "right to have rights" as a citizen of a nation-state, Graham actually empowered himself and prevented the United States from purging itself of the triple threat that he posed as an illegal alien, a racially suspect Jew, and an anarchist.

Not wanting to invite yet more arrests, Graham began living semiclandestinely. He remained in California—aside from a period in the 1970s when he resided in England under the name Frank Smith, evidently having obtained a false passport—among a small group of aging Italian anarchists in Los Gatos, and continued to contribute to American and British anarchist publications up until his death in 1985.[78] Vincenzo Ferrero died that same year at the age of one hundred, having likewise lived underground in Los Gatos, where he was known simply as "John the Cook."[79] Domenico Sallitto and Aurora Alleva also resided in Los Gatos, where, to avoid future harassment, Sallitto opted to apply for naturalization after World War II—which he could obtain only by falsely swearing he was not an anarchist. However, Patrick Farrelly, the immigration inspector who had attended the 1933 van der Lubbe debate, intervened to halt the application. Repeated attempts and appeals, undertaken with the aid of the ACLU, finally succeeded in bestowing American citizenship upon Sallitto in 1954, and he and Alleva continued to participate in the Bay Area's anarchist movement and the ACLU before passing away in 1991 and 1992, respectively.[80]

Ferrero, Sallitto, and Graham, like their Chinese comrades Chen Shuyao and Cai Xian before them, all successfully negated the American state's claims to sovereignty and territoriality. Ferrero became one of millions of illegal immigrants who exploited the permeability of theoretically inviolable national borders, even after his deportation had been ordered. Sallitto capitalized on authorities' deficient intelligence capabilities to avoid deportation and then to obtain rights and protections that legally should have been denied him, even as they were belatedly being extended to Asian migrants during and after World War II: the anticitizen posing as citizen. Conversely, by attaining the anarchists' ideal of statelessness, Graham rendered the state virtually powerless to act against him. Though they pursued different strategies, each man remained defiantly within, but not of, the nation.

1    "Court Hears Anarchist," *Los Angeles Times*, January 15, 1938; *Freedom of Thought Arraigned: Four Year Persecution of "MAN!"* (Los Angeles: Marcus Graham Freedom of the Press Committee, 1939), 15–18; "'Red,' Jailed, Has His Joke," *Oakland Tribune*, January 15, 1938.

2    Hannah Arendt, *The Origins of Totalitarianism*, rev. ed. (New York: Harcourt, 1968), 269–90; Coco Fusco, "Stateless Hybrids: An Introduction," in *The Hybrid State Films*, ed. Papo Colo and Coco Fusco (New York: Exit Art, 1991), n.p. On "anticitizens," see David R. Roediger, *The Wages of Whiteness: Race and the Making of the American Working Class*, rev. ed. (New York: Verso, 1999), 57.

3    Roediger, *Wages of Whiteness*; James R. Barrett and David R. Roediger, "Inbetween Peoples: Race, Nationality and the 'New Immigrant' Working Class," *Journal of American Ethnic History* 16, no. 3 (Spring 1997): 3–44; Matthew Frye Jacobson, *Whiteness of a Different Color: European Immigrants, and the Alchemy of Race* (Cambridge, MA: Harvard University Press, 1998); Thomas A. Guglielmo, *White on Arrival: Italians, Race, Color, and Power in Chicago, 1890–1945* (New York: Oxford University Press, 2003); Mae M. Ngai, *Impossible Subjects: Illegal Aliens and the Making of Modern America* (Princeton: Princeton University Press, 2004); David R. Roediger, *Working Toward Whiteness: How America's Immigrants Became White; The Strange Journey from Ellis Island to the Suburbs* (New York: Basic Books, 2005).

4    James C. Scott, *The Art of Not Being Governed: An Anarchist History of Upland South Asia* (New York: Yale University Press, 2009), x.

5    Marcus Graham, "Autobiographical Note," in *MAN!: An Anthology of Anarchist Ideas, Essays, Poetry, and Commentaries*, ed. Marcus Graham (London: Cienfuegos Press, 1974), vii–xii; M. D. Davis, "In Re: Robert Parsons," July 15, 1919, and G. J. Crystal, "Robert Parsons," April 19, 1919, File 359916, Old German Files (hereafter OG), Records of the Federal Bureau of Investigation, Record Group 65, National Archives and Records Administration (hereafter FBI); *The Anarchist Soviet Bulletin*, April 1919; "To You Workers of America Colored or White," circular, n.d. [1919], File 8000-357986, OG, FBI.

6    G. J. Crystal, "Robert Parsons," April 19 and April 21, 1919, File 359916, OG, FBI; Richard Polenberg, *Fighting Faiths: The Abrams Case, the Supreme Court, and Free Speech* (New York: Penguin, 1987).

7    M. D. Davis, "In Re: Robert Parsons," July 15, 1919, File 359916, OG, FBI; V. J. Valjavec, "In Re: Robert Parsons—Anarchist Activities," March 10, 1921, File 203991, OG, FBI.

8    Graham, "Autobiographical Note," xii–xvi. On the Councils of Action, see Stephen White, "Labour's Council of Action 1920," *Journal of Contemporary History* 9, no. 4 (Oct. 1974): 99–122.

9    Graham, "Autobiographical Note," xii–xv; "Charges Police Beat Him," *New York Times*, February 27, 1921.

10   V. J. Valjavec, "In Re: Robert Parsons," March 10, 1921, File 203991, OG, FBI; "An Open Letter to the Russian Premier Lenin," *Free Society*, December 1921; Graham, "Autobiographical Note," xiii.

11   Jane Perry Clark, *Deportation of Aliens from the United States to Europe* (New York: Columbia University Press, 1931), 215–31.

12   Ngai, *Impossible Subjects*; Dan Kanstroom, *Deportation Nation: Outsiders in American History* (Cambridge, MA: Harvard University Press, 2007); Linda K. Kerber, "The Stateless as the Citizen's Other: A View from the United States," *The American Historical Review* 112, no. 1 (Feb. 2007): 1–34; Rachel Ida Buff, "The Deportation Terror," *American Quarterly* 60, no. 3 (Sept. 2008): 523–51.

13   Erika Lee, *At America's Gates: Chinese Immigration during the Exclusion Era, 1882–1943* (Chapel Hill: University of North Carolina Press, 2003); Ngai, *Impossible Subjects*; Barrett and Roediger, "Inbetween Peoples"; Jacobson, *Whiteness of a Different Color*; Karen Brodkin, *How Jews Became White Folks, and What That Says About Race in Amer-*

*ica* (New Brunswick, NJ: Rutgers University Press, 1998); Jennifer Guglielmo and Salvatore Salerno, eds., *Are Italians White? How Race Is Made in America* (New York: Routledge, 2003); Guglielmo, *White on Arrival*; Roediger, *Working Toward Whiteness*; Eric L. Goldstein, *The Price of Whiteness: Jews, Race, and American Identity* (Princeton: Princeton University Press, 2006); John Higham, *Strangers in the Land: Patterns of American Nativism, 1860–1925* (New Brunswick: Rutgers University Press, 1955), 138 (quote).

14  Lauren L. Basson, *White Enough to Be American? Race Mixing, Indigenous People, and the Boundaries of State and Nation* (Chapel Hill: University of North Carolina Press, 2008), 143; Nathaniel Hong, "Constructing the Anarchist Beast in American Periodical Literature, 1880–1903," *Critical Studies in Mass Communication*, no. 9 (1992): 121–23; Cesare Lombroso, *Gli Anarchici* (1894; reprint, Millwood: Kraus Reprint, 1983); Stefan Kühl, *The Nazi Connection: Eugenics, American Racism, and German National Socialism* (New York: Oxford University Press, 1994), 70–71.

15  United States Congress, House of Representatives, Committee on Rules, *Attorney General A. Mitchell Palmer on Charges Made Against Department of Justice by Louis F. Post and Others* (Washington, DC: Government Printing Office, 1920), 26–27; Higham, *Strangers in the Land*, 220; Kate Holladay Claghorn, *The Immigrant's Day in Court* (New York: Harper & Brothers, 1923), 453–60.

16  See Kenyon Zimmer, "'The Whole World Is Our Country': Immigration and Anarchism in the United States, 1885–1940" (PhD diss., University of Pittsburgh, 2010), 331–32.

17  Ngai, *Impossible Subjects*, chap. 1; Roediger, *Working Toward Whiteness*, 139–45.

18  Joseph J. Cohen, *Di yidish-anarkhistishe bavegung in Amerike: Historisher iberblik un perzenlekhe iberlebungen* (Philadelphia: Radical Library, Branch 273 Arbeter Ring, 1945), 393; Hippolyte Havel to [T. L. Miles], November 13, 1925, Folder 6, Fraye Arbayter Shtime Archive, International Institute of Social History, Amsterdam, The Netherlands (hereafter IISH).

19  Ralph Cheyney and Lucia Trent, introduction to Marcus Graham, ed., *An Anthology of Revolutionary Poetry* (New York: The Active Press, 1929), 38. On the Rebel Poets, see Douglas Wixson, *Worker-Writer in America: Jack Conroy and the Tradition of Midwestern Literary Radicalism, 1898–1990* (Chicago: University of Illinois Press, 1998).

20  James Edward Smethurst, *The New Red Negro: The Literary Left and African American Poetry, 1930–1946* (Oxford: Oxford University Press, 1999), 217n11, 20; "New Langston Hughes Poems," *African American Studies at Beinecke Library*, February 12, 2009, http://beineckejwj.library.yale.edu/2009/02/12/langston-hughes-poems/ (accessed October 30, 2011).

21  Marcus Graham to Max Nettlau, May 10, 1930, Folder 502, Max Nettlau Papers, IISH; *Freedom of Thought Arraigned*, 15; "Cancel Warrant to Deport Canada Poet," *Bakersfield Californian*, November 11, 1930.

22  Allison Varzally, *Making a Non-White America: Californians Coloring Outside Ethnic Lines, 1925–1955* (Berkeley: University of California Press, 2008), 5, passim; Zimmer, "The Whole World Is Our Country," chap. 4; Donna Gabaccia, "The 'Yellow Peril' and the 'Chinese of Europe': Global Perspectives on Race and Labor, 1815–1930," in *Migra-*

*tion, Migration History, History: Old Paradigms and New Perspectives*, ed. Jan Lucassen and Leo Lucassen (New York: Peter Lang, 1997), 177–96.

23    Report of Edw. P. Morse, April 23, 1921, File 202600-1687-1, Bureau Section Files, FBI; Joseph Spivak, "Our Organized Movement," *The Road to Freedom*, October 1927.

24    Anthony Martocchia and Philip Lamantia interview, October 31, 1982, Oral History of the American Left, Robert F. Wagner Labor Archives, Tamiment Library, New York University; R. De Rango, "Ai Compagni," *L'Emancipazione*, March 1931.

25    Vincenzo Ferrero File, Busta 2034, Casellario Politico Centrale, Archivio Centrale dello Stato, Rome (hereafter CPC); Paul Avrich, *Anarchist Voices: An Oral History of Anarchism in America* (Princeton University Press, 1995), 163; Aurora Sallitto interview, January 1992, cassette tape, IISH.

26    Domenico Sallitto File, Busta 4537, CPC; Aurora Sallitto interview, IISH; David Koven, "An Anarchist Life: Domenic Sallitto, 1902–1991," manuscript, 1992, 1–2, Folder 137, David Koven Papers, IISH.

27    "Corrispondenze," *Il Martello*, December 21, 1929; Ferrero File, CPC.

28    Nino Napoletano, "Internazzionalizmo," *L'Emancipazione*, July–August 1931; "Cronaca Locale," *L'Emancipazione*, November 1927; R. P., "Cronaca del Movimento Locale," *L'Emancipazione*, December 1927; "Comunicati e Corrispondenze," *L'Emancipazione*, January 1928; Avrich, *Anarchist Voices*, 163.

29    Ibid.; "Comunicazioni," *L'Adunata dei Refrattari*, March 18 and August 19, 1933; *Man!*, March 1933 and April 1933.

30    Avrich, *Anarchist Voices*, 410.

31    R. Tong, "The Chinese Anarchist Movement in U. S. A.," *Man!*, August–September 1933; Him Mark Lai, "Anarchism, Communism, and China's Nationalist Revolution," in *Chinese American Transnational Politics* (Chicago: University of Illinois Press, 2010), 58–60; Jane Mee Wong, "Pingshe: Retrieving an Asian American Anarchist Tradition," *Amerasia Journal* 34, no. 1 (2008): 133–51.

32    "Cronaca del Movimento Locale," *L'Emancipazione*, April 1928 and May 1928; Tong, "Chinese Anarchist Movement"; Lai, "Anarchism," 60, 172n33; Avrich, *Anarchist Voices*, 165.

33    On "paper sons," see Lee, *At America's Gates*, 194–207. On noncitizen Asian radicals' difficulties, see Josephine Fowler, *Japanese and Chinese Immigrant Activists: Organizing in American and International Communist Movements, 1919–1933* (New Brunswick, NJ: Rutgers University Press, 2007).

34    "Self-Admitted Anarchist Who Carried No Bombs Tells Yacht Club Mooney, Billings Innocent," *Albuquerque Journal*, March 26, 1932; Slovak [Alfred G. Sanftleben], "Carbon Monoxide," *Man!*, March 1934; M. G. to A. I. [Agnes Inglis], December 30, 1935, Box 4, Agnes Inglis Papers (hereafter Inglis Papers), Joseph A. Labadie Collection, Harlan Hatcher Graduate Library, University of Michigan, Ann Arbor (hereafter Labadie).

35    "What Could Be Done?" *Man!*, July 1933; Melchior Seele [Raffaele Schiavina], "A New Deal?" *Man!*, January 1934.

36    "Anarchists and the Labor Movement," *Man!*, January 1934.

37    M. S. [Raffaele Schiavina], "The Problem of Minorities," *Man!*, June 1939.

38    "The Scottsboro Case of Injustice," *Man!*, May 1935. On Jews and other immigrants "learning whiteness," see Brodkin, *How Jews Became White Folks*; Goldstein, *The Price of Whiteness*; Jacobson, *Whiteness of a Different Color*; Guglielmo, *White on Arrival*; Roediger, *Working Toward Whiteness*; Robert M. Zecker, *Race and America's Immigrant Press: How the Slovaks Were Taught to Think Like White People* (New York: Continuum, 2011).

39    Dr. J. Globus, "The Racial Myth and Internationalism," *Man!*, August 1934.

40    See, for instance, Peter Kropotkin, "What Geography Ought to Be," *The Nineteenth Century* 18 (1885): 949–56; John P. Clark and Camille Martin, eds., *Anarchy, Geography, Modernity: The Radical Social Thought of Elisée Reclus* (Lanham, MD: Lexington Books, 2004), 100–102; Gigi Damiani, *Razzismo e Anarchismo* (Newark, NJ: Biblioteca L'Adunata dei Refrattari, 1938). On socialist and syndicalist views of race, see Mark Pittenger, *American Socialists and Evolutionary Thought, 1870–1920* (Madison: University of Wisconsin Press, 1993), chap. 9; Michael Miller Topp, *Those Without a Country: The Political Culture of Italian American Syndicalists* (Minneapolis: University of Minnesota Press, 2001).

41    Samuel Polinow, "Anarchism and the National Spirit," *Man!*, April 1933.

42    "The Burning of the Reichstag Trial," *Man!*, October 1933; Melchior Seele [Raffaele Schiavina], "Marinus Van Der Lubbe," *Man!*, November 1933; M. G., "The Vindication of a Revolutionist," *Man!*, December 1933; Marcus Graham, "The Role of the Socialists and Communists in the Assassination of a Revolutionist," *Man!*, February 1934; "An Open Challenge to Debate," *Man!*, March, 1934.

43    Koven, "An Anarchist Life," 2; "Comunicati," *L'Adunata dei Refrattari*, July 16, 1932; Auora Sallitto interview, IISH.

44    "Government's Foul Conspiracy to Destroy Man!," *Man!*, May 1934; *Freedom of Thought Arraigned*, 3–4; *Fight against Deportation: Free Ferrero and Sallitto* (New York: Ferrero-Sallitto Defense Conference, 1936), 5; "Freedom of Thought and Expression on Trial," *Man!*, April 1935.

45    Marcus Graham, "Was There a General Strike?" *Man!*, August 1934; Eolo, "Lo Sciopero Generale di San Francisco," *L'Adunata dei Refrattari*, July 28, 1934.

46    *Fight against Deportation*, 9–11.

47    Nathaniel Cantor, "The Fascist Political Prisoners," *Journal of Criminal Law and Criminology* 27, no. 2 (July–Aug. 1936): 169–79.

48    Ann Fagan Ginger, *Carol Weiss King: Human Rights Lawyer, 1895–1952* (Niwot: University Press of Colorado, 1993), passim (quote on 11).

49    Avrich, *Anarchist Voices*, 147–48; Koven, "An Anarchist Life," 4.

50    "Will It Be Murder?" *New York Post*, December 27, 1935; *Man!*, July–August 1935; "Comunicazioni," *L'Adunata dei Refrattari*, September 14, 1935; "Court of Appeals to Hear Sallitto's Case," n.d. [1936], in "Anarchism—Deportations and Raids—Ferrero-Sallitto Defense Conference," Subject Vertical File (hereafter SVF), Labadie.

51    Ferrero-Sallitto Defense Conference, press releases, January [1936?] and September [1937], in "Anarchism —Deportations and Raids —Ferrero-Sallitto Defense Conference," SVF, Labadie.

52    See, for instance, "End of a Four-Year Fight," *Coshocton Tribune*, February 7, 1938.

53    "30 Years in U.S., Italian Must Go," *New York Post*, December 27, 1935; Koven, "An Anarchist Life," 4.

54    *New York Post*, November 30, 1936; "The Shape of Things," *The Nation*, November 13, 1937, 519; "A Heaven-Sent Chance," *Emporia Gazette*, July 11, 1935.

55    Judy Kutulas, *The American Civil Liberties Union and the Making of Modern Liberalism, 1930–1960* (Chapel Hill: University of North Carolina Press, 2006).

56    Harvey Klehr, *The Heyday of American Communism: The Depression Decade* (New York: Basic Books, 1984); Fraser M. Ottanelli, *The Communist Party of the United States: From the Depression to World War II* (New Brunswick, NJ: Rutgers University Press, 1991).

57    Hiroshi Motomura, *Americans in Waiting: The Lost Story of Immigration and Citizenship in the United States* (New York: Oxford University Press, 2007); "The State," *Man!*, January 1933 (emphasis in original); "Cronache Sovversive," *L'Adunata dei Refrattari*, September 16, 1933; Harold Preece, "A Capitalistic Government at Work," *Man!*, January 1934; "Under the Reign of the Iron Heel—Government," *Man!*, February 1934; "Comunicazioni," *L'Adunata dei Refrattari*, December 7, 1935.

58    Sallitto File, CPC.

59    Carlo Tresca, "Ho Pestata la Coda ad una Biscia," *Il Martello*, May 2, 1939; Kutulas, *American Civil Liberties Union*, 53–54.

60    Clark, *Deportation of Aliens*, chap. 8–12; Lee, *At America's Gates*, 48; Ngai, *Impossible Subjects*, 82–86.

61    Charles P. Larrowe, *Harry Bridges: The Rise and Fall of Radical Labor in the United States*, 2nd rev. ed. (Westport, CT: Lawrence Hill & Company, 1977), 138; Elizabeth Dilling, *The Roosevelt Red Record and Its Background* (Chicago: The Author, 1936), 149; "The Shape of Things," *The Nation*, November 28, 1936, 619.

62    See Motion for Leave to File Brief as Amici Curiae and Brief in Support of Thereof, *United States of America ex rel. Domenic Sallitto, Appellant, v. Commissioner of Immigration, Ellis Island, New York Harbor*, 85 F.2d 1021 (2d Cir 1936), in case file "Sallitto, Domenick," American Committee for Protection of Foreign Born Papers, Labadie.

63    Avrich, *Anarchist Voices*, 148; "Anti-Perkins Move Applauded," *Los Angeles Times*, March 11, 1938.

64    *HR 8631: A Bill for the Relief of Vincenzo Ferrero*, 75th Cong., 2d Sess., 1938, unpublished US House of Representatives Committee Hearings, 75 HIm-T.107 and 75 HIm-T.108 (Bethesda: Congressional Information Service, 1988), 8, 16, 49–50, 31–32.

65    Ibid., 35, 37–39.

66    Ibid., 5, 31, 39, 41.

67    Tresca, "Ho Pestata la Coda ad una Biscia"; "Former Oaklander Is Refugee Abroad," *Oakland Tribune*, October 20, 1939; Lee, *At America's Gates*, 170.

68    *Freedom of Thought Arraigned*, 3, 9; "In Retrospect of Current Events: A Statement of Facts," *Man!*, August–September 1936; Graham, "Autobiographical Note," xxi; "U.S. Government Raids 'Man!' and Jails Editor," *Man!*, October 1937; MG to "Dear Friend," October 20, 1937, box 4, Inglis Papers.

69    *Man!*, June 1935; *Pour la liberté de pensée violée* (N.p. [Nîmes?]: Marcus Graham Freedom of the Press Committee, Section française, n.d. [1939]); D. Alonso to Marcus

Graham, n.d., Marcus Graham Papers, Labadie; American Civil Liberties Union, *Eternal Vigilance! The Story of Civil Liberty, 1937–1938* (New York: American Civil Liberties Union, 1938), 15.

70    *New York Post*, January 11, 1938.

71    "Editor Found in Contempt," *Los Angeles Times*, January 14, 1938; *United States v. Parson*, 22 F. Supp. 149 (SD Cal 1938); "'Red,' Jailed, Has His Joke."

72    *Graham v. United States*, 99 F.2d 746 (9th Cir 1938).

73    "Editor Held in Contempt," *Los Angeles Times*, June 27, 1939; *Oakland Tribune*, June 27, 1939.

74    *Graham v. United States*, 112 F.2d 907 (9th Cir 1940); "Silence about Birth Thwarts His Deportation," *San Francisco Chronicle*, June 7, 1940; "A 'Philosophical Anarchist' Gets 6 Months in Jug," *San Francisco Chronicle*, June 23, 1940; *Annual Report—American Civil Liberties Union*, 1941, 42.

75    M G to Comrade Inglis, June 8, 1940, and [Marcus Graham] to Dear Friend, n.d. [1940], box 4, Inglis Papers.

76    "Government's Foul Conspiracy to Destroy Man!" *Man!*, May 1934.

77    Joshua Starr, "Jewish Citizenship in Rumania (1878–1940)," *Jewish Social Studies* 3, no. 1 (Jan. 1941): 57–80.

78    Barry Pateman, correspondence with the author, April 23, 2011; Avrich, *Anarchist Voices*, 488n110.

79    Paolo Finzi, "Ricordando John, Cioè Vincenzo," *Bollettino Archivio G. Pinelli*, no. 32 (Dec. 2008): 39.

80    Elaine Elinson and Stan Yogi, "Immigrants Faced Deportation for Political Activity," *Wherever There's a Fight: How Runaway Slaves, Suffragists, Immigrants, Strikers, and Poets Shaped Civil Liberties in California*, 2009, http://www.whereveretheresafight.com/additional_stories/immigrants_faced_deportation_for_political_activity (accessed April 19, 2011); Koven, "An Anarchist Life," 4–6.

# 5

# Relief and Revolution

## Southern California Struggles against Unemployment in the 1930s

CHRISTINA HEATHERTON

Arise, you prisoners of starvation!
Arise, you wretched of the earth!

—The Internationale

¡Arriba, parias de la Tierra!
¡En pie, famélica legion!

—La International

THE WOMEN IN THE JAIL CELL WERE SINGING. THE JAIL, A DUSTY FACILITY in the farming town of Brawley, California, twenty-five miles north of the Mexican border, was full of striking lettuce pickers, their wives, and supporters. Crammed together in the women's section were a number of Mexican women who had been arrested in the strike, and one brassy white teenager. The teen couldn't speak Spanish, because, as she later recalled, "I'm a backward, stupid, provincial Anglo." To pass the time, the women taught each other songs. The teenager, Dorothy Healey, a Communist organizer from Los Angeles, tried teaching the women radical labor songs. The women, "part of that generation of Mexicans who had grown up with the Mexican Revolution," bested the young organizer. In Spanish, they sang the "Internationale," a song that commanded the "prisoners of starvation" and the *parias de la Tierra*, "wretched of the earth," to arise. In the early 1930s, this song was still an anthem that socialists, anarchists, communists, and fellow travelers alike—all those desiring an end to exploitation—could sing together. This song, remembered Healey, "bridged all the countries of the world." The women, who had lived through the Mexican Revolution, a struggle variously derided as the chaos of an underdeveloped nation and also praised as the first social revolution of the twentieth century, knew the lyrics well.[1]

Brawley, a small town in the Imperial Valley, was one of many rural California areas on fire in the early years of the Depression. In 1933, a year before general strikes would rock docks, mines, mills, and shop floors across the country, California's fields exploded in labor rebellions. Santa Clara cherry pickers, Lodi grape cutters, Yolo County orchard pruners, and Oxnard sugar beet workers, among others—close to fifty thousand workers in total—went on strike, accounting for half of all US farm worker strikes that year. In the largest single strike in agricultural history to that date, over eighteen thousand workers walked away from the cotton fields across the San Joaquin Valley. Spanning over one hundred miles, and affecting 65 percent of the state's crops, these thirty-seven strikes represented an unprecedented insurgency in the California fields.[2]

Farm workers fought for a closed shop, better wages, and union-controlled hiring, demands consistent with the industrial strikes of the period. While they faced conditions similar to those of industrial workers, California's farm workers were violently disciplined by forces such as racism, incarceration, deportation, and the uneven dispensing of local, state, and federal relief. The sustained vulnerability of farm workers was a key feature of this labor regime. For it to function, a floating reserve army of labor, available for work during harvests and subject to deportation or arrest during growing seasons, was required continuously. Of this situation, writer Carey McWilliams noted that "labor is an unemployed pool available on call, much in the manner of water or electricity." It was against these conditions that farm workers and their families and allies rebelled.[3]

In December 1933, striking lettuce workers in the Imperial Valley traveled two hundred miles northwest to Los Angeles to seek organizing aid from the Communist Party (CP). Given that the Party had assisted farm workers in the majority of strikes across the state that year (twenty-four out of thirty-seven) and had also participated in earlier Imperial Valley strikes, it was not surprising that the lettuce workers again sought its assistance. Dorothy Healey agreed to accompany the striking workers. In driving the long highway between Los Angeles and the Imperial Valley, the group traced an urban-rural continuum across the capitalist landscape, where migratory workers, crops, and capital moved in symbiotic circulation. For Los Angeles–based entities such as the new Bank of America, the Los Angeles Chamber of Commerce, and members of the Los Angeles Police Department, it was a path well trod. Throngs of migrant workers also made this trek after harvest seasons. As Carlos Bulosan would write of Filipino migrant workers like himself, "All roads go to California and all travelers wind up in Los Angeles."[4]

Before joining the lettuce workers, Dorothy Healey had been a leader in the Los Angeles Unemployed Councils, a CP-led project that organized unemployed workers for relief long before the New Deal promised any such federal provisions. In leaving the unemployed movement in Los Angeles to assist the strikers in the fields, Healey had unwittingly joined the forefront of a shared struggle. In rural areas like the Imperial Valley, workers were striking. In Los Angeles, unemployed workers were being thrown off of relief rolls and often coerced into working in the fields as scabs to break strikes. In such ways, the state's management of relief turned workers against one another across the urban-rural divide. Confronting these conditions required the nimble capacity to organize farm workers in the fields alongside unemployed workers in the city. During the Depression, such an organizational structure was provided by the CP and utilized by workers from revolutionary and anti-imperialist traditions, in particular, a Mexican revolutionary tradition.

The revolutionary struggle for relief in southern California during the Great Depression effectively connected organizing efforts across the capitalist landscape. Between the Unemployed Councils in Los Angeles and the agricultural strikes in places like the Imperial Valley, the struggle represented a distinct convergence of antiracist, Marxist, and Mexican revolutionary traditions. Organized resistance to capitalism was, of course, not new to the Mexican working class. Many of the Mexican and Mexican American workers had been influenced by extended confrontations with US capital during the Mexican Revolution.[5] They subsequently brought strategies, tactics, and militancy to the revolutionary struggle for relief and against repression in California in the early years of the Great Depression.

The struggle for relief by Mexican workers in the fields and unemployed workers in the city was a regional confrontation with class power. In the struggle, relief took material, ideological, and strategic forms. Relief was sought in the forms of unemployment insurance, food aid, and rent supplements, as well as expenditures for heat, education, and subsistence. It allowed workers to reproduce their lives and labor and also gave them a material base from which to challenge the exploitation of their labor. Through provisions of relief, workers were able to extend their strikes, press for better wages, and enhance their bargaining power for improved working conditions. This working-class struggle for relief also promoted a collective consciousness, wherein a radical redistribution of resources supplanted individualized notions of success and failure. Conversely, in the hands of growers and the region's capitalists, relief had a different meaning: it could be strategically denied or supplied to break strikes, damage workers' leverage, coerce labor, provoke police repression, or trigger deportation efforts. Encompassing multiple geographical and political dimensions, the struggle for relief revealed and represented a radical internationalist movement to confront racism and capitalism on different scales and fronts.

RELIEF AND THE OPEN SHOP

A coalescence of regional, national, and international capitalist interests significantly shaped southern California's landscape. While successful organizing in heavily unionized coastal cities such as Portland, Seattle, and San Francisco had achieved higher wages and improved labor conditions for the working class, capitalists envisioned Los Angeles as an industrial city that would buck the red trend on the Pacific coast. By the 1920s, major industrialists such as Harrison Gray Otis and Henry Ford, as well as the heads of Firestone, Bethlehem Steel, and Proctor and Gamble, devised plans to maximize the efficiency of production and diminish barriers to capital accumulation in the region. Their plans stressed strident antiunionism, low taxes, and strong police departments, all central elements to establishing and maintaining a racialized labor regime. Companies such as Goodrich Rubber, Continental Can, Pittsburgh Plate Glass, Willard Storage Battery, American Maize Products, and US Steel further contributed to the surge of capitalist investment in Los Angeles. In turn, the city's industrial capacity grew faster than that of any other area of the country in the 1920s. While these businesses fiercely competed against one another, they were willing to organize together to maintain the one thing that had brought them to the Golden State: a cheap, unorganized, racialized, and terrorized labor force, with a large segment permanently unemployed to depress wages and ambitions.[6] Under the aegis of the Los Angeles Chamber of Commerce, these interests aligned to pursue an "open shop" model, in which employers could conduct business "free from interruption and interference" of labor organizing. Ruling class forces sought to achieve in Los Angeles what had been impossible in other major US cities, to make it the "open ship citadel of America."[7]

The principal agency charged with implementing this vision was the Los Angeles Police Department, specifically a unit called the Red Squad. By the early decades of the twentieth century, these "archangels of the Open Shop" were notorious for their repression of organized labor and, increasingly over the course of the Depression, their harassment of organized unemployed workers. With the backing of the police commission, the courts, and the mayor, the Red Squad infiltrated labor groups, broke up legal and peaceful picket lines, disrupted lawful meetings, bashed meeting places, tortured protesters, and monitored organizers illegally with brute force and impunity. Hailed as an unparalleled success across the state, the Red Squad extended its reach outside of Los Angeles. Officials from the chambers of commerce of the Imperial Valley and San Joaquin Valley sought the Red Squad's expertise in their own labor conflicts. With officers dispatched from Los Angeles to the surrounding rural areas to help break strikes and target organizers, the Red Squad embodied and protected the tight interdependence of rural and urban spaces. Raw materials such as Acala cotton, for example, were farmed in these rural industrial agricultural spaces and then transported for use in LA's manufacturing industry. Preserving the open shop meant stretching police resources across this geography of accumulation and repressing labor at each phase of production. Tellingly, the head of the Red Squad maintained a special office not inside the police department headquarters but in the headquarters of the Los Angeles Chamber of Commerce.[8]

From the point of view of the region's capitalists, an open shop model had largely been realized on California's agribusiness farms in the form of a vulnerable, precarious, racially segregated, and largely unorganized labor force. Farm workers were "treated as so much scrap when it was needed," according to writer John Steinbeck. By the onset of the Depression, most of California's migrant agricultural laborers came from Mexico, under the widespread assumption that they would move back to Mexico after the completion of a job, leaving, as some growers proposed, nothing behind but profits. Depicted for over a century as "uncivilized" and unfit to "mix their labor properly with the land"—representations that justified the US expropriation of their lands—Mexicans were lauded in the early decades of the twentieth century as an itinerant labor force, in part to deflect nativist fears of racial and cultural contamination. In this way, the southern California landscape offered spatial expressions of historically produced racism. The racialization of Mexicans, intrinsic to US expansionism since the nineteenth century, developed alongside the organized and aggressive pursuit of Mexican labor and land by the US state and US-based capitalists on both sides of the border.[9]

The bucolic imaginary of rural landscapes often obscured the labor regimes of large-scale industrialized capitalist agriculture. Carey McWilliams, a labor advocate and state commissioner of immigration and housing, coined the term "factories in the field" as a corrective, to help reimagine the fields as factories and reinterpret farm workers as proletarians. He also dispelled the myth that farms were owned and operated by small independent famers, revealing that, in fact, half of all agricultural lands in California were owned by the Bank of America (then called the Bank of Italy). A government commission would likewise observe later that actual farm owners "track[ed] very little earth into their parlors." Organized into a group called Associated Farmers, California's corporate agricultural interests bore little resemblance to small family farms. Associated Farmers included industrial, railroad, utility, and banking interests, with corporate donors such as Southern Pacific Railroad, Bank of America, and Pacific Gas and Electric.[10]

Within this rural labor regime, capitalists, in collusion with the state, cultivated multiple mechanisms to control the movement of Mexican laboring bodies. The Border Patrol, first established in 1924, came to enforce immigration laws as a form of labor control. While individual Border Patrol agents were influenced by contradictory and competing notions of manhood, whiteness, belonging, and empire, the broad interpretations of immigration laws and enforcement priorities were often determined by the southern California regional power bloc. As historian Kelly Lytle Hernández describes, the patrol became "another weapon in the arsenal of agribusiness." In different periods of need, Border Patrol unevenly permitted Mexican laborers to cross the US-Mexico border and work in the California fields. Agents simultaneously kept their eyes trained on Mexican workers, ensuring that they neither left jobs before the end of harvests nor attempted to stick around after harvests, once their labor was no longer needed. Local police departments operated toward similar ends. They could redouble the controlling mechanisms of growers by, for example, evicting workers and their families from company-owned homes if they dared to oppose working conditions. The police could similarly evict people who lived in tent city "Hoovervilles" or hobo jungles adjacent to the fields, claiming that such encampments posed public health hazards. Given the supple definition of vagrancy laws, nearly anyone was vulnerable to arrest, particularly if found to be participating in strike meetings. Threats of arrest and deportation haunted every choice Mexicans made in and around the California fields, as the Border Patrol and police officers sought to keep workers terrorized and unorganized.[11]

Alongside immigration and local police forces, vigilante groups operated with relative impunity in the fields. As the *Daily Journal* noted in 1934, in Los Angeles jails, police "do their own assaulting," but in the Imperial Valley, "the police put prisoners outside and let the populace assault them." Vigilante groups, organized through clubs such as the American Legion or the Kiwanis, often operated as informal extensions of local law enforcement. These groups of "armed men," Dorothy Healey remembered, would "beat up the strikers and the strike leaders ... [then] ... go into the community and carry on the same as the Ku Klux Klan." Local law enforcement agencies openly and actively colluded with private vigilantes, enabling activities such as night rides, burning crosses, tar and feathering, mutilation, bombings, gassing, and clubbing. A 1934 Los Angeles police manual, later adopted by the statewide California Peace Officers Association, instructed the police to cultivate local citizens groups and encourage them to attend "special training schools" to learn "corrective measures" that police officers could not use legally. Across the state, labor organizers observed that "vigilantes attack 'independently'—but conveniently without police interference." California's reputation as a haven for vigilantism grew in the 1930s. In the words of a national pamphlet, the "West Coast saw the greatest and most consistent rise in the corrupt vigilante movement," with the Imperial Valley specifically identified as a "festering cancer of vigilantism."[12]

While deportation, policing, and vigilante violence operated as clear instruments of repression, one less obvious mechanism was also crucial to this regime: the local, state, and federal dispensation of relief. Espousing a commonly held belief, agribusiness leader Charles Collins Teague declared in 1928 that itinerant Mexican laborers were ideal for work in the

California fields because they did not need "to be supported through the periods when there was no work to do." Such racist characterizations had material consequences. According to a California State Emergency Relief Administration study, most Mexican agricultural workers had employment for an average of six months a year, making survival solely on wages nearly impossible, especially as wages declined during the Depression. When asked about this situation, Harold E. Pomeroy, executive secretary of the Associated Farmers, testified to a Senate subcommittee that Mexican workers were often "satisfied" with their earnings during the shorter period and thereafter able to enjoy what he called a "rather long holiday." For many workers and their families who faced immediate threats of starvation, untreated illness, homelessness, and extreme poverty, these intervening months hardly constituted a "holiday." Speaking for thousands of agricultural workers like him, Juan Serrano starkly noted at a 1931 statewide public hearing on unemployment, "My family is facing starvation."[13]

To survive after the harvest season, workers and their families cobbled together informal work (often gendered labor in the garment industry), mutual aid, and paltry but accessible forms of relief. In Los Angeles, where workers largely congregated, available relief took the meager forms of private charity administered through the Catholic Welfare Bureau or emergency relief from the Los Angeles County Outdoor Relief Division. Prior to the New Deal, urban areas absorbed much of the off-season costs of supporting agricultural workers from rural areas. Some local Los Angeles agencies and nativist groups opposed such distribution of relief, arguing that it constituted an informal subsidy to agribusiness. While relief indeed reduced rural employers' costs of sheltering, feeding, clothing, and generally reproducing workers, southern California growers were not overly concerned with workers' access to resources beyond their control. Rather, through the expansive spatialization of productive relations in southern California, growers were invested in maintaining and reproducing a vulnerable and mobile workforce. Both workers and employers therefore recognized the centrality of relief to broader struggles over production and reproduction.[14]

The vulnerability of Mexican workers on relief intensified alongside the expansion of mechanisms for arrest and deportation, especially as the economic crisis deepened. Formal measures made it increasingly difficult for farm workers to receive aid. In August 1931, the state legislature passed the Alien Labor Act that prohibited companies doing business with the government from employing "alien" workers on public jobs. In the same year, the legislature passed residency requirements for public relief, requiring applicants to prove that they had resided in the state for three years and within a particular county for one year. These new provisions excluded many migrant Mexican workers. In addition, the absence of relief could lead to confinement or deportation. Louis Barros, who picked peas in Castroville for fifteen cents a basket, discovered that he barely made enough to cover his nightly board of $1.25. He traveled to LA, where he soon found himself arrested for vagrancy. "Reaching Los Angeles too late one evening for the soup line," he wrote, "I was picked up by a detective and jailed." In a 1932 editorial, Barros explained that imprisonment was the "penalty workers pay for being unable to find jobs which do NOT exist." For Mexican workers like Barros, the inability to locate relief could easily translate into imprisonment and oftentimes deportation.[15]

As relief grew scarce, public sentiment turned sharply against migrant workers receiving aid, especially in Los Angeles, where the police intensified its surveillance of Mexican workers. Charles P. Visel, director of the LA Citizens Committee on Coordination of Unemployment Relief, helped to accelerate the process, arguing that "it would be a great relief to the unemployment situation if some method could be devised to scare these people out of our city." By coordinating local police and federal immigration agents in surrounding states, Visel arranged a large-scale roundup of Mexican workers in February 1931. Through political pressure and other scare tactics, local and federal agents worked with relief and welfare agencies to raid LA's Mexican communities and to drive approximately fifty thousand persons, many of whom were US citizens, south of the border. All in all, nearly half a million Mexican workers were forcibly and illegally "repatriated" during the Great Depression, as deportation emerged as a central tool to manage labor and relief.[16]

Through the conjoined practices of deportation, policing, vigilante violence, and relief policies, Mexican workers were among the most exploited and vulnerable among southern California's laborers. Repatriation efforts put extreme pressure on Mexican workers, forcing them to accept reduced wages and abysmal living conditions or face the prospect of deportation to Mexico. Repatriation in the early 1930s, however, produced unintended and contradictory consequences, such as the disappearance of a labor supply skilled and experienced enough to meet California growers' needs.[17]

With newfound leverage, Mexican workers began to challenge the terms of their employment with greater frequency and militancy. By the early 1930s, the heads of agribusiness grew worried that their fields were becoming fertile grounds for radicalism. And many of them blamed access to relief. "The Mexican on relief is being unionized and is being used to foment strikes among the few still loyal Mexican workers," George Clements of the Los Angeles Chamber of Commerce warned. "The Mexican casual labor is lost to the California farmer unless immediate action is taken to get him off relief." To a meeting of the Farmer's Union, *San Francisco Chronicle* editor Chester Rowell announced, "Make no mistake about it, if you yourselves do not settle this question of the migratory laborer, the Communists will." In the capitalist landscape of southern California, relief and radicalism appeared to be rising together.[18]

## MEXICAN REVOLUTIONARY TRADITIONS

Communists such as Dorothy Healey did, in fact, help migrant workers organize against agribusiness capitalists, but Communists did not introduce Mexican workers to this fight. For many Mexican farm workers in California, their struggles represented an ongoing confrontation with capitalism. The Mexican Revolution was itself a struggle against US capital. In the years following World War I, US capital continued to dominate the Mexican economy as it had since the beginning of the twentieth century. In the 1920s, 65 to 85 percent of all of Mexico's exports went to the United States, and nearly 75 percent of all of Mexico's imports came from the United States. In addition, US companies commanded 80 percent of all Mexican mineral production and close to 95 percent of all refinery production by 1929. Throughout the 1920s and into the Depression, the United States looked to Mexico for economic relief as a market for US manufactured goods, a source of raw materials, and a site for manufacturing. Individuals from Los Angeles invested more capital in Mexico than residents of any other city in the United States.[19]

The expansion of US investment, extraction, production, and transportation in Mexico also led to the expansion and radicalization of the working class there. By the early 1930s, the Mexican working class was enveloped in dramatic revolts. In 1933, over seventeen thousand workers walked off their jobs demanding better wages, housing, schools, and medical services. In 1934, Mexico saw a rash of major strikes launched across various industries. Strikes were mostly organized against foreign-owned industries such as the Huasteca Petroleum Company (owned by US Standard Oil) and the Mexican Telephone and Telegraph Company (an allied company of American Telephone and Telegraph). By the following year, over 100,000 workers were on strike from industries as diverse as mining, oil, railroad, telephone, and sanitation, representing one of the largest industrial strike waves in Mexico's history.[20]

Many of these strikes grew out of everyday indignities. The Huasteca strikes, for example, sprang from unrest over decrepit housing for workers. Workers protested unsanitary conditions and insufficient space for their children at company-run schools. Although demands for better housing and schools were not on their face revolutionary, the organization of workers for their basic rights and dignity informed the broader struggle for the control over production, the ownership of national resources, and the eradication of exploitative conditions. The strike wave across industries and revolts in the countryside in the 1930s, in turn, forced the implementation of the most radical tenets of the 1917 Mexican Constitution. The era witnessed the nationalization of the oil and railroad industries, the revoking of foreign capitalist interests, massive national education and literacy programs, and the most sweeping land redistribution programs in the history of the Americas.[21]

These experiences circulated on the California fields. Recalling his encounter with Mexican workers in the 1933 cotton strike, organizer Pat Chambers noted how workers discussed the "many revolutions and wars" waged so that "the Mexican people might be free, have some land of their own," and "have the right to live without fear of starving to death."[22] Such perspectives and backgrounds had profound effects on the militancy of farm workers in California and upon those who had direct and indirect relationships to the revolution. Communist organizers came to realize the value of this experience. In the Imperial Valley, Dorothy Healey soon noticed that her radical appeals were met with patient indulgence. While she talked about strategy, the workers explained to her, "Of course we're ready for revolution. When the barricades are ready, we'll be on the barricades, but don't bother us with meetings all the time. We know what to do, we know who the enemy is.... Just tell us when the revolution is ready. We'll be there."[23]

The Mexican strikers drew on a radical and historical consciousness of tactical alliances that they had gained during the Mexican Revolution. As Devra Weber's generative research demonstrates, the revolution operated as "a model of a collective struggle" that inspired the strategies and symbols of the strike. Former military officers organized patrols and sentries with other veterans. Within the strike camps, workers named streets after revolutionary heroes and sang revolutionary *corridos*. They reminisced about friends and relatives who had participated in revolutionary strikes. "The Mexican people are revolutionary as it is," insisted organizer Leroy Parra. With their knowledge of the Mexican Revolution, he believed that they were better able to see "the exploitation here in this country." While workers maintained different and conflicting feelings about the Mexican Revolution, these differences appeared to be "submerged" during the strike. Instead, the workers' memories of the revolution stressed shared historical opposition against the United States. For working people long exposed to the unrestrained incursions of US capital in Mexico, unity through antipathy made sense.[24]

This shared history made a deep impression on all of the striking workers. In his coverage of the cotton strike, Joe Evans observed that white workers and other workers of color learned that "Mexican workers were not 'greasers' as portrayed by Hollywood films." In the process of struggle, they came to see them instead as "courageous, determined, intelligent workers." "Never has there been greater courage shown," reported Evans, "than that of the Mexican workers in the course of this strike." Workers, in turn, developed a deep sense of solidarity and affinity. When growers at Corcoran tried to intimidate workers, setting up loudspeakers and demanding that the leaders come forward, a "spontaneous shout" came back proclaiming, "We are all the leaders!"[25]

Amid the major agricultural strikes in 1933, a bloc of growers, financiers, and local government officials across California united to stem the tide of radicalism. Discovering that farm workers were receiving relief in 1933 through the New Deal's Federal Emergency Relief Administration with few stipulations, they immediately sought to cut off access to public relief. While growers exerted disproportionate control over local relief, they had no control over the dispensation of federal aid. As Paul Taylor and Clark Kerr concluded in a report for a Senate subcommittee, the 1933 cotton strike effectively became the first large labor conflict in the United States in which a federal agency had offered support to striking workers. In this case, the federal government had specifically supported striking workers through food aid. This form of relief allowed strikers to feed themselves and their families, enabling the strike to persist.[26]

After the 1933 strike wave, agribusiness leaders quickly and successfully organized to wrest control over relief from the federal government. A Senate investigation into California labor abuses revealed that in 1934 cotton and walnut growers, Sunkist, Western Growers Protective Association of vegetable growers and shippers, and other employers helped convene a special labor committee of the Los Angeles Chamber of Commerce to regain local control of relief. Once relief was administered by state and local agencies sympathetic to agribusiness, farm workers remained at the mercy of growers. Collaborating with Los Angeles public agencies, charities, and government offices, California growers increased their pressure on relief officials. Soon, unemployed workers were being removed from local and state relief rolls and forced to work in the fields during strikes. Los Angeles relief recipients, particularly Mexican workers, were given an ultimatum: scab in the fields or relinquish eligibility for relief. Relief officers were instructed to offer jobs with guarantees of free transportation and sometimes an advance of one bag of groceries. Instructions to relief workers concluded with this admonition, "If [relief recipients] refuse, do not threaten them, only state that they need not expect any more favors from Los Angeles County."[27] By compelling workers into the fields and dictating the terms of their employment, state and local relief agencies operated as de facto labor recruiters for agribusiness.[28]

An editorial by a Mexican worker, who withheld his name in fear of reprisal, in October 1933 described how workers were being turned against each other:

> We go to the fields in the hot sun and work long hours—at 15c an hour. It is too little.... Our children get hungry, or women get sick. We cannot buy medicine. Then we try to get more wages—just a little more, to live on, not to get rich. What happens? The sheriff comes with lots of men. They have clubs, pistols, machine guns. They beat us with the clubs. They throw the gas that burns our eyes. Then the courts—they issue injunctions ... it means we cannot strike. They put us in jail ... they tell us there is a job for us in the country. We go there—and there is a strike going on. WE must break the strike to keep the workers from getting the more wages.[29]

Employers and law enforcement agents continued to work hand in hand to create an "open shop" in southern California.

Figure 5.1. Massive organizing efforts by farm workers and unemployed city workers during the Depression drove many to join or work with the Communist Party in California. "Why 1,000 More Joined the Party," *Western Worker*, November 27, 1933.

By 1935, the Los Angeles Chamber of Commerce and the state relief administration were working with agribusiness to tailor relief rolls according to the needs of growers. Between August and October 1935, seventy-five thousand workers were dropped from the rolls and forced into the fields. These local developments reflected national power struggles, as southern California agribusiness capitalists added their voice to a powerful bloc of southern capitalists, Dixiecrats, and landowners. The federal government responded by denying agricultural workers equal protection in New Deal legislations, such as the National Labor Relations

Act, the Social Security Act, and the Fair Labor Standards Act. The status of Mexican workers in California held national significance. "California is today the testing ground for fascism in this country," a *New Republic* commentator surmised. "If the present program of oppression and terrorism can be launched with active success in California, it can be utilized in other states as well." To confront the machinations of capital, organizing efforts had to operate across regions, in both cities and rural areas, with a concrete consideration of the global scale as well. Accordingly, workers in the fields posed the following question to their "comrades in the big cities": What would they do "to help smash the vigilantes' murder gangs and the policy to starve them back to work"?[30]

## LOS ANGELES UNEMPLOYED COUNCILS

California was a key destination for desperate job seekers during the Depression. With few jobs to be had, the Golden State quickly became the "transient capital of America." Upward of twelve thousand to fifteen thousand hopefuls a day drove, hitchhiked, jumped trains, and made their way across California's state lines in 1931 from the Dust Bowl, northern Mexico, the Pacific Northwest, the Pacific Islands, and the Jim Crow South. Los Angeles became home to most of California's job seekers and half of the state's jobless population. Unemployment reached crisis levels, with one out of five Angelenos unable to find work. Those lucky enough to secure employment were surrounded by a growing mass of the unemployed, crowded into the city's shelters, relief offices, jails, and peripheries. On the outskirts of downtown and in the banks of the culverted Los Angeles river, a new landscape had cropped up, a veritable jungle of shantytowns and ramshackle tent cities bearing the president's name, Hoovervilles. Squats of shacks and lean-tos rendered poverty publicly visible. Men hired by the city to sweep streets and clear brush in these outlying areas could barely finish a day's work, regularly fainting from malnutrition. The health board would soon recommend that the unemployed hunt pigeons for sustenance.[31]

In the early years of the Depression, there was no national unemployment insurance, no provisions for direct relief, and no federal legislation to help the millions without jobs. State-level assistance was paltry, inefficient, and discriminatory. To receive aid recipients often needed to qualify as mentally or physically disabled. Only a fraction of people in need could receive it. In 1931 unemployment hovered around 28 percent in southern California, with rates as high as 50 percent for black and Mexican workers in Los Angeles. Racist administration by local, state and regional agencies often meant that relief was doled out in variable sizes, with the smallest grants given to black and Mexican families. Public relief operated as a disciplinary measure, dispensed to few and intended to demean recipients to discourage their reliance upon it. Oftentimes, relief was administered through the auspices of the police department, a provision that drove away many applicants. As late as 1934 in fourteen states, receiving relief deprived persons of the right to vote. The disciplinary power of the relief system, both federal- and state-sponsored, generally lay not in an outright refusal of relief but in the systematic degradation of those who received aid.[32]

The official silence around mass suffering was deafening. Falling beyond the purview of the president, politicians, labor leaders, and social scientists, the poor seemed invisible to all but "the doctor, the judge, the gravedigger, and bum-bailiff."[33] Carving out existences on the peripheries of public consciousness, Herman Boren, an unemployed milling operator from San Francisco, stated, "'The way that homeless unemployed men have to live is worse than the way animals and insects live." In desperation, the writer Meridel Leseur observed, "A woman will shut herself up in a room until it is taken away from her, and eat a cracker a day and be as quiet as a mouse so there are no social statistics concerning her." If the poor were willing to suffer silently, there seemed no incentive for the government to intervene. Herbert Benjamin, national leader of Unemployed Councils, told a Senate Committee in 1931 that no real help would be forthcoming "until every man in Congress is shivering in his very pants because he thinks the unemployed are going to engage in struggle."[34]

With nearly a third of the US labor force out of work, Unemployed Councils spread quickly across the country. They demanded recognition and resources during the Great Depression, giving voice, expression, and mobilization to an otherwise unrecognized surplus population that had grown exponentially after the stock market crash of 1929. The councils became the nation's first poor people's organization, representing one of the first large-scale protest movements against the economic crisis. In contrast to segregated American work sites, Unemployed Councils produced spaces where working-class peoples of different genders, races, and ethnicities could engage in a common struggle for radical social change.[35]

Unemployed Councils had several objectives: organize the unemployed for immediate relief by door-to-door outreach; develop new leadership from the rank and file through block committees; and bring groups of people in need to welfare offices to demand jobs and relief. The Los Angeles Unemployed Councils assembled together an impressive range of activities. Before the New Deal legislations, they organized at charities and welfare bureaus for relief, demonstrated at City Hall, and negotiated with the board of supervisors to implement citywide increases in relief. Once federal relief became available through the New Deal, they organized at locals of the Relief Workers Protective Union. They protested against racially discriminatory hiring in public jobs. They called for an end to foreclosures, challenged evictions in courthouses, and moved furniture back into homes of the evicted. They organized in shelters against rotten food and for the right of all residents to have beds. They defended squatters living in Hoovervilles and forced officials to find alternative housing. They allied with veterans' movements to demand housing and bonus pay for starving World War I veterans. They fought for free medical care, public utilities, and transportation for the unemployed. The councils protested the incarceration of their members and the deportation of Mexican workers, tying their movement to broader revolutionary demands, including a call for a tax on the rich to end the Depression.[36]

Local organizing efforts in different LA neighborhoods, such as Boyle Heights, Echo Park, Hollywood, Huntington Park, and Long Beach, converged to citywide Hunger Marches in the plaza downtown. Later the councils coordinated statewide demonstrations in Sacramento. On caravan trips to the state capital, members would stop in small towns, organizing throughout the trip and recruiting new members along the way. The same process would repeat across the country leading up to Hunger Marches on Washington. With their efforts, "marching columns of unemployed became a familiar site." Observer Len De Caux wrote, "The communists brought misery out of hiding in the workers' neighborhood." In increasing numbers, the unemployed refused to suffer in silence.[37]

On March 6, 1930, the Unemployed Councils held an International Day of Struggle Against Unemployment. Over 1.2 million people came out in cities and towns across the United States and around the world. On that day, "the unemployed and homeless—poor farmers, black workers and sharecroppers in the deep South, miners in Appalachia," according to Los Angeles Unemployed Council member Elaine Black, "all became a strategic political force to be reckoned with." In Los Angeles, the protest drew a crowd of five thousand to ten thousand to the plaza, one of the biggest demonstrations in the city's history. Three years later, in 1933, the Hunger March drew an even bigger crowd of nearly forty thousand. Nationwide, these protests helped convert unemployment into a front-page issue that was impossible to ignore.[38]

Like many city residents, Elaine Black witnessed hundreds of people, demonstrators and spectators alike, arrested and beaten, some "almost clubbed to death." The Presidential Commission on Law Observance and Enforcement would later corroborate her statement, describing the attack on the Los Angeles demonstration as "an eight hour clubbing party." Truncheons, brass knuckles, tear gas, rifles, blackjacks, blades, and impunity made the Los Angeles Police Department's Red Squads a brutal force against demonstrators and often onlookers as well. The violence drove some away, but many more became transformed by the obvious injustice of police brutality and were emboldened to join Unemployed Councils. An unsympathetic *Los Angeles Record* article agreed, opining, "In the existing unemployment situation, they can count on making recruits among jobless men made desperate by hunger and indignant by senseless police cosackism."[39]

In 1931 Dorothy Healey moved to predominantly Mexican East Los Angeles on Soto Street near Hollenbeck Park. There she organized block committees of Unemployed Councils. She recalled, "You could go anywhere and knock on doors and you were going to find the unemployed." Through the councils, organizers went house to house in working-class neighborhoods, setting up meetings, convincing the unemployed to form block committees with their neighbors. In effect, the councils became an "informal neighborhood association" for the "destitute." With local organizing efforts at the level of neighborhood councils, women emerged as critical leaders and participants. People who joined were women like housewife Mildred Olsen. Olsen had been unable to feed her children or afford her rent or gas bills before local Unemployed Councils demonstrated with her at the local relief office. To a California State Commission on unemployment she testified, "We could go hungry; we could live in basements and skirmish in ash cans and our children go hungry; but by organized pressure we got our demands met."[40]

Unemployed Councils attracted and transformed women of different backgrounds. In addition to Elaine Black, a daughter of Russian Jewish immigrants, and Dorothy Healey, prominent figures of the movement included Japanese American organizer Mary Matsudo Imada and African American Adele Young. Though Healey would go on to have a long career in the Los Angeles CP spanning five decades, she found her work in Unemployed Councils revelatory and exemplary. In the councils, she saw "fragmented" and "atomized" unemployed participants "start to feel a consciousness." She recalled the transformation of participants in the organizing process:

> We didn't just agitate. People joined an organization, and those people, those unemployed, would lead the next demonstration, and you'd go on and set up a new block committee a block away that would meet every week and take its delegations down. You'd keep doing that so that you were constantly developing new leaders ... with new talents that were latent before but then became explicit.[41]

The struggle for relief opened up new political possibilities and coalitions.[42]

## RADICAL INTERNATIONALISM AND
## THE GLOBAL STRUGGLE FOR RELIEF

Alfred Wagenknecht, head of the CP's relief arm, complained that while "thousands of unemployed workers were kept intact," the ranks of the party did not increase proportionally as a result of Unemployed Councils. Not required to join the CP to participate in the councils, tens of thousands of persons streamed through their ranks, but not many became CP members. This was particularly true for Mexican workers. Although commentators have proposed that there was a fundamental incompatibility between Mexican nationalism and communism or, alternately, that Mexican workers were predisposed to anarcho-syndicalism and therefore reluctant to join the CP, such observations tend to overlook examples to the contrary. Mexican workers were very active in communist and socialist organizations and campaigns, including the Congresso and later the Congress of Industrial Organizations (CIO) and the Cannery and Agricultural Workers Industrial Union (CAWIU).[43]

In a 1932 editorial, Irving Kreitzberg wrote that there was great support among Mexican workers for CP campaigns, especially when efforts were made to include Mexican communities and when fliers were published in Spanish. Even absent these efforts, Mexican workers often spoke at rallies and spontaneously joined demonstrations. Mexican workers who did join the Party, like Jose Arispe, regularly organized with other Mexican workers. In 1939 Emma Tenayuca, a Communist organizer and Unemployed Council leader in Texas, considered this point in an article she cowrote titled "The Mexican Question in the Southwest." While she recommended that the Party pay greater attention to the specific needs of Mexican workers—recognizing that they formed distinct communities, affected by racial, cultural, and political discrimination—she argued that their liberation was tied to a broader radical movement. Tenayuca's claims help to explain the significance of the struggle for relief to the CP. Although the struggle did not necessarily increase Party membership, it intensified the struggle against racism, expanded opportunities for participation of nonwhite communities, and crucially expanded the dimensions of class struggle.[44]

While expressly organizing and raising consciousness around unemployment, the Unemployed Councils helped expose the unwaged relations that permanently structured the processes of capital accumulation. As Karl Marx had noted nearly a century earlier, the accumulation of capital required a "constant transformation of a part of the working population into unemployed or semi-employed 'hands.'" A permanent surplus labor population functioned to pressure the employed segment of the working class into accepting lower wages and more exploitative conditions. In southern California, this surplus labor population had disproportionately been composed of people of color. Although hunger and unemployment had become newly recognizable as a national condition during the Depression, they had long structured the lives and labors of workers of color, in particular migrant farm workers, female domestic workers, and industrial workers who were racially excluded from trade unions. What had been deemed "exceptional" for racialized sectors of the working class soon became a generalizable condition for growing numbers of workers. The economic crisis only deepened trenches of class struggle already established along the color line.[45]

Throughout the Depression, the Communist Party experienced a major upsurge in participation and membership. The western division attributed this jump to two primary campaigns: the organizing among farm workers through the CAWIU and the advent of the Unemployed Councils. Outgrowths of the new Trade Union Unity League (TUUL), an independent trade union organization that sought to organize workers traditionally excluded from trade unions, both organizing efforts found their greatest successes in California. The CAWIU and Unemployed Councils achieved particular success in southern California, ironically because of restrictions placed on labor organizing. The open shop policies of the region, coupled with the American Federation of Labor's unwillingness to share organizing space with the CP, meant that factories and white factory workers were largely out of reach, particularly in Los Angeles. In turn, the Party sought new constituencies. In the notoriously sectarian Third Period of 1928–1935, the Party was able to reach people of color who were farm workers and unemployed workers, half of whom were women. In southern California, these organizing efforts broadened the struggle against capitalism to include sites such as fields, homes, food banks, jails, deportation centers, and relief offices in addition to factories and other points of production. Given its new constituencies, the Party became more attentive, through its organizing, to the intersections between the color line and the class struggle.[46]

The struggle for relief forged meaningful solidarities between workers of various backgrounds to facilitate discussions of racial and class dynamics at local, national, and international scales. Pettis Perry, for example, who would become one of the most influential African American Communists in the country, had formative experiences organizing in southern California. Perry had left Alabama, barely escaping the clutches of Jim Crow racial terror. He worked in auto plants, canneries, and packinghouses and eventually found harvesting work in the Imperial Valley. There in the California fields he encountered radical Mexican farm workers alongside Communist organizers. He later joined the movement in Los Angeles, working as a full-time organizer around unemployed struggles. He became one of the Party's foremost critics of white supremacy and capitalism, concluding, "The working class will never come to power unless there is a relentless struggle against white chauvinism."[47]

Unemployed Councils were one of several new vehicles that generated greater participation of working-class people of color in radical politics. Other communist campaigns in the period included defense of the Scottsboro Boys in Alabama; support for jailed Unemployed Councils leader Angelo Herndon; opposition to Japanese imperialism; and support for striking farm workers. In multiethnic Los Angeles, these campaigns created greater spaces within which people of color could operate. Official membership in the CP tripled, and the ranks of sympathizers grew exponentially, drawing increasingly from black, Mexican, Japanese, and Chinese communities, as well as from already established Russian, Jewish, and poor white communities. Meetings often required translation into Spanish, Italian, and Japanese.[48]

Japanese American organizer Karl Yoneda made numerous appeals to the unemployed Japanese in Los Angeles as he helped coordinate a Japanese branch of Unemployed Councils. As a worker and organizer of farm workers, fruit stand workers, waiters, and newspaper writers in the early Depression years, Yoneda had become acquainted with Mexican, black, Filipino, Japanese, and poor white workers, encounters that helped to shape his analysis of race and class in the labor movement. Recognizing the complex position that Japanese farm workers occupied in the early 1930s, he appealed to Japanese berry pickers in El Monte "not to scab!" but to "join their Mexican and Filipino brothers in strike." Similarly, he condemned the Japanese boarding house owners, growers, and scab providers for being on the wrong side of the class struggle. Significantly, Yoneda was one of many voices to lead the Los Angeles chapter of the Party to protest against Japanese imperialism. With members like Yoneda, movements for unemployment relief were meshed with calls to free the Scottsboro Boys and demands such as "Hands off China" and "Down with Japanese Imperialism!" In such ways, a radical internationalist spirit infected the local work of Unemployed Councils.[49]

Otto Huiswoud, one of the first black members of the CP, believed that the Depression presented an opportunity for a "broad campaign among the Negro masses on the basis of everyday demands for a united revolutionary struggle of the entire working class against Yankee Imperialism."[50] Leading Pan-Africanist and communist George Padmore agreed. Addressing black workers throughout the colonized world in his magazine *The Negro Worker*, Padmore instructed his readers to follow the example of Unemployed Councils:

> The gigantic hunger marches of the unemployed workers in the USA—colored and white united—in England, and other European countries have struck deep fear in the hearts of the bosses and have caused a halt to the tide of many contemplated anti-working class measures in these countries. These splendid examples of proletarian mass action should serve as an inspiration to the unemployed colonial toilers to do likewise.

As Padmore's observations suggested, the struggle against hunger and unemployment was decidedly international. At the core of this struggle was an understanding that racism was a force repressing the working class as whole. As a journalist writing about the case of the Atlanta Unemployed Council, organizer Angelo Herndon concluded, "Maintenance of the color line is the core of anti-labor policy." Through their struggles in US cities and across regions, members of Unemployed Councils came to see their work as a part of a worldwide class struggle.[51]

The California strikes occurred amid a wave of radicalism circulating across the globe. By 1934, strikes were being staged by sugar cane workers in Puerto Rico, unemployed marchers in Trinidad, miners in northern Spain, and thousands of workers across Mexico, as well as sharecroppers, longshoremen, domestic, and unemployed workers in the United States. The struggles for relief and against racism in the California fields, Los Angeles Unemployed Councils, and Mexican industries exemplified and expanded a militancy proliferating across the world.

With their diverse composition, the farm worker strikes and Unemployed Councils in southern California enabled a critical conceptualization of geographies of capitalism. By organizing simultaneously in spaces such as the agricultural fields and among the urban unemployed, they offer a view of how capitalism was developing across regions and across the globe. These southern California movements integrated considerations of racism and imperialism in confronting capitalism. Taken together these movements for relief and against repression demonstrate how convergences of radical traditions emboldened the global antiracist class struggle in the 1930s and beyond.

1    Dorothy Healey, oral history interview, "Tradition's Chains Have Bound Us" (1982), Dorothy Healey Collections, Special Collections, California State University, Long Beach, 102; Dorothy Healey, interview in *The Internationale*, DVD, dir. Peter Miller (Icarus Films, 2000); Michael Denning, "Representing Global Labor," *Social Text* 92, 25, no. 3 (Fall 2007): 21–45.

2    Richard Walker, *The Conquest of Bread: 150 Years of Agribusiness in California* (New York: New Press, 2004), 285.

3    Ibid., 285; Carey McWilliams, *California: The Great Exception* (Berkeley: University of California Press, 1999), 156, 158.

4    Carlos Bulosan, *America Is in the Heart* (Seattle: University of Washington Press, 1973), 111.

5       I use the term "Mexican" throughout to refer to both Mexican citizens and American-born Mexican people residing in the southwestern United States.

6       David R. Roediger and Elizabeth D. Esch, *The Production of Difference: Race and the Management of Labor in U.S. History* (New York: Oxford University Press, 2012), 193–204; Mike Davis, "Sunshine and the Open Shop: Ford and Darwin in 1920s Los Angeles," *Antipode* 29, no. 4 (October, 1997): 358.

7       "The Forty-Year War for a Free City: A History of the Open Shop in Los Angeles," *Los Angeles Times*, October 1, 1929, 2; McWilliams, *California*, 144.

8       Communist Party Los Angeles County (CPLAC), "Two Decades of Progress: Communist Party LA County 1919–1939," September 1939, 13; Ruth Wilson Gilmore, *Golden Gulag: Prisons, Surplus, Crisis, and Opposition in Globalizing California* (Berkeley: University of California Press, 2007), 133; Dorothy Healey, "Tradition's Chains," 84; Edward J. Escobar, *Race, Police, and the Making of a Political Identity: Mexican Americans and the Los Angeles Police Department, 1900–1945* (Berkeley: University of California Press, 1999), 83–84; Frank Donner, *Protectors of Privilege: Red Squads and Police Repression in Urban America* (Berkeley: University of California Press, 1990) 59–60.

9       Camille Guerin-Gonzalez, *Mexican Workers and American Dreams: Immigration, Repatriation, and California Farm Labor, 1900–1939* (New Brunswick, NJ: Rutgers University Press, 1994), 45–47; John Steinbeck, *Their Blood Is Strong: A Factual Story of the Migratory Agricultural Workers in California* (San Francisco: Simon J. Lubin Foundation, 1938), 26; Laura Pulido, "Rethinking Environmental Racism: White Privilege and Urban Development in Southern California," *Annals of the Association of American Geographers* 90, no. 1 (2000): 12–40; Tomàs Almaguer, *Racial Fault Lines: The Historical Origins of White Supremacy in California* (Berkeley: University of California Press, 2009), 51–57.

10      Don Mitchell, *Lie of the Land: Migrant Workers and the California Landscape* (Minneapolis: University of Minnesota Press, 1996), 17–35; Carey McWilliams, *Factories in the Field: The Story of Migratory Farm Labor in California* (Boston: Little, Brown and Company, 1939), 233; "California: Gentlemen Farmers," *Time*, December 16, 1940; Clarke A. Chambers, *California Farm Organizations: A Historical Study of the Grange, the Farm Bureau, and the Associated Farmers, 1929–1941* (Berkeley: University of California Press, 1952), 45.

11      Devra Weber, *Dark Sweat, White Gold: California Farm Workers, Cotton, and the New Deal* (Berkeley: University of California Press, 1996), 121; Kelly Lytle Hernández, *Migra! A History of the U.S. Border Patrol* (Berkeley: University of California Press, 2010), 26, 44, 56.

12      C. H. Garrigues, "The Spotlight," *Daily Journal*, 1934; Healey, "Tradition's Chains," 100; Mike Davis, "Vigilante Man," in *No One Is Illegal: Fighting Violence and State Repression on the U.S.-Mexico Border*, ed. Justin Akers Chacón et al. (Chicago: Haymarket Books, 2006), 18; Peace Officers Association of the State of California, *A Peace Officer's Manual for Combating Subversive Activities*, January 20, 1935, 21–22; American League Against War and Fascism, Los Angles Committee, *California's Brown Book*, October 1934, 3; Isobel Walker Soule, "The Vigilantes Hide Behind the Flag" (National Committee for the Defense of Political Prisoners, 1937).

13 Committee on Education and Labor (CEL), Violations of Free Speech and Rights of Labor, *Hearings before a Subcommittee of the Committee on Education and Labor, United Stated Senate, Seventy-Sixth Congress* (Washington, DC: United States Government Printing Office, 1940), 19527; Jess Walsh, "Laboring at the Margins: Welfare and the Regulation of Mexican Workers in Southern California," *Antipode* 31, no. 4 (1999): 398–420; Roediger and Esch, *Production of Difference*, 196; McWilliams, *Factories in the Fields*, 322; "Reveal Jobless Suffering in San Jose and 'Frisco," *Western Worker,* January 1, 1932.

14 Cybelle Fox, "The Boundaries of Social Citizenship: Race, Immigration, and the American Welfare State, 1900–1950" (PhD diss., Harvard University, 2007), 142; "Mexican Workers Get Only 70 Pct. of What Others Do," *Western Worker,* November 6, 1933; McWilliams, *Factories in the Field,* 322.

15 George J. Sánchez, *Becoming Mexican American: Ethnicity, Culture, and Identity in Chicano Los Angles, 1900–1945* (New York: Oxford University Press, 1993), 211; Ricardo Romo, *East Los Angeles: History of a Barrio* (Austin: University of Texas Press, 1992), 164; "Jail Worker for Begging Food," *Western Worker,* January 1, 1932; Louis B. Perry and Richard Perry, *A History of the Los Angeles Labor Movement, 1911–1941* (Berkeley: University of California Press, 1963), 238.

16 Guerin-Gonzalez, *Mexican Workers and American Dreams,* 81; Cybelle Fox, "Three Worlds of Relief: Race, Immigration, and Public and Private Social Welfare Spending in American Cities, 1929," *American Journal of Sociology* 116, no. 2 (Sept. 2010): 466–68; Abraham Hoffman, "Stimulus to Repatriation: The 1931 Federal Deportation Drive and the Los Angeles Mexican Community," *Pacific Historical Review* 42, no. 2 (May 1973): 219; Francisco E. Balderrama and Raymond Rodriguez, *Decade of Betrayal: Mexican Repatriation in the 1930s* (Albuquerque: University of New Mexico Press, 2006), passim.

17 "Jail Worker for Begging Food," *Western Worker,* January 1, 1932; Douglas Monroy, *Rebirth: Mexican Los Angeles from the Great Migration to the Great Depression* (Berkeley: University of California Press, 1999), 210.

18 Donald L. Zelman, "Mexican Migrants and Relief in Depression California: Grower Reaction to Public Relief Policies as They Affected Mexican Migration," *Journal of Mexican American History* 5 (1975): 1–23; Weber, *Dark Sweat, White Gold,* 127; Raymond P. Barry, ed., *A Documentary History of Migratory Farm Labor in California* (Oakland: Federal Writers Project, 1938), 43–44.

19 Nora Hamilton, *The Limits of State Autonomy: Post-Revolutionary Mexico* (Princeton: Princeton University Press, 1982), 73, 106; James D. Cockcroft, *Mexico's Hope: An Encounter with Politics and History* (New York: Monthly Review Press, 1998), 111; Greg Grandin, *Empire's Workshop: Latin America, the United States, and the Rise of the New Imperialism* (New York: Metropolitan Books, 2006), 35; Jessica Kim, "Oilmen and Cactus Rustlers: Los Angeles, Mexico, and the Building of a Regional Empire, 1890–1941" (PhD diss., University of Southern California, 2012), 8.

20 Joe C. Ashby, *Organized Labor and the Mexican Revolution under Lázaro Cárdenas* (Chapel Hill: University of North Carolina Press, 1967), 23–24.

21 Adolfo Gilly, "Chiapas and the Rebellion of the Enchanted World," in *Rural Revolt*

in *Mexico: U.S. Intervention and the Domain of Subaltern Politics*, ed. Daniel Nugent (Durham, NC: Duke University Press, 1998), 261–333; Ashby, *Organized Labor and the Mexican Revolution*, 24–26.

22 Ed Royce, "A Scene from the Cotton Strike," *Western Worker*, October 30, 1933.

23 Healey, "Tradition's Chains," 96.

24 Weber, *Dark Sweat, White Gold*, 87–88, 94.

25 Joe Evans, "Only Communists Lead, Cotton Pickers Learn," *Western Worker*, November 20, 1933.

26 Paul S. Taylor and Clark Kerr, "Documentary History of the Strike of the Cotton Pickers in California 1933," in CEL, *Hearings*, 19994.

27 "Welfare Letter in L.A. Exposes Scabherding Role," *Western Worker*, November 20, 1933;"Cut 20,000 Mexicans Off Relief, Supplies Cotton Field Scabs," *Western Worker*, November 13, 1933; McWilliams, *Factories in the Field*, 286.

28 CEL, *Hearings*, 19530; Taylor and Kerr, "Documentary History," in *Hearings*, 19994.

29 "Tells Why Mexican Workers Join the Hunger March," *Western Worker*, October 2, 1933.

30 Ira Katznelson, *When Affirmative Action Was White: An Untold History of Racial Inequality in Twentieth-Century America* (New York: W. W. Norton, 2005), 22; Fox, "Boundaries of Social Citizenship,"17; Cletus Daniel, *Bitter Harvest: A History of California Farmworkers, 1870–1941* (Berkeley: University of California Press, 1981), 261; Bruce Minton, "The Battle of Sacramento," *New Republic*, February 20, 1935, 38–40; Ed Royce, "A Scene from the Cotton Strike," *Western Worker*, October 30, 1933; Sánchez, *Becoming Mexican American*, 224; McWilliams, *Factories in the Field*, 286.

31 Anne Loftis, *Witness to the Struggle: Imagining the 1930s California Labor Movement* (Reno: University of Nevada Press, 1998), 109; Errol Wayne Stevens, *Radical LA: From Coxey's Army to the Watts Riots, 1894–1965* (Norman: University of Oklahoma Press, 2009), 189, 192, 193; Louis Bloch, *Abstract of Hearings on Unemployment Before the California State Unemployment Commission* (April and May 1932); "Pigeons Urged to Feed the Poor," *Los Angeles Times*, December 22, 1932.

32 Francis Fox Piven and Richard Cloward, *Poor People's Movements: Why They Succeed, How They Fail* (New York: Vintage Books, 1979), 42; Irving Bernstein, *The Lean Years: A History of the American Worker, 1920–1933* (Baltimore: Penguin Books, 1966), 240, 287; Katznelson, *When Affirmative Action Was White*, 38; Theodore Draper, "Notes on Unemployed," unpublished, Theodore Draper research files, 1919–1970, Box 17, Folder 16, Manuscript, Archives, and Rare Book Library, Emory University.

33 Karl Marx and Frederick Engels, *Collected Works*, vol. 3 (New York: International Publishers, 1975), 284.

34 Bloch, *Abstract of Hearings*, 3; Meridel Leseur, "Women on the Breadlines," in *Communism in America: A History in Documents*, ed. Albert Fried (New York: Columbia University Press, 1997), 196; Moritz Hallgren, "Mobilizing the Poor," in Fried, *Communism in America*, 132.

35 Piven and Cloward, *Poor People's Movements*, 76.

36 Wild, *Street Meeting*, 183; "L.A. Jobless to Fight Relief Cut with Hunger March Oct 2," *Western Worker (WW)*, September 11, 1933; "Evicted Family Put Back in the House by Jobless," *WW*, September 18, 1933; "Relief Union in Fight on Eviction of Negro

Families," *WW*, September 25, 1933; "All Out for LA County Hunger March Oct. 2," *WW*, October 2, 1933; "LA Jobless Battle Cops at Welfare Office," *WW*, October 23, 1933; Jennie Grey, "12,000 in Militant March Force 10% L.A. Relief Raise," *WW*, November 20, 1933; "Public Works Mean Full Time Work for 45c Per Hr," *WW*, November 27, 1933.

37 "All Out for LA County Hunger March Oct. 2," *Western Worker*, October 2, 1933; Mike Davis, "The Necessary Eloquence of Protest," *The Nation*, March 17, 2009; Harvey Klehr, *The Heyday of American Communism: The Depression Decade* (New York: Basic Books, 1984), 49–68; Healey, "Tradition's Chains," 86; Sadie Amter, "Episodes at Cumberland: Reflections by Sadie Amter," *Daily Worker*, March 23, 1958; Len De Caux, *Labor Radical: From the Wobblies to CIO, A Personal History* (Boston: Beacon Press, 1970), 162–63.

38 Vivian McGurkin Raineri, *The Red Angel: The Life and Times of Elaine Black Yoneda* (New York: International Publishers, 1991), 23; Scott Allen McClellan, "Policing the Red Scare: The Los Angeles Police Department's Red Squad and the Repression of Labor" (PhD diss., University of California, Irvine, 2011), 173; Davis, "The Necessary Eloquence of Protest," 58 ; Grace M. Burnham, *Unemployment* (New York: International Publishers,1932), 34.

39 Raineri, *The Red Angel*, 23; Escobar, *Race, Police, and the Making of a Political Identity*, 81; Wild, *Street Meeting*, 191; "Brains Wanted," *Los Angeles Record*, February 28, 1930.

40 Healey, "Tradition's Chains," 48, 73, 72; Wild, *Street Meeting*, 181; Daniel J. Leab, "'United We Eat': The Creation and Organization of the Unemployed Councils in 1930," *Labor History* 8, no. 3 (1967): 300–315; Louis Bloch, *Abstract of Hearings*, 71.

41 Wild, *Street Meeting*, 193; Yoneda, *Ganbatte*, 21; Dennis McLellan, "Dorothy Healey, 91; "Lifelong Communist Fought for Workers," *Los Angeles Times*, August 8, 2006; Healey, "Tradition's Chains," 48–49; Bernstein, *The Lean Years*, 434.

42 Healey, "Tradition's Chains," 49.

43 Len Meyers and Chris Knox, "Organizing the Unemployed in the Great Depression: Fighting for Unity," *Workers Vanguard* 73, no. 18 (July 1975): 6–7; Bernstein, *Bridges of Reform*, 43; Douglas Monroy, "Anarquismo y Comunismo: Mexican Radicalism and the Communist Party in Los Angeles during the 1930s," *Labor History* 24 (Winter 1983): 42.

44 Zaragosa Vargas, "Tejana Radical: Emma Tenayuca and the San Antonio Labor Movement during the Great Depression," *Pacific Historical Review* 66, no. 4 (Nov. 1997): 553–80; Irving Kreitzberg, "For a Decisive Turn in Our Mexican Work and the Creation of a Mexican Department to Concentrate on the South-West," *Western Worker*, July 1, 1932; George H. Shoaf, "Jose Arispe—Story of Worker's Broken Home," *Western Worker*, May 15, 1932; "Red Suspect Under Arrest," *Los Angeles Times*, November 17, 1929.

45 Marx, *Capital*, 786, 789–90; William A. Sundstrom, "Last Hired, First Fired? Unemployment and Urban Black Workers during the Great Depression," *Journal of Economic History* 52, no. 2 (June 1992): 415–29; Bernstein, *The Lean Years*, 287; Theodore Draper, "Notes on Unemployment," 15.

46 Robin D. G. Kelley, *Hammer and Hoe: Alabama Communists during the Great Depression* (Chapel Hill: University of North Carolina Press, 1990); Christina Heatherton,

*The Color Line and the Class Struggle: The Mexican Revolution, Internationalism, and the American Century* (forthcoming).

47   Scott Kurashige, *The Shifting Grounds of Race: Black and Japanese Americans in the Making of Multiethnic Los Angeles* (Princeton: Princeton University Press, 2008), 81–82; Sides, *LA City Limits*, 32; Wild, *Street Meeting*, 194; Pettis Perry, *White Chauvinism and the Struggle for Peace* (New York: New Century Publishers, 1952), 18.

48   "Discrimination Against Negroes on LA Jobs," *Western Worker*, December 11, 1933; "Scottsboro Mother, Moore and Carter Tour So. Ca," *Western Worker*, September 25, 1933; Kurashige, *Shifting Grounds of Race,* 78; Josephine Fowler, *Japanese and Chinese Immigrant Activists: Organizing in American and International Communist Movements, 1919–1933* (New Brunswick, NJ: Rutgers University Press, 2007), 67; Shana Bernstein, *Bridges of Reform: Interracial Civil Rights Activism in Twentieth-Century Los Angeles* (New York: Oxford University Press, 2011), 40; Fried, *Communism in America,* 98.

49   Miscellaneous clippings, Box 1, Folder 2, Karl Yoneda Papers, Collection 1592, Special Collections, University of California, Los Angeles.

50   Otto Huiswoud, "The Effects of Unemployment on the Negro Masses in the USA," *Inspector,* April 2, 1931, 359.

51   George Padmore, "The Fight for Bread," *Negro Worker* 3, nos. 6–7 (June–July 1933): 3–4; Angelo Herndon, *Let Me Live* (Ann Arbor: University of Michigan Press, 2007), 316.

**PART FOUR**

Seeing Radical Connections

# 6

# Policing Gay LA

## Mapping Racial Divides in the Homophile Era, 1950–1967

EMILY K. HOBSON

ON THE EVENING OF JANUARY 27, 1952, A SEVENTEEN-YEAR-OLD NAMED Horace Martinez became a target of "vice" entrapment by the Los Angeles Police Department (LAPD). As Martinez later recounted, he and four friends had been passing time at Echo Park, a popular gathering spot in the neighborhood of the same name. The teenagers drank coffee at the park boathouse, and Martinez went to use the restroom, which he knew was a cruising site for men seeking sex. He noticed a man watching him closely inside. When Martinez asked the man what he was looking at, the man slapped him in the face; the teenager ran out of the bathroom yelling, "Help! Help! A queer!" The assailant was an undercover police officer named Ted Porter who chased Martinez, tackled him, and began beating him with his fists. Martinez's friends ran over. Although the youth were unarmed, Porter shot nineteen-year-old William Rubio in the chest, piercing his lung and knocking him into Echo Park Lake. Another plainclothes officer appeared, and the police arrested all five teenagers. Rubio regained consciousness in the county hospital and was held there nearly a month before being transferred to jail; the other teenagers were booked on robbery charges.[1]

In the aftermath of these arrests, the teenagers and their parents sought help from the Civil Rights Congress (CRC), a leftist organization active in the Echo Park neighborhood. Martinez, Rubio, Rubio's seventeen-year-old brother Victor, and seventeen-year-old Frank Canales were Mexican American. The fifth teenager, William Arnold, was an eighteen-year-old of Italian descent. The CRC interpreted the teenagers' case in a long pattern of LAPD abuse against working-class people and people of color, especially Mexican and black youth. They described "vice" policing as a catalyst of the arrests and denounced both antigay entrapment and brutality as abusive police practices.

At the same time that the CRC responded to these arrests, a recently formed organization of gay men—the Mattachine Society, one of the earliest and most influential organizations in the history of LGBT (lesbian, gay, bisexual, and transgender) activism—learned of the Echo Park case. Having just formed a Citizens Committee to Outlaw Entrapment, Mattachine stated, "The issue here is not whether the man is a homosexual, *but whether the Police Department is justified in using such methods.*"[2] The CRC and Mattachine shared ties to the local Communist Party and exchanged information with each other as they worked to challenge the charges levied against the teens. Victor Rubio and William Arnold were soon released, but over the spring and early summer William Rubio was tried for assault with a deadly weapon and with attempting to help a prisoner escape.[3] Martinez and Canales were found guilty of resisting arrest and striking an officer. While Canales served his sentence at home, the judge remanded Martinez to a youth facility for "psychiatric evaluation"— a typical outcome for those convicted of "morals" charges such as homosexuality. Martinez protested his innocence and avowed his hostility to gay men, but his arrest and conviction were framed by allegations of lewd behavior.[4]

A few weeks after the teenagers' trials, another entrapment arrest occurred that held a different outcome and became much better known in queer history. An undercover LAPD officer followed a thirty-four-year-old white gay man named Dale Jennings case home from Westlake (now MacArthur) Park. Like nearby Echo Park, Westlake was a well-known cruising spot. Jennings recounted that the officer was "a big, rough looking character who appeared out of nowhere ... and then followed me over a mile home. Thinking he had robbery in mind, I walked fast, took detours and said goodbye at each corner. Later I wondered how obvious I must have appeared to him to cause this persistence, until he remarked to another officer ... 'It's all I can do to keep up the old quota.'" Jennings stated that the officer pursued him into his apartment and, once inside, arrested Jennings for seeking homosexual sex.[5]

Jennings was one of the handful of men participating in the Mattachine Society and, together with others in the group, decided to turn his arrest into a test case. He demanded a jury trial and hired George Shibley, a civil rights lawyer known for having defended the twenty-one Mexican American men falsely accused of murder in the 1942 Sleepy Lagoon case.[6] In court, Jennings acknowledged that he was homosexual but denied that he had been seeking sex. The jury deadlocked and the city dismissed his case. Throughout Jennings's trial, Mattachine circulated fliers among gay men, arguing that police entrapment was a method of harassing homosexuals in public sites. The organization grew dramatically, especially after the case's dismissal. The Jennings case would eventually become marked as the first major victory of the "homophile" movement—the self-declared name for the first phase of sustained organizing among gay and lesbian people in the United States and Europe, dated from approximately 1948 to 1969 and understood as the precursor to gay liberation.[7]

In their first fliers on entrapment and their correspondence with the CRC, Mattachine drew strong connections between the Jennings case and the Echo Park arrests.[8] But the group's discussion of policing quickly shifted. By the time Jennings's trial was underway in June, Mattachine stopped mentioning the Echo Park case and more generally ceased to note links between practices of entrapment and brutality, the policing of gay life and the policing of communities of color.[9] Their reticence continued even as new cases surfaced involving antigay policing and police violence against men of color. In April, the *Los Angeles Times*, the *Daily News*, the Communist *Daily Worker*, and the Civil Rights Congress all took note that the officer who had assaulted Horace Martinez was charged with beating another Latino man, Ramón Castellanos, during a "vagrancy-lewd" arrest.[10] Mattachine ignored the Castellanos case and said less and less about racialized policing, even while solidifying an argument that homosexuals could be understood as being analogous to people of color because they were "a social Minority with ... group-culture characteristics (patterns, problems, and oppressions)."[11]

The members of Mattachine were white, primarily middle-class men in their thirties and forties who declared themselves to be homosexual; the Mexican American working-class youth arrested in Echo Park were presumptively straight, with one on record as being antigay. (Martinez declared that the group had gone to the park to rob a "queer," though Victor Rubio denied this story.) Yet while Dale Jennings, Horace Martinez, William and Victor Rubio, Frank Canales, and William Arnold held different relationships to sexual identity and met different outcomes in court, they shared a common experience of entrapment. Their arrests open a

Figure 6.1. Boathouse at Echo Park Lake, 1948.
Courtesy of the Los Angeles Public Library.

window onto the deep inseparability between the policing of race and the policing of sexuality in mid-twentieth-century Los Angeles.

In early 1950s Los Angeles, queer life was concentrated in working-class and racially mixed areas of the city. It was present in a wide range of sites, including bars, bathhouses, and parks, and was most visibly (though by no means exclusively) policed among men. Arrests for homosexual offenses were published in city newspapers and were difficult to defend; in Mattachine's words, "How do you prove you are not what you are not?"[12] Further, the LAPD used anti-gay policing as a means of regulating communities of color just as it used racist policing as a means of controlling queer life. As Mattachine's earliest flier on entrapment stated, it was "dangerous" to assume that anti-gay policing was "special and confined." Rather, homophobia was a tool of racial and political containment: "If Negroes and Whites ride in the same car, they open themselves to being stopped by police prowl cars and being accused of suspicion of Homosexuality. 'Nigger-lover' has two meanings in a cop's mouth, not one."[13]

Soon, however, Mattachine stopped making such arguments. Instead, homophile activists developed a more limited response to policing: they imagined race and sexuality as separate and homosexual life as radically distinct from communities of color.

Norman Klein has famously described Los Angeles as being structured by a "history of forgetting."[14] A history of forgetting the imbrications of homophobic and racist policing proved central to the growth of homophile activism in Los Angeles. This same forgetting has echoed across the field of queer history, where the Echo Park case remains virtually unknown. To date, the only published discussion of the case appears in Daniel Hurewitz's *Bohemian Los Angeles*, which traces the links between artistic, leftist, and gay communities in the early and middle decades of the twentieth century. Hurewitz rightly interprets the Echo Park case as a catalyst in Mattachine's politicization of homosexuality as a "minority" identity analogous to race. Yet he neglects to note how sexuality shaped the Echo Park arrests, describing only a "fight with the police" and never mentioning antigay entrapment.[15] Although Hurewitz evocatively illustrates the homophile movement and its cultural milieu, he isolates Mattachine's ideological trajectory from the material context that inspired it and overlooks how the group's use of analogy to define "minority" identity obscured the lived intersections of sexuality and race. LGBT history and public memory too often replicate the fault lines of the homophile movement, framing queer communities and communities of color as if they have developed independently or in isolation. Such segregated renderings have obscured the ways in which all policing of sexuality, queer or straight, is racialized, and the means by which homophobia and racism function through rather than simply alongside each other. In Lisa Duggan's words, "Homophobic rhetoric and stepped-up policing" have been "state tools for imposing *racial* norms," especially norms against interracial contact in public space.[16]

Los Angeles is a powerful site from which to identify relationships between sexual containment and racism and to challenge the ways these relationships have been forgotten. The city was both a central hub of the homophile movement and an aggressively policed place, especially beginning in 1950, when William Parker became chief of the LAPD. Indeed, the nearly exact overlap between the homophile era and the Parker era (1950–1966) was no mere coincidence. Parker's LAPD placed longtime locations of gay life—interracial, primarily working-class areas in and around downtown—under greater and greater surveillance, while leaving whiter areas in Hollywood and West Hollywood less monitored. Over time, police suppression of interracial contact and "vice" deepened both the physical and the conceptual segregation of the city's sexual life. Queer people of color increasingly gathered in house parties and other semiprivate sites, while white gay bars, organizations, and gathering places gained safety above ground but moved west.[17] The homophile movement bent itself toward claiming respectability and countering charges of "deviance," politicizing homosexual identity in terms that divided it from "street life." As Christina Hanhardt argues, gay issues became imagined as what would remain if the racial diversity, class marginality, and gender transgression of queer life could be "taken out."[18] These limits shaped sexual politics into the late 1960s and beyond. Parker-era policing constructed racial divides that became fundamental to the political rhetoric and everyday geography of gay LA.

*　*　*

Postwar Los Angeles was bent on segregation, pushing and pulling people from areas that had been racially mixed into more homogenous, isolated sites.[19] Defense industries brought waves of new residents, particularly black people, and as growth continued the city and its suburbs set defined racial limits. As George Sánchez has discovered, redlining practices categorized the Mexican American, Japanese American, Jewish, and black neighborhood of Boyle Heights as "hopelessly heterogeneous" and financially risky. Out of all the Boyle Heights residents who sought to buy homes where loans were available—that is, in Anglo neighborhoods—Jewish residents met the least hostility and gradually migrated across the city. Boyle Heights became more homogenously Mexican and more dominated by renters.[20] Housing trends thus converged with policing practices to designate interracial areas as especially dangerous and to grant the greatest economic, social, and cultural security to places defined as white. By the early 1960s, black and Latino people were increasingly isolated both from white Angelenos and from each another. Although communities began to overlap in new ways in the 1970s, racial segregation came to define postwar LA. Black residents became concentrated in south Los Angeles; white residents on the Westside, in the Valley, and suburbs; Mexican Americans in Echo Park, downtown, and East LA; and Asian and Native Americans scattered around the central city.[21]

Policing was integral to the segregation process. Scott Kurashige argues that the postwar LAPD "present[ed] one face of guardian to the suburbs and another of occupier to the inner city."[22] This style of policing held continuities with the past, but became especially visible while William Parker served as chief (1950–1966). Parker instituted a "professionalism" model that centralized power inside the department, prioritized internal control over public oversight, and heightened the use of crime statistics to explain criminality by race. Alternately termed "crime control," "proactive policing," or, in Parker's most famous formulation, "the thin blue line," the professionalism model envisioned the police as an embattled group that protected society against barely contained forces of chaos.[23] Officers moved off the sidewalk and into technologically equipped cars, targeting "street life" among black and Latino young men as the central source of crime.[24] Police brutality against black and Latino residents rose sharply. In addition to the events leading up to the 1965 Watts Riots, major controversies included police beatings of young Mexican American men in 1951 and 1952, known as the "Bloody Christmas" and Tony Rios cases; police assaults on black teenagers at Griffith Park in 1960; and a police shooting at a black Muslim temple in 1962. "Crime control" also rested on suppressing dissent. Parker responded to the Bloody Christmas and Rios cases by preventing an investigation by the civilian police commission and by implying that Communists drove allegations of police brutality.[25] Redbaiting restricted and isolated the city's most radical and multiracial activist groups, including the Civil Rights Congress, at precisely the moment that the Echo Park entrapment and beating case occurred.[26]

In targeting "street life," Parker's police professionalism stigmatized an overlapping range of behaviors, including black and Mexican youth culture, homosocial contact among working-class men, homosexuality and gender transgression, sex work, and interracial contact of various kinds. Concern over these behaviors carried deep and tangled roots, with concepts of perversion and deviance fueled by anxieties over racial, class, and urban upheaval. Notably, Progressive Era campaigns against vice in Los Angeles had centered less on homosexuality than on heterosexuality, and less on men than on women. Anxious over white women's presence in public leisure, reformers and police had defined racially mixed, working-class nightlife as illicit, pushed sex work into neighborhoods of color, and concentrated vice arrests among black and Latina women.[27] These patterns were widespread across the early twentieth-century United

States. In Chicago and New York, reformers closed brothels in middle-class white neighborhoods, then largely ignored the prostitution relocated onto black streets. As Kevin Mumford argues, this relocation produced "interzones" in which heterosexual sex work, interracial entertainment, and queer expression converged.[28] White men increasingly traveled to "Bronzevilles" and Chinatowns to purchase sex and entertainment from black and Asian women. Venues for same-sex contact also developed in these areas, linking homosexuality to commodified and interracial desire. Nan Boyd's history of queer San Francisco shows that gay and lesbian subcultures grew at the "intersection of sexualized and racialized entertainment zones."[29] More broadly, Roderick Ferguson observes, black vice districts, bachelor Chinatowns, and "premodern" Mexican immigrant homes became defined as sites of "multiplying, intersecting racial, gender, and sexual perversions" in contrast to a racially, sexually, and gender normative white American home.[30]

While discourses of "perversion" and "deviance" were wide-ranging and amorphous, their malleable quality helped construct the more fixed category of the "homosexual." Homosexuality was brought into focus not only through medicine and psychiatry but also by policing practices targeting the gay, lesbian, bisexual, and transgender life that was grounded in working-class and racially diverse spaces and that included interracial, cross-class desire. By the middle of the twentieth century, as Margot Canaday argues, US welfare, military, and immigration policy converged to construct a "straight state" that defined the homosexual as an "anticitizen."[31] The US state excluded homosexuals from benefits in the New Deal and GI Bill, discharged them from military service, and by 1952 and 1953 barred them from immigrating into the country or holding federal employment.[32] In the late 1930s and following World War II, a series of national sex crime panics collapsed consensual adult homosexuality with child sexual abuse and coded homosexuality as a form of urban disorder.[33] Yet while the straight state codified the "homosexual" as a social category, it did not radically isolate homosexuality from other categories of difference, nor did it define all heterosexuality as equally decent. Rather, it added the homosexual to a long list of people deemed "ineligible," "dishonorable," and "likely to become a public charge." Policing proved pivotal to this construction in that local departments were most concerned with homosexuality as a sign of blight or something that marked a neighborhood's criminal character.[34]

As the straight state emerged, the LAPD—and William Parker, who joined the force in 1927—learned to view homosexuals as a special threat. By the late 1930s, men seeking homosexual activity in Los Angeles could find it downtown in a circuit that included Pershing Square, the bus depot, Main Street, and a few bathhouses and bars.[35] The LAPD declared a "war on vagrants" in 1936, and the city established a "sex bureau" to target "degenerates" in 1937.[36] As with similar campaigns across the nation, these efforts at containment served to stratify homosexual expression along lines of race, class, and gender expression. Middle-class white men constructed an increasingly hidden, segregated gay subculture by making use of their greater access to private space. Meanwhile, the queer life that remained out in the open became ever more markedly working-class, gender transgressive, and racially diverse.[37] While small enclaves of white gay men developed among friends in the Echo Park and Silver Lake hills, the southwestern, working-class sections of those neighborhoods became known for their cruising grounds. Across town in Hollywood, gay men enjoyed relative protection because police refrained from booking film stars on homosexual offenses.[38] This geography became more entrenched as gay and lesbian life expanded during and after World War II. Arrests for "sex perversion" and "vagrancy" grew in working-class neighborhoods, and police began to arrest lesbians in growing numbers, directing particular hostility at butch women of color and interracial pairs that included white women.[39] In 1947, the city council adopted a resolution calling on the LAPD to use "every latitude in its power" to shut down gay bars. Parker affirmed his commitment to this goal soon after becoming chief in 1950.[40]

The homophile movement developed in this context. Los Angeles was the movement's birthplace and, over the course of the 1950s and 1960s, one of its most central hubs.[41] In 1947, the same year the city council urged a crackdown on gay bars, a Hollywood secretary circulated *Vice Versa*, the nation's first lesbian publication. In 1948 Harry Hay, a Communist Party member and resident of Silver Lake, formed Bachelors for Wallace, bringing together leftist white gay men under the banner of supporting the Progressive Party presidential candidate. Hay's group became the seed of the Mattachine Society, which was founded in 1950 and expanded during the Dale Jennings trial in 1952. By late 1953, amid anti-communist hysteria, a more conservative majority in Mattachine rejected the leadership of Hay and other radicals and turned the group away from leftist political language, while also embracing public and comparatively militant goals of social services and education.[42] In 1957, Mattachine moved its head-quarters to San Francisco, where it built coalitions with groups including the lesbian Daughters of Bilitis (formed in 1955). Los Angeles remained a significant center of homophile activity through ONE, Inc., which spun off from Mattachine in 1952, began publishing *One* magazine in 1953, and organized challenges to obscenity laws.[43] Through *One* and other publications, Los Angeles gay and lesbian activists traded information, tactics, and ideas nationally and transnationally.

Harry Hay and the early Mattachine Society politicized homosexuality in terms that were profoundly shaped by discussions of race, nation, and identity in Los Angeles's left. The "black belt thesis," developed by and among US black radicals, defined black people in the US South as an oppressed nation. This idea was adopted by the Comintern in 1928 and proved profoundly significant to Marxist thought in the United States.[44] By the 1940s, Communists and fellow travelers drew on the black belt thesis to term Los Angeles the "United Nations in a city."[45] The local Civil Rights Congress used this language to organize cross-racial campaigns against police brutality, false accusations, deportations, and arrests for political dissent.

On founding Mattachine, Harry Hay resigned from the Communist Party due to its ban on homosexual members; according to Bettina Aptheker, after Hay began to work publicly in the homophile movement, the Party expelled him to prevent his rejoining.[46] Hay nonetheless drew heavily on Communist language in forming Mattachine, comparing sexuality and race in much the way he had learned to compare race and nation. Mattachine's founding statement of "missions and purposes," written and approved in 1951, used "minority" identity as both a description and a goal: a way to refer to homosexuals collectively as a "people," and a means to call for a "highly ethical homosexual culture ... paralleling the emerging cultures of our fellow-minorities—the Negro, Mexican, and Jewish peoples."[47] Daniel Hurewitz observes that although the idea of a homosexual "minority" was initially controversial in Mattachine, comparing homosexuality to race built support because it framed the homosexual minority as one brought together by persecution rather than inherent difference, and defined a "camaraderie *about* sexual desires that was not constituted by those desires."[48] But although this conception of homosexuality as a minority identity helped galvanize a movement, it also set immediate and lasting limits.

Most centrally, Mattachine's call for a "highly ethical homosexual culture" suggested that existing homosexual life was unethical or depraved. Set against dominant cultural norms, the idea that homosexuality could become ethical was potentially radical. Yet this idea was articulated through a politics of respectability that constrained the redefinition activists sought.[49] Mattachine's founding statement defined the group as setting a "dignified standard," proposed that homosexuals could lead "well-adjusted, wholesome, and socially productive lives," and argued that "a homosexual ethic" would be "disciplined, moral, and socially responsible."[50] In comparing this "ethic" to "the emerging cultures of our fellow-minorities," the group lauded a politics of respectability in racial and ethnic politics as well. Indeed, their use of "emerging" implied that efforts toward respectability were a valuable stage in social development. Soon, homophile activists would build on their call for ethical homosexuality by distinguishing "modern" sexualities from those they saw as immature. David Churchill has found that across the 1950s and 1960s, homophile publications not only criticized cruising and drag queens in US and European cities, but also drew contrasts with "premodern" homosexualities in Africa, Asia, and the Arab world.[51] Mattachine laid important groundwork for this rhetoric by defining sexuality parallel to race and by demanding that homosexuals and people of color disavow the ascriptions of degeneracy that had historically marginalized them. Mirroring the heterosexuality of black respectability, Mattachine's homosexual respectability became middle-class and white.

This ideological framework was bolstered and motivated by Parker-era policing. While Parker's methods of crime control by no means centered solely on sexuality, they did reflect anxiety over sexuality at every turn. Parker approached homosexuality as dangerous because it occupied public space in nonnormative ways and was racially impure. As part of "street life," homosexuality was both visible within, and an accusation that could be used to control, communities of color and interracial, working-class spaces in Los Angeles. Further, policing homosexuality offered a means to displace the LAPD's own culpability in "vice."

Parker was appointed chief in the wake of a 1948 scandal that revealed that LAPD officers had received payoffs from a heterosexual prostitution ring.[52] In public statements, the chief characterized police professionalism as both a triumph over past corruption ("cleaning up" the department) and a means to use social scientific data on race and crime to create an orderly city ("cleaning up" LA).[53] Through professionalism, he defined the police as a neutral body that responded to evidence, rather than a force that helped to construct the criminal (including sexual) marketplace through entrapment, blackmail, and payoffs. He directed officers' energies toward homosexuality and interracial entertainment, two forms of vice in which they had not been previously implicated but which were widely viewed as dangerous threats. Daryl Gates, Parker's protégé and eventual successor as chief, recounted that because officers were squeamish about responding to homosexual behavior, Parker "instituted a strict, nearly foolproof system of investigating vice complaints to force officers to check out every call."[54] In addition to targeting cruising sites and downtown bars, Parker worked to shut down black jazz clubs that tolerated "degenerates."[55] Mattachine, in turn, argued that Parker's protocols fed corruption because vice officers not only propositioned men but "reap[ed] rich rewards from phony entrapments, staged seductions, undisguised blackmailings, and the sales of ... perjuries."[56]

In 1950, the LAPD began to publish materials that reflected the public relations side of Parker's professionalism approach. Past LAPD "digests" had been composed solely of tables of data, but the department's new "annual reports" were distributed widely and laden with photographs and snippets of text. They also obscured details by simplifying information, demonstrating Parker's tactics of internal control. The information in these reports varied over time and therefore is difficult to track precisely. However, the available evidence shows that, under Parker, LAPD officers sharply increased their arrests for homosexual offenses. (Homophobic policing that resulted in nonsexual charges, as in the Echo Park case, could not be quantified.)

In 1950, the LAPD recorded 2,430 "sex perversion" arrests for acts including "crime against nature, sex perversion, sodomy, and vagrancy lewd." This represented an 84.9 percent increase over the 1940s average of 1,290 such arrests per year.[57] In other words, in Parker's first year as chief, the department nearly doubled their arrests for "sex perversion." Further, this jump occurred even as arrests for other forms of "vice," including prostitution, pornography, and gambling, fell.[58] Arrests for "perversion," later termed "sex offenses," grew at rates that outpaced population growth in the city, reaching 4,355 in 1965 and not dropping substantially until 1970—after the end of the Parker era, the move of most gay bars out of downtown, and the rise of a large and vocal gay liberation movement.

Although racial and ethnic data for "sex offenses" were not consistently made public, figures from 1956, a year with a relatively detailed report, show racially disproportionate policing: white men were less likely, and black and Latino men twice as likely, to be arrested for "sex offenses" compared to their population.[59]

The most significant effects of this policing were apparent at the neighborhood level. Throughout the Parker era, sexuality—and particularly homosexuality—was most heavily policed in the area that the LAPD designated as the Central Division. Central encompassed downtown, Westlake, Echo Park, and portions of Silver Lake.[60] In 1950, the division held only about 10 percent of the city's population but experienced almost a quarter of all arrests, over a third of all vice arrests, 52.1 percent of sex perversion arrests, and 63.9 percent of arrests for prostitution.[61] By the mid-1960s, Hollywood Division would match Central in "sex offenses," but Central would continue to see the overwhelming majority of vagrancy arrests, many for "vagrancy-lewd."

Central was largely working-class and the most racially mixed area of the city. Its residents were principally Mexican American or Chicano and white, with smaller numbers of Filipino, black, Chinese, Native American, and other people. The downtown areas were especially diverse and transient. Officer Daryl Gates began working Central in 1951, and later termed it "a mixture of blacks, Hispanics, Asians, and whites, many of them newly arrived immigrants. [I] policed Skid Row, Main Street—with its B-girl bars and burlesque theaters—to East 5th and 6th Streets and Bunker Hill ... it was a bunch of beaten-down, dilapidated old tenements, rife with crime, narcotics, gambling, drunks, prostitutes, and wholesale scumbags."[62]

Many other Angelenos viewed downtown in very different terms: as a place to find pleasure, power, and home. Jim Kepner, a white, leftist gay activist and an archivist of gay history, remembered downtown's Pershing Square—on Olive Street between 5th and 6th—as the center of gay life in the 1940s and 1950s. In his words, the Square was vibrant with both sexual and political activity:

> There were gays there—aplenty—but I didn't really know much
> about hustlers. There was vice [police], but you ignored them most of
> the time. And there was the excitement of the singalongs, the politi-
> cal and religious debates (I got very involved in these), the chess
> games ... a shifting group of people who weren't afraid to be differ-

ent.... I remember the easy, non-threatening crowds day and night on every downtown street. I remember Sidney, who seemed devoted to picking up every Marine who stopped in Pershing Square (and they all knew what they were there for) and recording the details for Doctor Kinsey ... the nights when Officer Shirley, who liked to call himself the Mayor of Pershing Square, was doing his number with nightsticks flying, the many friends met, again and again.[63]

In Kepner's memory, Pershing Square was both continually policed and continually transgressive and resistant—a place where multiple forms of dissent flowed together. The Square helped support many local businesses with gay clientele, including bars, baths, and newsstands selling physique magazines. Bunker Hill, which was residentially largely Filipino, became known for Maxwell's bar (Second at Hill) and the Palace Baths (Fourth and Main). By the mid-1950s a downtown lawyer named Gladys Root offered defense for sex offense charges.[64] The Chicano novelist John Rechy has described the area coffee shop Cooper's Doughnuts as a popular hangout for "queens, butch hustlers, their friends, and their customers ... [many] Latino or black"; Rechy also notes that in 1959 Cooper's saw a small riot against a homophobic police raid.[65] Asian gay men interviewed by Eric Wat recalled that, as late as the mid-1960s, Main Street was a place where "drag queens could go into the street in drag," and that "Fifth and Sixth Streets from [Pershing Square] east to Main Street's bus terminals were known as 'queen's row.'"[66]

Most brokers of power, however, saw the gay central city as dangerous and repellant. Los Angeles real estate brochures defined black people and sexual "deviants" as criminal groups that would reduce property values, and film noir filmed or set in Bunker Hill (for example, *Act of Violence*, *Double Indemnity*) linked sexual perversity with racial threats.[67] Over the course of the late 1950s and early 1960s, the city's Community Redevelopment Agency bulldozed Bunker Hill housing to construct corporate highrises. To garner public support, they described the area as "well known to the vice squad as a haven for prostitutes, juvenile delinquents, narcotics peddlers, and 'moral offenders of both sexes.'"[68] Whitney Strub has shown that battles over obscenity also found a frontline downtown. In 1961 the LAPD closed nineteen downtown bookstores and newsstands for selling "lewd" material; although that material was largely heterosexual, the raids were accompanied by a surge of arrests targeting gay men.[69]

Figure 6.2. Pershing Square, 1951, before major redevelopment.
Courtesy of the Los Angeles Public Library.

Finally, to accelerate redevelopment, the LAPD conducted sweeps of Pershing Square in 1959 and 1964. The 1964 sweep was followed by a wholesale renovation in which the city ripped out trees and bushes, removed most benches, installed brighter lighting, and transformed the Square into an easy-to-police concrete zone. The *Los Angeles Times* and *Daily News* named "deviates" and "perverts" as the targets of the cleanup and park redesign.[70]

Beyond Central Division, two other LAPD districts—Hollywood and Newton—proved significant in the Parker-era policing of sexuality and of race. By the mid-1960s the largely white Hollywood Division emerged as the second most significant hub for homosexual arrests (now grouped as "sex offenses") and its most significant site of male prostitution. Yet Hollywood experienced relatively light policing overall, and its prostitution arrests remained numerically low. The primarily black Newton Division was much more heavily policed, and although its "sex offense" arrests were few, women were arrested for prostitution there at high rates. Indeed, as women's prostitution arrests fell in Central, they rose in black LA. According to the data from 1956, African Americans constituted just 5 percent of the city's population, but black women experienced the overwhelming majority of female arrests for prostitution (62.6 percent) and the largest proportion of all prostitution arrests regardless of race or gender (42.3 percent).[71] These arrests were shaped by perceptions of black women as hypersexual and by the displacement of streetwalking into black neighborhoods in the early decades of the twentieth century. Although generally ignored by homophile activists, arrests for heterosexual prostitution significantly affected the lives of lesbian and bisexual women. Queer narratives include multiple anecdotes of women, both butch and femme, charged with prostitution on the basis of their presence in a lesbian bar.[72]

The figures in LAPD reports point to several trends in the sexual, gender, and racial hierarchies of Parker-era Los Angeles. First, they affirm Central Division as a focal point of homosexual arrests, while showing that its significance fell as gay life was pushed out by redevelopment. In this same period, Hollywood became a significant site of antigay arrests but remained otherwise lightly policed. Second, the geography that had marked the 1930s and 1940s, in which white gay and lesbian life gained safety behind closed doors and queer "street life" was racially mixed and working-class, shifted over the course of the Parker era through a new form of gay visibility. By the early 1960s, gay and lesbian bars and theaters—particularly those dominated by white clientele—were moving into Silver Lake, Hollywood, and West Hollywood, the last of which was policed by the less aggressive sheriff's department rather than the LAPD.[73] New, more racially mixed gay sites also emerged in Westlake (at Central's western edge) and in the Wilshire area.[74] Yet by the end of the 1960s and the beginning of gay liberation, gay and lesbian life had shifted decisively out of downtown, and its visible geographies were significantly more white than they had been just a decade prior.[75] By the early 1970s, the best-known gay bars were concentrated in Hollywood and West Hollywood, and some establishments segregated themselves by asking men of color for two or three IDs. Black, Latino, and other gay and lesbian people of color constructed autonomous geographies in neighborhoods of color, often in semiprivate spaces such as house parties. When they congregated aboveground, they were subject to heightened containment by police.[76] Gay safety and visibility came to be remade as privileges of whiteness through both political rhetoric and everyday practices.

Alongside this pattern, by the close of the Parker era a new gay poli-tics—soon to be called gay liberation—was afoot. Inspired by the growth of black, Chicano, and other Third World radicalisms, this politics was both more militant and more anti-racist. Its activists drew on internal colonialism theory to call for the liberation of "gay ghettos" and demanded gender and sexual "self-determination" at the scales of the private home and the individual body. Gay liberationists across the country, both white and of color, claimed solidarity across race and class and began to define drag as oppositional rather than as a mark of underdevelopment.[77] But concrete anti-racist alliances remained elusive, most especially in Los Angeles. Though the homophile movement was founded in LA, San Fran-cisco was the site where, between 1965 and 1967, homophile groups forged coalitions with antipoverty and civil rights groups, shifting their stances on class, race, and gender norms to work with "street queens" in the Ten-derloin district.[78] Los Angeles activists did not follow suit; instead, racial divides continued to mark the geographies of gay LA.

William Parker died on July 16, 1966, but his legacy lived on.[79] On December 31, 1966, the LAPD raided two gay, primarily white bars in Sil-ver Lake, the Black Cat and New Faces. Silver Lake occupied a bohemian middle ground between increasingly "seedy" areas in downtown and Echo Park and the more privileged gay life expanding farther west. Undercover officers witnessed men in the Black Cat kissing at midnight and, a few minutes into New Year's Day of 1967, began beating patrons there and next door at New Faces. The officers severely injured several people and arrested sixteen. They charged thirteen bar-goers with lewd conduct, two others with drunkenness, and one with assault on an officer. Six weeks later, on February 11, 1967, some two hundred people gathered in front of the Black Cat and protested police harassment. This was the city's first public demonstration for gay rights.[80]

The Black Cat demonstration has been widely noted as LA's first gay protest, and its timing makes it a useful marker for shifts between the homophile and gay liberation movements. But the event was notable in another way as well: it revealed the history of forgetting that was set into motion during the 1952 Echo Park arrests and that solidified across the Parker era. The group that led the protest at the Black Cat, Personal Rights in Defense and Education (PRIDE), had formed in 1966 and defined itself as more militant than older homophile groups. Indeed, PRIDE timed its protest to demonstrate its interests in radical alliances, because a New

Left organization called the Right of Assembly and Movement Committee (RAMCOM) had proposed February 11 as the day to protest police violence on the Sunset Strip. PRIDE endorsed RAMCOM's effort, and the two groups called for a night of linked demonstrations by gay people in Silver Lake, hippies in Venice and the Strip, black people in Watts, and Chicanos in Pacoima and East LA.[81] But only the Silver Lake and Strip demonstrations occurred because neither PRIDE nor RAMCOM had relationships with activist leaders of black or Chicano LA. Beyond that, the list of protests the two groups proposed was telling: they defined gay, black, Chicano, and hippie identities as linked by police subjugation but segregated into distinct, clearly bounded sites. RAMCOM and PRIDE imagined gay and hippie identities as white, and black and brown identities as straight. Gay activists knew that the LAPD oppressed many communities, but they had learned to forget to ask how oppressions of sexuality and race overlapped. Their segregated mapping of protest revealed the lasting effects of the policing of gay LA.

1    Many thanks to Moon-Ho Jung, Chandan Reddy, Laura Pulido, Wendy Cheng, Susie Woo, and an anonymous reviewer for their feedback and insight on this essay, and to Felicia Perez for her discussions and support.
        Echo Park case folder, Civil Rights Congress Papers (hereafter CRC), Southern California Library for Social Studies and Research (hereafter SCL), Los Angeles.
2    Citizens' Committee to Outlaw Entrapment, "NOW is the time to fight" (flier, Echo Park case folder, CRC, SCL), emphasis in original.
3    The Echo Park case folder includes extensive notes from the CRC, fliers and correspondence from the Mattachine Society, and clippings from local newspapers. The *Daily Worker* provided the most consistent coverage of the arrests and ensuing cases, but I have not been able to determine the final outcome of William Rubio's trial.
4    Martinez told the CRC that the teenagers had previously assaulted a "queer" at the park and planned to do so again; Victor Rubio disputed this in his statement to the CRC (Echo Park case, CRC, SCL).
5    Jennings published his own account of the arrest and ensuing trial in *One* magazine in 1953. Reprinted as Dale Jennings, "To Be Accused, Is to Be Guilty," in *We Are Everywhere: A Historical Sourcebook of Gay and Lesbian Politics*, ed. Mark Blasius and Shane Phelan (New York: Routledge, 1997), 310–12.
6    Daniel Hurewitz, *Bohemian Los Angeles and the Making of Modern Politics* (Berkeley: University of California Press, 2007), 261.
7    Hurewitz, *Bohemian Los Angeles*, 261–63; John D'Emilio, *Sexual Politics, Sexual Communities: The Making of a Homosexual Minority in the United States, 1940–1970* (Chicago: University of Chicago, 1983), 70–71; Stuart Timmons, *The Trouble with Harry Hay: Founder of the Modern Gay Movement* (Boston: Alyson Publications, 1990), 163–

68; and Walter L. Williams and Yolanda Retter, *Gay and Lesbian Rights in the United States: A Documentary History* (Westport, CT: Greenwood Press, 2003), 74–75.

8    Citizens' Committee, "NOW is the time to fight"; and Joseph Harrison (pseudonym), Citizens' Committee to Outlaw Entrapment, letter to "Miss Meyers," Civil Rights Congress, April 28, 1952 (both in Echo Park case folder, CRC, SCL). Joseph Harrison was most likely a pseudonym for Harry Hay.

9    The CRC did not involve itself in the Jennings case but did criticize entrapment when discussing the Echo Park arrests.

10   The CRC collected information about this beating, as is evident in *Daily News* and *Los Angeles Times* clippings in the Echo Park case folder, CRC, SCL. Castellanos's name was published in these papers, as was common with arrests for sexually based offenses at the time.

11   Joseph Harrison (pseudonym), Citizens Committee to Outlaw Entrapment letter to Civil Rights Congress, May 15, 1952 (Echo Park case file, CRC, SCL).

12   Citizens Committee to Outlaw Entrapment, "An Anonymous Call to Arms," undated (Echo Park case file, CRC, SCL). The original sentence was in all capital letters.

13   Citizens Committee to Outlaw Entrapment, "Anonymous Call to Arms." Similar charges were levied against civil rights workers in Mississippi, as detailed by John Howard, *Men Like That: A Southern Queer History* (Chicago: University of Chicago Press, 1999).

14   Norman Klein, *A History of Forgetting: Los Angeles and the Erasure of Memory* (New York: Verso, 1997).

15   Hurewitz, *Bohemian Los Angeles,* 233. Hurewitz cites the same sources I have found, all of which show that vice entrapment was central to the case. John D'Emilio notes the case in his dissertation but not in *Sexual Politics, Sexual Communities.*

16   Lisa Duggan, "Down There: The Queer South and the Future of History Writing," *GLQ* 8, no. 3 (2002): 385 (emphasis in original).

17   These racialized geographies are tracked in Lillian Faderman and Stuart Timmons, *Gay L.A.: A History of Sexual Outlaws, Power Politics, and Lipstick Lesbians* (New York: Basic Books, 2006), and receive somewhat greater analysis in Moira Rachel Kenney, *Mapping Gay L.A.: The Intersection of Place and Politics* (Philadelphia: Temple University Press, 2001).

18   Christina B. Hanhardt, *Safe Space: The Sexual and City Politics of Violence* (Durham, NC: Duke University Press, 2013), 265.

19   On interracial Los Angeles before World War II, see Mark Wild, *Street Meeting: Multiethnic Neighborhoods in Early Twentieth-Century Los Angeles* (Berkeley: University of California Press, 2005). On postwar segregation in the city and its suburbs, see especially George J. Sánchez, "'What's Good for Boyle Heights Is Good for the Jews': Creating Multiculturalism on the Eastside during the 1950s," *American Quarterly* 56, no. 3 (2004): 633–61; Scott Kurashige, *The Shifting Grounds of Race: Black and Japanese Americans in the Making of Multiethnic Los Angeles* (Princeton: Princeton University Press, 2008); and Becky Nicolaides, *My Blue Heaven: Life and Politics in the Working-Class Suburbs of Los Angeles, 1920–1965* (Chicago: University of Chicago Press, 2002).

20   Sánchez, "What's Good for Boyle Heights."

21    Josh Sides, *L.A. City Limits: African American Los Angeles from the Great Depression to the Present* (Berkeley: University of California Press, 2004), 6. See also Sides, "Straight Into Compton: American Dreams, Urban Nightmares, and the Metamorphosis of a Black Suburb," *American Quarterly* 56, no. 3 (2004): 583–606; and Philip Ethington, Anne Marie Kooistra, and Edward D. Young, *Los Angeles County Union Census Tract Data Series, 1940–1990*, Version 1.01 (Los Angeles: University of Southern California, 2000).

22    Kurashige, *Shifting Grounds of Race*, 269.

23    Joe Domanick, *To Protect and to Serve: The LAPD's Century of War in the City of Dreams* (New York: Pocket Books, 1994); Martin Schiesl, "Behind the Shield: Social Discontent and the Los Angeles Police Since 1950," in *City of Promise: Race and Historical Change in Los Angeles*, ed. Schiesl and Mark M. Dodge (Claremont, CA: Regina Press, 2006), 137–73; Edward J. Escobar, "Bloody Christmas and the Irony of Police Professionalism: The Los Angeles Police Department, Mexican Americans, and Police Reform in the 1950s," *Pacific Historical Review* 72, no. 2 (2003): 178; and Edward J. Escobar, *Race, Police, and the Making of a Political Identity: Mexican Americans and the Los Angeles Police Department, 1900–1945* (Berkeley: University of California Press, 1999), 105.

24    Domanick, *To Protect and to Serve*, 110–11; Schiesl, "Behind the Shield," 138. By the late 1960s, the Black Panthers and others would identify these "brothers on the block" as central agents of social change.

25    Escobar, "Bloody Christmas."

26    Gerald Horne, *Fire This Time: The Watts Uprising and the 1960s* (Charlottesville: University Press of Virginia, 1995), 6. The Mexican American Community Service Organization (CSO) disavowed the communist sympathies of the CRC and had relatively more success in addressing the Bloody Christmas and Tony Rios cases. See Escobar, "Bloody Christmas," and Escobar, *Race, Police, and the Making of a Political Identity;* Schiesl, "Behind the Shield," 141–42; and Kenneth C. Burt, "Tony Rios and Bloody Christmas: A Turning Point between the Los Angeles Police Department and the Latino Community," *Western Legal History* 14, no. 2 (Summer/Fall 2001): 159–92.

27    Janet Appier, *Policing Women: The Sexual Politics of Law Enforcement and the LAPD* (Philadelphia: Temple University Press, 1998), 125; Douglas Flamming, *Bound for Freedom: Black Los Angeles in Jim Crow America* (Berkeley: University of California Press, 2005), 275. In addition, Domanick argues that antivice campaigns in the 1900s and 1910s planted "the seeds for the invasive philosophy of policing" in years to come (Domanick, *To Protect and To Serve*, 33).

28    Kevin Mumford, *Interzones: Black/White Sex Districts in Chicago and New York in the Early Twentieth Century* (New York: Columbia University Press, 1997), 76. On medical and sociological models, see Siobhan Somerville, *Queering the Color Line: Race and the Invention of Homosexuality in American Culture* (Durham, NC: Duke University Press, 2000).

29    Nan Alamilla Boyd, *Wide Open Town: A History of Queer San Francisco to 1965* (Berkeley: University of California Press, 2003), 69–70.

30    Roderick Ferguson, *Aberrations in Black: Towards a Queer of Color Critique* (Minneapolis: University of Minnesota, 2004), 13–14.

31  Margot Canaday, *The Straight State: Sexuality and Citizenship in Twentieth-Century America* (Princeton, NJ: Princeton University Press, 2009). The construction of normative citizenship in contrast to male migrant "vagrancy" is analyzed by Nayan Shah, *Stranger Intimacy: Contesting Race, Sexuality, and the Law in the North American West* (Berkeley: University of California Press, 2011). Also see Chandan Reddy, *Freedom with Violence: Race, Sexuality, and the U.S. State* (Durham, NC: Duke University Press, 2011).

32  In 1952 the McCarran-Walter Act prohibited homosexuals and communists from immigrating and maintained racial exclusions through national quotas. The Supreme Court upheld the homosexual exclusion in Boutilier v. INS (1967). Eithne Luibhéid and Lionel Cantú, eds., *Queer Migrations: Sexuality, U.S. Citizenship, and Border Crossings* (Minneapolis: University of Minnesota Press, 2005); Marc Stein, "*Boutilier* and the U.S. Supreme Court's Sexual Revolution," *Law and History Review* 23, no. 3 (2005). On exclusions from federal employment, see David K. Johnson, *Lavender Scare: The Cold War Persecution of Gays and Lesbians in the Federal Government* (Chicago: University of Chicago Press, 2004).

33  On moral panics in 1930s Los Angeles, see Appier, *Policing Women*, 140 and 154–55, and Hurewitz, *Bohemian Los Angeles*, 132–33. For a national view after the war, see George Chauncey, "The Postwar Sex Crime Panic," in *True Stories from the American Past*, ed. William Graebner (New York: McGraw-Hill, 1993), especially 175–77. For an example of 1950s rhetoric, see Derek Coleman, "When Homosexuals Kill!" *Men's Life*, November 1955, or coverage of the case of Stephen Nash, convicted in 1957 for the sexually charged murders of ten men and one boy.

34  Local police served as border agents both before and after McCarran-Walter, as convictions for "morals" charges were a consistent reason immigrants were deported in the early through mid twentieth century. Lionel Cantú, Jr., *The Sexuality of Migration: Border Crossings and Mexican Immigrant Men*, ed. Nancy A. Naples and Salvador Vidal-Ortiz (New York: New York University Press, 2009), 39–54.

35  Hurewitz, *Bohemian Los Angeles*, 49–50, and Faderman and Timmons, *Gay L.A.*, 82–83.

36  Hurewitz, *Bohemian Los Angeles*, 132–33.

37  Kenney, *Mapping Gay L.A.*, 23; Timmons, *The Trouble with Harry Hay*, 60; George Chauncey, *Gay New York: Gender, Urban Culture, and the Making of the Gay Male World* (New York: Basic Books, 1994), 227–67 and 348.

38  On gay film stars and the LAPD, see Domanick, *To Protect and To Serve*, 121.

39  Faderman and Timmons, *Gay L.A.* The same pattern is noted in San Francisco in Boyd, *Wide Open Town*, and in Buffalo by Elizabeth Lapovksy Kennedy and Madeline Davis, *Boots of Leather, Slippers of Gold: The History of a Lesbian Community* (New York: Routledge, 1993).

40  Whitney Strub, "The Clearly Obscene and the Queerly Obscene: Heteronormativity and Obscenity in Cold War Los Angeles," *American Quarterly* 60, no. 2 (June 2008): 377. Strub cites this phrase as the city council's.

41  Key histories of homophile activism include D'Emilio, *Sexual Politics, Sexual Communities*; Boyd, *Wide Open Town*; Hurewitz, *Bohemian Los Angeles*; Marcia Gallo, *Dif-*

ferent Daughters: A History of the Daughters of Bilitis and the Rise of the Lesbian Rights Movement (New York: Carrol & Graf, 2006); Martin Meeker, Contacts Desired: Gay and Lesbian Communications and Community, 1940s–1970s (Chicago: University of Chicago Press, 2006); and Meeker, "Behind the Mask of Respectability: Reconsidering the Mattachine Society and Male Homophile Practice, 1950s and 1960s," Journal of the History of Sexuality 10, no. 1 (Jan. 2001): 78–116.

42    See especially Meeker, "Behind the Mask," 79.

43    On obscenity challenges, see Strub, "The Clearly Obscene."

44    The black belt thesis was substantially developed by Harry Haywood and promoted by black workers in the South before the Comintern adopted it. Robin D. G. Kelley, Hammer and Hoe: Alabama Communists during the Great Depression (Chapel Hill: University of North Carolina Press, 1990), 13. Many Marxists in the United States blurred Stalin's distinction between "nations" and "national minorities" and, adapting Lenin, attributed "nation" status to all racialized diasporas or colonized groups. J. M. Blaut, "The Theory of National Minorities," The National Question: Decolonizing the Theory of Nationalism (London: Zed Books, 1987).

45    Hurewitz, Bohemian Los Angeles, 189–228.

46    Timmons, The Trouble with Harry Hay; Bettina Aptheker: "Queer Dialectics/Feminist Interventions: Harry Hay and the Quest for a Revolutionary Politics," keynote address at "Radically Gay: The Life and Visionary Legacy of Harry Hay," conference at the Center for Lesbian and Gay Studies, City University of New York, September 28, 2012.

47    "Mattachine Society Missions and Purposes" (1951), in Will Roscoe, Radically Gay: Gay Liberation in the Words of Its Founder, ed. Harry Hay (Boston: Beacon Press, 1996), 131. This statement was written in April 1951 and ratified in July 1951. By way of contrast, sexual difference has also been framed in "universalizing" terms. Eve Sedgwick, The Epistemology of the Closet (Berkeley: University of California Press, 1990); Marc Stein, "'Birthplace of the Nation': Imagining Gay and Lesbian Communities in Philadelphia," in Creating a Place for Ourselves: Lesbian, Gay, and Bisexual Community Histories, ed. Brett Beemyn (New York: Routledge, 1997): 253–88; and Chris Phelps, "A Neglected Document on Socialism and Sex," Journal of the History of Sexuality 16, no. 1 (Jan. 2007): 1–13.

48    Hurewitz, Bohemian Los Angeles, 254 and 257.

49    The question of homophile respectability has been widely debated, most thoroughly by Meeker, "Behind the Mask of Respectability," who argues that respectability was a tactic that enabled Mattachine to advance militant causes. I agree that respectability could serve as a "mask" and that homophile groups and activists used multiple political strategies and held varied stances toward bar culture and gender transgression. However, I argue that Mattachine's rhetoric about "ethical" behavior limited its formulation of sexual and racial politics and helped make the homophile movement largely white and middle-class. For a reflection on similar dynamics later, see Allan Bérubé, "How Gay Stays White and What Kind of White It Stays," in My Desire for History: Essays in Gay, Community, and Labor History, ed. John D'Emilio and Estelle B. Freedman (Chapel Hill: University of North Carolina Press, 2011), 202–30; and Kevin

Mumford, "The Trouble with Gay Rights: Race and the Politics of Sexual Orientation in Philadelphia, 1969–1982," *Journal of American History* 98, no. 1 (2011): 49–72.

50   "Mattachine Society Missions and Purposes," 131–32.

51   David S. Churchill, "Transnationalism and Homophile Political Culture in the Postwar Decades," *GLQ* 15, no. 1 (2009): 31–65, especially 43, 49, and 51. Examples include R. H. Stuart, "India and Ceylon," *Mattachine Review* 3 (Dec. 1955): 7; and Philip Jason, "Homosexuals in a Related Culture: A Brief Investigation, Part I," *Mattachine Review* 4 (July 1958): 8–10.

52   Domanick, *To Protect and To Serve*, 68 and 96; Tom Sitton, *Los Angeles Transformed: Fletcher Bowron's Urban Reform Revival, 1938–1953* (Albuquerque: University of New Mexico Press, 2005).

53   Kurashige, *Shifting Grounds of Race*, 269.

54   Daryl Gates, with Diane K. Shah, *Chief: My Life in the L.A.P.D.* (New York: Bantam Books, 1992), 42.

55   On Central Avenue jazz clubs, see Flamming, *Bound for Freedom*, 377; and Mina Yang, "A Thin Blue Line Down Central Avenue: The LAPD and the Demise of a Musical Hub," *Black Music Research Journal* 22, no. 2 (2002): 217–39. On gays' presence in these clubs, see Timmons, *Trouble with Harry Hay*, 60.

56   Citizens Committee, "An Anonymous Call to Arms."

57   Los Angeles Police Department, *Annual Report of the Police Department* (Los Angeles: LAPD, 1950), 29.

58   Los Angeles Police Department, *Annual Report* (1950), 29. The department did not publicize data on sexually based arrests in every annual report, and by the mid-1950s it grouped sex perversion under the broader category of "sex offenses (other than rape or prostitution)." Report data makes it evident that the bulk of "sex offense" arrests were made for homosexuality among men. Officers raiding gay and lesbian sites also made arrests on charges of "masquerading," violence, resisting arrest, or prostitution or pandering.

59   In 1956, nearly all "sex offense" arrests were men (96.6 percent). White men made up 75.9 percent of male arrests, significantly less than the 87.9 percent of the population categorized as white in the 1950 census. Black men made up 12.7 percent of sex offense arrests versus 5 percent of the population, and Latino men made up 10.1 percent of sex offense arrests versus 5.8 percent of the population. LAPD, *Statistical Digest 1956*.

60   In 1950 Central spanned east to the LA River, west to Vermont, north to Los Feliz Boulevard, and south to Pico Boulevard; it was later adjusted to span west to Hoover and Hyperion, more closely following census tracts. In 1970, the northwestern half of this area became the Rampart Division. In the late 1990s, that division saw a notorious scandal naming dozens of officers in unprovoked shootings and beatings, drug dealing, planting false evidence, perjury, and other wrongdoing.

61   My tabulation of *Annual Report of the Police Department* (1950), 29.

62   Gates, *Chief*, 39.

63   Jim Kepner, "Goodbye to Pershing Square," n.d., Pershing Square File, ONE.

64   The *Los Angeles Times* termed Root "the civic center's most flamboyant figure." "Sex Deviates Can Be Cured, Says Attorney," *Los Angeles Times*, August 12, 1959.

65   Faderman and Timmons, *Gay L.A.*, 1–2. Their description is based on Timmons's interview with novelist John Rechy, who was present at the raid.

66   Eric Wat, *The Making of a Gay Asian Community: An Oral History of Pre-AIDS Los Angeles* (Lanham, MD: Rowman & Littlefield, 2002), 48 and 56; Kenney, *Mapping Gay L.A.*, 84.

67   Eric Avila, *Popular Culture in the Age of White Flight: Fear and Fantasy in Suburban Los Angeles* (Berkeley: University of California Press, 2004), 80–81.

68   As quoted in Don Parson, *Making a Better World: Public Housing the Red Scare, and the Direction of Modern Los Angeles* (Minneapolis: University of Minnesota Press, 2005), 153.

69   Whitney Strub, "Clearly Obscene," 386.

70   "Revised Plan for Pershing Square," *Los Angeles Times*, January 20, 1964; "Round Up 150 in Pershing Sq.; Jail 11," *Daily News*, undated but clipped with other 1964 events in Pershing Square File, ONE. See also "Pershing Square Bums Hauled In," *Los Angeles Mirror-News*, November 18, 1959; "Reformation Slated for Pershing Square," *Los Angeles Times* August 19, 1963; and "Pershing Square Folk Switch to City Hall," *Los Angeles Times*, September 13, 1964.

71   My tabulations from the *LAPD Statistical Digest* (1956). Latina women and Japanese men were slightly more likely to face such arrest than their populations; white women were arrested for prostitution at very low rates.

72   Boyd, *Wide Open Town*, and Kennedy and Davis, *Boots of Leather, Slippers of Gold*. For anecdotes of such arrests in Los Angeles, see *On These Shoulders We Stand*, dir. Glenne McElhinney (Impact Stories, 2009). Faderman and Timmons also note that many butch women in Los Angeles were arrested throughout the 1950s for "masquerading" (cross-dressing).

73   In Silver Lake, the Vista Theatre attracted a same-sex-seeking clientele; Strub, "The Clearly Obscene," 390. On Hollywood and West Hollywood, see Kenney, *Mapping Gay L.A.*; Faderman and Timmons, *Gay L.A.*; and Kepner, "Goodbye to Pershing Square."

74   Emily Hobson, "If Café and Open Door," in *A People's Guide to Los Angeles*, ed. Laura Pulido, Laura Barraclough, and Wendy Cheng (Berkeley: University of California Press, 2012), 45–46; Whitney Strub, "Mondo Rocco: Mapping Gay Los Angeles Sexual Geography in the Late-1960s Films of Pat Rocco," *Radical History Review* 113 (Spring 2012): 20. By 1969, the Gay Liberation Front held meetings in Westlake. The city's first gay community center opened in Westlake in 1971 before moving to the Hollywood/West Hollywood border in 1975; Kenney, *Mapping Gay L.A.*, 84–86.

75   Gay liberationists also shifted the geography of gay LA by celebrating daytime nudity and "gay-ins" in Griffith Park. Strub, "Mondo Rocco," 23; Richard Meyer, "Gay Power Circa 1970: Visual Strategies for Sexual Revolution," *GLQ* 12, no. 3 (2006): 441–64.

76   Since the 1970s the major and frequently the only black gay bar or nightclub in Los Angeles has been Jewel's Catch One, located in West Adams at Pico and Crenshaw. Jewel Thais-Williams, a black lesbian, purchased the facility in 1972 and converted it from a primarily white working-class straight bar to a primarily black working-class gay bar and later a nightclub. Jewel's Catch One was subject to marked police harassment well into the 1990s. On this site and its importance to Los Angeles

queer of color history, see Kai M. Green's dissertation under development, "Into the Darkness: A Black Queer (Re)Membering of Los Angeles in a Time of Crisis" (University of Southern California); Kai M. Green, "Catching the Incurable Contagion: Black Los Angeles' Disco Queers," *Artbound*, May 20, 2013, http://www.kcet.org/arts/artbound/counties/los-angeles/los-angeles-disco-queers.html; and Alice Y. Hom, "Unifying Differences: Lesbian of Color Community Building in Los Angeles and New York, 1970s–1980s" (PhD diss., Claremont Graduate University, 2011). On black queer geographies more broadly, see Ferguson, *Aberrations in Black*; E. Patrick Johnson, *Sweet Tea: Black Gay Men of the South: An Oral History* (Chapel Hill: University of North Carolina Press, 2008); and Allen Drexel, "Before Paris Burned: Race, Class, and Male Homosexuality on the Chicago South Side, 1935–1960," in Beemyn, *Creating a Place for Ourselves*, 119–44.

77 Terrence Kissack, "Freaking Fag Revolutionaries: New York's Gay Liberation Front, 1969–1971," *Radical History Review* 62 (Spring 1995): 104–34; Justin David Suran, "Coming Out Against the War: Antimilitarism and the Politicization of Homosexuality in the Era of Vietnam," *American Quarterly* 53, no. 3 (2001): 452–88; Ian Lekus, "Queer Harvests: Homosexuality, the U.S. New Left, and the Venceremos Brigades to Cuba," *Radical History Review* 89 (Spring 2004): 57–91; Betty Hillman, "'The Most Profoundly Revolutionary Act a Homosexual Can Engage in': Drag and the Politics of Gender Presentation in the San Francisco Gay Liberation Movement, 1964–1972," *Journal of the History of Sexuality* 20, no. 1 (Jan. 2011): 153–81.

78 Beginning in 1965, the San Francisco chapter of Mattachine worked to gain War on Poverty funds for the Tenderloin and supported Citizen's Alert, a multiracial coalition against police violence that challenged harassment of gay people and hippies as well as people of color. From 1965 through 1967, Daughters of Bilitis and the Council on Religion on the Homosexual also worked to address Tenderloin poverty, as discussed in Hanhardt, *Safe Space*.

79 Thad Brown, Thomas Reddin, and Robert Murdock served short terms as chief after Parker. Ed Davis was chief for most of the gay liberation era, from August 1969 to January 1978.

80 *ONE Confidential* 12, no. 4 (April 1967): 5–10, and "CRISIS Police Lawlessness Must Be Stopped!!" flier (Black Cat File, ONE); Belinda Baldwin, "L.A., 1/1/67: The Black Cat Riots," *The Gay & Lesbian Review* 13, no. 2 (Mar.–Apr. 2006): 28–30; Kenney, *Mapping Gay L.A.*, 165–66. Until fall 2011, the Black Cat site continued to be home to a gay bar, Le Barcito, whose sign included a black cat's face. Le Barcito closed at the end of 2011 for financial reasons. In 2012 an upscale bar and restaurant, once again called the Black Cat, opened at the site; it is decorated with historic photographs of Los Angeles, including images of the 1967 gay protest.

81 "Monster of a Protest Set for Saturday," *Los Angeles Free Press,* February 10, 1967; "Pickets Greeted by Opposition Backing 'Their' Police, Drive-In," *Los Angeles Times,* February 16, 1967; *ONE Confidential* 12, no. 4 (April 1967): 5–10; Mike Davis, "Riot Nights on Sunset Strip," *In Praise of Barbarians: Essays Against Empire* (Chicago: Haymarket Books, 2007).

# 7

# Carceral Migrations

## Black Power and Slavery in 1970s California Prison Radicalism

DAN BERGER

BEGINNING IN THE LATE 1960S AND CONTINUING FOR THE NEXT DECADE with added intensity, California was home to a militant antiprison movement that rippled across the country.[1] Through the writings and actions of black prisoners in different facilities, this organizing brought unprecedented visibility to the prison as a race-making institution. That is, by confining and disciplining populations by race, among other criteria, the prison helped create racial identities. While mass incarceration has increased the prison's racializing force, the prison has long been a race-making institution—and prisoners have acted as cocreators of racial meaning in prison and beyond. Indeed, black dissident prisoners were at the forefront in shaping California's Black Power politics and in identifying California as the vanguard site of Black Power nationally. The publication of texts by prisoners or former prisoners in California, such as Eldridge Cleaver's *Soul on Ice* (1968) and George Jackson's *Soledad Brother* (1970), introduced a wide range of readers to the centrality of the carceral state to the formation of black politics in the era before the consolidation of the prison industrial complex, the contemporary era of mass incarceration and hyperpolicing that placed prisons at the center of a network of disciplinary institutions. The popularity of these books, along with similar works by other prisoners during this time, such as Etheridge Knight, generated great interest in the prison and its authors, turning the prison briefly into a site of literary as well as political excitement. Surveying this development in the early 1970s, the quick-witted leftist writer Jessica Mitford (who had helped secure the publication of *Soledad Brother*) wrote that "literary agents are scouting prisons for convict talent."[2]

Yet California's eminence in the visibility of prison-based tumult obscured that its roots lay partially in the American South. Those who led uprisings, wrote exposés, or otherwise populated what was called the "prison movement" in California were southern transplants, shaped by southern racial hierarchies and modes of resistance as well as by the particularities of the American West. In the shadow of sweeping civil rights legislation, these prisoners joined their understandings of the violent and racially polarized world of confinement within the southern collective memory of chattel slavery with the western experience of carceral discipline to articulate a critique of the prison as a form of slavery. Although these men and women experienced Jim Crow, not chattel slavery, they used slavery as a way to identify the state-sanctioned violence that structured black life. Prisoners advanced a critique of slavery that identified all black people, if not also all nonelites, as enslaved by white supremacy, what historian Steven Hahn recently called "slaves at large."[3] Activist prisoners, especially authors—figures that scholars such as Joy James and Dylan Rodríguez have labeled imprisoned intellectuals—argued that the racially disproportionate nature of confinement made the prison a vanguard institution of state racism. They maintained that the prison, like slavery, was a race-making institution facilitated through government policies and state violence.

In comparing the prison to the plantation, prisoners made an argument about political subjectivity. Dissident black nationalists and their Latino allies, placed in solitary confinement as a result of their challenges to the prison, developed the sharpest critique of the prisoner as a slave subject. They used slavery to name the structural alienation enforced by the prison—its civil and political death, its seeming total control over the life and actions of its captives. These prisoners defined race in general and blackness in particular as being perpetually entangled with slavery, and slavery as fundamentally a problem of the United States and the modern world. It is easy to read into their position a host of anachronisms, an imagined community detached from historical continuity. The differences are critical—especially the difference between a labor regime premised on natal alienation and a repressive regime rooted in the absence of labor. Radical prisoners were not making a claim about labor; many of the most eloquent proponents of seeing the prison as a form of slavery, in fact, did not work while incarcerated. Still, the prison-slave analogy held valuable insight for making sense of racial consciousness in this pivotal era. Radical prisoners offered a critique of those liberal optimists who delighted that new civil rights laws would spell the end of black subjection and black protest, and they identified blackness as a source of inspiration in the struggle for justice.

Prisoner radicalism therefore provides insight into the ways that social movements shaped racial identities in the waning days of the civil rights era. This is especially true in California, where George Jackson identified a political program that inspired a generation of prisoners to challenge not only their confinement but also the underlying racial logics of confinement itself in the United States. Jackson's writings inspired prisoners and others around the world during the 1970s, but his work inside California prisons and his connection to leading figures of the Black Panther Party centered in Oakland maximized his effect in the Golden State. For that reason, this chapter emphasizes the orbit around Jackson as a window into the wider world of prison protest at the dawn of mass incarceration. The cases under consideration here, especially Angela Davis (1970–1972) and the San Quentin Six (1971–1976), reveal the ways California prisoners mobilized critiques of slavery as a way to indict the prison as a manifestation of white supremacy and imperialism.

Prisoners were cutting edge "race radicals" in the dissolution of racial liberalism, offering a glimpse of the permanent-war America that was cohering in the 1970s.[4] Originating largely from a stratum of black communities that was emerging as the perpetually, if not permanently, unemployed, these dissident prisoners theorized the changing political economy that scholars now call neoliberalism. That is, they pointed to the state's extensive capacity to punish and its fundamental disinterest in the plight of the poor. Slavery, to them, was the new-old system of racial inequality that policed black communities. It named not only a system of racial animus but one of political economic oppression—from the exploitation of the plantation to the marginalization of the postindustrial city. In locating slavery as the centerpiece of American race relations, these prisoners were also identifying the growing class division among black communities. Their attempt to name their condition as one of slavery was both an attempt at forging (some might say forcing) black unity while pointing to the growing use of extreme deprivation as a form of labor management.

The centrality of black migration to the development of postwar prison protest suggests that the prison has not been as static and immobile a force as it might seem. Designed to restrict movement, the prison is para-doxically bound up with it. The prison generates movement in at least two ways: through physical migration and through political protest. As prison-ers, men and women forcibly migrate from cities to the rural areas where prisons are located. Once there, dissident prisoners seek to contest or mitigate their confinement in a myriad of ways. These two movements—migration and protest—often merged as prisoners challenged both their immediate conditions and the broader political economic circumstances that resulted in their imprisonment. Both of these movements converged in California in the 1970s as a result of the preceding generations of black migration out of the South. Between 1940 and 1960, the number of black people in Los Angeles increased from 63,774 to 334,916, quickly becoming roughly one-eighth of the city's population.[5] The defense industry beck-oned people west during the run up to World War II, and black southerners continued to head to California during the 1950s and 1960s as they sought a life outside of Jim Crow or were enticed by the Golden State's prom-ise of reinvention. These women and men, part of what historian James Gregory has labeled the southern diaspora, built the West Coast wing of the Black Power movement.[6] They brought their politics and experiences into prisons in Soledad and San Quentin, Folsom and Chowchilla. These politics flourished at the moment that southern-born musicians playing traditionally southern music—figures from B. B. King and James Brown to Merle Haggard and Johnny Cash—performed in prisons and incorpo-rated prison iconography into their albums.[7]

In their constructions of race and conceptions of freedom, dissident prisoners fused the geopolitics of the South and the North. As the bas-tion of chattel slavery and the region where the rigidity of racial hierar-chies was most visible and most violent, the South seemed to mirror the political geography of the prison. Southern modes of confinement had tethered race to crime since the dismantling of Reconstruction, while northern journalists and social scientists developed the ideological basis to equate blackness with criminality.[8] The connection between slavery and imprisonment did not begin with twentieth-century prisoners but rather with eighteenth- and nineteenth-century slaves. Indeed, African slaves identified their confinement as a prison from the point of kidnap, across the Atlantic, and onto the plantation.[9] While slavery may indeed be the "master metaphor" of black political critique since the mid-nineteenth century, invoked to explain all manner of racism, its saliency increased when leveraged from within the social death of the prison.[10] Further, when transported to the Pacific coast, the linking of enslavement and imprisonment challenged the premise of western (and specifically Californian) racial liberalism. Invocations of slavery among California prisoners, subsequently echoed by prisoners around the country, served to position slavery as central to a wider world of state violence and colonialism that extended well beyond the American South.

Prisoners used a critique of slavery to establish antiblackness as a fundamental component of the American West. Prisoners challenged the ability of states such as California to juxtapose their progressive racial climate against the supposedly backward South. The location of the critique's emergence was not incidental to its effect. Those incarcerated in American prisons have, since the end of Reconstruction, been disproportionately black.[11] And southern prisons in the 1960s came in for some deserved critique for their brutality.[12] Such criticisms emerged in the context of a national focus on the horrors of the Jim Crow South, and they were easily folded into a narrative of distinctly *southern*—as opposed to generically American—cruelties. But when prisoners such as Angela Davis, George Jackson, Ruchell Magee, Fleeta Drumgo, and many others spoke up, the critique was harder to write off as some kind of regional excess. All the more so given the California setting, since national narratives about slavery leave out the Pacific coast entirely. In popular mythology, the West Coast was the land of fresh starts and benighted liberalism, of multiracial democracy and free love. Prisoners challenged this mythology of western progress by identifying it with the regressive system of slavery. Rather than multiracial progressivism, prisoners described a Pacific coast rooted in white supremacist violence, characterized by the cruelest of racial hierarchies and the basest of punishments. And that this critique emanated from a population who most symbolically typified the lack of freedom made it all the more profound. People unaccustomed to looking west for slavery took notice.[13]

SOUTHERN ROOTS AND WESTERN ROUTES

As California prisoners described their "enslavement," they also extended the counter-intuitive use of the jail as a beacon of freedom for southern civil rights activists. Black activists in the South used the jail to publicize the abuses of segregation in the 1950s and 1960s, creating what literary scholar Houston Baker has provocatively labeled a "public sphere of incarceration." Beginning in the 1950s, Baker argues, black activists succeeded in turning "white policing and surveillance"—the mechanisms of the criminal justice system—into "a public arena for black justice and freedom."[14] In Baker's analysis, jail was the fulcrum of black visibility breaking open the segregationist stranglehold on black life in the South. Such spectacles, which of necessity passed through the jail cell, moved the "liberation struggle ... from 'invisibility' to legal civil rights victories."[15] Jail was a rite of passage for grassroots and prominent activists, including Martin Luther King, Jr., whose "Letter from a Birmingham Jail" (1963) became one of the hallmark texts of the civil rights movement, part of a canon that political scientist Joy James has dubbed "American prison notebooks."[16] Jail revealed the absurdity of the segregationist South, and as such was a worthy sacrifice in the broader black freedom struggle. The use of civil disobedience to challenge the Jim Crow regime turned what had traditionally been among the most taboo locations, the jail cell, into a vehicle to make public black oppression, commitment, and subjectivity. Civil rights activists did not take up the mantle of prisoner rights so much as use the jail as a strategic political metaphor of racial oppression and black liberation. I do not mean to equate the nonviolent activist briefly occupying a southern jail cell for violating the norms of Jim Crow with a northern prisoner facing an indeterminate sentence for crime born of poverty and racist policing. There were clear contextual and political differences between the two. Yet the latter person's ability to contest the prison owed in some measure to the tenacity of those in the former category.

While some southern civil rights activists went to jail for freedom, other black southerners went west in pursuit of it. Indeed, many of the most well-known imprisoned black activists and spokesmen of the period were raised in the South. As scholars have recently shown, the Black Panther Party for Self-Defense, which greatly contributed to prison activism, had southern origins, taking its name from an organization in Lowndes County, Alabama. The overlap was deeper than the name. As historian Donna Murch argues, the Panther emphasis on education and self-defense imported southern mores into the urban American West.[17] The two Panther leaders who were arguably most responsible for emphasizing the prison as a political site of struggle imbued with racial meaning were born in the South. Eldridge Cleaver ended up in Watts by way of Little Rock, Arkansas. Huey Newton was born in Louisiana, the youngest of seven kids, to sharecropper parents, before moving to Oakland.[18] Soledad Brothers John Clutchette and Fleeta Drumgo were from the Deep South; Clutchette was born in Texas, and Drumgo in Louisiana. Both moved to Watts as children with their respective families.[19] Another Louisiana native, Geronimo Pratt, arrived at the University of California, Los Angeles (UCLA) on the GI Bill after serving in the Vietnam War. Pratt developed the military capabilities of the LA Panthers prior to being framed for murder and spending twenty-seven years in prison. Johnny Larry Spain—who, like George Jackson, became a Black Panther after his incarceration and was among six prisoners charged with killing three guards and two prisoners the day Jackson was killed—was born to a white mother and a black father in segregated Mississippi. The target of physical abuse at school and verbal abuse by his mother's white husband, Spain was sent to live with a black family in California. Willie Tate, another of the six prisoners, was born in Selma, Alabama, and lived as a child in Texas before moving to California.[20] Other than Newton, whose family migrated to the Bay Area, most of those who became central to prison protest were southerners who migrated to Los Angeles, especially Watts. California prison radicalism, then, is the history not just of general westward migration but of postwar Los Angeles specifically.

Angela Davis provided perhaps the clearest example of how Pacific coast radicalism arose from a combination of southern lineage and western violence. Born and raised in Birmingham, Alabama—home to many of the pitched battles and the white terrorism that targeted civil rights activists—Davis came to California as a doctoral student in philosophy at UCLA, where she joined the Communist Party. Davis would soon cross paths with Ruchell Magee, another transplant born and raised in the South. Both were associates of George Jackson. In August 1970, Magee was a witness in the trial of a fellow San Quentin prisoner James McClain when Jonathan Jackson, George Jackson's brother, entered the Marin County courtroom with a satchel of guns. Magee quickly joined the seventeen-year-old Jackson in seizing hostages and was the only surviving participant after San Quentin guards opened fire on the group. Because several of the weapons were registered in her name, Davis was charged with knowingly supplying the guns that the young Jackson used.[21] Davis and Magee became codefendants for about a year, until their cases were severed due to differing legal strategies.

At the time Davis was a young, promising, and highly visible professor at UCLA, known for her prison activism on behalf of the Soledad Brothers and because of her highly publicized fight to remain on the faculty after an informant for the Federal Bureau of Investigation and the *San Francisco Examiner* had exposed her as a member of the Communist Party in 1969. As a well-known prison activist, professor, Communist, black Marxist cultural critic, and protofeminist, Davis enlisted the support of civil rights and Black Power activists, women's groups, and communists from around the world. Magee, however, was unknown to most people besides other prisoners. Their different strategic assessments, based on the difference between trying to *stay* out of prison versus trying to *get* out of prison, led them to sever their charges in July 1971 and stand trial individually. Before and after their cases were severed, however, Davis stressed her solidarity with Magee and objected to media depictions of them as being fundamentally at odds.[22]

Both Davis and Magee shared a belief in prison as a form of slavery, viewed the courthouse encounter as a slave rebellion, and fought to serve as their own attorneys. Self-defense in court was fundamental. It flouted the expected courtroom decorum and equipped the prisoner with greater agency in articulating a political position, turning the court from an instrument of elite rule into a vehicle for the spread of insurgent politics. In casting her trial as a fight over slavery, Davis suggested that black life— in the collective sense, not in terms of her individual self—hung in the balance. "My life is at stake in this case—not simply the life of a lone individual, but a life which has been given over to the struggles of my people, a life which belongs to Black people who are tired of poverty and racism, of the unjust imprisonment of tens of thousands of our brothers and sisters," Davis wrote from her jail cell.[23] She argued that the courtroom, through her individual predicament, represented something of the fate of all black people in America. For Davis, legal self-representation meant acting as cocounsel in her defense ("the prospects of justice and fairness in this case are inseparably joined to the issue of my self-representation," she wrote),[24] alongside an accomplished legal team that included long-time leftist lawyers Howard Moore, Leo Branton, Margaret Burnham, and Doris Brin Walker. The demand to serve as cocounsel in one's trial, as with so many tactics prisoners utilized at this time, was far more concerned with subjectivity than legality. Davis, Magee, and other prisoners who served as their own attorneys (even if in tandem with professional

Figure 7.1. Angela Davis, while awaiting trial, ca. 1971.
Photograph by Stephen Shames.

lawyers) sought to use the space of the courtroom to demonstrate their humanity. It was an argument against the alienation of enslavement; by asserting their personhood, their rational mind or legal expertise, they challenged the slave system's propensity to dehumanize through silence. By speaking on their own behalf they challenged the objectification that would have them be defendants. It was, in other words, self-defense in a literal sense, a challenge to the legal doctrine that held prisoners as "slaves of the state."[25]

The most formally educated of California's imprisoned intellectuals, Davis also offered the most extensive theorization of the prison as a form of slavery. In court, Davis and her attorneys challenged the prosecution's attempt to introduce into evidence a series of romantic letters she had written to Jackson while both were incarcerated; they argued that turning love letters into legal evidence reproduced the slave-system logic of criminalizing black women's sexuality. Slavery had defined its female captives as sexual objects that lacked rational capacities. While the total domination of captivity, alongside the ideology of black sexuality as lascivious, allowed white slave owners to sexually assault their captives, the system of social death refused to label such violations as rape, much less to prosecute them as crimes. As Saidiya Hartman writes, because slaves were thought to be sexually available while also being defined as less than human, rape—as a criminal act of unwanted sexual contact that violated a person's sense of self—did not apply to them.[26] The corollary, as seen in the Davis case, was that slaves were also incapable of love. By using her love letters to Jackson to demonstrate a criminal conspiracy, the prosecution foreclosed the possibility of black romantic intimacy. Here, in the denial of black love, was the gendering racism of the larger criminal justice system dating back to the plantation logics of the licentious sexuality of slaves. Davis's attorneys were able to get most of the letters barred from evidence, and, in an attempt to restore the possibility of black sexuality, they asked playwright Dalton Trumbo to turn the excerpts allowed by the court into a poem that they then read to the jury as part of the closing statement for the defense.[27]

Davis continued to challenge the salient sexual logics of slavery outside the courtroom. Writing from the Marin County jail, she offered an indirect response to the media's focus on her gendered body and those of all black women. "Reflections on the Black Women's Role of the Community of Slaves" (1971), one of several intellectual efforts Davis made in this time period to theorize slavery and freedom, was an attempt to counter the "black matriarch" thesis that held black women to blame for black subjection. That position was, she wrote, "an open weapon of ideological warfare" rooted in conceptions of the southern elite.[28] The essay made several key interventions: shifting the focus away from seeing armed revolt as the only form of challenging slavery, whether in the nineteenth century or the twentieth, Davis argued that "survival-oriented activities were themselves a form of resistance. Survival, moreover, was the prerequisite of all higher levels of struggle."[29] Further, in describing the plantation's gendered division of labor—where women and men worked in the fields but only women did domestic labor for both white masters and black slaves—Davis offered a much-needed feminist rendering of traditional accounts of slave life.

Her essay, then, was a response to the conservative gender politics that could be found both in mainstream sources such as the Moynihan Report and in writings by movement thinkers such as George Jackson and Eldridge Cleaver, the two hypermasculine initial spokesmen of American prison radicals, who declared black women as barriers to black liberation. Through a feminist analysis of slavery, Davis challenged the patriarchal conceptions of black womanhood across generations—from, as she later put it, the prison of slavery to the slavery of the prison. The prison, an institution that often racially segregated its already sex-segregated subjects, was an intensely gendered site. Davis's essay opened the door to a more feminist critique of the prison through a rereading of the plantation. As her essay located the origins of the specious "black matriarchy thesis" in slavery, so too did her essay help advance feminist challenges to the prison as an institution itself rooted in the gendered racism of slavery.[30] The essay also provided the space for other black women dissidents around the country to leverage a black feminist critique of slavery as part of a larger challenge to the sexism of white supremacist confinement. Former Black Panthers Safiya Bukhari (tried in Virginia) and Assata Shakur (tried in New Jersey), along with Joan Little in North Carolina, each drew consciously upon a long history of slave women's resistance in challenging their imprisonment during the second half of the decade. While these cases did not capture as much attention as the Davis case, the women involved nonetheless leveraged similar critiques as part of their freedom campaigns. They described the slave as a contradictory category, at once reflecting the depths of racist repression and the horizons of radical redemption. Davis spoke out on behalf of each woman, both in her writing and as part of her work with the National Alliance Against Racist and Political Repression, which formed out of the National United Committee to Free Angela Davis.[31]

## TOWARD A POLITICS OF FREEDOM AND ABOLITION

For prisoner activists on the Pacific coast, southern lineages merged with western experiences to shape their racial and radical politics, enabling them to understand the historical forces behind their confinement and to recognize confinement as a race-making institution. George Jackson (from Chicago, though with roots in Kentucky) was the most visible and eloquent on this matter, routinely defining prisoners as slaves who could transcend this condition through militant action. In letters and interviews, Jackson castigated the prison as the latest expression of black slavery. He claimed that "time has faded nothing. I recall the very first kidnap."[32] He argued that the American state was little more than a slave plantation. "Blacks are still doing the work of the greatest slave state in history," he wrote in a posthumously published letter. "The terms of our servitude are all that have been altered."[33] When prison guards killed Jackson in a bloody and bizarre incident in August 1971, the unanswered questions about his death became further proof to some that slavery—understood as the near-total state of subjection—continued to characterize US racial politics. For his supporters at the time and since, Jackson's death was a cold-blooded murder orchestrated by the state that had long displayed its desire to destroy him. It confirmed that slavery's logic of the expendability of black life was still in play, and that slavery and imprisonment mutually defined the black condition. Guyanese historian and activist Walter Rodney summed up the prevailing sentiment when he wrote in a political obituary for Jackson that "ever since the days of slavery the U.S.A. is nothing but a vast prison as far as African descendants are concerned."[34] James Baldwin was equally profound in arguing that Jackson's death confirmed the need to distrust the American state: "No Black person will ever believe George Jackson died the way they tell us he did."[35]

Other prisoners in the 1970s, including many of Jackson's contemporaries and students, saw themselves as rebellious slaves and framed imprisonment as an extension of slavery. They defined blackness as both the source and the scourge of imprisonment. According to Soledad Brother

Fleeta Drumgo, the prison was a "slave plantation" that bred passivity and attempted to indoctrinate its racialized subjects, "like we've been indoctrinated for 400 years." Drumgo declared that such schemes would fail because those inside "recognize our blackness."[36] At San Quentin awaiting trial, Ruchell Magee described slavery as a structural and affective reality for its black victims. "To some degree, slavery has always been outlawed and condemned on the outside by the hypocritical mockery of chattering lips. But on the inside of people and prisons, where slavery is embedded and proudly displayed as a Western way of life and a privilege of god himself, slavery is condoned on all of its numerous levels."[37] Magee, who was sentenced to another life in prison in January 1974 and remains in prison as of 2012, continued to define his incarceration as proof of the slavery that structures American society.[38]

Slavery could be found everywhere in how activists made sense of the prison as a tool of black subjection. Supporters of Angela Davis pointed to the massive media attention devoted to her capture to claim that her case was the current incarnation of the historical "response of slave owners to slave rebellions" and the Fugitive Slave Act.[39] The visibility accompanying her arrest exemplified that slavery continued to define the terms of black life in the United States. "One might have hoped that, by this hour, the very sight of chains on Black flesh, or the very sight of chains, would be so intolerable a sight for the American people, and so unbearable a memory, that they would themselves spontaneously rise up and strike off the manacles," author James Baldwin wrote in his poignant open letter to Davis. "But, no, they appear to glory in their chains; now, more than ever, they appear to measure their safety in chains and corpses."[40] Davis contributed to this association in several writings from her jail cell, including articles she wrote about slavery and sexuality, and about race and contemporary political repression. These articles contributed to a public persona of Davis as the epitome of black resistance to slavery. In interviews from jail, she described herself above all as "a Black woman … [who has] dedicated my life to the struggle for the liberation of Black people—my enslaved, imprisoned people."[41] Slavery continued to animate Davis's description of repression even after her acquittal on June 4, 1972. As scholar Cynthia Young notes, Davis began her 1974 autobiography describing her flight, time underground, and arrest—a narrative tool that "cannot help but echo slave narratives." It was fundamentally about "physical freedom, escape from impending captivity."[42]

Such declarations, common to black prison radicalism of the time, held that race both explained incarceration and could serve as a potential basis to undermine the prison's control. Slavery was an objective condition of confinement and an ideological condition of subjugation that could be transcended through a politics of resistance. From their experience in penal institutions, black prisoners challenged the prison as a mechanism of social control that tried to induce and compel consent to the prevailing rules of society. Jackson, for instance, told a reporter that "this camp brings out the very best in brothers—or destroys them entirely. No one leaves here unaffected."[43] To make the prison visible as a form of slavery was to seek the material, physical, and conceptual destruction of the prison, slavery, and apathy. Jackson wrote that the height of political consciousness was to recognize oneself as being trapped in a system of slavery yet to reject being a slave. "I have, I hope, trained all of the slave out of me," he wrote to attorney Fay Stender.[44] These prisoners framed slavery as an uninterrupted fact of black life in the United States; describing themselves as slaves enabled them to act as political agents. Used as a collective memory of oppression, slavery became a narrative tool in the development of black nationalism located within American prisons.[45] It followed, therefore, that not only the prison but slavery itself could be undermined by such sharp declarations of black militancy and individual confrontation with the state. Blackness was a source of resistance, representing persistent confrontation with the slave state. Much as the expansion of slavery in the nineteenth century sparked struggles against the state as itself a racial regime, so too did black migration in the context of the growing carceral control generate a new round of battles over the legitimacy of state authority. In each case, black opposition to slavery pointed to deep structural logics of state power. The radicalism lay in opposing the system that enabled such bondage—whether chattel or carceral—to occur. In challenging their positions as slaves on the plantation or in the penitentiary, black activists rejected the American state's claim to neutrality or beneficence. Prisoner critiques of American carceral slavery aimed to show that the civil rights demand for "freedom now" remained equally as relevant in the age of "law and order" as it was in the age of Jim Crow.

The description of the prison as a form of slavery, while most associated with black prisoners, afforded antiracist coalition and theorization among other prisoners of color, particularly in the context of the American

West. The San Quentin Six, as they came to be called, were six black and Latino men who were imprisoned at the San Quentin Adjustment Center on August 21, 1971. They were charged for the deaths of three guards and two prisoner trustees, men who were shot or had their throats slit in the melee accompanying George Jackson's death. All told, they faced forty-six charges of murder, assault, and conspiracy. Of the six, three had been born in the South (Fleeta Drumgo, Johnny Spain, and Willie Tate), and two traced their roots to the global South (Luis Talamantez is of Mexican descent; Hugo Pinell is from Nicaragua). (The sixth, David Johnson, was born and raised in San Diego.) The inclusion of two Latinos in the case served in part to expose the deep links between slavery and colonialism, within and beyond the US borders. That the group defined their condition as one of enslavement elevated what was becoming a standard prisoner critique of slavery to relate to both imperialism and ghettoization.

The six were indicted after Jackson's death in 1971, but the trial would continue until 1976. It was the longest and most expensive trial in California's history up to that point. While the struggle over legal representation did not define the San Quentin Six trial in the way it had with Magee and Davis, the specter of slavery continued to loom large over the case. The men hoped, like their predecessors, to use the courtroom to bring prison conditions to light: the long-term isolation, the repression of political activity, the constant humiliation and death threats. This was the slavery of prison, they argued. The defendants were shackled throughout the trial. The trial judge, Henry Broderick, authorized the men to be shackled for the length of the trial after jurors said that the sight of men in chains would not prejudice them. The prisoner-as-slave was in part an argument about accoutrements, and the use of chains became a central challenge in the case of the San Quentin Six. After fighting for their right of legal self-representation, the men fought for their physical self-representation—their bodily integrity in court. With the exception of Tate, who had been paroled two months before the trial began, five of the defendants "appeared in court chained and shackled to their chairs [which were bolted to the floor].... [These five] defendants were transported together from San Quentin to the Hall of Justice in a specially constructed bus in which each was enclosed in a separate compartment. In the courtroom they sat behind a bulletproof screen." The divider was thick enough that a public address system was necessary for the spectators to hear the proceedings.[46] At various points throughout, the defendants were chained not just at

Figure 7.2. San Quentin Six supporters protest the slavery of imprisonment, ca. 1975. Photograph by Jacob Holdt.

the hands and feet but at the hips and neck as well. Police also shaved the heads of the five imprisoned defendants in advance of the trial, further displaying them as wards of the state. Willie Tate said that the trial was dominated by the "symbols of slavery."[47] This treatment continued outside of court: lawyers for the men protested that their clients were chained and separated by a plexiglass barrier during their legal meetings. This arrangement forced the individuals involved to yell in order to be heard. Doing so, the attorneys protested, violated attorney-client privilege by making the content of their meetings known to the guards who watched the meetings from directly outside the room in which they took place.[48]

The defendants, lawyers, and supporters all decried the case as one of western slavery in full effect, and a 1975 ruling by federal court judge Alfonso Zirpoli held that the men's conditions of confinement amounted to cruel and unusual punishment.[49] Jurors in their criminal case seemed to agree that the men suffered abuse, but their mixed verdict suggests that they did not believe that the men were enslaved. Drumgo, Talamantez, and Tate were acquitted entirely and soon released from prison. The three of them had been intimately involved in California's radical prison movement: Drumgo was a Soledad Brother, Tate had been a jailhouse lawyer, and Talamantez served as a peacekeeper between black and Latino prisoners and as a thorn in the side of prison officials. The men had been sent to prison on lengthy or life sentences for minor crimes; their release ended long nightmares for each of them.[50] Spain was found guilty of conspiracy and two counts of murder, Pinell of two counts of felony assault, and Johnson of felony assault on a guard. Johnson received a suspended sentence and three years' probation, and, since he would have been paroled years earlier had it not been for this case, was released from prison. Spain, the youngest of the defendants at twenty-six and the only one who was a member of the Black Panther Party, and Pinell, thirty and perhaps the one closest to George Jackson, were both sentenced to life in prison.[51] In an analysis of the trial at the time, prison left-wing journalist Karen Wald hypothesized that the mixed verdict was a product of the mid-1970s suspicion of both the powerful and the powerless.[52] The case, in any respect, marked a turning point in prisoner challenges to slavery. In the early 1970s, prisoners used the courtroom to leverage critiques of slavery as commentary on the subjectivity of confinement. While such claims continued to animate prisoner publications, legal claims beginning with the San Quentin Six case and lasting into the early 1980s pursued a narrower and more technical charge of slavery. Here, prisoners across the Sunbelt challenged the accoutrements of incarceration and the use of forced labor inside. This effort crystallized in the 1980 Supreme Court decision in *Ruíz v. Estelle* that put the Texas state prison system into federal receivership as a result of the violently racist system of punishment and coercive labor inside.[53]

Activists who were not incarcerated also embraced the analysis of the prison as a form of slavery, in the process contributing to seeing the Pacific coast as a product of chattel state violence. Like the people they supported inside prisons, these outside agitators looked to the legacy of slave resistance for models of action. Their inspiration ranged from small acts of subversion to the symbolic terrain informing prison activism. Black journalist Reginald Major argued that he and other black people who attended the Angela Davis trial were "constitutionally incapable of making the line up [to be let into court] on police time. The tardiness was not so much a protest as the beginnings of resistance, a quiet ideological tensing up in rejection of absolute police authority."[54] Major's assessment suggests that rejecting the temporal niceties of court was an act of resistance inherited from slaves. Other activists took up the mantle of slave resistance more formally. Much as prisoners championed Nat Turner as an archangel of revolutionary deliverance, prison activists who were not incarcerated took as inspiration those who helped slaves to escape their bondage. For instance, small collectives of prison activists in seven cities in the early 1970s organized themselves as the Harriet Tubman Prison Movement (HTPM). The group formed to provide free reading materials to prisoners, supply free transportation for families to visit their incarcerated loved ones, and support a minimum-wage law for working prisoners. In focusing on literacy (here, in the form of access) and mobility (in the form of prison visits), the HTPM, as with other prison activists who pursued similar approaches, utilized some of the standard modalities for black empowerment against slavery.[55] These tactics posited the memory of slavery and slave resistance as foundational to representational strategies of prisoners. That is, prisoners confronted the same state practices that denied slaves education and mobility. In fighting for these issues, prisoners and their supporters represented their struggle as an ongoing confrontation with slavery.

An iconic attachment to slave rebels has long been present within black radical discourse. But as members of the Black Power movement—

including the Black Arts movement—prisoners had more than a symbolic purpose in invoking slavery and its discontents.[56] This history informed their efforts at self-representation, both literally and figuratively. Prisoners labored to represent themselves in court and to publics that would otherwise not see them. This attachment to representation held that dignity and self-control were vital threats to the prison's capacity to enslave. As a result, prisoners demonstrated self-determination where they could: adopting Swahili or Arabic names, becoming jailhouse lawyers, and serving as their own attorneys or cocounsel in court. These acts were less dramatic than escape attempts and attacks on guards, yet they were perhaps more important, for they, like the work songs and familial bonds of the plantation, constituted the building blocks of a prisoner-slave community.[57]

The prison protest reveals that the locus of black radicalism traveled in one generation from the rural and urban South to urban Los Angeles, and then again from the industrial metropolis to the small towns where prisons were (and are) located. Much as the contemporary prison industrial complex creates an internal diaspora of people taken from the cityscape to the countryside, prison protest of the 1970s emerged from and in conversation with the southern diaspora. Their westward movement generated a movement within prisons that itself helped make sense of the ways racism continued to structure black life in the wake of civil rights legal victories. It was not the mere importation of southern experience; rather, prisoners melded their southern roots with their experiences of the carceral state in the ghettoes, juvenile detention facilities, and prisons of California and beyond. From the plantation of the rural South to the concrete jungle of the urban North and West, prisoners identified slavery as the conceptual and material building block of the American state and its attendant racial hierarchies. As they sought to undermine the prison's power, these migrants hoped to abolish the American plantation in all its forms and all its locations. The continental legacy of abolition bridged the southern plantation experience with the national prison experience.

1    Thanks to Moon-Ho Jung, Stephanie Camp, Luther Adams, and Dylan Rodríguez for their incisive comments on earlier versions of this article. Thanks also to the other participants of the Race, Radicalism, and Repression conference—especially Donna Murch, Judy Wu, and Emily Hobson—for their valuable feedback.

As with any historical claim, periodizing prison activism is not without its challenges. In the formative but problematic book *The Rise and Fall of California's Radical*

*Prison Movement* (Stanford: Stanford University Press, 1994), Eric Cummins dates its origins to the Caryl Chessman case in the 1950s. Other texts on prison radicalism usefully suggest that resistance of different kinds has always accompanied practices of confinement. See Heather Ann Thompson, *Blood in the Water: The Attica Uprising of 1971 and Its Legacy* (New York: Pantheon, forthcoming); Alan Eladio Gómez, "Resisting Living Death at Marion Federal Penitentiary, 1972," *Radical History Review* 96 (2006): 58–86; Network of Black Organizers, ed., *Black Prison Movements USA* (Trenton, NJ: Africa World Press, 1995).

2  Jessica Mitford, "Kind and Usual Punishment in California," *Atlantic Monthly*, March 1971, 52. See also Lee Bernstein, "The Age of Jackson: George Jackson and the Culture of American Prisons in the 1970s," *Journal of American Culture* 30, no. 3 (2007): 310–23.

3  Steven Hahn, *The Political Worlds of Slavery and Freedom* (Cambridge, MA: Harvard University Press, 2009).

4  My terminology of race radicalism and racial liberalism builds on the framework set forth in Jodi Melamed, *Represent and Destroy: Rationalizing Violence in the New Racial Capitalism* (Minneapolis: University of Minnesota Press, 2011); and Chandan Reddy, *Freedom with Violence: Race, Sexuality, and the U.S. State* (Durham, NC: Duke University Press, 2011).

5  Daniel Widener, *Black Arts West: Culture and Struggle in Postwar Los Angeles* (Durham, NC: Duke University Press, 2010), 57.

6  James N. Gregory, *The Southern Diaspora: How the Great Migrations of Black and White Southerners Transformed America* (Chapel Hill: University of North Carolina Press, 2005).

7  Michael Streissguth, *Johnny Cash at Folsom Prison: The Making of a Masterpiece* (Cambridge, MA: Da Capo Press, 2004); John Hayes, "Man of Sorrows in Folsom," *Radical History Review* 98 (2007): 119–35; "San Q Rocks—Freemen Back Cons as Prison Seethes," *Berkeley Barb* 6, no. 6 (Feb. 9–15, 1968): 1.

8  See Robert Perkinson, *Texas Tough: The Making of America's Prison Empire* (New York: Henry Holt, 2010); David M. Oshinsky, *"Worse than Slavery": Parchman Farm and the Ordeal of Jim Crow Justice* (New York: Free Press, 1996); Khalil Gibran Muhammad, *The Condemnation of Blackness: Race, Crime, and the Making of Modern Urban America* (Cambridge, MA: Harvard University Press, 2010); Cheryl Hicks, *Talk With You Like a Woman: African American Women, Justice, and Reform in New York, 1890–1935* (Chapel Hill: University of North Carolina Press, 2010).

9  See Stephanie M. H. Camp, *Closer to Freedom: Enslaved Women and Everyday Resistance in the Plantation South* (Chapel Hill: University of North Carolina Press, 2004), 13; Angela Davis, "From the Prison of Slavery to the Slavery of Prison: Frederick Douglass and the Convict Lease System," in *The Angela Y. Davis Reader*, ed. Joy James (Malden, MA: Blackwell Publishers, 1998), 74–95.

10  Thanks to Stephanie Camp for the formulation of slavery as perhaps *the* "master metaphor" of black intellectual life.

11  In addition to the books listed in note 9 above, see Douglas A. Blackmon, *Slavery by Another Name: The Re-Enslavement of Black Americans from the Civil War to World*

*War II* (New York: Doubleday, 2008); and Ethan Blue, *Doing Time in the Depression: Everyday Life in Texas and California Prisons* (New York: New York University Press, 2012).

12 Heather Ann Thompson, "Blinded by a Barbaric South: The Ironic History of Penal Reform in Modern America," in *The Myth of Southern Exceptionalism,* ed. Joseph Crespino and Matthew Lassiter (New York: Oxford University Press, 2009).

13 For an excellent study of the racial apartheid underlying California's progressive veneer, see Daniel Martinez HoSang, *Racial Propositions: Ballot Initiatives and the Making of Postwar California* (Berkeley: University of California Press, 2010).

14 Houston Baker, "Critical Memory and the Black Public Sphere," in *The Black Public Sphere: A Public Culture Book,* ed. The Black Public Sphere Collective (Chicago: University of Chicago Press, 1995), 18–19.

15 Ibid., 33.

16 Joy James, "American 'Prison Notebooks,'" *Race and Class* 45, no. 3 (2004): 35–47.

17 Donna Murch, *Living for the City: Migration, Education, and the Rise of the Black Panther Party in Oakland, California* (Chapel Hill: University of North Carolina Press, 2010). See also Hasan Kwame Jeffries, *Bloody Lowndes: Civil Rights and Black Power in Alabama's Black Belt* (New York: New York University Press, 2009).

18 Dennis Hevesi, "Huey Newton Symbolized the Rising Black Anger of a Generation," *New York Times,* August 23, 1989, B7; John Kifner, "Eldridge Cleaver, Black Panther Who Became G.O.P. Conservative, Is Dead at 62," *New York Times,* May 2, 1998, B8.

19 Min S. Yee, *The Melancholy History of Soledad Prison* (New York: Harper's Magazine Press, 1973), 130–31.

20 Jack Olson, *Last Man Standing: The Tragedy and Triumph of Geronimo Pratt* (New York: Doubleday, 2000); Lori Andrews, *Black Power, White Blood: The Life and Times of Johnny Spain* (New York: Pantheon Books, 1996); "The San Quentin Six" (circa 1974), pamphlet, 6–7, in Raúl R. Salinas Papers (hereafter RRS), Box 7, Folder 12, Green Library, Stanford University.

21 For more on this case, see Dan Berger, *Captive Nation: Black Prison Organizing in the Civil Rights Era* (Chapel Hill: University of North Carolina Press, forthcoming); Bettina Aptheker, *The Morning Breaks: The Trial of Angela Davis* (1975; reprint, Ithaca: Cornell University Press, 1997).

22 Reginald Major, *Justice in the Round: The Trial of Angela Davis* (New York: Third Press, 1973); Sol Stern, "The Campaign to Free Angela Davis and Ruchell Magee," *New York Times Magazine,* June 27, 1971. In a letter to Huey Newton from jail, Davis complained that the media were denying her support of Magee. Angela Davis to Huey Newton, April 3, 1971, in Huey P. Newton Foundation (hereafter HPNF), Series 2, Box 41, Folder 15, Green Library, Stanford University.

23 Angela Y. Davis, "Notes for Arguments in Court on the Issue of Self-Representation," in *If They Come in the Morning* (New York: Signet, 1971), 252.

24 Ibid., 246.

25 Robert Chase, "Slaves of the State Revolt: Southern Prison Labor and a Prison-Made Civil Rights Movement," in *Life and Labor in the New, New South,* ed. Robert Zeiger (Gainesville: University Press of Florida, 2012), 177–213.

26    Saidiya V. Hartman, *Scenes of Subjection: Terror, Slavery, and Self-Making in Nine-teenth-Century America* (New York: Oxford University Press, 1997), 80–110.

27    The letters can be found in Angela Davis Papers, Carton 39, Folder: Letters to George Jackson, Mieklejohn Civil Liberties Institute (hereafter MCLI), Bancroft Library, University of California Berkeley. See also the summaries presented in Aptheker, *Morning Breaks*; Major, *Justice in the Round;* and Mary Timothy, *Jury Woman* (San Francisco: Glide Publications and Emty Press, 1975).

28    This article, exploring themes that had long interested Davis, appeared in *The Black Scholar* 3, no. 4 (Dec. 1971): 2–15, and is reprinted in James, *Angela Y. Davis Reader,* 111–28. The quote comes from page 126.

29    Ibid., 116.

30    Rebecca N. Hill, *Men, Mobs, and Law: Anti-Lynching and Labor Defense in U.S. Radical History* (Durham, NC: Duke University Press, 2008); Regina Kunzel, *Criminal Intimacy: Prison and the Uneven History of Modern American Sexuality* (Chicago: University of Chicago Press, 2008).

31    Angela Y. Davis, "JoAnne Little: The Dialectics of Rape," in James, *Angela Y. Davis Reader,* 149–60; Safiya Bukhari, *The War Before* (New York: The Feminist Press, 2010); Assata Shakur, *Assata* (London: Zed Books, 1987); Assata Shakur, "Women in Prison: How We Are," in *The New Abolitionists: (Neo)Slave Narratives and Contemporary Prison Writings,* ed. Joy James (Albany: SUNY Press, 2005); Victoria Law, "Sick of the Abuse: Feminist Responses to Sexual Assault, Battering, and Self-Defense," in *The Hidden 1970s: Histories of Radicalism,* ed. Dan Berger (New Brunswick, NJ: Rutgers University Press, 2010), 39–56; Emily Thuma, "Not a Wedge but a Bridge: Prisons, Feminist Activism, and the Politics of Gendered Violence, 1968–1987" (PhD diss., New York University, 2011).

32    George L. Jackson, *Soledad Brother: The Prison Letters of George Jackson* (1970; reprint, Chicago: Lawrence Hill Books, 1994), 233. For a critique of Jackson's ability to "recall" the Middle Passage, see Robert Reid-Pharr, *Once You Go Black: Choice, Desire, and the Black American Intellectual* (New York: New York University Press, 2007), 127–28.

33    George Jackson, *Blood in My Eye* (Baltimore: Black Classics Press, 1990), 10.

34    Walter Rodney, "George Jackson: Black Revolutionary," November 1971, reprinted in History Is a Weapon, http://www.historyisaweapon.com/defcon1/rodneyjackson.html (accessed March 19, 2009).

35    Quoted in George Jackson, *Soledad Brother* (Chicago: Lawrence Hill Books, 1994), x.

36    Fleeta Drumgo, quoted in "Interviews with the Soledad Brothers," aired on KPFK on August 17, 1970, archived in the Prison Movement collection, audio file PM 058, Freedom Archives, San Francisco.

37    Students for a Democratic Society, "Tape on Ruchell Magee," circa 1972, flyer, in New Left Collection (hereafter NLC), Box 56, Folder: Black Panther Party, Hoover Institution Archives, Stanford University.

38    See *Midnight Special* 3, no. 6 (June 1973): 23; Bettina F. Aptheker, *Intimate Politics* (Emeryville, CA: Seal Press, 2006), 288–91.

39    Aptheker, *Intimate Politics,* 246. This speech appeared in the leftist news weekly *National Guardian* in October 1970.

40 James Baldwin, "An Open Letter to My Sister, Angela Y. Davis," in *If They Come in the Morning*, 19.

41 Joe Walker, "Angela Davis: What's on Her Mind?," *Muhammad Speaks*, January 1, 1971, reprinted as a pamphlet by the Committee to Free Angela Davis, copy in Jessica Mitford Papers (hereafter JMP), Box 49, Folder 6, Harry Ransom Center, University of Texas Austin.

42 Cynthia A. Young, *Soul Power: Culture, Radicalism, and the Making of a U.S. Third World Left* (Durham, NC: Duke University Press, 2006), 187.

43 "Iron Box: The Prison Life and Death of George Jackson," audio file PM 023, Freedom Archives; originally a BBC program, aired on KPFA. Jackson's insistence on the prison's ability to influence everyone formed the basis of Michel Foucault's famous work on the prison, *Discipline and Punish: The Birth of the Prison* (1975). See Hill, *Men, Mobs, and Law*, 296.

44 Jackson, *Soledad Brother*, 210.

45 See "Soledad Brothers Defense Fund," pamphlet, n.d. (circa 1970), 7, in NLC, Box 57, Folder: Black Power. More generally, see Berger, *Captive Nation*; Robert Chase, "Civil Rights on the Cell Block: Race, Reform, and Violence in Texas Prisons and the Nation, 1945–1990" (PhD diss., University of Maryland at College Park, 2009).

46 Cummins, *Rise and Fall of California's Radical Prison Movement*, 259–60; Bill Monning, "San Quentin 6: 'Justice' Shackled," *The Conspiracy*, 5, no. 6 (May 1975): 3, 13, copy in National Lawyers Guild Papers (hereafter NLGP), Oversized Box 7, Bancroft Library, University of California at Berkeley.

47 "Johnny Spain Appeals 1976 San Quentin 6 Conviction," *Black Panther*, May 20, 1978, 3; James R. Bendat, "The San Quentin Six Trial: Do Chains Have a Place?," *Los Angeles Times*, May 22, 1975, 7; Karen Wald, "The San Quentin Six Case: Perspective and Analysis," in *Punishment and Penal Discipline: Essays on the Prison and the Prisoners' Movement*, ed. Tony Platt and Paul Takagi (San Francisco: Crime and Social Justice Associates, 1980), 169. Tate quoted in Alice Yarish, "What It's Like to Be Free and One of the San Quentin 6," *San Francisco Examiner and Chronicle*, July 13, 1975.

48 The Prison Law Collective, "Adjustment Center Challenge by SQ6," *The Conspiracy*, April 1974, 13.

49 My discussion of the case builds on a series of interviews I conducted with the San Quentin Six defendants David Johnson, Luis Bato Talamantez, and Willie Sundiata Tate, and the attorneys Fred Hiestand, Mark Merin, and Larry Weiss.

50 Drumgo's nightmare, however, would continue in a different manner. He was gunned down on an Oakland street by two men in November 1979. See Aptheker, *Morning Breaks*, 287; Fleeta Drumgo funeral program, in Kendra and Franklin Alexander Papers (hereafter KFAP), folder: Davis, Angela, Southern California Library, Los Angeles. See also the October 4 (circa 1972) untitled press release, in NAARPR files, Box 3; "Who Are the San Quentin Six?" (circa 1975), in KFAP, folder: San Quentin 1971–1972.

51 Spain was released from prison in 1988, four years after the attorney Stephen Bingham returned to the United States and was acquitted in the case. Because the original conspiracy rested on Bingham's alleged involvement, his acquittal opened the

door for Spain to appeal his conviction. See Andrews, *Black Power, White Blood,* for more on Spain. Pinell, however, remains in prison in California. As of 2011 he was incarcerated at Pelican Bay State Prison, a control unit prison within the prison. In July 2011 he was one of thousands of prisoners who embarked on a hunger strike at Pelican Bay.

52   Wald, "San Quentin Six Case," 169, 173–75.

53   See Chase, "Civil Rights on the Cell Block"; and Perkinson, *Texas Tough.*

54   Major notes, however, that black journalists and spectators abandoned this form of resistance when the verdict in Davis's trial was ready. Then, he writes, "we were up front." Major, *Justice in the Round,* 290.

55   "Harriet Tubman Prison Movement," circa 1973, pamphlet, in Tony Platt, private collection.

56   Lee Bernstein, *America Is the Prison: Arts and Politics in Prison in the 1970s* (Chapel Hill: University of North Carolina Press, 2010); James Edward Smethurst, *The Black Arts Movement: Literary Nationalism in the 1960s and 1970s* (Chapel Hill: University of North Carolina Press, 2005).

57   John W. Blassingame, *The Slave Community: Plantation Life in the Antebellum South* (New York: Oxford University Press, 1979); Sterling Stuckey, *Slave Culture: Nationalist Theory and the Foundations of Black America* (New York: Oxford University Press, 1988); H. Bruce Franklin, *The Victim as Criminal and Artist: Literature from the American Prison* (New York: Oxford University Press, 1978).

# PART FIVE

# Fighting a State of Violence

# 8

# Hypervisibility and Invisibility

## Asian/American Women, Radical Orientalism, and the Revisioning of Global Feminism

JUDY TZU-CHUN WU

DURING THE US WAR IN VIET NAM, THE HANOI-BASED VIET NAM WOMEN'S Union and the Union of Women for the Liberation of South Viet Nam both played integral roles in fostering a global women's antiwar movement. Through meetings, correspondence, and the circulation of print as well as visual media, the two Viet Nam women's unions (VWUs) actively nurtured US women's interest in American foreign policy and military activity in Southeast Asia. Their ability to fuel a sense of moral outrage among women across national, cultural, racial, and class boundaries stemmed from a belief that all human beings, and especially all women, could share a sense of commonality and purpose. To convey this message, the VWUs reached out to women around the world and articulated a gendered critique of imperialism and militarism. Their efforts to promote an international antiwar movement was premised upon a belief in global sisterhood, projecting and cultivating a female universalism that simultaneously challenged and transcended racial and cultural divides.

This chapter revisits the concept of global sisterhood from a different vantage point. Studies on global feminism have noted the disproportionate power and the misperceptions of white middle-to-upper-class women from the "West" in shaping these international alliances.[1] I examine instead how "Third World" women, both those from the global South as well as racialized women in the United States, fostered and deployed female internationalism during the "long" decade of the 1960s. In particular, I foreground the agency and perspectives of both Asian and Asian American women during the US War in Viet Nam. The political efforts of women from Southeast Asia resonated deeply with women of Asian ancestry in the United States. Over the course of the war, Asian American women were rendered largely invisible in American social movement circles. Cast as the "model minority" by the popular media in the 1960s, Asian Americans generally came to represent a counterpoint to social activism, a minority group seemingly disengaged from politics altogether. Mirroring similar conclusions about Japanese Americans, for example, the *U.S. News and World Report* argued in 1966 that "at a time when it is being proposed that hundreds of billions be spent to uplift Negroes and other minorities, the nation's 300,000 Chinese Americans are moving ahead on their own—with no help from anyone else."[2] For Asian American women, this image of the model minority was compounded by projections of hypersexuality and submissiveness.[3] Asian American women were racialized and gendered as the antithesis of political activism.

In contrast to the invisibility and marginalization of Asian American women, Vietnamese women occupied highly visible and exemplary roles as anti-imperialist revolutionaries in global as well as US-based antiwar and women's movements. The significant roles of Asian women within the international activist imaginary, which has yet to be fully recognized in the scholarship on radical movements, provides an opportunity to elaborate on a concept I call *radical orientalism*.

The activists who questioned the US War in Viet Nam wanted to name American policies and cultural practices as a form of imperialist domination, an effort to control governments, economies, and societies abroad in the name of modernization and democracy. These critics tended to distance themselves from what they perceived as the militaristic, materialistic, and racist values of mainstream US society. Instead, they wanted to identify with Asian people and with societies resisting colonialism (or formal control by another country) and neocolonialism (or indirect control). Consequently, these individuals ironically followed in an orientalist tradition of reinforcing a dichotomy between the East and the West, specifically between decolonizing Asia and imperial America. The radicalness of their orientalism stemmed from how they inverted and subverted previous hierarchies: American travelers idealized the East and denigrated the West. They turned to Asian countries and peoples for political, personal, and at times religious inspiration. Radical critics therefore replicated an orientalist logic that cultural theorist Edward Said identified, whereby the decolonizing East helped to define the identities and goals of activists in the West.[4]

In addition to the hierarchical inversion, radical orientalism differed from dominant forms of orientalism in that Asian individuals actively shaped Western understandings of Asia. In Said's critique of Occidental representations of the Orient, the East is inert and silent; instead, the West speaks for the East. Even in Vijay Prashad's discussion of Western radical appropriations of Eastern philosophies and religions, Asian people and culture tend to be frozen in time, valorized for an essentialized "spiritual patina."[5] The perceptions of Western antiwar travelers, however, were not just their projections of Asia. Asian individuals, political movements, and nations cultivated connections with US activists of diverse backgrounds and interpreted decolonizing Asia for these visitors. These Asian representatives were political beings grounded in a particular historical movement for national liberation against the West, communicating their interpretations of their identities, histories, ideologies, and goals with activists from the West. In other words, the East and the West worked together to foster a radical orientalist sensibility.

The depictions of Vietnamese female warriors played a crucial role in this radical orientalist framework. They directly countered classical orientalist depictions of exotic, sexualized, and victimized Asian women. Instead, these Third World female liberation fighters served as models of revolutionary womanhood. In doing so, however, these radical portrayals reinforced an orientalist binary, in which the East again served as a mirror for Western self-definition. Now representing a contrasting image of revolutionary hope to oppressive gender roles in North American societies, Asian women helped female reformers in the West to redefine their aspirations and political goals.

There is a tension between radical orientalism, which posits a binary sense of opposition between the Orient and the Occident, and global sisterhood, which emphasizes the possibility of genuine dialogue and collective identification among women across various borders. I believe that this tension was a productive and generative one that allowed women of varying backgrounds from the West to develop a sense of sisterhood with women from the East. These global political alliances were inspired by heroic representations of Asian women's anticolonial activism. In turn, these depictions of revolutionary womanhood both reinforced and challenged an orientalist logic. They fostered identification through an essentialized sense of East/West duality, but they also offered the possibility of Asian female agency and defiance. Radical orientalism and global sisterhood were mutually imbricated, not polar opposites.

The productive tension between a binary sense of opposition between the Orient and the Occident and an identification with radical Asia was particularly acute for Asian American women. Because of their marginalization within American political movements, women of Asian ancestry in the United States aspired to connect with their revolutionary Asian sisters in Southeast Asia. Their sense of sisterhood both recognized the disparate subject positions of Asian and Asian American women yet was also premised upon a sense of commonality rooted in racial, gender, and political likeness. Inspired by these encounters, both groups of women formulated innovative critiques of war and colonization that foregrounded the experiences and bodies of Asian women in understanding US militarization and empire.

This chapter analyzes the efforts of Asian and Asian American women in fostering global sisterhood. Given vast cultural, racial, and political divides, the process of fostering a female internationalism relied upon face-to-face contacts between women of diverse backgrounds that would expand their political imagination and sense of communion beyond the nation-state. Actual encounters between Asian and American women provided opportunities for dialogue and for the recognition of each other's humanity. In addition, the reporting of these encounters, which were circulated through articles, books, reports, letters, interviews, speeches, short stories, poetry, photographs, film, and artwork, helped to create a common language, a shared sense of time, and an internationalist commitment toward mutual responsibility.[6]

The first section examines how the VWUs attempted to communicate their political message to various groups of American women activists, particularly those who identified as "traditional" maternalist peace advocates and as second-wave feminists. The second section reveals how the US War in Viet Nam shaped the political aspirations and identifications of "Third World" women based in racialized communities in the United States, illustrating especially how Asian American women came to be political activists and theorists of war, race, and gender. The third section focuses on the relationship between global sisterhood (which seeks to promote universal commonality) and radical orientalism (which fosters political communion through a recognition of binary difference). These layered efforts to promote an international women's antiwar movement were not free of conflict or misunderstanding, but highlighting Asian and Asian

American perspectives offers an opportunity to reframe Western women's peace activism as part of a global movement that emerged through dialogue and negotiation as well as through projection and romanticization.[7]

## FOSTERING GLOBAL SISTERHOOD

In its campaign to promote a worldwide movement against the US War in Viet Nam, the Viet Nam women's unions cultivated relationships with individual women and with female organizations from a variety of political leanings and backgrounds. Members of the VWUs invested personnel, time, and energy to establish relationships with women in the West through conversations, meetings, and letters. Their efforts to foster global sisterhood used multiple strategies rather than a uniform message to create overlapping and distinct international female constituencies. Specifically, the VWUs articulated maternalist gender equity, as well as gender separatist ideals. These messages appealed to women in the West who ascribed to diverse political beliefs and who came from varying class and racial backgrounds.

The earliest contacts that the VWUs had with women in the West were with maternalist peace organizations, such as the US-based Women Strike for Peace (WSP). Women Strike for Peace originated in 1961 with the efforts of predominantly middle-class and middle-aged white women to protect their families from nuclear annihilation. As historian and former WSP activist Amy Swerdlow explained,

> On 1 November 1961 an estimated fifty thousand women walked out
> of their kitchens and off their jobs, in an unprecedented nationwide
> strike for peace. As a radioactive cloud from a series of Russian
> atom bomb tests passed over American cities and the United States
> threatened to retaliate with its own cycle of nuclear explosions, the
> striking women sent delegations to their elected officials.... They
> demanded that their local officials pressure President John Kennedy
> on behalf of all the world's children, to end nuclear testing at once
> and begin negotiations for nuclear disarmament.[8]

This initial strike eventually led committed women to form Women Strike for Peace. The members of the organization, as historian Andrea Estepa has argued, had "wide-ranging professional identities," but they chose to publicly identify themselves as "housewives and mothers."[9] These women proclaimed their right to condemn the threat of global and nuclear warfare based on the desire to protect their own and other people's families. In other words, they were not rejecting gender difference but embracing it to define a special role for women on the global stage.

These maternalist motivations for peace inspired WSP to engage with peace activism during the US War in Viet Nam and with Vietnamese women. Women Strike for Peace's contact with the VWUs began in 1965, when two WSP members were among the first Americans to visit Hanoi after the commencement of the US bombing of North Viet Nam. That same year, a ten-person delegation from WSP met with representatives from North and South Viet Nam in Djakarta, Indonesia, to affirm women's unique abilities to cross Cold War barriers and foster peace.[10] These political and personal relationships continued to develop as WSP sent international delegations to Europe, Canada, Cuba, and North Viet Nam throughout the remainder of the war.

The efforts of WSP would not have been possible without the VWUs, who initiated the invitation to WSP representatives to visit Hanoi and then met and corresponded with them around the world. In addition to these personal contacts, the VWUs also circulated print and visual materials to help Western women gain an understanding of how Vietnamese women both suffered from but also resisted colonialism and military aggression. One important example of this antiwar literature was *Vietnamese Studies No. 10*, a publication devoted to the topic of *Vietnamese Women* (hereafter referred to as *VW*). The 1966 booklet, published significantly in English in Hanoi, was presented to US visitors, both at international gatherings and during their travels to Viet Nam. The portrayal of Vietnamese women in this work, which numbered over three hundred pages, resonated with the political ideologies and sympathies of women from a variety of backgrounds in the West.

*Vietnamese Women* consisted of eight sections, with chapters on broad topics, such as "The Vietnamese Woman, Yesterday and Today," as well as more intimate and localized portrayals of either individual women or women from particular villages or regions. The overall effect was to personalize and humanize women in North and South Viet Nam by providing a narrative of personal and social uplift through four historical stages: (1) Vietnamese women's lives under patriarchal and colonial oppression under French rule beginning in the mid- to late nineteenth century; (2)

Vietnamese women's efforts to challenge traditional gender roles through involvement in national liberation movements, first against the French and then against the United States; (3) the transformation of Vietnamese women's lives through socialist reconstruction projects in the North after the end of the First Indochina War against the French in 1954; and (4) how the opportunities for improving Vietnamese women's lives continued to be threatened by American imperialism and the Second Indochina War, which was being fought against the United States and the South Vietnamese government. Somewhat predictably, VW argued that the oppression of Vietnamese women, particularly for the vast majority who were members of the peasantry, was centrally connected to class and national oppression. For Vietnamese women to achieve liberation and equality, then, they had to not only struggle against patriarchal family and societal norms but also strive for national independence and socialist revolution.

The way this political message was conveyed, particularly through intimate portraits, appealed to Western women in various ways. For "maternalist" peace activists, like many members of WSP, the destructive effect of war on heteronormative family life in Viet Nam resonated strongly. Numerous portrayals of women in VW emphasize the temporary or permanent separation of husbands and wives, as well as mothers and children, because of war. The tragedy of war, then, was conveyed through the tragedy of heteronormative and maternal loss. One folksong quoted in VW expressed this longing between a young woman in North Viet Nam and her fiancé who departed to fight in the South: "Our destinies are bound together, I will wait for you/Even if I should have to wait a thousand years."[11]

The emphasis on family separation also was conveyed through other forms of communication. For example, Nguyen Thi Binh, who met with members of WSP in Djakarta and became one of the most recognizable Asian female figures in Western women's political circles, came from a relatively elite and educated background. Unlike most WSP members, Binh became an authorized political leader, eventually serving as the foreign minister of the Provisional Revolutionary Government of the Republic of South Viet Nam and its chief negotiator at the Paris peace talks. Despite the disjuncture in status between Binh and most members of WSP, Binh sought to connect with maternalist peace activists through a language of sisterhood and motherhood. For example, in a fifteen-minute film produced for Women Strike for Peace in 1970, Binh explained,

I am so happy as a South Vietnamese woman and mother to have
the opportunity to speak to you.... May I express my sincere thanks
to the Women Strike for Peace for its contribution to the anti-war
movements and its sympathy and support to our people, particularly the South Vietnamese women.... Our aspirations for peace are
all the more ardent, for over twenty-five consecutive years now, our
compatriots, we women included, have never enjoyed a single day of
peace. Let me tell you that in my own family, several members have
been killed while some others are still jailed by the Saigon regime.
I myself have had not much time to live with my husband and my
children. The moments my son and daughter were allowed to be at
my side have become so rare and therefore so precious to them.[12]

Binh's emphasis on the destructive effect of warfare on family life both
reflected the experiences of women in Viet Nam and also resonated with
maternalist activists in the West who stressed the sanctity of motherhood
and home life. [13]

Given the emphasis placed on protecting the family, Vietnamese wom-
en's resistance of colonialism and war, which necessitated transcending
traditional gender roles and at times engaging in or supporting acts of
violence, can be framed as heteronormative or maternalist agency. An
imprisoned female revolutionary during the struggles against French
imperialism wrote on her prison cell before she was executed:

A rosy-cheeked woman, here I am fighting side by side with you men!
On my shoulders, weighs that hatred which is common to us.
The prison is my school, its mates my friends.
The sword is my child, the gun my husband.[14]

In this poem, instruments of violence are equated with members of a
heteronormative family, with the evocation of the sword as a child and
the gun as a husband justifying the embrace of these objects as a means
to fulfill traditional familial responsibilities. Given colonial and wartime
conditions that did not allow for a peaceful existence of kinship units,
the female warrior bore the responsibility of defending her home and
homeland in order to become a wife and mother.

While this defiance of traditional gender roles in the name of maternal-
ism might have struck a chord with "traditional" women's peace activists

in the United States, the experiences and representations of Vietnamese women also offered a range of political possibilities for a diverse array of American women who initiated second-wave feminism in the 1960s and 1970s.[15] For liberal feminists seeking access and equality in the realm of work and politics, the experiences of Vietnamese women during both the war and socialist construction offered insights into the process of renegotiating public gender roles. For example, *Vietnamese Women* began by noting that while "it is easy to inscribe the 'liberation of women' in the programme of a political party, it is much more difficult to get it into legislation, and more difficult still to integrate it into the customs and manners of the time."[16] Significantly, the publication did not regard women in the West as the vanguard of change, stating instead that "at present, women in all Western countries are still asking for equal salary and wages with men.... And they are not to get it very soon."[17] Strikingly, the authors regarded women in the West as being engaged in a similar struggle and perhaps even falling behind the so-called Third World. *VW* documented at length the rights and advances women had achieved under the Democratic Republic of Vietnam, such as suffrage, equal pay, and holding prominent positions of political and economic leadership. At the same time, the publication also frankly acknowledged barriers to greater gender equity, conveying both advances and challenges through individual stories and charts with clear quantitative data.[18]

Other aspects of the Vietnamese analysis of women's oppression and agency would have appealed more strongly to women's liberation activists in the United States, who sought to identify and subvert the workings of patriarchy in all realms of life, not just in work and politics but also in the intimate realm of personal, familial, and sexual relationships.[19] For example, Vivian Rothstein, an activist with Students for a Democratic Society before her involvement in the women's liberation movement in Chicago, gained political inspiration to focus on female empowerment through her travels to Hanoi in 1967. Rothstein noted that her invitation to North Viet Nam was at the insistence of the Viet Nam Women's Union, which at the time had a clear understanding of how women could and should perform important roles in political movements for social transformation. She recalled that in fact the North Vietnamese women had a greater understanding of women's potential than she or her fellow male New Left organizers did. After all, the Hanoi-based VWU traced its history back to the founding of the Indochinese Communist Party in

1930. In North Viet Nam, Rothstein observed how the women's union sought to inspire and mobilize women. The organization had chapters at various levels, ranging from local villages to the national level and operating in schools, workplaces, health clinics, and government units. In all of these settings, the groups trained women for political leadership and advocated for their collective interests. Viet Nam Women's Union representatives conveyed to their US visitors "how important it was to organize the women ... and how powerful American women could be" as well.[20] When Rothstein returned to the United States, she helped form the Chicago Women's Liberation Union, which she modeled on the VWU.

The Vietnamese women not only served as political mentors through their analysis and institutions, they also provided functioning examples of women's communities. The Vietnamese organized all-female economic production teams, guerrilla units, and even regular military battalions while leading hybridized and improvised family structures in the midst of war. Although products of emergency circumstances, these practices nevertheless offered empowering demonstrations of how women, through separatist institutions, could transform the society around them. Finally, the emphasis on using the personal to offer political instruction, a strategy that the VWU used to mobilize the largely peasant constituency in Viet Nam, corresponded strongly to one of the key mantras of the women's liberation movement.

As the Vietnamese effectively reached out to maternalist and feminist women in the West, tensions and disagreements also arose between Asian and American women. That Vietnamese women's military feats in defense of their homes and villages often came at the expense of American lives likely gave pause to some women in the United States, particularly those who were committed to pacifism or who had family members serving in the military. Liberal feminists seeking opportunities to integrate into the existing social structure in the United States likely disagreed with the call for socialism, while the largely unquestioned heteronormativity embedded in maternalist politics frustrated American feminists striving for a more radical critique of sexual and gender relations.[21] Despite the political differences between Indochinese and American women of varying backgrounds and beliefs, the face-to-face meetings, letters, and publications initiated by the VWUs worked effectively to foster political and personal connections with maternalist and feminist women's activists in the West.

The Vietnamese women engaged in struggles of national liberation served as role models and political educators not only for maternalist peace activists and second-wave feminists but perhaps most profoundly for "Third World" women in the United States. These racialized women of African American, Chicana or Mexican American, Latina, Indigenous, and Asian American backgrounds adopted the title "Third World" in the late 1960s to express solidarity with Third World peoples globally.[22] Understanding themselves as internal colonial subjects, they allied with one another based on similar experiences of disfranchisement and marginalization within the United States. In addition, they identified with people in the Third World who were fighting for self-determination and national liberation from colonialism and neocolonialism. Furthermore, as women of color, they began in the mid- to late 1960s and 1970s to articulate an intersectional analysis of the social hierarchies that they experienced.[23] They discovered and explored a connection to Vietnamese women because of their shared political analysis of overlapping oppression based on race, colonialism, class, and gender.

For example, Betita Martinez, a Chicana activist based in New Mexico who had political roots in the southern civil rights movement, visited Hanoi in 1970.[24] Her sense of commonality with Vietnamese women was due not only to gender but also to what she perceived as a comparable colonized status. Likening the Vietnamese countryside to New Mexico, Martinez also observed how the vast majority of Vietnamese people were peasants, an identity celebrated by the Chicano/a movement.[25] In addition, akin to Mexican American demands for self-determination and reclamation of their ancestral homeland of Aztlán, the Vietnamese were engaged in a struggle for political independence and defense against military aggression and ecological destruction.[26] In Martinez's eyes, both the Vietnamese and Chicanos/as shared an indomitable sense of resistance: "The spirit of the people was like a force of nature itself, creating life in the shadow of death. The white people of the West with their unnatural soul and their unnatural weapons are a death people.... The Vietnamese are a life people [like Chicanos]. And anyone who thinks that a life people can really be conquered is a fool."[27]

For Third World women in the United States, the opportunity to interact with and learn from nonwhite female leaders was especially empowering. After meeting women from Southeast Asia at a Canadian conference in 1971, Maria Ramirez and Nina Genera, two Chicana activists based in the San Francisco Bay Area, recalled that it marked their first opportunity to witness and interact with Third World women in the vanguard of an ongoing revolution.[28] For Asian American women, this sense of racial as well as political identification was particularly acute. Largely invisible within social movement circles in the United States, they were able to find political role models through the hypervisibility of Vietnamese peasant women. Pat Sumi, a Japanese American antiwar activist who traveled with Black Panther Party leaders Eldridge Cleaver and Elaine Brown to North Korea, China, and North Viet Nam in 1970, explained,

> Women in Vietnam have a tradition of being liberation fighters....
> We met this seventeen-year-old woman. In her village there was an all-woman guerilla unit that shot down two American airplanes, while taking responsibility for the rice fields around the battery where the antiaircraft guns are. They produced more on that rice field than any other comparable plot in the village. And the whole group sang poetry and songs for us.[29]

Although most women activists in the United States did not travel to Vietnam, they nonetheless would have been able to read similar profiles of Vietnamese women in movement publications.

Pat Sumi was not unique in her admiration of Vietnamese women. A significant number of Asian American women were among the approximately one thousand North American antiwar activists who attended the Indochinese Women's Conferences (IWC), held in Vancouver and Toronto, Canada, in 1971. The IWC represented the first opportunities for North American women to have direct contact with their Asian "sisters"—women from North Viet Nam, South Viet Nam, and Laos, a country bordering Viet Nam that had become enmeshed in the US War in Viet Nam. There were 120 Asians from the United States and Canada at the Vancouver gathering, according to a Japanese American delegate, roughly half of the approximately 200 to 250 Third World women in attendance.[30] Because Asian Americans resided predominantly in the US West, they likely attended in smaller numbers at the Toronto conference, which was intended for residents of the East Coast and the Midwest.

Asian American women who could not travel to Canada could read extensive coverage of the IWC in the *Asian Women's Journal*, a pioneering and widely circulated publication devoted to Asian American women's issues. Originally issued in 1971, the same year as the conferences, the journal was eventually reprinted three times. It featured biographies of the Southeast Asian women who participated in the IWC as well as personal testimonies, poetry, and artwork by Asian American attendees, including an interview with Pat Sumi.[31] Sumi had not only traveled to socialist Asia in the summer of 1970 but had also played a key role in organizing the IWC. And she represented Third World women, whose political trajectories and consciousness emerged out of racial liberation movements, in contrast to the white maternalist peace activists and second-wave feminists who were prominent in organizing the IWC.

Recognizing political differences among IWC organizers and participants, Sumi demanded separate meetings for women of color to engage with Indochinese delegates autonomously. "Since we have been denied an equal participation *with* white groups, we can only ask for equal but separate conferences," she explained in a statement. "The possibility of a confrontation between Third World and white women's groups at a joint conference would be disrespectful to the Indochinese women and would further reinforce the tensions that exist among North American women."[32] Sumi's proposal received support from at least some white women. "Why should Third World women unify with white women who claim to recognize the need of self-determination for the Indochinese," a contingent from Los Angeles argued, "but who do not recognize the right of self-determination of all peoples in this country, as manifested in the 'small' way of planning a conference for people instead of with them."[33] As a result of this call for separate conferences, the IWC in Vancouver was divided into three sections: "old friends" or maternalist activists; "new friends" or women's liberation activists; and Third World Women.

The IWC attracted the interest of Asian American women because female revolutionaries from Southeast Asia crystallized three main tenets of Asian American women's emerging political identity—their racial, international, and gender consciousness. Donna Kotake, a Japanese American who attended the Vancouver conference, recalled the political inspiration that the Indochinese women offered. Raised in a farming community in the San Francisco South Bay and attending San Jose State University in 1971, Kotake was undergoing a political awakening. Growing up in the United States, she explained, your whole identity was not Asian. Your identity was just, like, you wanted to be a white person.... So, to us at that point, ... identifying ourselves as Asian Americans, wanting to learn more about our own histories, and you know, being proud of the histories ... and I think really hooking up with other non-whites was a really big deal.... So, you know, there's the identity going on as being Asian and there's a third world coming, coalitions coming together, and there's this international thing with Vietnam, and at the same time people talking about China and seeing what a shining example of, you know, what it could be like to be free, people who care about ... people and a country that provides ... for everyone.[34]

Kotake and other activists of her generation were discovering their racial identity as Asian Americans. Instead of desiring whiteness, Kotake recognized herself as a member of a resistant pan-ethnic group that had a distinct history and culture connected to Third World struggles in the United States and around the world.

Her political consciousness having been raised through the Asian American movement press and conversations with individuals such as Sumi, Kotake experienced a profound connection with the Indochinese women in Vancouver. They shared her racial and gender status and her anti-imperialist politics. When asked how the IWC influenced her, Kotake responded, "Just feeling the strength of the women and realizing how much women can do ... it really made me feel incredibly proud about being a woman."[35] Another Asian American woman who attended the conference emphasized that the presence of Asian female bodies enhanced the political message of the Indochinese delegates. She wrote, "Their physical presence had tremendous impact on the hundreds of Third World and white women. Here were six Asian women—physically small, sincere, friendly, often appearing extremely tired. Yet, whenever one spoke, it was with such clarity and with a background of personal involvement that the meaning of a people's revolution became a reality."[36]

At the time of the conference, Asian American women were developing a gendered and racialized analysis of the war that emphasized the transnational connections between Asians in Viet Nam and those in the United States. Activist Evelyn Yoshimura articulated this perspective in an essay titled "GI's and Racism," which first appeared in the Asian American movement newspaper *Gidra* and was then reprinted in *Asian*

*Women's Journal.* Yoshimura argued that the US military relied upon and reproduced racial hatred for Asians to motivate American soldiers to fight in Asia. By promoting the "view of Asian people as sub-human beings ... the U.S. military ... can instill the values and mentality that is necessary to become effective killers."[37] These racial attitudes, which were cultivated among US soldiers during basic training on the US mainland and then on military tours in Southeast Asia, were carried and reproduced back and forth across the Pacific.

The figure of Asian women played a central role in the racial education of US military personnel. As Yoshimura stated, US soldiers learned to regard "Asian women as a symbolic sexual object."[38] Through the systematic creation of red light districts in Asian countries where US troops were stationed, the US military institutionalized the practice of American GIs frequenting Asian prostitutes in what sociologist Joane Nagel calls the "military sexual complex."[39] Not limited to individual excursions, these practices became integral to military culture and discourse through ritualized retellings of these experiences. An Asian American Marine recalled of his boot camp experience,

> We had these classes we had to go to taught by the drill instructors, and every instructor would tell a joke before he began class. It would always be a dirty joke usually having to do with prostitutes they had seen in Japan or in other parts of Asia while they were stationed overseas. The attitude of the Asian women being a doll, a useful toy, or something to play with usually came out in these jokes and how they were not quite as human as white women ... how Asian women's vaginas weren't like a white woman's, but rather they were slanted, like their eyes.[40]

Such racialized and sexualized depictions of Asian women, used to foster male bonding among US soldiers, guided US military policies and practices in Southeast Asia—in the brothels and in the general prosecution of war.

The Indochinese women who traveled thousands of miles to meet women in North America bore witness to the US military sexual complex and the gendered effect of militarism. Among the six female delegates from Southeast Asia, women who either suffered traumatic abuse or who could testify to wartime atrocities tended to receive the most attention in activist publications. Dinh Thi Hong, for example, had a powerful effect on conference attendees. A middle-aged housewife from South Viet Nam, Hong had not been politically engaged in the movement for liberation before she was imprisoned. Suspected of supporting the opposition to the South Vietnamese government, she was detained and tortured in a series of the regime's most notorious prisons. In her autobiographical narrative, she recalled having "pins [planted] in my fingertips," having "electrodes ... attached to my ears and to my fingers, nipples and genitals ... and [being] tortured with electricity until I was unconscious." In addition, her interrogators "forced water, lye and salt into my stomach and trampled on my stomach until I vomited blood and was unconscious." Illustrating the visceral and sexualized nature of torture, Hong's detailed account appeared in several movement publications produced by the New Left, Third World, and women's organizations.[41]

Such accounts of atrocities reminded North American women of the horrific nature of the US war in Southeast Asia and the particular effect it had on women. While many antiwar activists no doubt had absorbed similar information through movement publications, the effect of hearing these stories in person was much more profound. Furthermore, the IWC took place just after lieutenant William Calley's conviction for his role in the My Lai massacre. On March 16, 1968, Calley had commanded one of three platoons that entered a village suspected of supporting the "Viet Cong" (Army intelligence had actually misidentified the village). In the aftermath of the Tet Offensive on urban military and political outposts throughout South Viet Nam, US soldiers became determined to hunt down and punish communist sympathizers. Practiced in violent search-and-destroy missions, the American troops executed over five hundred residents of My Lai in one day. They murdered women, the elderly, and young children, none of whom shot at the Americans. GIs also sexually tortured and raped women before executing them. A soldier recalled, "I cut their throats, cut off their hands, cut out their tongue, their hair, scalped them. I did it. A lot of people were doing it, and I just followed. I lost all sense of direction."[42]

After years of delay and deflection on the part of the US military, Calley was finally found guilty of mass premeditated murder and assault with intent to commit murder in March 1971. Although he would ultimately serve only a few months in military prison and a few years under house arrest for his crimes, Calley's conviction made the My Lai massacre a focal point of the IWC in Vancouver, which convened only two days after the verdict was announced.[43] Asked repeatedly about Calley, the Indochinese delegation used the occasion to highlight the level of violence and destruction the US military committed everyday in Southeast Asia.[44] Without acquitting Calley's role, Phan Minh Hien, a teacher and a representative of the Women's Union for the Liberation of South Vietnam, stated, "While Calley is the person who gave the order, he was merely carrying out the orders of the US administration." For Hien, Calley's crimes were America's crimes, since "the U.S. administration sent U.S. troops into Vietnam, 'that is why the U.S. youths commit crimes against our country ... why the Vietnamese people have to fight ... and why U.S. youths get killed.'"[45]

As the Vietnamese delegates explained how the US War in Viet Nam depended on gendered and sexualized violence in Asia, Asian American women emphasized the transnational nature of that violence. "We, as Asian American women, cannot separate ourselves from our Asian counterparts," Evelyn Yoshimura argued. "Racism against them is too often racism against us.... The mentality that keeps Suzy Wong, Madame Butterfly and gookism alive turns human beings into racist murdering soldiers and also keeps Asian Americans from being able to live and feel like human beings."[46] Harkening back to decades of fictive representations of Asian women as available and vulnerable objects of Western military men and US military campaigns in Asia, Yoshimura invoked a larger history of colonial violence and racial subjection across the Pacific.[47] As the appellation Third World women suggested, racialized women in the United States recognized how colonization and gender oppression operated in tandem both abroad and at home.

### RADICAL ORIENTALISM AND GLOBAL SISTERHOOD

The Indochinese Women's Conferences provided an example of how ideas and practices could critique and transcend national boundaries. The political leadership of Indochinese women inspired an array of American sisters—who identified themselves as maternalist, feminist, and Third World activists—to combat American militarism and imperialism. Yet even as these women forged international alliances, they also reinforced a binary between women from the East and those from the West. The North American attendees of the IWC tended to perceive Indochinese women as either victims of war or revolutionary heroines, as a people subjected to and resisting Western violence. In contrast, the women from South-

Figure 8.1. A Vietnamese Madonna and Child that appeared on the cover of *Memo*, the newsletter for Women Strike for Peace, December 1966. Swarthmore College Peace Collection, Swarthmore, Pennsylvania.

east Asia encouraged their audience to view everyone as equally capable of political activism. The tension between difference and commonality was nevertheless an enabling one that helped to forge an international sisterhood, predicated upon and in excess of a radical orientalist outlook.

The politics of rescue or a feminist orientalist outlook readily shaped the perspectives of some Western women. Following the IWC conferences, the newsletter for Women Strike for Peace, *Memo*, published a series of letters from its readers under the headline "They Must Be Saved," a phrase that positioned North American women as the potential saviors of Asian women.[48] Reinforcing this message was a widely circulated image among peace activists that appeared on the cover of *Memo* in December 1966. Featuring a Vietnamese mother holding a baby in her arms, the image portrayed the mother as utterly hopeless and forlorn. As she gazes down and away, three white angels descend toward her to offer solace, evoking the role to be played by women of the West. Published during the Christmas season, the Vietnamese Madonna image underscored a maternalist message, calling for the salvation of a fellow mother and, perhaps more importantly, her child, whose gaze connects directly with the viewer.

In contrast to the politics of rescue, a radical orientalist sensibility also shaped the perceptions of feminist activists from the West. Seeking to critique the militaristic West, American radicals followed in an orientalist tradition of demarcating a divide between the East and the West, specifically between decolonizing Asia and imperial America. By inverting previous hierarchies, however, they pursued a radical politics that idealized the East and denigrated the West. As targets of Western imperialism, racism, and sexism, Indochinese women represented the ultimate underdogs to the US military. Yet, by fighting against nearly impossible odds with a sense of strength, clarity, and unity, the Southeast Asian representatives reminded North American women what was possible both individually and collectively. Replicating and challenging an orientalist logic, the revolutionary East served to define the identities and goals of activists in the West.

Asian American women were particularly invested in this form of radical orientalism as a means to express their affinity with Asian female revolutionaries and to forge a revolutionary political agenda. In contrast to the relative invisibility and marginalization of Asian American women in movement circles, Vietnamese women occupied a hypervisible role as revolutionary leaders. A widely circulated image in US movement newspapers, including the *Black Panther* and *Gidra*, featured an Asian female peasant cradling a rifle in one arm and a baby in the other.[49] Equally ready to engage in armed struggle and to nurture her child, indeed to engage in armed struggle to nurture her child, this figure embodied revolutionary womanhood and motherhood, conveying the interconnectedness of multiple liberations: by fighting for her family, her class, and her nation, the female Vietnamese peasant was freeing herself. If female peasants in an underdeveloped nation could defend themselves against the most technologically advanced and wealthy country in the world, what might be possible for activists, particularly Asian American female activists, within the United States?

The desire to view Asian female warriors as political role models was particularly acute as various identity-based political movements emerged in the United States in the late 1960s and early 1970s. In contrast to the divisions that fractured various women's political communities in the West, the Southeast Asian women at the IWC stressed the need for self-sacrifice and alliances. Lacking the resources to fight a conventional war, the Vietnamese turned to guerrilla warfare, a tactic that necessitated

Figure 8.2. Peasant woman with baby and gun. Cover of *Gidra*, March 1970, reproduced in Steve Louie and Glenn Omatsu, eds., *Asian Americans: The Movement and the Moment* (Los Angeles: UCLA Asian American Studies Center Press, 2001), 17.

cultivating political support among the "people." "Cadres must make the masses love them," a representative explained at the IWC. "This is a question of principle. If the masses love the cadres, they will listen to what they say and give them protection." That love, she continued, flowed from shared sacrifice. "That is why you must be exemplary," she said. "You must be exemplary in sacrifices. You must be the first to give your life, and the last to get rewards."[50]

For the Indochinese delegates, the strategy of building a political base was applicable to struggles beyond armed conflict. In response to a question as to whether the antiwar movement should pursue violent forms of protest, the women from Southeast Asia explained, "Revolutionary force is in two parts: (1) political force and (2) armed force. When we say political force we refer to the consciousness of people.... You need this political force.... The force must be large and strong, of people determined and courageous, who can take repression. When one is killed or jailed, another takes the place."[51] Instead of recommending armed resistance for the US peace movement, the Indochinese women explained that they had no choice but to fight militarily. "We need military force to drive out the aggressors and take the power," they stated. "In different stages of struggle, sometimes political force is to the forefront, sometimes military force. But always military force must be combined with political force." The military ought to be inseparable from the people, they argued, since "isolation in the fight is very dangerous."[52]

For the Indochinese delegates, the importance of cultivating broad political support extended beyond national borders. As members of the Laotian delegation explained, "The policy of the United Front ... is to win more supporters and isolate the administration. It is a tactical policy, a policy of increasing our friends and decreasing the enemy."[53] The Vietnamese delegates also shared that they had

> followed anti-war activities in Canada and the U.S.A. We have taken
> note of the demonstrations, petitions, and many other actions. They
> all help in our struggle against U.S. aggression. The most important
> thing is to mobilize larger forces to undertake these actions. If we
> are larger and more united, we can achieve greater success. We need
> unity and solidarity between the many groups.... As Ho Chi Minh
> said, "Unity, unity, larger unity; success, success, bigger success."
> The greater the difficulties, the broader must be the force in order to

defeat the enemy. The more we consolidate, the more we weaken and divide the enemy.[54]

The IWC provided a venue to articulate and pursue a common, transpacific struggle against US imperialism.

In response to the frustration expressed by antiwar activists that their organizing efforts achieved few results, the Indochinese counseled patience and persistence. The Vietnamese and Laotian delegates, regardless of their age, espoused a broader historical consciousness that recognized and built on previous generations' struggles. The Indochinese encouraged their American counterparts to do the same, addressing a tendency among some young American activists to search constantly for new political ideologies, strategies, and identities. They explained, "We must also be prepared for all the struggles to take a long time. Actions must go on, but the results may not be seen for a long time.... We say to you: Be patient. Be flexible. Be vigilant. And wage a *persistent* struggle."[55]

These words of advice led North American women to regard the Indochinese women with awe and to view themselves even more critically for their failure to create unity and commonality of purpose. As an Asian American delegate pondered in a poem about the conference

How can your people maintain such discipline, understanding and
    humanity?
One million soldiers have been killed or wounded
three million civilians have been killed or wounded
one hundred fifty thousand children are orphaned
fifty thousand people are imprisoned
thirty nine thousand women over the age of twelve are prostitutes.[56]

In the poem, the author expresses a sense of separation between the Southeast Asian women and herself (and presumably other North American attendees of the IWC) by asking how "your people" could endure and resist such violence and upheaval. Despite a sense of racial and gender affinity, she recognizes her subject position as a person of Asian ancestry in the West, geographically distanced from the direct site of colonial and military conflict. In addition, she ascribes an essentialized and romanticized identity to the Vietnamese, depicting them as a collective people suffering under and resisting American oppression.

The same poem, however, suggests that the Indochinese emphasized a collective identity that transcended orientalist binaries. The voice of an Indochinese woman responds to the question addressed to "your people" by stating, "For twenty five years we have been defending our land. What our fathers began we continue. What we do not finish our children will continue and even their children's children until the enemy is driven out. / Until the People win. Until there is peace."[57] The evocation of "we" is a collective call, an open-ended coalition that included multiple generations of Vietnamese people as well as a broader international community of "the people" struggling for peace. Through their words and actions, the Southeast Asian women reminded their North American audience that the Indochinese, according to Asian Women's Journal, "were not too different from ourselves as women. We need not have false feelings of inadequacy."[58] By working together, women around the world might achieve liberation and peace.

Although premised on a cultural binary between the East and the West, the radical orientalist rendering of Asian women as revolutionary warriors simultaneously fostered a sense of global sisterhood across racial, national, and political divides. Female internationalism from this angle helps us to reevaluate the concept of global sisterhood in two significant ways. First, in contrast to classical understandings of orientalism, which has regarded women in the "Third World" as oppressed recipients of Western benevolence and feminist rescue, radical orientalism showcased the agency of Vietnamese women in initiating international partnerships and serving as political mentors for women in the West. The VWUs certainly hoped that women from the West would help them end the war, but they also believed that they had a reciprocal and perhaps even greater ability to offer political instruction and guidance. Global sisterhood as a political strategy, in short, was not just imposed by the West but also crafted and promoted by the East.

Second, the political discourses that fostered global sisterhood in the IWC suggested that an international female political community need not hinge on a monolithic analysis of gender oppression across time and space. The political messages that Vietnamese women conveyed through face-to-face meetings and the circulation of print and visual media carried multiple meanings and inflections. Discussions of war and motherhood, the sexualized and racialized nature of violence, and women's revolutionary potential spoke in different ways to different groups of women. For some, the global dialogues affirmed a more universal understanding of women's lives and experiences. For others, such as Asian American women, their connections were rooted more in a unique sense of difference based on racial, gender, and colonized status.

What emerged, then, was not "sectarian" identity politics, as is often charged against social movements of the 1960s, but a radical politics of engagement. Following her travels to North Viet Nam, Vivian Rothstein was most impressed by the VWU's emphasis on organizing a "majoritarian" movement, characterized by efforts to build broad political consensus and coalitions.[59] Literally engaged in a struggle for life and death, women in Viet Nam sought to cultivate the broadest range of allies possible. Global sisterhood, for them, was never about developing a rigid universal theory on women's oppression. Rather, while recognizing the conflicts and disparities across geopolitical boundaries, the VWUs sought to involve women of varying backgrounds and political beliefs to engage and learn from one another's ideas and experiences. It was a remarkable lesson in how those from the global South could provide leadership to those in the global North and how a global sisterhood might accommodate differences, foster dialogues, and generate political unity.

1    Inderpal Grewal, *Transnational America: Feminisms, Diasporas, Neoliberalisms* (Durham, NC: Duke University Press, 2005); Chandra Mohanty, "Under Western Eyes: Feminist Scholarship and Colonial Discourses," *Feminist Review* 30 (Autumn 1988): 61–88; and Leila J. Rupp, *Worlds of Women: The Making of an International Women's Movement* (Princeton: Princeton University Press, 1997).

2    "Success Story of One Minority Group in U.S.," *U.S. News and World Report*, December 26, 1966, reprinted in *Roots: An Asian American Reader*, ed. Amy Tachiki, Eddie Wong, Franklin Odo, and Buck Wong (Los Angeles: Asian American Studies Center, University of California, 1971), 6.

3    Yen Le Espiritu, *Asian American Women and Men: Labor, Laws, and Love* (Thousand Oaks, CA: Rowman and Littlefield Publishers, 1996).

4    Edward W. Said, *Orientalism* (New York: Vintage Books, 1979).

5    Vijay Prashad, *The Karma of Brown Folk* (Minneapolis: University of Minnesota Press, 2000).

6    This analysis of the role of activist media in fostering internationalism is building upon Benedict Anderson's analysis of print media in fostering nationalism. Benedict Anderson, *Imagined Communities: Reflections on the Origin and Spread of Nationalism*, rev. ed. (New York: Verso, 1991)

7    This study utilizes English-language materials, including those written and disseminated by the Vietnamese Women's Unions, as well as the oral histories of American,

Canadian, and Vietnamese antiwar activists. The interviews were conducted in English, at times with the assistance of translators.

8    Amy Swerdlow, *Women Strike for Peace: Traditional Motherhood and Radical Politics in the 1960s* (Chicago: University of Chicago Press, 1993), 15.

9    Andrea Estepa, "Taking the White Gloves Off: Women Strike for Peace and 'the Movement,' 1967–73," in *Feminist Coalitions: Historical Perspectives on Second-Wave Feminism in the United States*, ed. Stephanie Gilmore (Urbana: University of Illinois Press, 2008), 87.

10   Swerdlow, *Women Strike for Peace*, 214–15.

11   *Vietnamese Women* ([Hanoi: Xunhasaba], *Vietnam Studies No. 10*, 1966), 42.

12   "Madame Nguyen Thi Binh Speaking to American Women," transcript of film, October 1970, 1, Women Strike for Peace Collection (WSPC), Series A, 2, Box B, 2, Swarthmore College Peace Collection, Swarthmore, PA.

13   Jessica Frazier, "Collaborative Efforts to End the War in Viet Nam: The Interactions of Women Strike for Peace, the Vietnamese Women's Union, and the Women's Union of Liberation, 1965–1968," *Peace and Change* 37, no. 3 (July 2012): 339–65.

14   *VW*, 33.

15   Scholars have been increasingly critical of the waves analogy, because this framework tends to privilege certain forms of white middle-class women's activism as indicators of feminism. They also question differentiating distinct strands of feminism that emerged during this time period, such as liberal, radical, socialist, and lesbian. After all, individuals tended to evolve in their political understandings, participate in multiple organizations and collectives, and embrace diverse political views. However, some of these terms do capture key political distinctions, and Vietnamese women appealed to these diverse agendas among self-identified feminist activists in the West. Gilmore, *Feminist Coalitions;* and Nancy A. Hewitt, ed., *No Permanent Waves: Recasting Histories of U.S. Feminism* (New Brunswick, NJ: Rutgers University Press, 2010).

16   *VW*, 3.

17   Ibid.

18   Ibid., 307.

19   Agatha Beins, "Free Our Sisters, Free Ourselves! Locating U.S. Feminism through Feminist Publishing" (PhD diss., Rutgers University, 2011); Agatha Beins, "Sisters Rise Up! Feminist Identities and Communities in the Women's Liberation Movement," seminar paper, NEH Summer Institute: "Sequel to the 60s," June 2008, Schlesinger Library, Harvard University; and Agatha Beins, "Radical Others: Women of Color and Revolutionary Feminism," draft chapter for book manuscript, "Liberation in Print: Feminist Periodicals and the Production of a Social Movement Identity," read fall 2011.

20   Vivian Rothstein, telephone interview with author, Los Angeles, March 9, 2007.

21   Judy Tzu-Chun Wu, "Rethinking Global Sisterhood: Peace Activism and Women's Orientalism," in *No Permanent Waves*, ed. Hewitt, 193–220; and Wu, *Radicals on the Road, Internationalism, Orientalism, and Feminism* (Ithaca: Cornell University Press, 2013). For a discussion of controversies about sexuality at the 1975 international women's conferences, see Jocelyn Olcott, "Cold War Conflicts and Cheap Cabaret:

Sexual Politics at the 1975 United Nations International Women's Year Conference,"
*Gender and History* 22, no. 3 (Nov. 2010): 733–54.

22   Max Elbaum, *Revolution in the Air: Sixties Radicals Turn to Lenin, Mao, and Che* (London: Verso, 2002); Daryl J. Maeda, "Black Panthers, Red Guards, and Chinamen: Constructing Asian American Identity through Performing Blackness, 1969–1972," *American Quarterly* 57 (2005): 1079–1103; Daryl J. Maeda, *Chains of Babylon: The Rise of Asian America* (Minneapolis: University of Minnesota Press, 2009); Daryl J. Maeda, *Rethinking the Asian American Movement* (New York: Routledge Press, 2012); Lorenza Oropeza, *¡Raza Sí! ¡Guerra No! Chicano Protest and Patriotism during the Viet Nam War Era* (Berkeley: University of California Press, 2005); Laura Pulido, *Black, Brown, Yellow, and Left: Radical Activism in Los Angeles* (Berkeley: University of California Press, 2006); Cynthia A. Young, *Soul Power: Culture, Radicalism, and the Making of a U.S. Third World Left* (Durham, NC: Duke University Press, 2006).

23   Frances Beal, "Double Jeopardy: To Be Black and Female" (1969), reprinted in *Triple Jeopardy: Racism, Imperialism, Sexism* (New York: Third World Women's Alliance, 1969); Maylei Blackwell, *¡Chicana Power! Contested Histories of Feminism in the Chicano Movement* (Austin: University of Texas Press, 2011); Benita Roth, *Separate Roads to Feminism: Black, Chicana, and White Feminist Movements in America's Second Wave* (Cambridge: Cambridge University Press, 2003).

24   Betita Martinez, telephone interview with author, San Francisco, December 7, 2006.

25   Loreno Oropeza points out that by 1960, 80 percent of Mexican Americans were living in urban areas. However, the Chicano/a movement was heavily invested in the symbolic identity of being "agricultural people tied to the land." Oropeza, *¡Raza Sí! ¡Guerra No!*, 86.

26   "Viet Nam War—Why? Their People ... Our People ...," *El Grito del Norte* 29 (Aug. 1970). Martinez also reported on the treatment of ethnic minorities in Viet Nam, and emphasized that these groups had the right to bilingual education. Loreno Oropeza makes a similar argument about the significance of the Viet Nam War for the Chicano/a movement.

27   Oropeza, *Raze Si! Guerra No!*, 99–100.

28   Maria Ramirez and Nina Genera, interview with author, Chabot, California, February 27, 2007.

29   "Life in New Asia," *Getting Together* 1, no. 6 (Nov.–Dec. 1970): 15.

30   Kiku Uno, "Open Letter to Sansei," *Asian Women's Journal* (Berkeley: University of California, Berkeley, 1971 / Asian American Studies Center, University of California, Los Angeles, 3rd printing, October 1975), 82; citation is from the 1975 edition.

31   Cindy Takemoto, "Pat Sumi: Off the Pedestal," *Asian Women's Journal*, 107.

32   "We as Third World Women ...," n.d., Kathleen Hudson Women's Bookstore Collection, F-111, Subject Files, Folder "Indochinese Women Conference," Simon Fraser University Archives and Records Management Department, Vancouver, British Columbia, Canada.

33   "Statement from a Number of the White Women in Los Angeles Who are Working on the Indochinese Women's Conference," 2, n.d., Kathleen Hudson Women's Bookstore Collection, Subject Files, Folder "Indochinese Women Conference."

34  Donna Kotake, interview with author, San Francisco, May 31, 2006.

35  Maeda, *Chains of Babylon*; Kotake interview.

36  Uno, "Open Letter to Sansei," 82.

37  Evelyn Yoshimura, "GI's and Racism," *Asian Women's Journal*, 74.

38  Ibid.

39  Cynthia Enloe, *Bananas, Beaches, and Bases: Making Feminist Sense of International Politics* (Berkeley: University of California Press, 1990); Katharine H. S. Moon, *Sex Among Allies: Military Prostitution in U.S.-Korea Relations* (New York: Columbia University Press, 1997); Heather Marie Stur, *Beyond Combat: Women and Gender in the Vietnam War Era* (Cambridge: Cambridge University Press, 2011); Ji-Yeon Yuh, *Beyond the Shadow of Camptown: Korean Military Brides in America* (New York: New York University Press, 2002); Joane Nagel, *Race, Ethnicity, and Sexuality: Intimate Intersections, Forbidden Frontiers* (New York: Oxford University Press, 2003), 191.

40  Yoshimura, "GI's and Racism," 74.

41  The delegation from Southeast Asia consisted of three teams of two female and one male translator each for North Viet Nam, South Viet Nam, and Laos. A fourth delegation from Cambodia had intended to travel to Canada as well but was unable to do so. Vo Thi The (age fifty), a professor of literature at the University of Hanoi and an officer in the Viet Nam Women's Union, had visited Canada previously in 1969. Given her seniority and experience, she served as an overall leader of the 1971 delegation. Nguyen Thi Xiem (age forty), a gynecologist and obstetrician, was the vice president of the VWU. Dinh Thi Hong (forty-six), a housewife, and Phan Min Hien (thirty-one), a teacher, represented the Women's Union for the Liberation of South Vietnam. Two additional teachers, Khampheng Boupha (forty-seven) and Khemphet Pholsena (twenty-nine), represented the Laotian Patriotic Women's Association. Each group was accompanied by a male translator: Nguyen Tri (forty-six), from North Viet Nam; Trinh Van Anh (thirty-three), from the South; and Soukanh Srithirath (thirty-four), from Laos. "The Indochinese Women's Conference," *Goodbye to All That* (newspaper published by San Diego Women), April 20–May 4, 1971, 3, 4.

42  Quoted in Michal R. Belknap, *The Vietnam War on Trial: The My Lai Massacre and the Court-Martial of Lieutenant Calley* (Lawrence: University Press of Kansas, 2002), 65.

43  Belknap, *Vietnam War on Trial*, 4.

44  Kathleen Gough, "An Indochinese Conference in Vancouver," 10, [n.d.], Anne Roberts Women's Movement Fond, Folder 1, Simon Fraser University Archives and Records Management Department, Vancouver, British Columbia.

45  "U.S. Govt. Blamed for My Lai Deaths," *Winnipeg Free Press*, March 31, 1971, reproduced in *The Visit* (March–April 1971), Voice of Women Supplement/La Voix des Femmes Supplementaire (July 1971).

46  Yoshimura, "GI's and Racism," 76.

47  Jodi Kim, *Ends of Empire: Asian American Critique and the Cold War* (Minneapolis: University of Minnesota Press, 2010); Paul A. Kramer, *The Blood of Government: Race, Empire, the United States, and the Philippines* (Chapel Hill: University of North Carolina Press, 2006); Robert G. Lee, *Orientals: Asian Americans in Popular Culture*

(Philadelphia: Temple University Press, 1999); and David Roediger, "Gook: The Short History of an Americanism," *Monthly Review* 43 (Mar. 1992): 50.

48    "Impressions from the Conference of Indochinese and North American Women, April 1971, Sponsored by Voice of Women, WILPF, WSP," *Memo* 2, no. 1 (Fall 1971): 16.

49    This image appeared in the *Black Panther* 20 (September 1969): 3; and on the cover of *Gidra* (March 1970), with an accompanying article on "Vietnamese Sisters," reprinted from *Sisters United* 1 (January 1970): 10.

50    "Learning How to Do It," *The Pedestal* (May 1971): 11.

51    Kathleen Aberle, "An Indochinese Conference in Vancouver," *Bulletin of Concerned Asian Scholars* 3, nos. 3–4 (Summer–Fall 1971): 20.

52    Ibid., 21.

53    Ibid., 23.

54    Ibid., 19.

55    Ibid., 19, 21.

56    Juanita Tamayo, "Tripping to Vancouver," *Asian Women's Journal*, 81. The poem was originally published in *Kalayaan*, a Filipino American activist publication.

57    Tamayo, "Tripping to Vancouver."

58    "Indochinese Women's Conference," *Asian Women's Journal*, 78.

59    Rothstein interview.

# 9

# Radicalizing Currents

## The GI Movement in the Third World

SIMEON MAN

IN OCTOBER 1971, THE USS *CORAL SEA* PREPARED FOR ITS DEPARTURE FROM the Alameda Naval Complex to the South China Sea. Amid the escalated air war in Southeast Asia that resulted from president Richard M. Nixon's recent call to "Vietnamize" the war, its voyage was to be routine and expected, certainly nothing spectacular. Events aboard the docked aircraft carrier, however, signaled anything but business as usual. One month before its scheduled departure, seven of its crewmen announced their refusal to go to Vietnam. At a press conference on October 11, the dissident sailors claimed that thirty-seven crew members including themselves would leave the carrier when it departed for the war zone. Asserting a "moral obligation to voice [their] opinions," they collected over thirteen hundred signatures in a petition to publicize the crew's widespread objection to the war and their demands to keep the carrier docked. As the events unfolded and the brass meted out punishments to the dissenters, the wider Bay Area community swiftly responded in support. Antiwar activists staged protests at the gate of the naval air station, while some churches opened their doors to provide sanctuary for deserters. On November 12, after a month of struggle and anticipation, the *Coral Sea* finally departed San Francisco Bay. All told, 250 men abandoned the ship. From the safe havens of the Bay Area, some of the deserters issued a statement of solidarity with those on board, and with US military servicepersons in general: "Just as we have left the Coral Sea, we know that increasing numbers of brothers and sisters in the military will find the courage to resist the intimidation of their commanding officers, and refuse to fight."[1]

As antiwar activists rejoiced and resumed their struggle in the Bay Area, the *Coral Sea* continued on into the Pacific, navigating across US military bases in Okinawa, Japan, and the Philippines en route to Vietnam. When the carrier arrived at these bases over the next two months, a diverse group of activists, including some GIs, American organizers, local activists, and base workers anxiously waited to welcome the disaffected sailors. The *Coral Sea* had transported the crewmen across the waters to another world of radicalism—the kind that fueled the dreams of Third World revolutionaries stateside yet few had experienced firsthand. In the months before the ship's arrival in the Philippines, a wave of labor strikes led by Filipino base workers had brought US military operations at Clark Air Base to a near standstill. In their demands to the US military for equal pay, and their rights to work and to strike, the base workers found unlikely alliances with the GIs stationed there, some of whom joined the strikers at the picket lines as others held out clenched fists and made peace signs at the gate. "The Filipinos are my brothers," an American airman proclaimed against orders to repel the strikers. "I will not fight them. Theirs is a legitimate cause." By the time the *Coral Sea* docked at Subic Bay in January 1972, such expressions of solidarity between American GIs and Filipino workers circulated widely. As the sailors disembarked, the GIs and their organizers handed out copies of underground newspapers and other literature to acquaint them with the wider movement they took part in. They held meetings for the sailors to air their complaints openly, and even introduced them to Filipino comrades who related their experiences as kindred subjects of US militarism.[2] An ocean away from the antiwar protests of the Bay Area and the US mainland, activists in the Philippines and elsewhere nurtured a political space for those who no longer wished to participate in the Vietnam War. The movement of the *Coral Sea* in the closing months of 1971 may have symbolized a new phase of the US war in Vietnam, but, apart from this apparent shift, it also produced other currents of radicalism in the Pacific.

The events surrounding the *Coral Sea* tell us much about the international and transnational dimensions of antiwar radicalism in the late 1960s and early 1970s. If the first part of the story about Bay Area activism is familiar to scholars of the US antiwar movement, the second half remains more obscured. In 1969, after President Nixon announced plans to withdraw American troops from Vietnam as part of his "Vietnamization" policy, American activists began to turn to Asia as the locus of their antiwar organizing work. Vietnamization, they knew, signaled not an end to the war but a military strategy centered on the increased utiliza-

tion of South Vietnamese Army forces and intensified aerial bombard-
ments that reactivated the chain of US bases in the Pacific. As the war in
Vietnam escalated by these other means, so the antiwar movement took
on different forms. The Pacific Counseling Service, founded in 1969 by a
group of pacifists in the Bay Area to offer legal counseling to GIs opposed
to the war, occupied a pivotal role in this transformation. In the spring
of 1970, PCS, as it was more popularly known, expanded its operations
from the US West Coast to Japan, Okinawa, and the Philippines, the pre-
cise locations that housed the military bases and the arsenal for Nixon's
escalated air war. There, PCS organizers opened "GI centers" in proxim-
ity to US air and naval bases, where they continued working to politicize
American servicemen against the war and other issues. Vietnamization,
as this chapter will argue, set the conditions for US antiwar activism to
proliferate across the Pacific. If Vietnamization was conjured in part to
stem the tide of domestic antiwar dissent, it had the unintended effect of
inciting rebellion elsewhere.

In traveling abroad, however, PCS organizers did not simply replicate
their work in different places for different constituents; they transformed
their activism in the process. As part of a radicalizing New Left that drew
inspiration from Third World revolutionary movements, PCS organizers
gravitated to the politics of these militarized locales, integrating themselves into political struggles that were at once both deeply local and
global, and that formed parts of a longer, more expansive struggle against
US militarism and imperialism. In the context of ongoing decolonization
and demilitarization movements in places such as Okinawa and the Philippines, simply organizing GIs against the war no longer sufficed. Instead,
PCS organizers and other American activists labored to turn their dreams
of Third World internationalism into reality by forging political alliances
between GIs and Okinawan and Filipino base workers, an affinity of class
and color that they presumed would sow the kind of political consciousness necessary to advance socialist revolution in the United States. As
they carried on their work, they drew the attention of local and US military authorities alike, who targeted them as subversives who not only
undermined the US war effort but also threatened to unravel the political
alliances that would preserve the US empire in Asia for the post–Vietnam
War era. By 1973, as the war drew to an end and as some American antiwar
activists pursued a politics beyond the war, PCS organizers began returning to the US mainland, many of them deported from the Philippines dur-

ing martial law, and continuing their anti-imperialist activism through different channels. In what follows, I chart the story of a short-lived yet remarkable global insurgency that rocked the US empire at the end of the Vietnam War, and in so doing illuminate the radical circuits that spanned the Pacific—going both directions—that should prompt a rethinking of the roots and routes of antiwar and Asian American radicalism in the 1960s and 1970s.

## PACIFIC COUNSELING SERVICE AND THE US NEW LEFT

The Pacific Counseling Service began its first GI project in Monterey, California, in March 1969, amid the largest concerted rebellion to shake the US military in recent memory. A marine colonel assessed two years later, "The morale, discipline and battle-worthiness of the U.S. armed forces are, with a few salient exceptions, lower and worse than at any time in this century and possibly in the history of the United States."[3] A culture of GI dissent flourished as part and parcel of the national antiwar movement in the late 1960s and early 1970s, driving soldiers, sailors, and marines to rebel from within the military. In individual and coordinated instances, GIs went absent without leave, deserted, rioted, refused or shirked combat, and committed "fragging" against their superiors. But if GI rebellion during the Vietnam War reflected the imperatives of the era's antiwar movement, it also marked a critical moment in the longer formation of the US empire. In the decades after World War II, unbridled militarism and racialized class inequalities proceeded apace to make the military into a budding site of antiracist working-class resistance. More than just a "working-class war" that pulled disproportionate numbers of poor people into the military's ranks, the war in Vietnam was, at root, a colonial conflict that exposed the limits of American claims to democracy and racial equality. Particularly among black, Chicano, Asian American, Pacific Islander, and American Indian GIs who were drafted or compelled to enlist, many witnessed a kind of racial violence in Vietnam that rang all too familiar in their own lives. By the time their communities at home began to radicalize the agenda of the antiwar movement, transforming the call from "bring home the troops" to "stop killing our Asian brothers and sisters," GIs of color likewise drew upon the symbols of Third World liberation to proclaim racial solidarity with decolonizing subjects of the US empire.[4]

The San Francisco Bay Area occupied a key site of these events and political transformations. Home to several major military installations, including the Alameda Naval Air Station, Fort Ord, the Presidio, and the Oakland Army Base, the Bay Area was well situated for antiwar activists to confront the war machine directly. By the time PCS got started in Monterey in 1969, the Bay Area already formed a vibrant hub of antiwar activism involving students, pacifists, the clergy, and GIs. Growing unabated since president Lyndon B. Johnson's initial push for US troops in 1965, opposition to the Vietnam War deepened in early 1968 following the Tet Offensive, when the National Liberation Front launched attacks against US and allied forces that once and for all shattered the myth of US military omnipotence before domestic and international publics. Antiwar activists in the Bay Area, with a growing number of dissident GIs stationed nearby, were driven to action. On April 27, 1968, a group of forty active-duty servicemen headed an antiwar demonstration in San Francisco to mark the first GI-led civilian peace rally in the country. Two and a half months later, nine AWOL servicemen publicly took "sanctuary" at a local Presbyterian church and announced their resignation from the military, an event that galvanized media attention around the fledgling GI movement. In these instances of early GI resistance, GIs and their supporters emphasized their moral opposition to the war, a political stance informed by the Quaker tradition of pacifism and encouraged by the religious left. Thus, when Sidney Peterman, a Unitarian minister in Monterey and a longtime member of the activist peace organization the American Friends Service Committee, proposed the establishment of a GI legal counseling office by the name of West Coast Counseling Service, he found receptive ears among the local churches and religious groups already at the forefront of the antiwar movement. With an initial cohort of activists drawn from earlier GI organizing efforts in the Bay Area, Peterman opened the PCS office to provide draftees and GIs with legal support to keep them out of the military and the war.[5]

If PCS grew out of the peace activism of the Bay Area, it was also a part of the wider GI movement unfolding across the United States. Beginning in 1968, activists of the New Left established GI coffeehouses near US military bases throughout the country, to offer a "free" space for GIs to gripe openly about the military and to cultivate their antiwar consciousness. Loosely affiliated and localized, the coffeehouses functioned as the cultural base for the growing GI movement nationwide, bringing dissident

Figure 9.1. Active-duty GIs and civilians march for peace in San Francisco, September 1968. Image from *Task Force* 1, no. 2 (Oct. 1969). Courtesy of GI Press Project.

GIs and civilians together and nurturing their camaraderie beyond the confines of military life. As New Left activists understood, the coffeehouses marked an important development of the antiwar movement by figuring the "GI" as a nascent political actor with deep organizing potential. By 1969, coffeehouses had emerged across the United States wherever military bases sprawled. With funding from national organizations such as the United States Servicemen's Fund, established by New Left organizers to foster the GI movement, the coffeehouses soon assumed the political centers of countless local GI-civilian groups charged with organizing GIs through activities including the printing and distribution of GI newspapers. Out of the GI coffeehouses thus emerged a wider web of collectives and initiatives that broadly signaled the transformation of the New Left and the beginnings of the GI movement in the United States.[6]

Sid Peterman was inspired by these developments when he proposed his GI counseling office in Monterey in the spring of 1969. Through his Unitarian church, he had engaged in GI counseling to some extent, but the time was ripe to commit more fully to the work. With funding secured through the Unitarian Universalist Association, the Unitarian Service Center, the Clergy and Laymen Concerned About Vietnam, and a handful of organizers, including some Vietnam veterans, clergymen, and conscientious objectors, PCS began its work near Fort Ord. Alan Miller was among the initial cadre. A white Presbyterian cleric from Minnesota, Miller had spent parts of the early 1960s organizing in the civil rights movement in the South before moving to the Bay Area in 1965, enticed by the new political energies out West. As an administrative person working with the local college ministries, he quickly gravitated to student antiwar activism, and helped conscientious objectors find alternative service through the church. His antidraft activities soon roused the attention of the Federal Bureau of Investigation (FBI). In the summer of 1968, lengthy surveillance of his activities led officials to interrogate him concerning the case of one Selective Service registrant who had refused induction after being "counseled, aided and abetted" by him. His activities likewise drew the attention of Sid Peterman. Miller's theological background, his experience working with GIs, and his broad commitment to social justice were qualities that ought to animate PCS, Peterman believed. The demands of Fort Ord, where forty thousand army trainees prepared for Vietnam deployments, certainly required organizers with such dedication. And they wasted no time. In the first six months, Miller and the other PCS organizers handled more than seven hundred legal cases involving GI rights, and helped 120 soldiers obtain "conscientious objector" status.[7]

Miller's early political activities might have attracted the FBI's vigilance, but they only precipitated the more organized surveillance of PCS soon after its emergence. PCS's early success indeed elicited swift response from local and national authorities. The Seaside Police Department began infiltrating the PCS office sometime during its first year, compiling reports of its activities that later would appear before the House Committee on Internal Security when it conducted hearings to determine the extent of GI subversion. In September 1969, the Department of Defense (DOD) sought to stem the growth of the GI movement by issuing a "Directive on Dissidents," the most comprehensive policy to date for "handl[ing] dissident and protest activities among members of the armed forces." The directive outlined rules about the possession and distribution of printed materials, off-post gathering places, the publication of underground newspapers, and on- and off-post demonstrations, all activities that sustained the GI movement. Although it admitted to the legality of most of these activities, the directive also gave base commanders wide discretion in implementing guidelines.[8] Meant to suppress GI dissent at its inception, the DOD directive gave PCS activists the justification to continue their organizing work, even as it portended the systematic repression to come.

The Pacific Counseling Service expanded elsewhere on the West Coast toward the end of 1969, about the time that the GI movement as a whole deepened its political commitments and steered further left. With a dozen or so organizers, PCS opened offices in Oakland, San Francisco, and San Diego, and soon went north to Tacoma, Washington, to coordinate the work already underway near Fort Lewis. In Tacoma, PCS aligned with the GI-Civilian Alliance for Peace, the local GI collective that had just concluded an unprecedented campaign led by Socialist Worker Party students at the University of Washington to rally GI support for the United Farm Workers Union and their boycott of nonunion grape growers, after the DOD attempted to break their strikes by increasing orders of "scab" grapes for the army. Dale Borgeson, an army draftee from Minnesota who became a GI organizer at Fort Lewis during this time, soon joined the PCS ranks and would play a pivotal part in its expansion to Asia within the year. Meanwhile, the extension to San Diego coincided with the December 14 moratorium demonstration at nearby Oceanside and the founding of the Movement for a Democratic Military, the only GI organization at the time to openly espouse an antiracist and anti-imperialist politics. In the largest demonstration in the country on that day, an estimated one thousand servicepeople converged with a crowd of four thousand to rally near the Camp Pendleton Marine Corps Base. GIs carried signs that read "Bring our brothers home, keep us here!" and "End racism through solidarity!" The historic demonstration galvanized a multiracial coalition of GIs under the banner of Third World unity, and broadly signaled the GI movement's departure from its pacifist roots. It was the kind of radical politics PCS organizers increasingly pursued. As Alan Miller and others explained in their 1970 report, "Because of the racist patterns in American society and the fact that draft counseling services are primarily available to white, middle class young people, a disproportionately high number of service personnel are ... members of the black, brown or third world communities." Hence, "much of the work of PCS is directed toward the support of non-white GIs."[9] Acknowledging their efforts on behalf of non-white servicemen, Third World movement publications such as the *Black*

*Panther* and the San Francisco–based *New Dawn* soon directed black and Asian American draftees to PCS offices.[10]

The early formation of PCS thus took place at a critical juncture in the radicalization of the New Left. Taking their cue from the Asian, Chicano, and Black Power movements, the largely white middle-class activists of the New Left had learned to look beyond the boundaries of the United States to take inspiration from liberation movements around the world. In 1969, the New Left exemplified this shift by forming the Venceremos Brigade, a group of American activists brought to Cuba to harvest sugar cane with local workers and to show their solidarity with the Cuban Revolution. For GI movement organizers, such global struggles meant that the pursuit of a strictly antiwar politics no longer sufficed; they would need to further instill an antiracist and anti-imperialist consciousness among the servicemen. Pacific Counseling Service met this challenge by turning toward Asia as the locus of its GI work. In the spring of 1970, just as Sid Peterman and others planned to begin organizing GIs abroad, they renamed their collective by replacing "West Coast" with "Pacific," making it the Pacific Counseling Service. Expanding to Asia, they thought, would allow them not only to organize the majority of GIs that had been overlooked by the movement stateside but also to facilitate GI alliances with "Third World" activists as part of the GIs' political education. Working in revolutionary Asia proved all too enticing, and before long, Peterman embarked across the Pacific. Meanwhile, in Monterey the PCS staff eagerly sought to bring the lessons of revolutionary struggle to the soldiers at Fort Ord by inviting Pat Sumi to speak. A Nisei activist and a participant of the Venceremos Brigade, Sumi had returned most recently from her tour of North Vietnam, North Korea, and the People's Republic of China as part of the US People's Anti-Imperialist Delegation, a group of eleven American activists and journalists that represented the broad spectrum of the US Third World Left. Sumi's famed sojourn had placed her on the radar of the PCS organizers, who believed that her presence in Monterey would captivate the GI audience, especially if she could speak about "Cuba and socialism."[11]

Sid Peterman made his first of many trips to Asia in early 1970, at the invitation of some Japanese antiwar activists in Tokyo. Responding to their request to open a GI counseling office in Japan, the PCS founder went on a two-month tour to survey the political situation. His trip confirmed what he already knew about Beheiren (the Citizens' Federation for Peace in Vietnam), a loosely organized collective of former Communist

Party members, intellectuals, and students that was at the forefront of the Japanese antiwar movement. Founded in 1965 with the goals of ending Japan's complicity in the war and securing peace and self-determination for the Vietnamese, Beheiren had worked closely with GIs and American activists since its formation. With the escalation of US troops to Vietnam and increasing numbers of soldiers passing through Tokyo on R & R, Beheiren founded the Japan Technical Committee for Assistance to Anti-War US Deserters in 1965, which would garner international attention by 1967 for helping four US sailors escape to Sweden. In December 1969, in concert with the moratorium demonstrations in the United States, Beheiren helped GIs at the US Marine Corps Air Station at Iwakuni start a chapter of the American Servicemen's Union, one of the largest and most influential GI organizations at the time. Given Beheiren's remarkable history of organizing GIs, its outreach to PCS seemed only logical. Pleased with what he saw, Peterman returned to Tokyo in April 1970 for an "indefinite period," armed with just six hundred dollars a month to establish the first PCS office in Asia, in the same building as Beheiren's national headquarters.[12]

Word spread quickly that a GI counseling center had made its home in Tokyo, and before long, US military personnel on R & R and from surrounding areas in Japan made their way to the office to seek support. Beheiren's alliance proved indispensable during PCS's early transition, enabling it to expand its work to other nearby bases by the middle of the year. On July 4, 1970, when thirteen imprisoned American marines at Iwakuni led a rebellion against the "brutal and dehumanizing conditions" on the brig, PCS and Beheiren leaped to their support. Together, they organized a joint defense team and helped transform the "Iwakuni 13" into a symbol of GI resistance in Asia.[13] Capitalizing on the momentum of this "unique occurrence," Beheiren and PCS worked with the Iwakuni marines to found the Hobbit coffeehouse, a place of political socialization mirroring its stateside counterparts. At the coffeehouse, GIs freely interacted with and learned from Japanese activists, developing, in the words of a PCS organizer, "a friendship that's not a monetary exchange with a 'sweet cream' lady." As the organizers were quick to point out, the political alliance they had forged with Japanese activists aimed, at the most fundamental level, to restructure the kinds of racialized and gendered relationships between Asians and Americans dictated by the US military empire. Their success in doing so, however, did not go unnoticed by the local and base authorities. Responding to their "proselytizing" of

GIs around the base towns, the US military discontinued all R & R flights to Tokyo in 1971, while the Japanese government threatened to deport the American activists. By the summer of 1972, following a series of raids, the military police at Iwakuni had declared the Hobbit "off-limits" to American military personnel.[14] The GI movement in Asia posed a new kind of problem unforeseen by US military and state officials, yet one that they responded to swiftly and aggressively.

## VIETNAMIZATION AND THE NIXON DOCTRINE

As much as their transpacific movements reflected the radicalization of the New Left, the American activists traveled on routes not solely of their making. On November 3, 1969, just before news of the My Lai massacre surfaced in the media and took the nation by storm, President Nixon announced his "Vietnamization" policy to mollify the growing antiwar public. The phased withdrawal of US ground troops from South Vietnam had begun in June, the president reassured the public, and would be completed on a steady schedule "as the South Vietnamese become strong enough to defend their own freedom."[15] Contrary to what the name implied, however, Vietnamization not only intensified the war by other means but also internationalized it anew. The policy underscored Nixon's intention to prosecute the war from afar, ostensibly beyond the view of the dissenting home front. But even as domestic rancor against the draft and the war fissured, Vietnamization was already transforming US military bases in Japan, Okinawa, and the Philippines into outposts for the intensified aerial campaigns that marked the final years of the US war. After 1969, the air force and the navy—with the full might of American firepower—assumed an unprecedented role in the war, with direct consequences for US bases in the Pacific. Instead of suppressing the GI movement, Vietnamization set the stage for its proliferation across Asia.

The increased military operations on these bases renewed international tensions and debates about US base policies throughout the Pacific Rim. In Japan, Okinawa, and the Philippines, antiwar and labor activists denounced the US violation of bilateral base agreements, which disallowed the use of the bases for military operations in Vietnam and elsewhere without the prior consent of their governments. Protests, localized but by no means isolated, erupted almost spontaneously in the wake of Nixon's escalation of war. To the base workers and others who had long lived in the shadows of US power in their countries, the Vietnam War not only represented an act of US aggression nearby but also served to remind them of the limits of their postcolonial sovereignty. Across these militarized and semicolonial territories, an insurgent antiwar politics remained inseparable from more incisive critiques of US foreign policy. In due time, such politics came to animate the GI movement. In an unprecedented instance in April 1972, PCS organizers and GIs from several US bases converged in Tokyo for a joint press conference, where they issued a collective statement against the Vietnam War. The statement began, "We protest the United States' claim of 'winding down the war' and 'Vietnamization,' ... for this fabrication now entails renewed massive bombing raids causing the genocide of the Vietnamese." Going one step further, they read, "We most strongly protest the United States' military's mockery of the Japanese-American security treaty, openly violating the provision that no troops be transferred to the Republic of Viet Nam without prior Japanese approval."[16] Dissident GIs and GI organizers in Asia thus learned to identify with the politics of those who shared a different and more entangled relationship with US imperialism, namely base workers and other antibase and labor activists for whom the Vietnam War was but a phase of a larger problem.

United States officials, it turned out, understood the broader implications of the war just as well. "Our Vietnam policy must be viewed in a wide context," so advocated Marshall Green, the assistant secretary of state for East Asia and Pacific Affairs in May 1970. As much as Vietnamization had seemed a radical departure from the conduct of war in Vietnam, Green reminded his State Department colleagues that it also signaled a continuation of US military policies in Asia since the start of the Cold War. Since 1950, US military aid funneled to "our Asian allies" has significantly strengthened the armed forces of these countries, increasing their sizes and improving their training in order to permit the United States to reduce the presence of US forces abroad. Green stated on another occasion that "striking Asian examples of successful modernization" in countries such as South Korea, Japan, and Taiwan served to remind US officials that the long-term investments in the buildup of Asian military programs had been money well spent. Yet that very "success" also meant that it was time to scale back. Especially in an era of mounting discontent over the rise of American power, the United States needed to allow its Asian allies to assume greater responsibilities, to find "Asian solutions to

Asian problems."[17] Vietnamization, as a program that replaced US troops with US-trained South Vietnamese forces, was but one manifestation of this wider shift in US policy toward Asia at the start of the 1970s.

The Nixon Doctrine, as the policy shift came to be known, framed Vietnamization as part of the broader realignment of US power in the Pacific. Announced by the president at a press conference in Guam in July 1969, the doctrine spelled out the intent of the United States to share the burdens of Cold War security and Third World development with other "modernized" Asian nations. Japan figured centrally within this formulation. In November 1969, prime minister Eisaku Sato gave a speech at the National Press Club in Washington that spelled out Japan's new role in Asia as part of the Nixon Doctrine. Sato declared the dawning of a new era for Japan—the "New Pacific Age"—when the nation would "take the leading role ... towards nation-building efforts of the Asian countries." Assured by a quarter century of US tutelage, the prime minister spoke confidently as a junior partner: "Japan, in cooperation with the United States, will make its contribution to the peace and prosperity of the Asian-Pacific region and hence to the entire world."[18] No longer the imperialist nation with unchecked dreams of leading a "Greater East-Asia Co-Prosperity Sphere," Japan had grown to become the kind of ally imagined by US state officials. The country's dynamic postwar economic growth, facilitated by US military aid, had secured its role as a vital economic engine throughout post–World War II Asia. Indeed, Japan's erstwhile colonial ambitions in Asia materialized two and a half decades later through the Nixon Doctrine. As the end of the Vietnam War came into sight, the United States and Japan had already begun working to secure the latter's part in the rehabilitation of Southeast Asian economies after the war.

As Sato and Nixon sat down in November 1969 to renew their alliance, however, the looming question over the future of Okinawa posed complications. A Japanese colonial "prefecture" since 1879, Okinawa emerged from the bloody battles of World War II not as an independent nation but as yet a colonial territory, this time administered by the US military. After Japan regained its autonomy in 1952, Okinawa remained a US colony to serve as the stationing point for US forces in the Pacific for the indefinite future. The cause of simmering tension between Japan and the United States ever since, the "Okinawa problem" erupted once again at the end of the 1960s amid rising discontent among Okinawan and Japanese activists over Nixon's escalating war in Southeast Asia, and their consequent demands for the reversion of Okinawa from US military control to the Japanese government. Sato and Nixon addressed these concerns in their 1969 meeting and reached an agreement. They issued a joint communiqué specifying the "return" of Okinawa to Japan by May 1972, under the condition that the US military would continue to occupy its bases for as long as it deemed necessary. In effect, the agreement aimed to placate antiwar and pro-reversion sentiments among Japanese and Okinawan leftists while assuring the continued presence of the US military on the Ryukyu Islands. But with an eye toward the future, US officials also understood that the return of Okinawa to Japan would promise Japan's investment in the security of East and Southeast Asia in the post–Vietnam War era. The communiqué, and the reversion treaty signed the following year, thus symbolized for the two countries a "reaffirmation of common political and security interests in the Pacific."[19]

For those who worked in the military bases in Okinawa, however, the events surrounding reversion signaled a cause for ongoing political engagement. In December 1969, one month following the Nixon-Sato meeting, the US military command in Okinawa declared its intent to fire 2,400 base workers as part of the move toward reversion. The announcement elicited immediate response from the workers. Zengunro, the base workers' union in Okinawa with a long history of militancy, promptly passed a strike vote demanding, first and foremost, the removal of all US bases from Okinawa; but as long as the bases remained, they also demanded the right to retain their jobs. Thirty-five thousand base workers struck for five consecutive days in January 1970, fired by visions of a deeper democracy in which labor struggles remained inextricable from those against US militarism and the resurgence of Japanese imperialism. With a firm grasp of their complex subordination under the US military—as workers and as colonial subjects—Zengunro base workers did something more unprecedented still: they reached out to American GIs for support. As PCS later recalled, the effect of the base workers' outreach to GIs, accomplished largely through English-translated leaflets and posters, was "immediate and positive." GIs smuggled copies of the posters and plastered them on barrack walls, and demonstrated solidarity with the workers by flashing "V" signs and power salutes. In pursuit of more substantive actions, some GIs even initiated a series of meetings with Zengunro leaders, "to exchange views on racism, imperialism, third world liberation, and on the possibilities of joint action." Their alliance persisted through May 1971, when, on the heels of

Figure 9.2. This image appeared in the GI paper *Camp News* 3, no. 6 (June 15, 1972), with the original caption: "Brothers meet with Okinawan students supporting base workers during a strike in 1971." Courtesy of GI Press Project.

the signing of the reversion treaty, Okinawans went on a general strike to protest the terms of the reversion agreement with firm support from GIs. At a public rally in Koza, GIs leafleted statements of solidarity in the streets, which read in Japanese and English: "We are moved by the sight of the Okinawan people fighting.... Brothers and sisters, your struggle is beautiful. We must crush American imperialism through our solidarity!"[20]

Worlds removed and yet brought together by shared circumstances under the US military, GIs and Okinawan base workers found common ground in the events surrounding Okinawa reversion. If Vietnamization "took" PCS activists abroad and allowed them to organize GIs in Asia, then the Nixon Doctrine transformed the work that "GI organizing" entailed. Dale Borgeson, the GI organizer from Tacoma who joined Sid Peterman

in Tokyo in December 1970 before going to Okinawa, learned to appreci-
ate the revolutionary potential of such unlikely, if temporary and frag-
ile, political alliances between GIs and Asians. While struck by the same
"spontaneous anti-military, antiwar sentiments among the GIs" in Japan
and Okinawa as anywhere else he had witnessed in the United States,
Borgeson also saw the possibility "to educate the GIs about what was going
on in Okinawa," to transform their understanding of the US military and
the war into a broader critique of US militarism and neocolonialism.[21] An
alliance with Zengunro base workers, in this case, would help channel
GI antimilitary sentiments into an anti-imperialist struggle against the
United States, Japan, and their interimperial alliances.

Such insurgencies did not elude authorities. Indeed, as they gained
momentum they demanded the collaborative surveillance of US base officials and local police forces, which never failed to remind the Americans of
their newfound vulnerabilities even as they served to reinforce the stakes
of their actions. When US military officials in Koza banned PCS organizers from entering a stockade to counsel imprisoned GIs, for example,
they filed trespassing complaints with the Japan Self-Defense Forces that
effectively granted the latter authority to enforce the ban.[22] Dissident
GIs and PCS activists in Okinawa thus came to be targeted as radicalized
subjects of the US empire, subjected to political repression the origins of
which proved increasingly difficult to distinguish and disentangle. Nonetheless, PCS pushed forth its agenda, expanding GI projects to wherever
US military activities and GI agitation demanded them. In August 1971,
less than a month after Borgeson arrived in Okinawa, Alan Miller, then
the administrative coordinator working from San Francisco, assigned him
to the Philippines. The political crisis surrounding an impending declaration of martial law there had grown increasingly desperate, and the
timing for a new GI project could not have been better. If organizing in
Japan and Okinawa in 1970–71 had introduced the American activists
and GIs to another world of radicalism, then events in the Philippines
the following year would test their political commitments against a state
violence of a different scale.

CLARK AND SUBIC BAY UNDER MARTIAL LAW

Borgeson arrived in the Philippines on August 22, 1971, the day after a
bomb ripped through a political rally in downtown Manila held by the

opposition Liberal Party, killing ten people. The event marked the latest in a string of mass violence under Ferdinand Marcos's rising dictatorship, and reminded Borgeson of the palpable dangers that confronted dissidents such as him. Upon arrival Borgeson met Melinda Paras, a young Filipina American activist from Wisconsin who recently had gone to the Philippines to participate in the growing national democratic movement. A member of the Venceremos Brigade to Cuba in 1969 and Kabataang Makabayan (KM), a nationalist youth organization affiliated with the Communist Party of the Philippines, Paras would become instrumental in forging collaboration between American and Filipino activists in the coming year. She knew the local political landscape. In November 1971, just before Jane Fonda's antiwar troupe, the FTA Tour, arrived in the Philippines to politicize GIs at Clark and Subic Bay, Paras had warned the show's organizers and performers about the dire political situation in the country. The FTA's "political vaudeville," already performed before thousands in the United States under the banner of "Free—or Fuck—the Army," would not sit well with Philippine authorities, she cautioned. "Countless" leaders of KM had been "incarcerated ... kidnapped and murdered" by the Philippine Constabulary previously; and given the FTA's mission of "arousing just dissent among the puppet troops of the US imperialists, and in support of our liberation struggle, your groups may also fall prey to the harassment of the Marcos fascist puppet regime." The bleak political climate notwithstanding, Paras reaffirmed her faith that the FTA would pull off a successful event, particularly if they could build positive relations with the Philippine media. "The press can be a very valuable asset in resisting the suppression of the people's democratic rights and civil liberties," therefore "good relations with the mass media [must] be maintained at all times during your tour." On the eve of the greatest antiwar GI demonstration ever staged overseas, the Americans received firm reassurance that they had the support of KM, a gesture that convinced them of the vital place of GI organizing within the national democratic struggles in the Philippines.[23]

The FTA show opened on the evening of November 28, 1971, outside Clark Air Base. Performing before 1,500 US airmen, military dependents, and Filipino civilians, the FTA launched the first of its four performances in the Philippines much as it had done in the United States, by denouncing US militarism, the Vietnam War, and the racial and gendered oppressions of the military. But an ocean away from home, the cast members deviated from their usual program. They enacted skits depicting the history of US colonialism in the Philippines and the exploitation of resources and indigenous peoples, explicitly linking the oppression of Filipinos with that of African Americans in the United States. During one performance, a group of Filipino students interrupted by shouting, "Down with US imperialism!"—a rejoinder welcomed by the performers. Over the next few days, the FTA performed to ten thousand more people, many of them Filipinos, and drove handfuls of GIs to the newly established GI Center near Clark.[24] The shows gave the American organizers just what they needed to jumpstart their activities in the Philippines. With the indispensable work of KM activists and the FTA performers, PCS and some affiliated American lawyers launched the GI movement in the Philippines, a broadly conceived political insurgency that fused antiwar politics with popular resistance against US neocolonialism and Marcos's fascism.

Anticipating the "subversive" nature of the FTA shows, the Department of Defense dispatched some officials to report on the events. The DOD observers, sitting among rowdy audiences, appeared more amused than alarmed. As indicated in their reports, the shows were "amateurish" in quality, their substance "an insult to the intelligence of most persons attending."[25] Their trivialization of the shows and its reception, however, only reflected wider disillusions about US colonialism's racial legacies in the Philippines. In March 1970, for example, when a senior military official called for the closure of the Manila R & R site in response to increasing "anti-American" sentiments there, some others argued against it, suggesting that "there is a firm rapport between the Negro servicemen and Filipinos that leaves Manila free of racial problems experienced elsewhere."[26] Such a foolhardy statement—coming not long after General William Westmoreland declared racial conflicts the preeminent problem confronting the US armed forces—revealed less a reality than a colonial fantasy about Filipinos' enduring support for the continued US military presence. Little did US officials imagine that the racial "rapport" between blacks and Filipinos was the outcome of an anticolonial and antiracist politics long in the making in the crucible of the US empire.[27] To the DOD observers at the FTA shows, open GI rebellion seemed a distant possibility. Yet, despite their attempts to downplay the shows' influences, their reports indicated a situation far direr than officials realized, as Filipinos and black GIs reaffirmed their mutual solidarity against US racism and imperialism.

On a broader level, the FTA shows exploded the myth of the Philippines as a "showcase of democracy," an image carefully cultivated throughout the post–World War II era as the linchpin of US power in decolonizing Asia. By condemning the US and Philippine governments in the ongoing impoverishment of the Filipino people and the escalation of the Vietnam War simultaneously, the FTA revealed the "showcase of democracy" as a gross misnomer, if not a slander of reality. Yet, by this time, even some US leaders were ready to cast the slogan aside. The rising political unrest in the Philippines was not lost on US officials, the implications of which threatened to unravel the "friendly" relations between the two countries. In 1969, the Senate Foreign Affairs Committee sent a team of state officials to the Philippines to investigate the political situation. The findings of the mission confirmed that "flagrant corruption and fraud in certain areas of the government," coupled with escalating unemployment across the provinces, had contributed to "the rebelliousness of the young people." The country was swept up in "nationalistic fervor," which had been quickly "exploited by a small Communist element to stir revolutionary zeal among some of the youth." By their admission, the Philippines seemed to have reverted to an unbridled nationalism that threatened to cast the nation beyond the "Free World." Marcos's inability to institute necessary reforms to reverse the current trend "could spell the end of democracy in the Philippines."[28] This assessment, as it turned out, proved all too prescient.

If America's model of democracy in Southeast Asia appeared to be waning, Borgeson and other American activists arrived at an opportune time to pick up and reclaim the slogan. In January 1971, just as PCS planned to start a project in the Philippines, Eric Seitz of the National Lawyers Guild (NLG) also expressed interest in expanding the guild's work to Southeast Asia. An organization of progressive lawyers with a long history of labor and civil rights activism, NLG had implanted its legal work firmly in the antiwar movement by the 1970s, having established the Military Law Office to work alongside PCS in Asia. In the spring of 1971, Seitz toured the Philippines and met with student and base worker union leaders, including some GIs who were "militant, working class, many of them black and brown," who all convinced him of the need for the guild's presence.[29] By September, Seitz and his team of five lawyers had solicited the help of Borgeson and Melinda Paras to establish an office in Manila. Although slow to start, their workload picked up as soon as momentum gathered around the upcoming FTA shows. In November, the GI newspaper at Clark introduced the airmen to the NLG lawyers, immediately next to an advertisement for the FTA. The enthusiasm generated from the FTA shows quickly established the reputation of the guild and PCS among the GIs, and by December, the two groups decided to move their offices from Manila to Angeles City and Olongapo, within the vicinity of Clark and Subic Bay Naval Base, respectively. Over the next two months, Borgeson and the guild lawyers maintained a "very busy pace" at the GI Centers, handling thirty-five cases involving courts martial and other complaints, and even discussing Philippine politics with the GIs. "Crowded with GI's from early in the morning to late at night," the GI Centers served as the hub of the GI movement in the Philippines, by then "smoldering" with activities.[30]

Their success did not go unnoticed by Philippine and US authorities. In February, base officials at Subic Bay reacted to the growing influence of PCS and the guild by denying base passes to the attorneys, typically an "ordinary courtesy" for Americans working on US bases. The increase in conscientious objector applications being filed at Clark also led the staff judge advocate there to complain to the Philippine Immigration office about the American activists, which prompted a visit to the GI Center by officials of the Bureau of Immigration on February 12. Typical harassments of this sort tended to get resolved when US citizens showed their valid documentation. The activists' apparent intransigence, though, soon led authorities to pursue more serious charges and confrontational tactics. On March 15, armed with a lead from immigration authorities that PCS and the guild were involved with local "subversive groups," the Philippine Constabulary and the US Army Military Police jointly raided the GI Center at Clark. With no one present at the time, they left, only to return the following month. This time, under the pretext of searching for an escaped American convict, the armed agents seized PCS and NLG files, and concluded the raid by arresting one GI counselor on false charges of having an invalid visa. Upon hearing of these incidents, Alan Miller immediately notified congressman Ronald Dellums, a longtime advocate of civil rights and GI rights, urging him to protect the civil liberties of the GIs and American civilian workers in the Philippines. Dellums fired off a cable to the Clark Base commander and to the US ambassador to the Philippines, demanding an explanation for the string of police attacks. Before either had time to respond, however, the constabulary and American agents attempted another raid on May 12. Without a search warrant this time, the authorities garrisoned the house with armored vehicles for two hours, to intimidate the Americans with a display of force. The police finally left without further incident, but the event left the activists shaken and fearful that "the next one may well result in the death of several people."[31]

As Philippine and US military authorities stepped up their efforts to repress the GI movement in the Philippines, PCS's and the guild's appeals to elected officials became more frequent and urgent. In one letter to Dellums and three senators, Alan Miller noted that "matters have now reached an extreme situation," and urged them to start an investigation to "protect the freedoms of both civilian PCS counselors and GI's stationed at Clark." Prompted by the call, US senator Sam J. Ervin, Jr., the chairman of the Subcommittee on Constitutional Rights, wrote to the secretary of defense to inquire into the matter. Unsurprisingly, the response was unfavorable. Based on its own investigation, the DOD found that guild attorneys had received the "full cooperation" of the staff judge advocate upon their initial arrival at Clark. Despite efforts by the US Air Force "to establish [a] good professional working atmosphere, NLG relations with the military have not always been a model of felicity." Not only did the lawyers seek to "create dissension and disloyalty" among the overseas servicemen, but they had also "fallen into disfavor with the Philippine Government" by their open support of KM and criticisms of the Marcos regime. In short, the guild engaged in work that fell beyond legitimacy, the implications of which threatened to undermine both governments. "Activities of this nature," the DOD concluded simply, "will not be sanctioned."[32]

The DOD understood the implications of the radical activities of PCS and the guild all too well. In their day-to-day organizing, PCS and guild activists sought to expose GIs to the realities of Philippine life beyond the US bases, to cultivate their awareness about the nationalist democratic struggles unfolding all around them. At the GI Center, for example, they read and discussed the writings of the popular nationalist historian Renato Constantino, which introduced the GIs "to a different way of looking at the US presence there" by raising questions about the legacies of US colonialism and the role of the US military bases. What they could not comprehend entirely through reading, they saw with their own eyes. On several occasions, the PCS and guild activists organized excursions to Manila, where some of the GIs got a ground-eye view of "the political upheaval in the country," including anti-Marcos demonstrations downtown and at the University of the Philippines. As a kind of politicized tourism, these trips formed a vital part of the GIs' political education by exposing them to the anti-imperialist politics that encompassed, but necessarily exceeded, the antimilitary and antiwar concerns of the GI movement. If PCS and guild activists introduced GIs to the politics of the Third World, then the Filipino people likewise got a glimpse of the GI movement at Clark and Subic Bay. In May 1972, Constantino interviewed Borgeson about PCS and the guild, and wrote an article for the *Manila Chronicle* that "gave us very terrific coverage." The article, as Borgeson recognized, cemented the GI movement within the political consciousness of the national democratic movement in the Philippines.[33]

Press coverage of the GI movement did not end with Constantino's article, but increased through the month of May as Filipino activists focused agitation around the US bases and their role in the escalation of the Vietnam War. US ambassador Henry Byroade sought to placate their concerns by insisting that the US government had not misused the bases for the war, a statement backed by Marcos and other Philippine state officials. Rather than pacifying skeptics, the claim translated into a call for unified action by Filipino antiwar and antibase activists and rallied GIs to their cause. On May 17, some GIs from Clark and Subic Bay planned to hold a press conference in Manila to divulge the true nature of the bases to the Philippine public. But authorities caught wind of the plan, and the evening before, the Military Police raided the GI Center at Subic Bay and arrested the two GIs scheduled to speak. The "kidnapping" did little to intimidate other GIs. The next day, the conference went on as scheduled, with two sergeants from Clark stepping in to cover for "their missing Navy brothers." Before the Philippines media, staff sergeant Wayne Evans and sergeant Tom Andric disclosed information about US military operations at Clark and its direct involvement in the Vietnam War. The GIs were "very well received by the press," a guild activist later assessed, "and the coverage here was excellent."[34]

The two men revealed that a squadron of F-4 fighter-bombers had been recently deployed from Clark Air Base to Thailand, along with more than five hundred support personnel, as part of the resumed bombing of North Vietnam. The revelations confirmed what many critics knew all along, but some Philippine legislators wanted to hear more. That afternoon, senator Benigno Aquino invited Evans and Andric to testify before a closed session of the Philippine Senate Committee on Foreign Relations, where the two GIs further revealed Clark and Subic Bay as staging areas in the escalated air war. When asked about why they chose to testify, Evans replied, "We came to this committee to let the Filipino people know the great danger to them in allowing Clark Air Base and Subic Naval Base to be used in the war in Vietnam. We fear the people of the Philippines are in grave danger of reprisals if the situation in Vietnam worsens." Senator Aquino praised their courage and thanked them on behalf of the Filipino people, "for telling the truth about the use of the U.S. bases here." After their testimony, base authorities immediately confined Evans and Andric, pending criminal investigation. But they had accomplished their tasks. According to a Filipino columnist, the two GIs had "served their noble purpose, for they have already told the truth about the use of the US bases in the Philippines—and none of these uses are for either defense or peace." Their statements at the press conference and the senate hearing cast the credibility of the US embassy and President Marcos into serious doubt, and won the favor of the Philippine public. As the *Manila Chronicle* put it, "The issue is now one of credibility, whether to believe the two American servicemen who have been involved in the operations of these bases, or the President." The overwhelming answer came three days later, when approximately ten thousand Filipino workers and students besieged the US embassy on the international day of protest against US aggression in Vietnam. The demonstrators demanded an immediate end to all US bombing, before being violently dispersed by the police.[35]

The events surrounding the press conference and the senate hearing marked the culmination of the GI movement in the Philippines, and confirmed the worst fears of US officials: that PCS and NLG organizers, "under a cover [and] front of GI counseling and legal defense," had worked "to reach service personnel for the purpose of subversion and political indoctrination; to provide a link between service personnel and indigenous leftist movements; and ... to destroy the effectiveness of the US armed forces in furtherance of the 'socialist revolution' in the United States."[36] By their estimation, such political activities had spiraled beyond control. But before long, an easy solution presented itself. On September 21, 1972, Marcos issued Proclamation No. 1081, declaring martial law in the Philippines. The president immediately ordered the arrests of political dissidents and oppositional leaders, suspended habeas corpus, and, in short, unleashed a reign of terror across the country. As active supporters of the national democratic movement, PCS and NLG activists did not escape unscathed. The Philippine Constabulary's well-rehearsed surveillance and harassment of the GI Center had paid off, and on October 16, it raided the center at Subic Bay one last time to arrest the two remaining GI organizers. A guild lawyer initially escaped the incident, but was apprehended the next day from the putative safe confines of the US military base. By this time, the base commander was all too ready to dispense with his legal responsibility to protect the American lawyer, and aided the constabulary to bring a swift end to the problem. Over the next few days, the staff of the guild and PCS offices in San Francisco worked frantically to develop a strategy to deal with the crisis, enlisting the help of the media, members of Congress, the American Civil Liberties Union, and the State Department for the release of the American civilians. By the end of the week, without pressing formal charges, the Marcos regime ordered the three American activists deported back to the United States. With the remaining defense cases at Clark abandoned, and just as the USS *Kitty Hawk* docked at Subic Bay with a new crew of weary and agitated sailors, the GI movement in the Philippines came to an abrupt end.[37]

## CIRCUITS OF ASIAN AMERICAN RADICALISM

Doug Sorensen, Bart Lubow, and Gene Parker, the three deported guild and PCS activists, may have left their work unfinished in the Philippines, but they continued to rally against martial law upon their return to the United States. When they arrived in San Francisco on October 27, 1972, they immediately convened a press conference to shed light on the political situation. "The Philippines' struggle for national democracy," they urged, "must not become another Vietnam War." Their message found receptive ears among the many Filipino activists who had met in San Francisco the previous month to deal with the impending crisis. The activists represented the spectrum of the US Filipino left, including Kalayaan, the San Francisco-based anti-imperialist coalition that was then at the forefront of the anti-eviction movement at San Francisco's International Hotel. Upon hearing news of martial law, the conference organizers formed the National Committee to Restore Civil Liberties in the Philippines (NCRCLP), a coalition that would play an active role in organizing opposition against the Marcos dictatorship for the next two years. On October 28, the NCRCLP invited the GI organizers to testify at their symposium, where Lubow and Parker not only confirmed the dire conditions in the Philippines but also affirmed the resilience of those continuing the struggle for national democracy. As reported in the *New Dawn*, the newspaper of the J-Town Collective, an anti-imperialist group from San Francisco, "These two brothers talked about US involvement in the Philippines and the miserable life and poverty of the people, but more importantly, of the people's heroic struggle against the Marcos regime." The deported organizers continued for several more weeks, speaking to activists across the country, before getting reassigned to other PCS projects in Hawai'i and Okinawa.[38]

As some of the PCS activists returned to GI organizing and as other guild lawyers gravitated to different progressive legal work, Melinda Paras and Dale Borgeson stayed in the Bay Area to engage further in Filipino anti-imperialist politics. The two had arrived in San Francisco just before the others, with Paras likewise having been deported and Borgeson having escaped the emergency by being in Japan at the time. After getting politicized around the Vietnam War in the Midwest three years earlier, the two had traveled the world and back, returning to a political community that neither had started from but that both now found a home in. Their time in the Philippines, according to Borgeson, had strengthened their "ties with the Philippine activist movement" such that to get "pulled from one movement into another" only seemed natural. In February 1973, Borgeson left the Bay Area for Seattle, to rejoin his friends from his antiwar activist days at Fort Lewis. As a "departing gift," Paras and other Filipino activists gave him a copy of Carlos Bulosan's *America Is in the Heart*, which he read on his train ride up the Pacific coast. "I was very moved by it," Borgeson recalled, at once aghast at the violent history endured by an earlier generation of Filipino migrant workers, yet empowered by their resolve to struggle and to build a labor movement. Reading Bulosan as he traveled along the same route as the venerable activist had done decades earlier, Borgeson got a glimpse of the history of Filipino labor activism whose relevance to contemporary struggles would become clear soon enough. When he arrived in Seattle, Borgeson linked up with young Asian American activists amid their ongoing struggles for Filipino cannery workers' rights and to preserve the International District. Charged to help spread the message against martial law, Borgeson quickly became immersed in the local politics of yet a different imperial metropole.[39]

Just as he had witnessed in Okinawa and in the Philippines, in Seattle Borgeson found a group of dedicated activists who understood all too well the linkages between "domestic" working-class struggles and global revolutions against the US empire. His anecdotes about his own radical and repressive encounters in the Philippines captured the imagination of people such as Gene Viernes and Silme Domingo, two Filipino activists who at the time were leading a class-action discrimination lawsuit on behalf of nonwhite cannery workers against their employer. In the fall of 1973, Borgeson helped initiate the Seattle chapter of the Katipunan ng mga Demokratikong Pilipino (Union of Democratic Filipinos; KDP), an organization started in the Bay Area earlier that summer by Melinda Paras and other Filipina/o activists, with the twin goals of ending racism in the United States and martial law in the Philippines. Racism and fascism in the Philippines were roots and branches of the US capitalist empire, the KDP founders insisted, such that the struggle against one necessitated the struggle against the other, guided by a broader internationalist vision of democracy. Nowhere was this "dual program" of the KDP more dramatically exemplified than in the labor struggles of the Pacific Northwest in the 1970s, where the efforts to democratize Local 37—the Filipino cannery union of the International Longshore and Warehouse Union with a long tradition of transpacific labor radicalism—eventually exposed the connections between the US empire and the Marcos dictatorship and the dangers therein. In 1981, shortly after Viernes traveled across the Pacific to speak with Philippine labor activists about workers' conditions under martial law, he and Domingo were gunned down outside their Seattle union office by agents of the Marcos regime.[40] In the end, and as ever before, a threat to the Philippine government was a threat to the US empire, a fact that the Viernes-Domingo murders would come to epitomize for Filipino activist communities in the United States and the Philippines.

The Viernes-Domingo murders remain a critical event in the annals of Asian American labor activism; yet that the story of the GI movement in Asia should end here is no anomaly. If these episodes appear irrelevant to one another, contained by their respective historiographies, they nonetheless bear the traces of deeper connections forged over the course of kindred acts of revolutionary dreams and travels. Like the thousands of Filipino labor migrants who traversed the Pacific and the Pacific coast before and after them, PCS antiwar activists traveled imperial routes sedimented over long histories of US militarism in Asia. They went overseas in 1970, propelled by Nixon's call to "Vietnamize" the war, and came back with an altered view of the war entirely. Organizing GIs across the vast US military empire had exposed the organizers to issues that far exceeded the war in Vietnam—including Okinawa reversion and martial law in the Philippines—that reframed their approach to the GI movement beyond the scope and period of antiwar politics. Indeed, by the time Borgeson had moved on to organize with the KDP in the mid-1970s, the Pacific Counseling Service continued to recruit new organizers to work in Okinawa, where the effects of ongoing US militarism at the close of the Vietnam War remained starkly transparent. As PCS reported in 1974, the recent transition to an "all-volunteer" force had led to bases in Okinawa comprising "more than 50% Black and Third World" GIs, even as "the military remains as racist an institution as it ever was." These men and women in the US military, aside from being subjected to persistent military racism and sexism, further provided the manpower for a post-Vietnam military that was invested in maintaining a "constant near-war situation," threatening to wage new wars as part of America's response to the "Vietnam syndrome" in ensuing decades.[41] Although PCS folded in 1976, having lost much of its funding from progressive organizations that had moved to other concerns, its short career nonetheless reveals a history of militarism, empire, and radicalism that lives on in our present. The history of the GI movement in Asia at the end of the Vietnam War should remind us of the imperial and anti-imperial circuits that spanned the Pacific in the long twentieth century, connections that at once made the US empire and global dreams of revolution possible.

1    For their comments on earlier drafts of this essay, I thank Michael Denning, Matthew Jacobson, Mary Lui, Monica Martinez, Ana Minian, Sam Vong, and the participants of the Asian American studies working group at Yale. I also thank the two anonymous reviewers for their thoughtful criticisms, and Moon-Ho Jung and Jessie Kindig for their comments on the penultimate draft. I am grateful to Dale Borgeson and Alan Miller for sharing their personal materials and recollections.
      "Crewmen Protest Coral Sea's Return to War," San Francisco Chronicle, October 12, 1971, 14; "Stop Our Ship" news release, Pacific Counseling Service and Military Law Office Records, BANC MSS 86/89c, the Bancroft Library, University of California, Berkeley (hereafter PCS-MLO); "Sanctuary for the Brothers of Coral Sea," PCS-MLO; "City Action Regarding the U.S.S. Coral Sea," PCS-MLO; "Statement by Crewmembers of the USS Coral Sea, December 9, 1971," PCS-MLO.
2    "The Brass Hassles Filipinos Too," The Whig, November 1971, 3; NLG-MLO 3rd Monthly Report, February 1, 1972, PCS-MLO.

3      Quoted in David Cortright, *Soldiers in Revolt: GI Resistance during the Vietnam War* (1975; reprint, Chicago: Haymarket Books, 2005), 3.

4      On the history of GI resistance during the Vietnam War, see Cortright, *Soldiers in Revolt*; Derek Seidman, "Unquiet Americans: GI Dissent during the Vietnam War" (PhD diss., Brown University, 2010). On the racial politics of GI resistance, see Kimberley L. Phillips, *War! What Is It Good For? Black Freedom Struggles and the U.S. Military from World War II to Iraq* (Chapel Hill: University of North Carolina Press, 2011); Daryl J. Maeda, *Chains of Babylon: The Rise of Asian America* (Minneapolis: University of Minnesota Press, 2010); Lorena Oropeza, *Raza Si! Guerra No! Chicano Protest and Patriotism during the Viet Nam War* (Berkeley: University of California Press, 2005).

5      On the Bay Area and the GI movement, see Derek Seidman, "The Bay Area and the Rise of the GI Movement," paper delivered at the Race, Radicalism, and Repression Conference, Seattle, WA, May 14, 2011; Cortright, *Soldiers in Revolt*, 57. On the "Nine For Peace," see pamphlet at the digital library of the *Sir No Sir!* website, http://www.sirnosirarchives_and_resources/library/pamphlets_publications/9_for_peace/cover.html (accessed November 1, 2013). On the formation of PCS, see "Investigation of Attempts to Subvert the United States Armed Services," *Hearings Before the Committee on Internal Security, House of Representatives,* 92nd Congress, 1st and 2nd Sessions (HISC), 6868–69. West Coast Counseling Service was renamed Pacific Counseling Service in May 1970. For readability I simply refer to the organization as PCS throughout the chapter.

6      Cortright, *Soldiers in Revolt,* chapter 3; Seidman, "Unquiet Americans," chapters 2 and 3.

7      "Background Information on the Pacific Counseling Service," n.d., PCS-MLO; US Department of Justice, FBI Report on Alan Stanley Miller, June 28, 1968, Alan Miller private collection.

8      DOD Directive No. 1325.6, September 12, 1969, PCS-MLO.

9      On the expansion of PCS on the West Coast, see "Background Information on the Pacific Counseling Service," PCS-MLO. On the GI-Civilian Alliance for Peace and the GI Movement in Tacoma, see Jessie Kindig, "Demilitarized Zone: The GI Movement at Fort Lewis during the Vietnam War" (MA thesis, University of Washington, 2009); Jessie Kindig, "GI Movement: Antiwar Soldiers at Fort Lewis," Antiwar and Radical History Project, at http://depts.washington.edu/antiwar/gi_mvmt.shtml (accessed April 16, 2012); Dale Borgeson, phone interview with author, February 4, 2012; "Military Moratorium Sunday, Dec 14: Civilians and GIs March in Oceanside," *Attitude Check,* December 1969, 1; PCS Report, 1970, PCS-MLO.

10      HCIS hearings, 6621; *New Dawn,* November 1972, 6.

11      HCIS hearings, 6490, 6742.

12      Letter, Alan Miller to Jane Fonda, January 6, 1972, PCS-MLO; "Beheiren: An Introduction to the Japanese New left "Peace for Vietnam Committee," pamphlet, n.d., PCS-MLO; Richard DeCamp, The GI Movement in Asia," *Bulletin of Concerned Asian Scholars,* vol. 4, no. 1 (Winter 1971): 110; Thomas R. H. Havens, *Fire Across the Sea: The Vietnam War and Japan, 1965–1975* (Princeton: Princeton University Press, 1987), 55.

13      Beheiren pamphlet, November 5, 1970, PCS-MLO.

14     PCS release, "Hobbit Open Soon," n.d., PCS-MLO; "Anti-War GIs Organized in the Pacific Area," newsclip, 1971, PCS-MLO; NLG letter, July 7, 1972, PCS-MLO.

15     President Nixon's Speech on "Vietnamization," November 3, 1969, The Wars for Vietnam, 1945–1975, at http://vietnam.vassar.edu/overview/doc14.html (accessed May 7, 2012).

16     Press release, Japan Joint GI Conference, April 1972, PCS-MLO.

17     Marshall Green, "The Nixon Doctrine: A Blueprint for the 1970s," Department of State publication, January 1971; Marshall Green, "A Strategic Appraisal of the Pacific Area," speech, Marshall Green Papers, Hoover Institution Archives.

18     Quoted in Green's statement before the Subcommittee on Foreign Operations, November 26, 1969, 3, Marshall Green Papers.

19     Ibid. On the "Okinawa problem," see C. T. Sandars, *America's Overseas Garrisons: The Leasehold Empire* (New York: Oxford University Press, 2000), 161–66.

20     Havens, *Fire Across the Sea*, 205; PCS Report, January 4, 1972, PCS-MLO; "Chibario! Okinawa's Struggle for Freedom," VVAW/WSO pamphlet, ca. 1972, PCS-MLO.

21     Dale Borgeson, phone interview with author, February 4, 2012.

22     People's House Progress Report, May–June 15, 1973, PCS-MLO.

23     Ibid.; letter, Kabataang Makabayan to PCS, FTA, October 13, 1971, PCS-MLO.

24     DOD Report, "Jane Fonda Far East Trip: Nov–Dec 1971," reprinted in HCIS, 7099–101.

25     Ibid.

26     Closure of Manila R&R Site, March 1970, Box 261, Folder: "Morale and Welfare, R & R, 1970," Historian's Background Material Files, RG 472, National Archives and Records Administration.

27     Willard B. Gatewood, Jr., *Black Americans and the White Man's Burden, 1898–1903* (Urbana: University of Illinois Press, 1975).

28     "Excerpt of Special Study Mission to Asia of the Senate Foreign Affairs Committee," reprinted in *Congressional Record*, September 27, 1972, 92nd Congress, 2nd Session.

29     The National Lawyers Guild operated in the Philippines and elsewhere in Asia under the appended name Military Law Office (MLO). Eric Seitz, "Proposal for Establishing NLG-MLO in Asia," 1971, PCS-MLO; letter from Seitz to George Logan, January 22, 1971, PCS-MLO; letter from Seitz to Angela Davis, May 21, 1971, PCS-MLO.

30     *The Whig*, November 1971, 2; PCS Work in Asia, 1972, PCS-MLO; Borgeson phone interview with author, February 11, 2012; "Subic GI Center Opens," *Seasick*, January 1972, 1; "NLG-MLO 3rd Monthly Report," February 1, 1972, PCS-MLO.

31     NLG-MLO 3rd Monthly Report, February 1, 1972, PCS-MLO; letter, Senator Ervin to Secretary Laird, March 17, 1972, PCS-MLO; NLG-MLO 4th Monthly Report, March 7, 1972, PCS-MLO; NLG-MLO 5th Monthly Report, April 27, 1972, PCS-MLO; memorandum, PCS to Senators Alan Cranston, John Tunney, George McGovern, Mark Hatfield, April 24, 1972, PCS-MLO; letter, Miller to Dellums, Cranston, Tunney, and McGovern, May 1972, PCS-MLO.

32     Letter, Miller to Dellums, Cranston, Tunney, and McGovern, May 1972, PCS-MLO; letter, J. Fred Buzhardt, DOD, to Ervin, Jr., June 19, 1972, PCS-MLO.

33     Borgeson, phone interview with author, February 11, 2012.

34     NLG-MLO 6th Monthly Report, May 27, 1972, PCS-MLO.

35  "GIs Expose U.S. Aggression from Philippines," June 1, 1972, PCS-MLO.

36  Naval Investigative Service information report, January 29, 1973, Subject: GI Center at San Antonio, R.P./Raid by Philippine Authorities, Alan Miller private collection.

37  NLG-MLO Monthly Report, August–November 1972, PCS-MLO.

38  Ibid.; "Philippines Martial Law Symposium," *New Dawn* 2, no. 4, November 1972, 6; NLG-MLO Monthly Report, August to November, 1972, PCS-MLO.

39  Borgeson, phone interview with author, February 13, 2012.

40  Ibid.; Estella Habal, *San Francisco's International Hotel: Mobilizing the Filipino American Community in the Anti-Eviction Movement* (Philadelphia: Temple University Press, 2007), 70–71, 181.

41  PCS-Pamphlet 1974, PCS-MLO; "GI Organizers Needed!" PCS, May 1975, PCS-MLO.

# Contributors

**DAN BERGER** teaches comparative ethnic studies at the University of Washington, Bothell, where he specializes in the study of race, prisons, and social movements in postwar US history. He is the author or editor of several books, including *Captive Nation: Black Prison Organizing in the Civil Rights Era* (University of North Carolina Press, forthcoming).

**KORNEL CHANG** teaches history and American studies at Rutgers-Newark, State University of New Jersey. He is the author of *Pacific Connections: The Making of the U.S.-Canadian Borderlands* (University of California Press, 2012). He is currently working on *Occupying Knowledge: Expertise, Technocracy, and De-Colonization in the U.S. Occupation of Korea*, a project that examines the role of technocrats and expert knowledge in the US occupation of Korea.

**CHRISTINA HEATHERTON** is assistant professor of American studies at Trinity College. Her work focuses on racial capitalism, culture, and social movements. She is currently completing a book titled *The Color Line and the Class Struggle: The Mexican Revolution, Internationalism, and the American Century*. She is the editor of *Downtown Blues: A Skid Row Reader* (Freedom Now Books, 2011) and co-editor with Jordan T. Camp of *Freedom Now! Struggles for the Human Right to Housing in LA and Beyond* (Freedom Now Books, 2012).

**EMILY K. HOBSON** is assistant professor of history and gender studies at the University of Nevada, Reno. She is currently completing her first book, *Lavender and Red: Race, Empire, and the Gay and Lesbian Left* (under contract with the University of California Press). Her work has appeared in the *Journal of Transnational American Studies* and *The People's Guide to Los Angeles*, among other venues.

**MOON-HO JUNG** teaches US history and Asian American studies at the University of Washington. He is the author of *Coolies and Cane: Race, Labor, and Sugar in the Age of Emancipation* (Johns Hopkins University Press, 2006). He is currently at work on a book project titled *The Unruly Pacific: Race and the Politics of Empire and Revolution, 1898–1941* (under contract with the University of California Press).

**DENISE KHOR** is assistant professor of American studies at the University of Massachusetts, Boston. Her research focuses on Asian American history, comparative ethnic studies, and film history and visual culture. She is currently completing her first book titled *Pacific Theater: Movie-Going and Migration in Asian America, 1907–1950*.

**GEORGE LIPSITZ** is professor of black studies and sociology at the University of California, Santa Barbara, where he serves as chair of the advisory board of the Center for Black Studies Research. His publications include *How Racism Takes Place* (Temple University Press, 2011), *The Possessive Investment in Whiteness* (Temple University Press, 1998), *A Life in the Struggle* (Temple University Press, 1988), and *The Fierce Urgency of Now* (coauthored with Daniel Fischlin and Ajay Heble, Duke University Press, 2013).

**SIMEON MAN** is assistant professor of history at the University of California, San Diego (beginning 2015). Before joining UCSD, he received postdoctoral fellowships from Northwestern University and the University of Southern California. He is currently working on his first book, *Soldiering through Empire: Race and the Making of the Decolonizing Pacific* (under contract with the University of California Press).

**JUDY TZU-CHUN WU** is professor of history and women's, gender, and sexuality studies at Ohio State University. Her books include *Dr. Mom Chung of the Fair-Haired Bastards: The Life of a Wartime Celebrity* (University of California Press, 2005) and *Radicals on the Road: Internationalism, Orientalism, and Feminism during the Viet Nam Era* (Cornell University Press, 2013). She is a coeditor of *Frontiers: A Journal of Women's Studies*.

**KENYON ZIMMER** is assistant professor of history at the University of Texas, Arlington. His research focuses on migration and radicalism, with a special interest in the transnational history of anarchism. He is currently completing a book titled *Immigrants against the State: Yiddish and Italian Anarchism in America, 1885–1940*.

# Index

Civil Rights Congress (CRC), 188–90, 194, 197

Cleaver, Eldridge, 213, 218–19, 223, 249

Clements, George, 168

Clutchette, John, 219

colonialism and neocolonialism, 248, 269, 281

color line: Communist Party, class struggle, and, 179; Depression and, 178; Du Bois on, 14–15; gender and, 94; Herndon on, 181; IWW and, 89; Jews and, 135

Communist International (Comintern), 144, 197

Communist Party, US (CP or CPUSA): anarchist debate with, 139–41; Angela Davis and, 220; Ferrero-Sallitto case and, 144–45; homophile movement and, 189, 197; Mexican workers in California and, 160–61, 168, 169, 177–81; redbaiting, 194; as vanguard group, 52–53

Communist Party of the Philippines, 282

Conaty, Nora, 103

concentration camps, 5, 18

Congress of Industrial Organizations (CIO), 177

Constantino, Renato, 286–87

Continuous Journey Order (Canada), 79

"coolie" trade, 10–11. *See also* laborers, Asian

"coolie" trope, IWW contestation of, 86–87

*Coral Sea*, USS, 266–67

counterpublics and film culture in Hawai'i, 104–6, 112

Crenshaw, Kimberle, 38–39, 51

creoles of color in Louisiana, 69n41

Cuban Revolution, 274

Cullen, Countee, 134, 143, 149

cultural reception and renegotiation of expressive culture, 62–65

Cummins, Eric, 232n1

Czolgosz, Leon, 131

**D**

Damiani, Gigi, 139

Das, Taraknath, 77, 78, 79, 83, 90, 98n26

Davis, Angela, 219–24, *221*, 225, 230

Dayal, Har, 77, 90

De Bow, J. D. B., 10

De Caux, Len, 175

Dellums, Ronald, 285–86

Department of Defense (DOD), 272–73, 283, 286

Depression relief and Mexican workers in southern California: Brawley, CA, example, 159–60; Communist Party and radical internationalism, 160–61, 168, 169, 177–81; federal vs. state and local control of relief, 170–73; forms of relief, 161–62; Los Angeles Unemployed Councils and, 161, 174–81; Mexican Revolution experiences and, 168–73; open shop model and, 162–64, 171, 179; Red Squad (LAPD) and, 163, 176; relief as control regime, 164–68, 174; strikes, 160, 170–71, 181; unemployment levels, 173

Dewey, George, 15

Dickstein, Samuel, 147

"Directive on Dissidents" (DOD), 272–73

*Discourse on Colonialism* (Cesaire), 48

domestic violence, 50–51

Domingo, Silme, 291

Drumgo, Fleeta, 219, 225, 227, 229, 235n50

Du Bois, W. E. B., 14–15, 43

Duggan, Lisa, 192

**E**

Eliot, Thomas D., 11

*L'Emancipazione*, 135–37

engaged scholar trap, 59–61

Ervin, Sam J., 286

Estepa, Andrea, 242–43

Evans, Joe, 170

Evans, Wayne, 287–88

expressive culture and historical thinking, 63–65

**F**

Farrelly, Patrick J., 146, 152

fascism: anarchists and, 136, 139; Mexican workers and, 173; in Philippines, 283, 291

Federal Bureau of Investigation (FBI), 6, 272. *See also* Bureau of Investigation

Federal Emergency Relief Administration, 170

Federation of Japanese Labor (Hawai'i), 119

"feeling good about feeling bad" trap, 61–62

feminism: black feminist critique of slavery and prison, 223; social effects of, 50–51; Viet Nam women's unions and, 246–47; waves analogy, 262n15. *See also* Asian and Asian American Women and global feminism during the Vietnam War

Ferguson, Roderick, 195

Ferrero, Vincenzo, 135–36, *140*, 141–49, 152

Ferrero-Sallitto Defense Conference, 142–48

Fields, Sara Bard, 144

Filipino Federation of Labor (Hawai'i), 119

Filipino workers: base worker activism at Clark Naval Base and Subic Bay, 281–89; in Hawai'i, 115; labor activism in Seattle, 290–91; racial epithets against, 17

Fish, Hamilton, 12

Flynn, Elizabeth Gurley, 85, 86–87

Fonda, Jane, 282

Ford, Henry, 162

Fort Ord, California, 272

Foucault, Michel, 235n43

*Free Society*, 131

"free trade" and history of race, 8–14

Friedman, Bella, 137

FTA Tour, 282–84

Fusco, Coco, 129

## G

Galleani, Luigi, 133, 134, 135

Gandhi, Mohandas, 80

Garvey, Marcus, 65

Gates, Daryl, 199, 200

gay liberation movement, 204–5. *See also* homosexuality and race in Los Angeles

Genera, Nina, 249

*Ghadar*, 76, 81, *82*

Gibson, Randall Lee, 14

GI-Civilian Alliance for Peace, 273

*Gidra*, 256, 257

GI movement and Pacific Counseling Service (PCS): at Clark Air Base and Subic Bay, Philippines, 267, 281–89; coffeehouses for GIs, 270–71, 274–75; *Coral Sea* case, 266–67; Japanese antiwar movement and, 274–76; in Okinawa, 278–81, 292; PCS, GI dissent, and the New Left, 269–76; in San Francisco Bay Area, 266–67, 270–73, 289–90; in Seattle, 290–91; Vietnamization policy, Nixon Doctrine, and, 267–68, 276–81

Glenn, Evelyn Nakano, 113

Goldman, Emma, 133

Gordon, Avery, 45

Graham, Marcus (born Shmuel Marcus), 128–31, 133–34, 137–41, 149–52

Green, Marshall, 277–78

Gruppo Emancipazione, 135–37, 145

## H

Hahn, Steven, 214

Hamer, Fannie Lou, 65

Hanhardt, Christina, 193

Hansen, Miriam, 104–6, 112

Harriet Tubman Prison Movement (HTPM), 230

Hartman, Saidiya, 222

Hasegawa, Robert, 120

Hawai'i: 1909 strike, 103–4, *105*; contract labor system, end of, 106; *haole* developed as racial category, 113; Japanese labor uprisings in, 88–89; Reciprocal Treaty between US and, 13–14; ruling elite in, 113; welfare capitalism in, 109, 112, 114, 120

Hawaiian Creole English, 118, 124n36

Hawaiian Sugar Planters' Association (HSPA), 103, 104, 109–10, 112

Hawaiian theaters and labor movement: counterpublic formations and, 104–6, 112, 118; educational American films, 115; Japanese films and entrepreneurship, 107–12; Laupahoehoe plantation theater proposal, 112–14, 118–20; masculine images and, 118–19; silent western films, 115–18; social isolation, effects on, 117; social reform and regulation, 112–15; theater troupes, 106–7; theatrical performance and labor organizing, 102–4

Race, Radicalism, and Repression on the Pacific Coast and Beyond conference, 6

race studies, *konesans* and *balans* and, 38–39

radical social movements: contemporary characteristics of, 51–52; historical inquiry and, 40–41; larger democratic effects and, 49–51; neoliberal policy and, 48. *See also specific movements*

Rahim, Hussain, 80, 90–91, 99n31

Ramirez, Maria, 249

Ramnath, Maia, 78

Ramos, Santiago, 118

Rawick, George, 53–54, 61

Rebel Poets, 133

Reclus, Élisée, 139

redbaiting, 194

redlining, 193

Red Scare (1919–20), 132–33

Red Squad (Los Angeles), 163, 176

"Reflections on the Black Women's Role of the Community of Slaves" (Davis), 222–23

Reinecke, John, 124n36

relief. *See* Depression relief and Mexican workers in southern California

Relief Workers Protective Union, 175

religion, 114

respectability, politics of, 198, 209n49

Reuther, Walter, 67n14

revolutionary manhood in Pacific Northwest: conflicting versions of manhood, 74; Indian revolutionary nationalists in diaspora, 75–80; interracial radical alliance, 72–73, 89–92; IWW and redemption of Asian manhood, 83–89; limits of, 92–95; manhood rhetoric and colonial gender politics, 80–83

Right of Assembly and Movement Committee (RAMCOM), 205

Riley, Charles, 72

Riordan, John, 85, 100n40

Rios, Tony, 194

Rizal, José, 19

Robeson, George M., 12

Robinson, Cedric, 52

Rodgers, John, 12–13

Rodney, Walter, 224

Rodríguez, Dylan, 214

Romero, Oscar, 61

Roosevelt, Franklin D., 145–46

Roosevelt, Theodore, 15, 17, 19–20, 21

Root, Gladys, 201

Rosenfeld, Seth, 6

Rossi, Angelo, 136

Rothstein, Vivian, 246–47, 261

Rowell, Chester, 168

Rubio, Victor, 188–89, 190, 205n4

Rubio, William, 188–89, 190

*Ruíz v. Estelle*, 230

Russian Revolution, 52

**S**

Sacco, Nicola, 55, 143

Said, Edward, 239–40

Salaam, Kalamu ya, 44

Sallitto, Domenico, 135–37, *140*, 141–46, 149, 152

Sallitto, Nina, 141, 142, 143

Sánchez, George, 193

San Francisco: Chinese-born anarchists in, 137; general strike (1934), 141–42; homophile movement in, 204, 212n78

San Francisco Bay Area: GI movement in, 266–67, 270, 289–90; Italian anarchists in, 135–42, 152; San Quentin Six, 227–29, *228*

San Quentin Six, 227–29, *228*

Sasaki, K., 93–94

Sato, Eisaku, 278–79

scholars, isolated and engaged, 57–61

Scott, James C., 129

Scottsboro Boys, 138, 179–80

Seattle: Filipino labor activism in, 290–91; New Delhi bombing and, 76; Sasaki case, 93–94; South Asian migrant repression in, 78; United India House, 77; Wing Luke Museum of the Asian Pacific American Experience, 5. *See also* revolutionary manhood in Pacific Northwest

Sedition Act (1901), 20

segregation, racial, 193–94, 217–18. *See also* Jim Crow laws (US South)

Seitz, Eric, 284

Serrano, Juan, 166